WOMEN AND JOURNALISM

This book offers a rich and comprehensive analysis of the roles, status and experiences of women journalists in the United States and Britain. Drawing on a variety of sources and dealing with a host of women journalists, ranging from nineteenth-century pioneers to Paula Zahn and Kate Adie, the authors investigate the challenges that women have faced in the struggle to establish their reputations as professionals. *Women and Journalism* provides an account of the gendered structuring of journalism in print, radio and television, and speculates about women's still-emerging role in on-line journalism. Women's role in the management of mainstream newspapers and television stations is assessed, with a consideration of what difference gender can and does make. Women's accomplishments as war correspondents are tracked to the present, including their work covering the war in Afghanistan.

The book is unusual in its contrasting women's contributions to mainstream and to alternative news media. It examines the strategies that women have adopted to resist their marginalization in male-dominated media management by charting women's independent press, radio, television and Internet initiatives in the United States and Britain. With respect to mainstream journalism, women have been redeployed within the rise of a postmodern style of journalism distinguished by an emphasis on confessional and therapy 'news', often in the name of a market-led 'post-feminism'. The authors conclude by addressing women's contribution to public discourse and their role in the age of interactive news media.

Deborah Chambers is Reader in Sociology of Culture and Communication at Nottingham Trent University. Her publications include *Representing the Family* (2001); *Practice and Politics in Cultural Research: Cultural Studies as Method* (2004) with Richard Johnson, Parvati Raghuram and Estella Tincknell; and *Changing Social and Personal Relationships* (forthcoming). **Linda Steiner** is Associate Professor in the Department of Journalism and Media Studies at Rutgers University. She is editor of *Critical Studies in Media Communication* and is on the editorial boards of *Journalism: Theory, Practice and Criticism*, *Journalism and Mass Communication Quarterly* and *Feminist Media Studies*. Her most recent publications include *Critical Readings: Media and Gender* (2004). **Carole Fleming** is Senior Lecturer in Broadcast Journalism at Nottingham Trent University, and is the author of *The Radio Handbook* (Second Edition, 2003)

WOMEN AND JOURNALISM

Deborah Chambers, Linda Steiner
and *Carole Fleming*

Routledge
Taylor & Francis Group

LONDON AND NEW YORK

First published 2004
by Routledge
2 Park Square, Milton Park, Abingdon, Oxon, OX14 4RN

Simultaneously published in the USA and Canada
by Routledge
270 Madison Ave, New York NY 10016

Routledge is an imprint of the Taylor & Francis Group, an informa business

Transferred to Digital Printing 2005

© 2004 Deborah Chambers, Linda Steiner and Carole Fleming

Typeset in Times by M Rules

Printed and bound in Great Britain by TJI Digital, Padstow, Cornwall

British Library Cataloguing in Publication Data
A catalogue record for this book is available from the British Library

Library of Congress Cataloging in Publication Data
A catalog record for this book has been requested

ISBN 10: 0-415-27444-3 (hbk)
ISBN 10: 0-415-27445-1 (pbk)

ISBN 13: 978-0-415-27444-9 (hbk)
ISBN 13: 978-0-415-27445-6 (pbk)

Contents

Authors' biographies

Deborah Chambers is Reader in Sociology of Culture and Communication in the Department of English and Media Studies at Nottingham Trent University. She has taught and researched at undergraduate and postgraduate level in British and Australian universities on social and cultural theory; gender and popular media; youth and sexual morality; and research methods. Her publications include *Representing the Family* (2001) and *Practice and Politics in Cultural Research: Cultural Studies as Method* (with Richard Johnson, Estella Tincknell and Parvati Raghuram, 2004). *Changing Social and Personal Relationships: An International Perspective* is forthcoming (2005).

Linda Steiner is Associate Professor and former Chair in the Department of Journalism and Media Studies at Rutgers University, where she teaches news reporting, gender/race/media, and media ethics at undergraduate level; and audience studies and qualitative methods at Ph.D. level. Many of her publications focus on feminist media ethics, the structure of feminist media, and the history of journalism education. She is former associate editor of *Journalism and Mass Communication Quarterly,* and incoming editor of *Critical Studies in Media Communication.*

Carole Fleming lectures at undergraduate and postgraduate level in the Centre for Broadcast Journalism at Nottingham Trent University. She has worked as a reporter in provincial newspapers and as a radio journalist for both the BBC and commercial radio. She has researched and published on the radio industry in the UK, and is currently completing research on news values and audience targeting in broadcast news.

Acknowledgements

We would like to thank the Department of English and Media at Nottingham Trent University and the Department of Journalism and Media Studies at Rutgers University for providing a stimulating intellectual community. At Nottingham Trent University, the research leave awarded to Deborah Chambers by the Research Unit 65 in Communication, Media and Culture was greatly appreciated and we owe special thanks to Sandra Harris, Head of Department, and John Tomlinson, Research Leader, for this crucial support. Particular thanks also go to Olwyn Ince, for her considerable help as research assistant in the gathering of information for the project at NTU. Lynne Hapgood contributed to a first draft of Chapter 1 and to enjoyable discussions about early proposals for the book, for which we are most grateful. We thank the anonymous referees and reviewers who provided valuable support and advice. At Routledge, we wish to convey our gratitude to Christopher Cudmore for bringing us together across the Atlantic to write this book, and also to Rebecca Barden and Lesley Riddle who supported its completion. This book is dedicated to our families.

A note on usage

Writing a book for readers on both sides of the Atlantic presents its own challenges, particularly when the authorship is also transatlantic. Since the publisher is British we have written the book in British rather than American English. This is unproblematic on the whole, but the accepted terms for racial groups are not the same on both sides of the ocean. Thus we have used a mixture of terms – African American, women of colour, black journalists, white women, and so on – and have tried to be sensitive of context ('women of colour' being used with regard to the US, for example). We have avoided the initial capital in 'Black' or 'White' as this is unusual in British usage. We have also avoided the use of black or white as nouns, as this is potentially offensive in both cultures.

Introduction

WOMEN AND JOURNALISM IN THE
UNITED STATES AND BRITAIN

Women journalists present a paradox. Their presence as professional writers and presenters of news is now commonplace, yet they continue to be marked as 'other', as 'different' from their male colleagues. In print news, official rhetoric proclaims that a journalist's gender is irrelevant. However, while maleness is rendered neutral and male journalists are treated largely as professionals, women journalists are signified as *gendered*: their work is routinely defined and judged by their femininity. We find that women have not achieved equality either in several 'serious' fields of news such as politics and business or in the highly popular and lucrative area of sports news. Women are still concentrated in sectors considered to be 'soft' news, such as those with an emphasis on 'human interest' stories, features and the delivery of a magazine-style of journalism. In television – where spectacle counts – emphasis on the decorative value and even the sexualization of women journalists is overt.

Women television news presenters and correspondents continue to be subject to regular comments and complaints about their appearance: their clothes, hair and voices are scrutinized far more intensively by both management and viewers than those of their male counterparts. In a comment still relevant today, Patricia Holland (1987: 133) said of women newsreaders on British television during the late 1980s, 'The imposed limits of femininity, it seems, cannot easily be cast off, particularly in the hard world of news reporting'. The personal lives and bodies of women journalists are often dissected and debated in the news media. This treatment comes from news media's top management, apparently in response to audiences' curiosity. Indeed, the high social visibility of women journalists in popular discourses contrasts with their relative invisibility in boardrooms and at other senior management meetings.

This book examines the status, practices and experiences of women journalists working in the United States and Britain from the nineteenth century to the present. We analyse women's influence on changing news agendas, news values and the very parameters and meanings of public knowledge and 'news', using historical sources to contextualize women's contemporary position in the profession. Our aim is to show how news processes on both sides of the Atlantic have been largely, although not exclusively, shaped by gender and how the organization of the news and of the newsroom, as well as assumptions about gender and women, have affected women's performance and potential as journalists.

Within a historical frame but with an emphasis on the last fifty years, we investigate how women have helped change journalism and their role in journalism. We analyse women's influence on the ways that audiences use and respond to news. We also examine how conventions and assumptions about gender play out differently in specific areas of news journalism such as war reporting, discussed in Chapter 10. Chapters 7, 8 and 9 tackle women's alternative news media, stretching from women's print periodicals during the suffrage movement in the late nineteenth century to feminist experiments with radio and television, and on to even more recent uses of Internet sites.

Our argument can be summarized as follows: although the number of women in journalism has risen impressively over the past two decades, this rise has been patchy. Women have not yet reached a critical mass in 'serious' news beats. Moreover, they remain a minority in the top management jobs in news organizations, where a glass ceiling continues to limit women's promotion to key decision-making positions (see Chapter 4). Women continue to face sexism in the newsroom. Given that social conventions insist that women assume the major burden of childcare, working mothers suffer from a newsroom culture demanding long hours and offering a lack of childcare facilities. They have resisted and forced a certain amount of change; they have pushed for and then utilized equal opportunity policies. They have challenged sexism in the newsroom. Women's expansion in numbers at the lower rungs of the professional hierarchy and in television broadcasting, where an attractive and youthful femininity is still demanded, have coincided with key changes in the agendas, styles and topics of news. Their central participation in these changes has led, however, to the stereotyping of this emergent style of news journalism as 'feminine' news.

This shift in news styles raises important questions about the distinctions between the rise of a market-led set of news values in mainstream journalism described below, especially in Chapter 11, and alternative news media. We argue that a market-led post-feminist journalism masquerades as a kind of news that promotes women's issues. To paraphrase Patricia Holland (1987: 136), the history and even more recent experiences of women in journalism demonstrate repeatedly that 'women's right to speak in public may easily be subverted' by drawing attention to their femininity and the habitual questioning of their communicative competence. However, as we demonstrate, women have a long history of working in and for alternative media, where they can foreground women's issues and even promote radical causes and needs, such as those of the lesbian community and of women of colour. We argue that women journalists' roles in recent developments in mainstream news journalism and also alternative news media (including Internet newsgroups) raise important questions about women's part in advancing women's voices in the public sphere. We examine feminist contributions to debates about Jürgen Habermas's (1989) concept of the 'public sphere' to explore these issues.

Women journalists as spectacle

Women journalists find that they are not only deliverers but also objects of news. During the period we were writing this book several women journalists became spectacles, part of the news themselves, in a manner which was peculiar to their femininity. For example, a marketing campaign in the US in 2002 to promote CNN anchor Paula Zahn raised a number of issues about the status of women in news journalism, when the promotions department – apparently without approval from Zahn or CNN top management – ran a fifteen-second television advertisement for Zahn showing her profile and lips, with a voice saying, 'Where can you find a morning news anchor who's provocative, super-smart, oh yeah, and just a little bit sexy?' The words 'PROVOCATIVE' and 'SEXY' flashed on the screen and the sound of a zipper being unzipped was heard when the music stopped (De Moraes 2002: C1). Zahn is a highly experienced journalist who has interviewed dozens of prominent political leaders and heads of state. She has worked in several major cities across the United States, was an anchor and co-host for both CBS and ABC, and hosted her own daily news programme: *The Edge with Paula Zahn* at Fox News Channel, until Fox fired her for engaging in employment talks with its arch-rival CNN. She started working for CNN on 11 September 2001.

When Zahn made it clear that she was offended by the advertisement, CNN Chairman Walter Isaacson called the campaign 'a major blunder'. James Kellner, chairman of Turner Broadcasting, which owns CNN, immediately demanded that the advertisement be pulled. He had already been challenged for hiring a television actress from the police drama series *NYPD Blue* (among others) to anchor the *Headline News*. The ad was quickly scrapped and the issue died down with only a few cynics noting that Zahn, who reportedly earns $2 million a year, has been inducted into the Celebrity Legs Hall of Fame Internet site (Ager 2002).

Many column inches and much airtime was devoted to Yvonne Ridley who was sent in 2002 by the *Sunday Express* to Islamabad, where she crossed the border into Afghanistan and was captured by the Taliban. As discussed in Chapter 10, after being released Ridley received hostile press from several fellow British journalists for placing herself and her local guides in danger. Ridley was also condemned for taking unnecessary risks because she was a single mother with an eight-year-old daughter. As Helen Carter of the British broadsheet newspaper the *Guardian* asked provocatively, 'Should Yvonne not have put herself at risk because she was a woman and a mother?' (Carter 2001: 9). Moreover, Ridley's three marriages were scrutinized by the news media.

BBC foreign correspondent Kate Adie (2002) recounts in her autobiography, which was serialized in the *Guardian*, her experience of being pursued by the news media as the sole woman in a twelve-member press team covering the Gulf war in 1990. Already a household name by the time she was assigned to Kuwait and Iraq, she was preoccupied with trying to fit into the military uniform and keep tabs on the extensive equipment – from water bottles to a nuclear biological chemical kit – the British Army gave all reporters. In addition, she said:

> I was also bothered by the attentions of the newspapers. Obsessed with a Woman Going to War, at least one paper sent a reporter to track my moves and get 'a few embarrassing snaps'. And at home, a woman MP [Member of Parliament] wrote a snide piece containing the ridiculous fiction that I'd lost my pearl earrings and 'soldiers had been hunting for them in the sand' . . . The feeling of being sneaked up on by a fellow hack intent on making life difficult was unsettling. I was finding things quite hard anyway, although the Army had not once showed me any prejudice or seemed in the least irritated by having to accommodate a female in a unit of 2,000 men. I was in my mid-40s, relatively fit and keen to do my best, but I was worried that I'd fail to make the grade in some way. And if I did, I felt I'd be letting down a lot of women back in Britain who thought that I ought to be able to hack it. I didn't want to stand out and 'be the exception': I just wanted to get on with the job – without complaining: a whingeing woman was just what the papers would have loved.[1]

Interestingly, Adie says her single status has drawn comment throughout her well-publicized career. She is regularly asked: 'Why aren't you married?' and 'Has your career prevented you from finding a partner?'

Some biographers have even sexualized their female subjects in a way that is virtually unheard of with respect to male journalists. One of the most egregious examples is that of Marguerite Higgins, a Pulitzer prize-winning war reporter, whose biographers describe her attractiveness and stance of sexual liberation as much as her ambition (Schilpp and Murphy 1983, May 1983). Julia Edwards (1988: 191), whose discussion of other women foreign correspondents is celebratory, if not adulatory, attacked Higgins, her Columbia journalism school colleague, comparing her to Marilyn Monroe: 'pretty, talented, sexy, and painfully insecure'. Even Edwards, however, is forced to note that while Higgins's enemies accused her of sleeping with men to obtain her stories, her lovers were mainly fellow correspondents. Moreover, Edwards

(1988: 196) concedes that male foreign correspondents who cheated on their wives aroused no criticism.

We argue in this book that women have been the object of the public gaze 'as' women, that is, for their status as mothers or their single-woman status, for their oddity or difficulties as *women* war reporters or as *women* bosses, and for the sexism they face from male colleagues.

'But I don't do weddings': women's entrance into the profession

While there is a great deal of noise about women journalists in the media, how women have dealt with both professional and personal issues in terms of training, recruitment, promotion prospects, and how they have confronted sexism has attracted far less noise. Comparing the history, roles and status of women journalists in the United States and in Britain sheds light on organizational factors attributable to gender or, more specifically, to sexism. It is not our intention to add 'great women' to the 'great men' approach to history in this book. Instead, we believe in the importance of the patterns that emerge from their lives, understood collectively and historically, including what they have said about their experiences in their memoirs, autobiographies and interviews, as well as taking into account what others have said. Our aim is to arrive at an understanding of how, when and where women's gender has mattered in the context of journalism. And certainly some specific themes emerge from these stories about women journalists fairly consistently over two centuries, including their demand to be treated as equals and as 'professionals'. Whenever possible, we consider how the assumptions about 'women' as a category are often disguised assumptions about white women. The claims that newsrooms were open to women long ignored the extent to which newsrooms, especially mainstream newsrooms, remained closed to women of colour.

Importantly, the issue for women journalists is not always one of being denied jobs on account of gender. For decades women were refused most reporting jobs by men who said: 'It's no job for a woman'. These days, it is more complicated. Whereas maleness is taken for granted, women are 'signs' within the masculine narratives of news discourses (Rakow and Kranich 1991). The intersecting themes that run through this book and the manifold ways in which gender is still meaningful, can be seen in the story of Liz Trotta who, by her own admission, is no feminist but who seems to have confronted at some level nearly every variety of sexism invented. Having originally been told by the *New York Times* editor that 'It's not a job for a woman', Trotta (1991: 21) was eventually hired by a network executive who specifically wanted a 'girl reporter'. Trotta (1991: 37) said she wanted to persuade WNBC 'that I wasn't "a girl reporter" but a reporter who happened to be a girl'. When a network producer wanted her to cover the wedding of President Lyndon Johnson's daughter, Trotta (1991: 58) said firmly, 'But I don't do weddings . . . Oh, I don't mean to be rude, but I don't work on women's stories.' Yet NBC promoted her to publicize its news, and capitalized on her persona as 'girl' reporter. Later, she faced an NBC field producer who was constantly knocking on her hotel room door.

> Parrying his amorous advances became part of my daily routine. At that point sexual harassment was not even a concept, let alone an actionable offense, so I swallowed hard and decided it was just another affront to be absorbed by any woman who wanted to succeed.
>
> (Trotta 1991: 66)

Eventually she complained and the offending male field producer was transferred.

Relevant sources on women in journalism

In the last few decades, large-scale surveys of journalists have generally included gender along with other factors of age, social class, race, educational background, training, rank, responsibilities and so on. Such statistical data allow comparisons of men's and women's career patterns and professional advancement (Gallagher 1995, Weaver and Wilhoit 1996, Delano and Henningham 1995, Henningham and Delano 1998). However, given that such surveys are rarely designed to focus specifically on gender issues, the findings of gender difference are often schematic rather than conclusive. For example, survey data indicating that male journalists are on average older than female journalists does not explain its significance in terms of women's career patterns and advancement. The age difference may suggest that women do not stay in the profession as long as men; but this data does not explain whether this difference is attributable to the lack of promotion prospects for women, lack of childcare support, a male-dominated newsroom culture, or something else. In parallel, we draw on content analyses to shed light on the extent to which there are differences in the ways that men and women gather and report the news. For example, analyses of news content suggest that, compared to men, women reporters tend to focus on issues affecting women's lives, personalities and personal views more often, approach women as news sources more often and use a broader definition of news in developing a human-interest angle (Covert 1981, Mills 1997, Meyers 1997, Skidmore 1998, Christmas 1997). Nonetheless, this kind of evidence, as with any other kinds of data, must be contextualized rather than essentialized.

We draw on qualitative as well as quantitative sources in our analysis of women journalists' recruitment and promotion patterns, and also in our discussion of gendered newsroom cultures and values. A range of research based on in-depth interviews with women journalists also supports our analysis, providing insights into women's experiences in particular journalistic specialities and indicating their interpretations of such issues as equal opportunities, newsroom cultures and attitudes of male colleagues to women journalists. In the first two chapters we provide a historical context for an understanding of the issues and debates about the current position of women journalists discussed later. Chapter 1 traces women's contribution to mainstream journalism from the mid-nineteenth century to the early twentieth century, when women were being allowed into the profession on men's terms, that is, from the early days of an expanding mass media to the Second World War, when women began to break into jobs once reserved for men because men were sent to war. We focus on the social pressures women experienced and the lengths they had to go in order to be taken seriously by their male counterparts and the media public.

While some women were able to break into the male enclave of newspaper journalism from the mid-nineteenth century, Chapter 1 emphasizes that women were treated as consumers rather than producers of news. When newspapers began to rely increasingly on advertising revenue from the 1880s onwards, a new form of 'women's journalism', mainly fashion and society news, emerged to attract women readers. For educated middle-class women, journalism was regarded as a glamorous career enabling them to break out of feminine confinement to the domestic sphere. None the less, women were associated with – and assigned to – journalistic styles and topics widely deemed as outside 'serious' reportage. The emergence of 'women's pages' ensured that women journalists played a central role in feature writing and stories aimed at women. In 1903, an entire, if shortlived, paper was aimed at 'gentlewomen' in the UK, the *Daily Mirror*. Beyond that, women's role in mainstream journalism was producing sensationalism and human-interest stories.

A dilemma facing women journalists from the start was that the very notions of 'objectivity' and 'impartiality' were anchored within a partial, male-oriented construction of knowledge, reportage and 'news' which produced a patriarchal framework for the professionalization of the occupation. News about women's issues was ignored or sensationalized and women readers were widely regarded as interested only in 'gossip'. Certain issues were either rarely aired in the mainstream news media or reported unsympathetically, such as women's social and economic subordination and the demand for women's political, educational, employment and domestic rights. The fact that femininity was associated with the domestic sphere assured women journalists' prominence as curiosities and as suppliers of 'women's news' to draw women readers. However, until the introduction of equal opportunities principles and laws in the late twentieth century, it was only in alternative news media that women consistently enjoyed opportunity to take on decision-making roles as editors and controllers of the press.

The two world wars not only provided opportunities for women to enter journalism in larger numbers but also to advance their careers by entering the field of 'serious' news, including war reporting. It may even be argued that women initiated the human-interest approach to war reportage. Women were long barred from war reporting by being denied accreditation by the military, but some found ingenious ways of circumventing these barriers. In any case, many women were pushed out of newsrooms when the wars were over.

However, the emergence of the women's pages and features in early-twentieth-century newspapers not only prompted a rise in the number of women journalists but also provided a space for airing, from the late 1960s, feminist debates. As Chapter 2 describes, the women's page gave rise to new styles of newspaper journalism. Despite its accent on human-interest stories, the women's page often subverted the conventional values of 1950s' suburban domesticity with the introduction of important feminist debates about equal opportunities in employment, equal pay, childcare, divorce, abortion and so on.

Radio began in the United States in 1920, three years earlier than in Britain. Programming in both countries was generally aimed at housewives, with an emphasis on fashion and beauty, as Chapter 1 shows. In Britain, the strict moral code of the BBC established by Lord Reith ensured that women journalists would play only a peripheral role in British radio for decades after its inception. Although women were denied access to the airwaves, they played a major part in shaping broadcasting behind the scenes, even rising to senior positions, as with the case of Hilda Matheson, who became the BBC's Head of Talks in 1927 and who spearheaded a more informal style of reporting.

The voice of British radio, however, was strictly masculine; except for the rare administrator, women were audiences and consumers, and were not heard on air. Women fared better in American radio during this period: Judith Cary Waller became the first woman manager of a radio station by 1922. As with print, the Second World War provided significant opportunities for women to advance in American radio as presenters and war correspondents. By the 1940s women were in charge of educational and public services on all four of the US radio networks. However, women were held back in both the US and Britain by men's assertion that women's voices were too high-pitched and thus lacked authority. Women seeking jobs on-air, as with print, were confined to programmes aimed at women.

In the UK, women were virtually barred from reading the national news on BBC radio. They were not employed as newsreaders on a regular basis until the 1970s. Men were typically awarded the more interesting reporting jobs such as foreign assignments and riots. Women were assigned celebrity interviews and human-interest stories. One programme bucking the trend was the BBC's *Woman's Hour*. This radio programme was originally designed to help women returning to the domestic front after the Second World War, but it quickly extended its remit to include women's social inequality and related issues. By the mid-1970s it was accepted that women reading the news on British local radio provided much-needed diversity to break up the relentless dominance of male DJs who introduced the music.

Women in the United States were likewise able to enter television broadcasting at a much earlier stage of the medium's history than in Britain, with Frieda Hennock being appointed as first US woman commissioner for the Federal Communications Commission in 1948. In 1971, six women were newsreaders on NBC alone. By contrast, during BBC Television's early years, British women were banned from reading the news until 1960, when Nan Winton was appointed – even then, only on an irregular basis. Objectivity was associated with masculinity. Magazine programmes on television aimed at women were, like radio, typically composed of fashion, cookery and childcare tips, relegating women's interests to the domestic sphere. Not until 1975 did BBC Television employ Angela Rippon as its first regular female newsreader. This marked the beginning of the pattern of employing women news anchors for their appearance rather than their journalistic skills. While greying and balding men were able to continue as presenters, older women were identified as inappropriate to the medium. During the 1970s producers and directors of programmes, editors of newspapers and decision-makers across the news media were invariably men.

From the 1970s onwards in both Britain and the US, women were employed by news organizations in larger numbers when the crisis of shrinking numbers of women readers was exposed by the strong competition between newspapers, radio and television. Women readers and audiences were wooed by female journalists with a new kind of news that related to their lives. Likewise, women journalists were called upon to provide feature stories on American and British television and to contribute personalized, human-interest accounts of the women's page, even of such major events as the Vietnam War. In Chapter 2 we show how the style influenced definitions of news right across the media. Newspapers began increasingly to emphasize both contextualization of the news and personalized accounts.

Education and training of women for journalism

Important contrasts between the education and training of journalists in Britain and the US have impacted on the employment patterns and progress of women in the profession. We argue that the availability of an academic degree eventually had a crucial effect on the advancement of women journalists by providing opportunities to train in a relatively egalitarian environment.

With university degrees in journalism being offered at the start of the twentieth century in the US but not until the end of the twentieth century in Britain, the professionalization of the occupation has been slower in the UK. Chapter 3 shows that the British on-the-job model of journalism training, on a trade union basis, significantly disadvantaged British women wishing to enter the field.

Yet women at universities in the US had to endure academic textbooks that addressed students as male and assumed all journalists would be male. These early texts offered no analysis of gender divisions and the gendered structuring of the profession. We assess the extent to which such programmes acknowledged women's interests in acquiring 'serious' professional education as journalists or offered specialized training to cover topics aimed at women. Analysis of vocational literature, textbooks and other teaching materials shows that journalism education has long discouraged women who entered journalism programmes from pursuing journalism as a serious career. Although today, options and courses are provided on gender issues, key journalism texts still fail to address gender centrally. Moreover, the presence of women lecturers in journalism classrooms influences the performance of female students: the more women teaching the subject, the better female students perform (Grunig 1993).

Women's contemporary status in journalism

Over the last twenty or twenty-five years, in both the US and UK, women have begun to achieve critical mass in certain subfields and to break through the barriers to decision-making positions. However, we argue that women's increasing presence in the profession does not necessarily indicate their empowerment within media structures. Chapter 4 explains that they remain concentrated at the lower echelons of the profession while men continue to dominate top management positions in the newspaper, radio and television industries.

The phrase 'glass ceiling' refers to an invisible barrier to promotion that women experience in many professions. We argue that it has not yet been shattered. It is true that women are now able to negotiate non-hierarchical management models more conducive to their needs and to introduce new ways of working, including flexible hours, job shares and childcare support in order to undermine the culture of long hours traditionally associated with journalism. As yet, however, there is no evidence of women managers effecting an acceleration of the promotion of women from junior ranks. Women also report that they continue to experience sexism in the newsroom, with 60 per cent indicating they have either experienced or witnessed prejudice against women (Henningham and Delano 1998: 148, Ross 2001).

Although women are still largely absent in such areas as political reporting, they have contributed to a distinctive shift in news agendas and priorities, as Chapter 5 describes. While there is little consensus between women themselves about whether the rise in the number of women journalists have made a difference to news values and newsroom culture, it has been argued that women have transformed newsroom culture by their central involvement in widening definitions of news. However, the evidence is contradictory and suggestions that women have spearheaded changes in definitions of news values have been questioned. For example, as we discuss in Chapter 10, some women journalists and scholars argue that women tackle a wider range of wartime events than do men (Edwards 1988, Elwood-Ackers 1988, Rouvalis and Schackner 2000).

However, other researchers dispute the idea that women write differently from men (Weaver and Wilhoit 1996, Weaver 1997, Henningham and Delano 1998). Many of the changes in news values have been prompted by commercial imperatives and, as such, women continue to be typecast by being assigned fashion, lifestyle and education or health issues, a practice that implies they are incapable of dealing with 'hard' news. Nevertheless, Chapter 5 offers evidence suggesting that traditional masculine news narratives have been challenged by women's increased presence in the profession.

Chapter 6 examines in detail how women sometimes challenged sexism and gender discrimination in journalism. By obtaining the support of already established trade unions, guilds and press associations, women have challenged discriminatory practices regarding hiring decisions, salary levels, assignments and promotions, especially in Britain. When women failed to rouse interest and support from these organizations, as was often the case, especially in the US, they created their own. Some of these were established within specific news organizations, others were state-wide (in the case of the US), or regional, while still others coalesced around specific interests.

Working both with these organizations and independently, women not only advocated women's employment interests but also registered grievances with national hearing bodies and filed legal suits. Several US cases where women took legal proceedings against employers inspired useful attention in and about the news media. The case of Christine Craft, a US television reporter who sued her employer after she was fired for being 'too old, too ugly, and not deferential to men', exemplifies the kinds of suits women took on. That said, even when women were victorious in court, the court-ordered remedies frequently failed to mandate sustained or systematic changes on the part of employers. So these efforts generally produced only short-term gains for the individual complainants, rather than leading to a large-scale transformation of the workplace. In Britain, equal employment practices in public-service broadcasting have sometimes been effective, but mostly in the lower-status regions rather than the prestigious London headquarters of the BBC.

The cultural and structural barriers to promotion, the ghettoization of women in particular fields of journalism and their lack of promotion have persuaded many women to develop and use alternative news media to advance women's causes and to publicize women's issues, concerns and experiences. Women have developed more co-operative and collective ways of working together to transcend the patriarchal management practices and hierarchical structures that excluded them from decision-making roles within mainstream media. Women have used their own specialized media to create, defend, explain and celebrate new identities, new roles and new worlds for women.

Chapter 7 distinguishes mainstream from alternative and advocacy journalism, and explores the role women have played in developing such alternative productions as women's newspapers, newsletters and magazines to sustain feminist movements, such as the suffrage movement, and support social change. We focus on women's achievements as activists and their use of alternative print news as a vital avenue for publishing and disseminating their views and events during the nineteenth and early twentieth centuries, especially during the first wave of feminism in the US and Britain. Chapter 8 addresses how alternative periodicals challenged the mainstream media of the 1980s that purveyed images of a self-assertive, self-motivated superwoman within a congratulatory but depoliticized discourse. Well-known popular feminist publications, such as *off our backs* and *Ms. Magazine* in the US, and *Spare Rib* in Britain, demonstrate that radical feminist newspapers and magazines within independent publishing were themselves important contributions to the public reshaping of women's news.

In Chapters 8 and 9, we explore the journalistic successes and failures of smaller institutions representing various sexual, political, professional or vocational interests – including lesbian groups, women in management and black women – for an understanding of the forms and processes of alternative women's journalism in both countries. While mainstream images of women were addressing women as career women yet also largely as consumers, radio and television documentaries were speaking to women as participants in policy formulation, as democratic citizens, by promoting women's issues and advocating equality. Chapter 9 describes the development of women's radio stations and programming, women's broadcast and cable television programmes and women's Internet newsgroups. The alternative press, radio, television and Internet newsgroups, have allowed and even encouraged women to participate in the process of changing women's lives, beginning by training women to use printing and the press, broadcasting and Internet techniques.

Although high levels of burnout are routine in women's alternative media, this form of journalism constitutes an important realm of journalistic practice that has in turn impacted on mainstream journalism. Alternative media have been crucial in promoting social change, recruiting and bolstering new converts, and in inventing effective ways to defend social movements to wider society. Echoing the earlier struggles of women in journalism at the end of the nineteenth century, the marginal status of women globally has prompted these continued initiatives through the use of the Internet and has promoted the formation of links between women in Western and developing nations. The Internet is proving to be a successful medium for socially excluded groups since it provides the potential to transcend national boundaries and establish cyber communities. Throughout its history, women's alternative news media has addressed the public as *citizens* rather than as *consumers*.

Chapter 10 examines women's work as war correspondents during transnational conflicts from the late nineteenth century to the so-called war on terror of 2001. Women journalists' presence was strongly seen during the Vietnam War, but even then they ventured into a masculine environment and Gloria Emerson continued to encounter prejudice from the military and from fellow male reporters. During the 1982 Falklands War, the British government forbade women to travel to the Falkland Islands, evidence that progress for women war correspondents continued to be slow. But, successful foreign correspondents such as the BBC's Kate Adie are still judged by their appearance rather than their competence. Nevertheless, we find that women have disrupted the emphasis on 'bullets and bombs' typical of traditional masculine reporting styles and contributed a new style of reporting war news emphasizing civilian sufferings, the systematic rape of women, and other intended and unintended 'side-effects' of war.

Women have proved their flexibility and adaptability by forging new approaches to war journalism: they have developed original angles, tending to focus more on the human suffering resulting from wars and less on military actions. In doing so, they confirmed their ability to attract news audiences. After the September 11th 2001 attacks on the US, women journalists – reporting on American bombing of Afghanistan and the overthrow of the Taliban forces – were conspicuously displayed on television news broadcasts. Despite the fact that most women broadcast journalists were anchored in the studios, it led to a public news media debate about the risks of sending women war reporters out to war zones. As wives and mothers they continue to suffer from a kind and level of hostility and public disapproval that men with families do not face.

We identify some worrying current trends which indicate a return to practices and representations of feminine individualism under the guise of a celebration of 'popular culture' while ignoring political, pedagogic and professional feminism. Chapter 11 examines how women are contributing to this shift, involving not only an emphasis on human-interest stories but also the rise of confessional and therapy news. Recent trends in mainstream journalism indicate a shift to a postmodern approach that addresses audiences first and foremost as consumers. It emphasizes personal writing styles, sensationalism, celebrities and a sexualization of presentation, exemplified by what van Zoonen (1998) calls a 'Ken and Barbie' format. The rise in the number of women in journalism has coincided with this market-led, depoliticized 'post-feminist' redefinition of news; women journalists are being used to attract women readers and audiences (McRobbie 1994, 1997, Whelehan 2000). We argue that a post-feminist discourse is linked to a devaluation of serious news, such as foreign affairs, developing world issues, poverty and social exclusion; children's, ethnic minorities' and women's rights and economic issues and industrial relations.

Women and public discourse in the age of new media

The book concludes by speculating about women's future within new media. Chapter 12 evaluates women's journalism in the age of new media technology by mapping the dramatic shifts that have taken place in the last decade surrounding the digitalization of media and information technology. We explore the rise of on-line journalism by looking at the likely impact on changing work structures and on the content and style of journalism and ask whether women are likely to play a central part in this emerging medium. We go on to examine whether women journalists have engaged in a reformulation of the public sphere in the last century. Jürgen Habermas (1989) produced a normative theory of democratic participation in politics. He celebrated a public sphere – distinct from the state and from commercial market relations – in which citizens' opinions could develop through analytical and rational debate. It is a site where citizens can criticize the state and engage in debate and conversation, rather than buying and selling. Habermas (1989) argues that the emancipatory potential of the public sphere, in which equal citizens can debate freely through universal access, is being eroded under capitalism. Within his account of the rise and fall of a bourgeois public sphere, Habermas asserts that democratic debate on issues of public concern is being undermined. Bearing in mind women's past and recent achievements, we engage with Habermas's thesis and examine whether they have negotiated and reformulated the 'public sphere' of mass communication.

This final chapter offers predictions about the future of journalism and the public sphere for women as audiences/readers, users of media and professional communicators. It asks whether a democratization of public discourse is likely to release women journalists from gendered structures and stereotypes through interactive technology or whether the concentration of ownership and control will place further constraints on their employment practices and occupational status, thereby reinforcing a commercialization and 'sexualization' of journalism. It can be argued that the conventional distinctions between professional communicators and public-as-consumers are being sharpened by the accelerating framing of news as commodity. On the other hand, the emergence of cyber communities through the Internet and other interactive media may open up important possibilities for communities of women to contribute to the democratization of the public sphere and blur the distinction between mainstream and women-led alternative news media.

1

Early women journalists: 1850–1945

As with most paid occupations during the late nineteenth and early twentieth century, journalism was male-dominated and hierarchical. Editors and publishers regarded women as consumers rather than as producers of news. Only when advertising became necessary to newspapers' survival in the last decades of the nineteenth century were women actively sought as journalists to produce articles that would directly appeal to women readers and around which lucrative advertisements targeting women consumers could be placed. That is, women were hired as 'women journalists' to attract female audiences. While most male editors assumed that women lacked reporting skills and could never acquire them, those who did employ women assigned them to topics in which men – as readers and journalists – were uninterested.

In colonial America there were several notable examples of women involved in newspapers, but their presence was usually connected to the journalism of their husbands, fathers or brothers. A hundred years later, women clearly had an independent presence in journalism. US census figures demonstrate that out of 12,308 journalists in 1880, only 288 were women. By 1900, out of a total of 30,098 journalists, 2,193 were female (Steiner 1997b: 4). And the numbers and percentages continued to grow during this period. US census figures indicate that in 1920 women were 16.8 per cent of the reporters and editors, and by 1950, they were 32 per cent of journalists. The role of women in American and British society as a whole was changing and newspapers began to reach out to a wider audience as literacy and education levels rose. The women who managed to enter paid journalism were highly educated, white (with the exception of the black women writing for the black press) and from middle-class backgrounds. Some women were forced to earn a living as writers and journalists because they were single and/or because their family's economic circumstances had declined. Others managed to move into journalism with the help of family connections as wives or daughters of male journalists. None the less, as this chapter documents, women occupied a subordinated 'ghetto status' at least until the turn of the twentieth century and, in many respects, beyond that period. They were often confined to marginal areas of news – fashion, domestic issues and a form of 'society news,' that is, essentially glorified gossip about the lives of the rich and famous. Although many women resented and even attempted to resist this status, often at great personal cost, in the nineteenth and early twentieth century journalism remained characterized by a sharp gender division of labour in newsrooms, structured by male dominance in terms of numbers, status and managerial control. This chapter outlines not only women's achievements but also their experiences of prejudice and sexist stereotyping when they entered the profession.

The rise of women journalists

During the nineteenth century societal attitudes in the United States and Britain discouraged women from journalism. Generally regarded as a 'craft', even a rough and tough craft, journalism was deemed unsuitable for educated ladies. For example, Edwin Shuman (1899: 148–9), a US newspaperman who wrote a couple of early textbooks about reporting practices, asserted: 'The work of news-gathering, as a rule, is too rude and exacting for [women] . . . Local reporting work deals too exclusively with men and the affairs of men to give women a fair chance in it.' Towards the end of the nineteenth century women began to demand and often need a more active role outside the home. Those white, middle-class and well-educated women who managed to enter journalism were confined to writing about topics and in a style that contrasted sharply with the straight factual reporting of their male colleagues.

Women's journalism dealt with what were considered to be 'light' topics, such as fashion, the arts, domestic issues and society gossip. Male journalists dealt with the 'serious' and higher-status news of political and economic issues. Even when women did write about politics or social issues, they were encouraged to provide what has come to be referred to as the 'human-interest' angle by demonstrating how events affected people in their everyday lives. The role of early women journalists was to provoke an emotional response from readers. That said, this angle and the perceived glamour of journalism are also part of what drew women to journalism. Then, as now, journalism dealt with famous and influential people. So even if women were confined largely to society news, they enjoyed access to the rich and famous that no other profession open to women offered. Moreover, if on the whole they were paid less than men, they still were able to earn a living as journalists, a not insignificant fact to women who were orphaned, single, widowed or divorced, or whose fathers, brothers or husbands were poor managers of money.

In Britain, newspapers went through profound changes during the second half of the nineteenth century. Taxes on newspaper advertising were abolished in 1853; stamp duty was withdrawn in 1855; and taxes on paper were removed in 1861. In the United States in that period there was increasing excitement about democratization and the emergence of 'the common man' (the gender reference was intentional). Newspapers also expanded, often designed to bring news to that common man. Cheaper paper, the lowering of postage rates and several improvements in printing technology meant that larger newspapers could be produced faster and more efficiently. The innovation of the telegraph in 1844 was among the technological developments that had a direct and immediate consequence for journalism in both countries.

Not surprisingly, newspaper publishers promoted and invested in Samuel Morse's invention; first, individual papers used the telegraph to get news reports back to the newsroom, but by the mid-nineteenth century newspapers were organizing wire services. Improved systems of distribution, especially national railway systems, allowed for the emergence of a mass circulation popular press. By the end of the nineteenth century all newspapers in the US and Britain relied on advertising revenue, as opposed to sponsorship or the cover price, to subsidize production costs. To attract advertisers, publishers needed to capture the readership advertisers wanted, and so broadened the topics the newspapers covered.

The daily press of mid-Victorian Britain was characterized by 'serious' journalism that dealt with politics, finance and commerce, and this was supplemented by the so-called 'pauper press', comprised mainly of weekly titles sold for a few pennies and aimed at a largely working-class readership. From the 1850s onwards, however, newspapers for the middle classes like the British *Daily Telegraph* began to realize the economic advantage of widening their appeal to the working class. They adopted a lighter journalistic style that sought to entertain as well as inform readers: 'Politics and opinion started to be supplemented, if not replaced, with material of a "human note": crime, sexual violence and human oddities' (Williams 1998: 51).

Many newspapers aimed to attract more women readers by introducing what came to be labelled as 'women's journalism', a style of news writing confined to society news, reports on changing fashions and feature articles on domestic issues. These stories for women readers were written by women reporters. In Britain, significant changes in the law between 1884 and 1896 gave women greater rights within marriage; wider educational opportunities delivered by the 1870 Education Act produced a population more literate than ever before; technological progress had increased mobility and communication; and programmes of urban and industrial change were improving living conditions and increasing both men's wages and leisure time. Similar transformations occurred in the United States where, for example, illiteracy dropped by half (to 10.7 per cent of the population) between 1870 and 1900, while public[1] school attendance rose from 57 per cent to 72 per cent (Emery and Emery 1984: 232). Moreover, during that period, a number of women's colleges were established, and several state universities became coeducational. In 1918, women in Britain finally won the right to vote, followed, after virtually a 'Century of Struggle', in America in 1920. (This refers to the federal level; women could already vote in several states.)

Two women who were both illustrative and exceptional were Margaret Fuller from the US and Harriet Martineau from Britain. The two women, who became friends when Martineau travelled to the United States to campaign against slavery, had remarkably parallel social background and education, and both needed to support their families. Fuller grew up in Cambridge, Massachusetts, home of Harvard College, where it was not unusual for girls to be very well educated from an early age. Her father introduced a strict educational regime and taught her to translate passages from Virgil at the age of six. In her twenties, influenced by a blend of Unitarianism and Goethe's philosophy, Fuller embarked on a search for intellectual ways of developing the self to higher levels of consciousness. After her father died, Fuller, then twenty-five, was forced to support her family financially, which motivated her to take up writing professionally. Having established herself as a scholar and writer of literary essays, Margaret Fuller became literary editor of the *New York Tribune* in 1844 and two years later she became America's first woman foreign correspondent, as Chapter 10 on women war correspondents elaborates.

Harriet Martineau was born in 1802 the sixth of eight children in an upper-middle-class English family. Her father, a Unitarian, belonged to an elite literary circle, and believed in educating girls. Although largely self-taught, Harriet Martineau was, like Margaret Fuller, exposed to the kind of topics normally taught only to boys and she kept up a concentrated form of independent enquiry all her life. To stave off poverty when her father died in 1826, Martineau, then twenty-four, was forced to support her mother and herself. As she was deaf and therefore unable to work as a governess as her sisters did, Martineau chose writing as a career, producing a foundational treatise on the principles of sociological research called *How to Observe Morals and Manners* (1838). Said to be the first woman journalist in Britain, Harriet Martineau earned her income as a professional writer, and her *Illustrations of Political Economy* (1832–4) sought to prove that women could live on their own income. In 1852 she became a lead writer for the *Daily News*. When she worked for the *Daily News*, Martineau wrote from Ambleside in the Lake District (where Margaret Fuller once visited her) and sent her material to the paper in London by railway and coach. The copy would be published the next day. The never-married Martineau herself speculated that she might not have succeeded as an author if she had experienced the confines of a typical middle-class Victorian marriage. She saw the evils and disadvantages of married life and remarked 'I am probably the happiest single woman in the whole of England' (Pichanick 1980). With obvious parallels to Margaret Fuller's life trajectory in the United States, the combination of a rigorous and formal education within a middle-class background, the need to find a career to support her family, an inability to become a governess and her single status were pivotal to Martineau's career as a feminist, scholar, writer and journalist. Strongly committed to social justice, Martineau worked against slavery and campaigned for the establishment of the Poor Laws.

Flora Shaw became in 1892 the first woman on the permanent staff of *The Times* (of London), where her work would have certainly been regarded as glamorous and the envy of middle-class British women typically confined to the domestic sphere. A passionate colonialist, Shaw had been informally employed by *The Times* since 1890, writing an unsigned column. In 1892 she was sent to South Africa. Her reports, written in the form of letters, caused a sensation. The assistant manager of the paper, Moberly Bell, commented that in his two years at the paper, 'I can honestly say that nothing of the sort . . . has created such comment' (quoted in Sebba 1994: 38). She went to Australia, New Zealand and Canada before returning to take up a permanent editorial position.

Journalism began to be seen as a viable occupation for women in the US in the 1890s. This greatly distressed many male journalists, such as Edwin Shuman (1903: 157), who commented, 'Why any woman who can get $800 a year for teaching should wish to take up the harder work of newspaper reporting is difficult to understand.' Men claimed that the work was too arduous for women and that women exposed to the rough-and-tumble environment of the newsroom would lose their high ideals, their sweet and tender ways, indeed, their femininity. Many male journalists endorsed the findings of Edward Bok, editor of the *Ladies Home Journal*, that 'a girl cannot live in the free-and-easy atmosphere of the local room or do the work required of a reporter without undergoing a decline in the innate qualities of womanliness or suffering in health' (quoted in Steiner 1992: 10). How many women were actually deterred by this rhetoric cannot be known, but certainly many women pursued opportunities in journalism, and then went on to advocate them for others. In her 1893 book entitled *What Can a Woman Do: or Her Position in the Business and Literary World*,[2] journalist Martha Louise Rayne included a chapter on journalism, which Rayne described as 'agreeable, wide-awake work, with no more drudgery than there is in other occupations, and with many compensations'. Likewise, in her 1904 *Text Book for The Young Woman Journalist* the British journalist Frances Low claimed, 'The occupation of journalism is daily becoming more attractive to the average fairly well-educated woman' because of the 'constant variety of work and scene, contact with all sorts and conditions of men and women, and opportunities to know something of the deeper side of life' (Low 1904: 2, 6).

Low's advice also points to the nature of journalism work at this time: it had no specific entry qualifications. Although this also had disadvantages, in an era when educational opportunities for women remained uneven, the relative openness of journalism meant that women who were reasonably well educated, middle class, confident and persistent could gain entry.[3] Along with teaching or writing, becoming a journalist at that time was 'one of the very few routes open to intelligent women with some education to rise beyond humble origins or out of a failed marriage' in both countries (Sebba 1994: 3). Again, women's persistence was often motivated by the vulnerability of economic decline, as well as the desire to escape the confines of Victorian married life. However, only white women were able to take advantage of this relatively open access; very few mainstream papers hired men or women of colour.

The impact of the New Journalism on women

The rise of the New Journalism in the big cities of the United States during the 1880s was undoubtedly a key element in generating openings for women journalists between the 1880s and the outbreak of the First World War on both sides of the Atlantic. New Journalism blended two former traditions, the elite political press and literary and essay journals on the one hand, and the popular 'penny' or 'boulevard' newspapers and story papers on the other. It was characterized by large headlines, prominent illustrations and 'lively writing', like today's newspapers. It broadened the traditional topics of financial and political news covered by newspapers. The aim was to obtain large circulations and raise profits, so advertising took up wide columns (Marzolf 1983). The British adapted the American model with the aim of combining sensationalism with social reform. As Marion Marzolf (1983) argues, American New Journalism was so influential that it transformed the style and look of modern daily newspapers across Europe.

One controversial aspect of this New Journalism was its sensationalism, its determination to build a readership by nurturing an appetite for scandal and drama on its front pages. Information was presented in a way intended to arouse public emotion, whether hostile or empathetic. In its most extreme and popular forms, the New Journalism was scorned as 'Yellow Journalism'. The new emotional and sensational style was used to appeal to a new market of unsophisticated readers, but political affairs and public welfare were also strongly promoted, with political support given to the urban working classes. It was therefore heavily criticized for losing objectivity and impartiality. Significantly, this was the very moment when women journalists began to be appreciated for their ability to attract readers through their style of writing and approach to stories.

Representing the paradigmatic case in the United States, Joseph Pulitzer first experimented with the murder/sin/sex formula at the *St. Louis Dispatch*. The formula was more fully celebrated when Pulitzer bought out the *New York World* in 1883. Pulitzer recognized the growing economic power of women and their importance to advertisers, and the *World* is credited as being one of the first newspapers to include a women's page (Smith 1979: 159). In Britain, Alfred Harmsworth, knighted as Lord Northcliffe, launched the *Daily Mail* in 1896 with the statement: 'get me a murder a day'. By the turn of the century his formula of crime, adventure and human-interest stories made it the first British mass circulation paper, with a circulation of 989,000. Like Pulitzer, Northcliffe recognized the economic benefits of 'women's journalism'. Although the populist *Daily Mail* shied away from the overt sensationalism of British Sunday newspapers, 'priding itself on being a respectable family paper' (Williams 1998: 56), its daily page 7 'magazine' section offered women readers stories covering the latest fashions and features on domestic matters. In 1903 Northcliffe launched the *Daily Mirror* as 'a paper for gentlewomen, written by gentlewomen' under the editorship of Mary Howarth (Lee 1976b: 82). However, the paper did not sell and in 1905 it was revamped as an illustrated newspaper (Williams 1998: 57).

The New Journalism of the late nineteenth century produced three key changes. First, it gave women opportunities to enter the profession as they took on the task of interviewing and writing stories about women. Second, women were sought as subject-matter, both because they seemed to embody the drama of social change and because women's growing independence was 'a source of significant social anxiety' (Malone 1999: 70). Chapter 11 on contemporary 'postmodern' journalism evokes some strong parallels. A third change was in political issues, such as the suffrage movement, which were treated in sensationalist terms or as 'human-interest' stories, but provided an opportunity for the popular newspapers to challenge the formal, documentary style of the elite press and to stir readers' sense of outrage or compassion.

A direct aim of New Journalism was to make newspapers function as agents of social reform. Not unlike today's trends in news reporting, a new style of reporting was seen as necessary in order to 'speak directly to the people'. British Editor W. T. Stead defended the use of sensationalism to 'arrest the eye of the public and to compel them to admit the necessity of action'.[4] A number of British newspapers such as the *Star* and *Daily Chronicle* engaged in 'government by journalism' by advocating social reform. Women reporters became 'sob sisters' in this context. For example, the British journalist Annie Besant exposed the appalling conditions of working girls in an 1888 article headlined 'White Slavery in London'. Besant documented the industrial complaints of the sweated match girls who worked at the Bryant and May Match Company.[5] The *Link* article encouraged the match girls to go out on strike for three weeks. As a result of supplying details to Besant, three women from the factory were sacked so she helped them to form a matchgirls' union. Other newspapers including the *Pall Mall Gazette* and the *Star* took up the story, detailing the horrific lives and sweated labour of the match girls. Eventually the company was forced to improve conditions and its treatment of workers.

Women journalists were also exploited by editors who assigned them to perform investigative stunts precisely because these would be regarded as extraordinarily daring for women (and to a lesser extent, even for men). As Beasley and Gibbons (1993: 111) state: 'Women reporters ascended in balloons, descended in diving bells, dressed like beggars and waifs, feigned madness, and posed as servants in the homes of society figures to pursue exciting and scandalous tidbits for their readers.' As the most famous 'stunt girl' in the US,

Elizabeth Cochrane, who wrote under the byline Nellie Bly, inspired a tradition of intrepid women journalists. She entered journalism in the early 1880s after writing a letter to the *Pittsburgh Dispatch* to protest an article entitled 'What Girls Are Good For'. She never looked back. After joining Joseph Pulitzer's *New York World*, she initiated a mode of infiltration that consistently led to policy changes. She pretended to be mad so that she would be committed to an insane asylum and could thereby investigate mistreatment of patients; she let herself be arrested in order to expose conditions in women's prisons; and she worked in stores and factories in order to publicize the plight of workers. In 1889 the *World* cashed in on her enthusiasm for adventure and sent the twenty-four-year-old reporter around the world in an attempt – successful, as it turned out – to beat the record of the fictional Phineas Fogg in Jules Verne's *Around the World in Eighty Days* (Kroeger 1994).

Women in the black press

The history of black women's press activity in the United States begins well before the Civil War.[6] Relatively few women worked for the abolition papers in the United States, which are discussed in Chapter 8. Women were much more active in the daily and weekly black papers that emerged after the Civil War's end, such as the *New National Era*, published during the days of Reconstruction. Certainly the number of black papers dramatically increased after the Civil War, for a variety of reasons. For example: African Americans were able to earn more and could be sought by advertisers; more African Americans were getting an education; and social service and reform groups emerged to support the black press. Some of the papers were geographically based (where there were black communities) while others were specialized – especially those associated with either political or religious organizations.

Already in 1889, Lucy Wilmot Smith, who wrote for a number of African American religious (Baptist) and women's weeklies, wrote about eight prominent African American women journalists for an article published in the *Journalist*, a national trade paper for journalists that was the forerunner of *Editor and Publisher*. Many of the women she discussed would not now be described as 'reporters'; they wrote columns advocating a kind of genteel ideology of racial progress and 'uplift'. None the less, Smith, born in Kentucky in 1861, asserted that educated black women – having always been forced to work and strive for recognition – were doing even better than white women, especially in journalism: 'the brotherhood of the race, men whose energies have been repressed and distorted by the interposition of circumstances, give them opportunities to prove themselves; and right well are they doing this, by voice and pen' (quoted in Penn 1969: 381).

Thus, while white women writing for the white press were of several minds regarding the attention paid in the newsroom to their gender, African American women proudly wrote 'as' African American women. For them, journalism was not a profession but a calling that they took up specifically and explicitly as African American women. While distinct and intersecting barriers of gender and race kept them, for the most part, out of mainstream newspapers, they certainly were writing for the press. More to the point, they were important to the black press.

In one of the earliest histories of 'race journals', written in 1891, Penn (1969) mentions Mary Cook, who started writing on a regular basis in 1887, the year she graduated from college. Under the name Grace Ermine, she edited a column in the *South Carolina Tribune* and, like Smith, wrote columns for the *American Baptist* and for *Our Women and Children*, a magazine published in Louisville, Kentucky that used a number of women writers. Penn's discussion of Cook's work underscored her gentleness and spirituality, but she could be very direct and pointed in describing the continuing racism of the white community in the South.

The most popular black 'lady writer' was Victoria Earle Matthews (1861–1907). Earle's mother was a slave who escaped to New York, leaving her children in Georgia. Eventually she earned enough money to regain custody of her two surviving daughters, who had been reared as white in the master's household (allegedly, the master was their father) (Hutson 1971: 510). Earle only briefly attended school in New York. Earle began writing as a substitute for a number of papers in New York; soon she was writing for a variety of religious papers, and especially for black papers, including *New York Age*, the *New York Enterprise*, the *Brooklyn Eagle* and the *New York Globe*. She also became the New York correspondent for black papers around the country, including the *Boston Advocate, Washington Bee, Richmond Planet* and the *Cleveland Gazette*. Matthews became even more famous as one of the founding members of the National Federation of Afro-American Women, which eventually became the National Association of Colored Women. She also served on the editorial board of that organization's magazine, the *Woman's Era*. An active lecturer (for example, she spoke at the World's Columbian Exposition in 1893 in Chicago) and advocate of political reform, she founded the White Rose Industrial Association, which opened a home for black girls just arrived in New York, to make sure that they were not preyed upon by unscrupulous men. She and her husband, a coachman, had one son, who died at the age of sixteen.

After the turn of the century, the black press grew in strength and in number, in part because the growing number of successful black-owned businesses needed, wanted and supported advertising in the black press. Major black papers appeared in Philadelphia, New York, Baltimore, Chicago, Boston, Pittsburgh, as well as somewhat smaller ones in St. Louis, Kansas City, Buffalo, Norfolk, Houston, Dallas, Denver and Los Angeles (the *California Eagle*, which lasted from 1879 to 1967). These papers, like the white papers, wanted women to write columns for women, and again, many of the women wrote for several papers. For example, using a couple of *noms de plume*

Mary Britton, who graduated from Berea College in 1874 in her home state of Kentucky, wrote for several black general and family papers, including those based in Cleveland, Lexington, Indianapolis and Cincinnati. Ione Wood, born in New Jersey, wrote for various publications, especially on temperance.

A few women managed to cover the African American community for both black and white newspapers. For example, as a teenager Delilah Beasley (1871–1934) submitted brief items about local church and social activities in Cincinnati, Ohio, where she grew up, to a couple of black newspapers, as well as to a 'mainstream' paper, the *Cincinnati Enquirer* (Streitmatter 1994). Having moved to California, in part to do research on black pioneers, Beasley wrote an article for the *Oakland Tribune* in 1915 protesting the unambiguous racism of the film *Birth of a Nation* and promoting the accommodationist philosophy of Booker T. Washington. Streitmatter's excellent history of the black press quotes an explanation that Beasley published in the *Oakland Sunshine*, a black paper, for her interest in writing for the white press:

> News of special interest to us as a people ought to be discussed in our own papers among ourselves. But, if a bit of news would have a tendency to better our position in the community, then it should not only be published in our own race papers, but in the papers of the other race as well.
>
> (Streitmatter 1994: 76)

'Journalism for women'

Women journalists in the first half of the twentieth century faced a central paradox: those who refused to accept restrictions on what they could write about and who were not suitably feminine at work were branded as personally deviant, while those who accepted the limitations imposed on them and allowed themselves to be treated as feminine were professionally marginalized. By marking out the gender of women journalists as odd and abnormal while treating the gender of male journalists as neutral, male editors created an effective barrier to women's success.

In mainstream newspapers, women journalists had to fight to avoid being sidelined into society and fashion news or providing a light, 'feminine' view of a story. Certainly, books of the period about journalism and for would-be journalists in the United States insisted that this was the proper sphere for women. For example, Charles Olin would have limited women to occasional sidebars:

> Her story is not supposed to add anything of importance to the report of her brother journalist, its whole value lying in the fact that it is written from a wholly feminine standpoint, in a bright feminine manner, with little touches of feminine sympathy, pathos and sentiment.
>
> (Olin 1906: 51)

Between 1920 and 1940, efforts were made to elevate the status of society news in the United States. Dix Harwood's 1927 book *Getting and Writing News* admitted that society pages rarely enjoyed much dignity, although he claimed:

> [T]he society desk is oftentimes one of the most valuable offices on the paper if the occupant be a woman of high intelligence with a nose for news . . . and a woman of poise and dignity – a woman whom hostesses will be forced to treat as an equal.
>
> (Harwood 1927: 148–9)

But these attempts to raise the profile of society news seem weak and unconvincing. Echoing the explicit sentiments of many men, Morton Sontheimer, in his 1941 *Newspaperman*, admitted that 'The women's department jobs almost invariably go to women, not because men can't do them but because they won't' (Sontheimer 1941: 228). Sontheimer concluded, therefore, that news staffs should be no more than 5 per cent female.

Some women were more resentful of their ghettoized status than others. Elizabeth Jordan, for example, received her first job in the 1880s editing the woman's page of a Milwaukee newspaper owned by a family friend, but she was less than delighted by this opportunity to supply 'light and warmth to the women of the universe'. She said in her autobiography, 'It is a miracle that the stuff I had to carry in "Sunshine" did not permanently destroy my interest in newspaper work' (Jordan 1938: 14). As it turns out, in 1890 she was hired by the *New York World*, where she promised to do anything but society news: 'I drew the line at that' (Jordan 1938: 48). She achieved great success at the *World*, and in 1899 she became an editor of *Harper's Bazar* magazine, indicating that it was easier for women to reach decision-making positions in magazines than in newspapers.

In some cases, like that of British journalist Emillie Peacocke, entry into journalism was aided by family connections. Encouraged by her father, John Marshall, who was the editor and co-proprietor of the *Northern Echo*, she joined the paper in 1898, at the age of fifteen, as a trainee reporter. But her journalistic background and training did not insulate her from prejudice. In 1902 she applied for the post of sub-editor on the *Yorkshire Daily Observer*. Although her application was apparently the best of the hundred or so received, she was told, 'We cannot possibly see our way to offering a position as sub-editor to a lady. The difficulties and objections are in our view insuperable' (quoted in Abrams 1994: 11). Undaunted, Peacocke went on to become one of Fleet Street's first full-time female reporters. She began at the *Daily Express* in 1904, and moved to the *Sunday Express* in 1918 as editor of the women's page. Although this was a position she would have shunned in earlier years, as she commented later, 'in the 1920s, the control of the new Woman's Department, was from every point of view a tempting proposition, calling for a new appraisal as opportunities for women were opening on every front' (quoted in Sebba 1994: 56).

As Rebecca Abrams (1994) suggests, dismissing the impact of the early women's pages on women's progress in journalism is tempting, because they rarely reflected the personal lives or political convictions of the women who wrote them. For example, Peacocke's column for the British *Sunday Express* featured the busy daily routine of 'Mrs. Becker', a fictional housewife, yet the author was a committed feminist and working mother (Abrams 1994). This highlights how women journalists were valued specifically as women, writing for women on topics concerning women's traditional role in the home. It also suggests the contrast between the fiction they wrote and the reality of their lives as paid employees in a male-dominated profession. Nevertheless, the creation of women's pages at least provided a recognized space for discussing women's issues and granted a foothold for women in journalism. As the next chapter explains, that foothold was to prove to be important for many women journalists after the Second World War.

One British journalist who began her career in the 'woman's page ghetto', but went on to redefine women's pages, was Mary Stott. Like Peacocke, Stott came from a family of journalists. Both her parents were journalists, but it was her uncle, a chief sub-editor on the *Leicester Mail,* who offered her a job as a proofreader in 1925. A year later she was appointed woman's editor, much to her dismay: 'I went back to the reporters' room and put my head on the filing cabinet and wept! I wanted to be a proper journalist, I didn't want to be stuck with women. I wanted to be doing the same things as the men' (quoted in Abrams 1994: 11). Despite battling against women's page journalism, Stott never really escaped it. Her answer in the end was to change the nature of the pages. In 1957 she became the editor of the women's pages in the *Guardian* and is credited with helping to transform them from offering coverage of fashion and domestic matters to those of social and political concern.[7]

Another route open to women journalists then, as now, was to work for non-mainstream publications (see Chapter 7). In America, women such as Ida B. Wells brought news and a commitment to a cause to her African American readers through the *Memphis Free Speech*. In Britain, the tradition was just as powerful, and, in the last two decades of the nineteenth century, a number of women used the press to publicize their campaigns. Helena Swanick, a Cambridge graduate, wrote for the *Manchester Guardian* before becoming the editor of the suffragist paper, the *Common Cause* from 1910 to 1912. Helen Blackburn also supported the suffragettes through her editorship of the *Englishwoman's Review* from 1881 to 1890.

Some male press owners and producers were forced to accept women who proved they could hold their own. Men even ended up praising them in terms of their honorary masculinity. But not all editors were overtly or consistently sexist. Notable exceptions include, in Britain, Sir John Robinson on the *Daily News*, W. T. Stead of the *Pall Mall Gazette* and C. P. Scott at the *Manchester*

Guardian, all of whom were supportive of women journalists in Britain and provided opportunities where few existed. In the United States, Stanley Walker, editor at the *New York Herald Tribune*, proudly espoused sexist notions. Walker characterized women reporters as slovenly, impolite, humourless; according to him, they are suckers for romance and 'don't understand honor or fair play . . . as men understand it' (Walker 1934: 248). Yet, Walker certainly provided Ishbel Ross with opportunities for work and success. The Scottish-born Ross, who got her first break as a reporter when she covered the arrival in Canada of suffrage leader Emmeline Pankhurst, quickly made and sustained a national reputation as a plucky and highly competitive reporter and was eventually appointed to the *Herald Tribune*'s editorial board. At Stanley Walker's suggestion she wrote *Ladies of the Press* (1936), which remains a useful resource about famous women journalists in the nineteenth and early twentieth centuries. Ross also wrote four novels as well as twenty non-fiction books and many magazine articles.

In certain instances the employment of women in journalism was a form of enlightened patronage although, ultimately, all such appointments increased the power and influence of women in journalism. For example, C. P. Scott nurtured the careers of a number of talented women in Britain, but only if they were his wife's university friends or women he met socially, such as Caroline Lejeune, who established herself as a film critic on Scott's advice, working for the *Guardian* from 1922 to 1928 and the *Observer* from 1928 until 1960. It should also be noted that male journalists in the early part of the twentieth century (and beyond) also used personal connections to gain entry to journalism. The 'old boy' or 'old school tie' network operated as a serious barrier to women. However, the proportion of women who resorted to personal contacts to get a job created the impression that only 'well-connected' women were suitable to be journalists, and this created another entry barrier for women from working-class backgrounds.

Women generally faced opposition and prejudice and had few role models to guide them. Even though the number of women journalists increased during the early twentieth century, they consistently failed to break through to the front page – the 'critical test' that was generally agreed by the journalism world to be the heart of real journalism (Belford 1986: 2).

The First World War, which is often perceived as a time of liberation for women workers, was a mixed blessing for women journalists. It disrupted hard-won successes and created a hiatus in the development of women's careers that extended well into the 1920s. It could be argued that the war gave women some degree of greater independence and awareness. Housewives were called up to work in munitions and other factories or volunteered to do war work. Middle-class women trained for nursing and clerical duties, and thousands of women from the leisured classes worked for their local communities. Certainly, opportunities to replace men who went to fight gave many women a glimpse of their own potential as journalists. Emma Bugbee, for example, only succeeded in getting a desk in the *New York Herald Tribune* newsroom in 1915, despite being qualified for the position years before. In general, papers and magazines halted production or published fewer pages, and official war coverage dominated the press, making the peacetime tone of many features and columns inappropriate. Meanwhile, in Britain, the First World War correspondents were little more than disseminators of military propaganda, effectively silenced by The Defence of the Realm Act, 1914.

While the war affected the United States, American journalists were not as restricted as their British counterparts. America's late entry into the war combined with its physical isolation from the fighting allowed journalists of both sexes more freedom for a longer period, while in the UK information was strictly controlled from the outset. Most contributions by women to the reporting of the war were to emerge later in books, diaries, essays and letters – forms of writing that fell outside the rules of press censorship but much of which tells the story of the war and human suffering.[8] Denied the opportunity to report on the war from the front line, women's main contribution to war reporting was to explain its impact on civilian populations. Nevertheless, in doing so, women arguably contributed to the establishment of a new style of war reporting, as discussed in later chapters. A similar situation occurred during the Second World War. Men went off to report from the front line, which created some opportunities for women at home, but in general these opportunities were relinquished at the end of hostilities. None the less, the war did help to consolidate the position of some women, like Hilde Marchant, who wrote for the British *Daily Express* and later the *Daily Mirror* and who for a short time was one of the best-paid reporters in Fleet Street (Sebba 1994: 160).

Radio broadcasting: a voice for women?

While standard histories of early radio make little mention of women's contributions, women participated in radio as a hobby from the outset, especially as wives or daughters of male radio hobbyists. Radio quickly became popular with audiences in the US, and therefore with advertisers. In 1921 some thirty radio stations were operating and by 1923 the number had increased to 600. By 1930 40 per cent of US households had radio sets. One consequence of the huge growth in the number of radio stations and in audiences was a need for more performers. This itself created certain opportunities for women – in music and acting, and in programming. By the beginning of the Second World War, radio news was an important source of national and world news in the US and included the world news round-up produced by CBS correspondents in Europe and elsewhere. Television was still in its infancy in the US. In 1941, when the Japanese bombed Pearl Harbor there were television stations on the air only in New York, Philadelphia, Chicago, Los Angeles and Schenectady, NY (home of General Electric), and few people owned receivers. Radio, however, was available in 80 per cent of US households (Sloan, Stovall and Startt 1989: 314, 316).

British broadcasting

The British government granted a licence to a consortium of wireless manufacturers who created the British Broadcasting Company in 1923. It was initially set up as a commercial organization that derived its income from a proportion of the sale of radio sets in its early years, along with a proportion of a licence fee collected by the General Post Office. In 1926 the Crawford Committee called for broadcasting to be free from commercial domination, and the following year a public service broadcasting institution, the British Broadcasting Corporation, was established by Royal Charter, funded entirely by licence fees and headed by John Reith.

As Director General, John Reith, knighted in 1927, ran the BBC according to his own strict Presbyterian moral code. This severely restricted women's recruitment and promotion within the corporation. Although he retired in 1938, Reith's influence extended for decades thereafter through the strict public service ethos he established to 'inform, educate and entertain' (in that order) the British public. Divorced and married women were not allowed to work for the BBC until the 1960s. In particular, Reith was determined to establish through the BBC a distinct national identity that included a set standard of spoken English known as Received Pronunciation. Not only did this effectively exclude regional accents from the airwaves, it also meant that the majority of on-air voices belonged to men. Women were banned from reading news bulletins on the BBC right up to the 1970s, in part because early microphones were designed for the male vocal range and tended to make women sound 'tinny', but also because the BBC management believed that the female voice was too closely associated with gossip and lacked the authority necessary for news reading (Shingler and Wieringa 1998: 46).

A senior programme producer of the 1930s recalls being severely reprimanded for allowing the violinist Daisy Kennedy to perform. Reith's objection was that she was a divorced woman and therefore should be shunned (Shingle and Wieringa 1998: 66).[9] One woman who helped shape BBC news was Hilda Matheson. Reith appointed her as Head of Talks in 1927, impressed by her connections gained as the political secretary of one of the first women to become a Member of Parliament, Nancy Astor (Hunter 2000: 42). At this time the BBC's news bulletins were restricted to after 6.30 p.m. so that they did not compete directly with newspapers, and they were written by the Reuters news agency. Print journalists' cumbersome style of writing was unsuitable for radio, so Matheson developed a style of writing that sounded more natural when read aloud. In 1928 she commissioned a report into the way the newly formed News Section should operate. The eleven-page report recommended that news agencies should provide their full wire service to the BBC, and that bulletins should be structured with home news first, followed by overseas news and sports news. The report was 'the most important document on news values ever produced for the BBC' (Hunter 2000: 43). It changed the Corporation's approach to news.

From the beginning, the BBC targeted women as an audience. One of its first programmes was *Woman's Hour*, which ran for nine months in 1923. It was cancelled on the recommendation of the Women's Advisory Committee, in part because it was broadcast at 4 p.m. when few women had time to listen to it, but also because of objections from the National Federation of Women's Institutes, which objected to grouping women in the same way as children, who also had their own special 'hour' (quoted in *Woman's Hour* 2002). Undeterred, the BBC launched a special series of 'household talks' for women in 1928. Throughout the 1930s these talks were broadcast every morning when, it was believed, women could take a break from their chores and learn something over their cup of tea. Most of the talks concerned detailed domestic methods (for example, how to clean wallpaper using stale bread), but some dealt with politics or domesticity in foreign countries. While many of the experts used in these talks were male – especially doctors and nutritionists – the talks began in the 1930s to be aimed at a working-class audience (quoted in *Woman's Hour* 2002).

Improvements in technology led to developments in mobile recording units, which were first used outside London in 1937. Although cumbersome and awkward to use, the mobile units allowed the sounds and voices of 'real' people (as opposed to public figures, politicians and experts) to be used on air. Olive Shapley, an assistant producer for the north region, based in Manchester, was part of one of the first teams to use the new equipment for a feature on shopping. Over the next few years, until the outbreak of war, Shapley made countless radio documentaries that 'broke new grounds for radio both in their technique and their subject matter' (Scannell and Cardiff 1991: 345). She tended to feature the lives of 'ordinary' people drawn from the working classes, from canal workers to lorry drivers, and from miners' wives to the homeless. Her technique was to keep her links to a minimum and allow the natural sounds and voices of those directly involved to tell the story in their own words. In the days of scripted radio and Received Pronunciation, this was revolutionary – and not always well received (Shapley 2000: 34). As with women's pages in newspapers, these little pockets of feminine broadcasting were important, even though they were limited and very slow to develop, because they provided an entrée for women that would later be exploited.

US broadcasting

Judith Cary Waller was the first manager of a Chicago radio station owned by the *Chicago Daily News* that went on the air in 1922. With a background in advertising, Waller is credited with inaugurating live coverage of sports events (she obtained permission to broadcast home games of the Chicago Cubs baseball team) and with founding one of the longest-running experiments in radio education, The American School of the Air (Hilmes 1997). She was made Public Service Director when WMAQ was sold to NBC in 1931. Indeed, by the 1940s, the directors of educational and public service programming at all four networks in the US were women.

However, as in Britain, women were for the most part assumed to be active as the audience, not the on-air producers of radio programming, since it was claimed that they lacked the authoritative male voice. Ironically, it was the woman who wrote the first 'Listener's Point of View' column, in 1924, for *Radio Broadcast* magazine, that sparked the debate over whether women's voices were appropriate on air. Jennie Irene Mix had received a letter from a record dealer speculating that the reason for poor sales of records with women's voices is that the voice of women 'is very undesirable and to many, both men and women, displeasing' (quoted in Hilmes 1997: 142). Mix's informal survey of male station managers found some support for the idea. The following year a survey of 5,000 listeners apparently found that men's voices were preferred to women's by 100 to 1.

Women's on-air role was essentially confined to programmes designed specifically for women. Ruth Crane Schaefer told an interviewer that she 'had to find a job' during the Depression – and managed to get hired in 1929 to organize commercials for WJR in Detroit. But she quickly took over *Mrs. Page's Household Economy*, dispensing information about cooking and cleaning, six days a week. Then, in 1946, by which time she was president of the National Association of Women Broadcasters, she took over a television show, *The Modern Woman* (Beasley and Gibbons 2003: 167–74). During the Second World War, just as many American newspapers were forced to hire women or move women into more prominent news positions, to replace men serving in the military, so radio stations scrambled to find staff, including in Europe.

An important radio voice in the US was Dorothy Thompson (1894–1961). Journalism historians usually discuss Thompson as a columnist and writer, but given that Thompson was the single female radio commentator during what was perhaps the golden age of radio commentary, she is worth mentioning here. In 1914 Dorothy Thompson graduated from Syracuse University, wanting to be a writer. After suffering a number of rejection letters for her short stories she took a menial job with a women's suffrage organization, although she soon moved on to writing and organizing publicity stunts for the campaign (Kurth 1990). After the First World War, Thompson and a good friend went to Europe as freelance correspondents, where they both received assignments to cover a Zionist conference. She persevered, mentored by a number of experts in politics and journalism, and learned to be resourceful, that is, to use bribery and disguise in order to obtain and transmit her stories. By 1925, Thompson was officially named head of the combined Berlin bureaus of the *New York Evening Post* and the *Philadelphia Public Ledger*. She interviewed many major figures in and out of politics, including Trotsky, Atatürk and Freud. Peter Kurth (1990: 79), one of her biographers, notes that Thompson never lacked for passionate suitors, a fact she relished. That said, she is credited with a wonderful brush-off: 'Yes, dear, but right this minute I've simply got to get to the bottom of this Bulgarian business.' She kept working through her first marriage, to a fellow foreign correspondent, although when she married novelist Sinclair Lewis in London in 1928 she quit journalism for a while.

Having returned to Europe, Thompson interviewed Adolf Hitler in 1931. From then on, she regularly denounced Hitler and the Nazis, as seen in her articles and book *I Saw Hitler!* (1932). Identified as 'a leading opponent of the Hitler regime' (Kurth 1990: 201), she was ordered by an agent of the Gestapo, on behalf of Adolf Hitler, to leave the country in 1934, making her the first American correspondent to be expelled from Germany. In 1936, she began a column for the *New York Herald Tribune* that eventually was syndicated to as many as 170 daily papers, with some of her fiery columns collected in a book. *On the Record* was not a 'woman's column', but dealt with politics, economics, the military and indeed the entire human condition, from a position of 'liberal conservatism'. A majority of her columns were devoted to attacking Hitler.

Some of the other female reporters hired to deliver radio news also had print backgrounds – such as Sigrid Schultz, who was already in central Europe for the *Chicago Tribune* and another Illinois newspaper woman, Helen Hiett (Hosley and Yamada 1987: 7). Betty Wason, another woman hired for the CBS's *World News Roundup*, claimed that CBS complained that her voice was too young and feminine for war news and that the public objected to it. Van Wagoner Tufty claimed her daily afternoon radio show was not a woman's programme, 'but the news as reported by a woman' (quoted in Hosley and Yamada 1987: 37).

More often, these women explicitly claimed to bring to the fore a woman's viewpoint. But this does not indicate that they were all happy about it or had actually volunteered to do this. Hosley and Yamada (1987: 62) note that CBS debuted a radio soap opera called *Wendy Warren and the News* about the adventures of a 'girl reporter'. Before the soap opera began, a man would perform a short 'real' newscast, and then the actress who played Wendy Warren would read a minute of 'women's news'. Once the United States entered the Second World War, women were hired across the US to replace the radio broadcasters who had been drafted. The news department at a Cleveland, Ohio station was 'all girl' – except, of course, for management. A 1944 survey reported that women outnumbered men as radio announcers by twelve to one (Hosley and Yamada 1987: 61).

Conclusion

The first hundred years of journalism in the United States and Britain show that women had to overcome many obstacles to get into the newsroom. Many editors refused to believe women capable of the job, and those who were hired had to fight for the opportunity to write about the same topics as men and in the same style as men. The norm was that middle-class women, particularly married women, did not work. According to the US census of 1920, only 9 per cent of married women were gainfully employed. This rose only to 11.7 per cent by the 1930 census. In the UK the figures are very similar, with 10 per cent of married women employed according to the 1931 census. Editors might worry that even hiring a young single woman was a waste of their mentoring and supervisory energy since in all likelihood she would quit upon marriage or upon bearing children. This posed serious problems for women who needed to earn a wage to support themselves or their families. None the less, by the Second World War women journalists were established on both sides of the Atlantic. Already in 1920 and then continuing for decades, newspapers across the US ran a syndicated comic strip called 'Winnie Winkle the Breadwinner', which, if it mocked women's consumerism and vanity, also pointed to a now-standard cultural figure. And certainly women had achieved a beachhead in journalism.

In broadcasting women faced an additional barrier to their acceptance. Early microphones designed for the male vocal range made their voices sound high-pitched and robbed them of authority. And there were doubts about women's suitability to speak in public about serious political and economic matters. For decades this kept many of those women working in radio confined to programmes geared towards homemakers or children.

Despite the many parallels between the United States and Britain in the way women journalists progressed, there are also some striking differences. In broadcasting, the commercial route taken by radio in the US provided hundreds of radio stations across the country which gave women a chance to gain experience on small local stations before moving to more prestigious ones. In Britain, radio was a public service broadcasting monopoly run by the BBC and rigidly controlled from its London centre, so there were fewer chances for women to prove their ability in the new medium. Moreover, women's advancement was curtailed by a number of patriarchal codes: the strict Reithian moral code that barred married and divorced women from the BBC, the industry's reluctance to treat women's voices as authoritative or as acceptable to the technology, and the gender-structured conventions of listening.

In both the United States and Britain, women journalists were expected to be 'different' from male colleagues in both what they wrote and the way they wrote it. They were expected to make significantly distinctive contributions to news production compared to their male counterparts and were employed to produce a type of 'women's journalism' consisting of society news, women's pages and something that came to be called 'human-interest' news. This emergent news genre not only emphasized consumerism, fashion and housework but also reported events in a style aimed at evoking emotion, compassion and sensationalism. Again, especially in the US, women could and did muscle their way into covering literally everything from sports to international affairs, although by no means in the same numbers as men. Moreover, as the following chapters explain, while long deterred from the 'serious' news of politics, economic and foreign affairs, women were sanctioned to spearhead the rise of a more accessible and contextualized form of journalism and a corresponding shift away from a strict emphasis on facts. As such, women journalists came to be associated with this trend towards a 'human-interest' style of news and were gradually actively sought for their ability to attract wider news audiences.

2

Women journalists in the post-war period

Many of the advances in journalism made by women between 1939 and 1945, when they filled positions vacated by men who fought in the Second World War, were lost over the immediate post-war period when men returned and reclaimed their newsroom jobs. In some cases, women were asked to hand back their jobs to the men they had replaced. In other cases, they were replaced by newly recruited men. For example, Marjorie Paxson had been working for a United Press bureau in the Midwestern US, where she and another woman covered everything but executions and college football (since women were not allowed in the press box). Paxson (1991: 21) says she signed a waiver agreeing to give up her job at the end of the war. Sure enough, in 1946 she was released – although the Associated Press hired her as a radio writer, for higher pay.

Mary Stott's experience is also typical of what happened to women journalists on both sides of the Atlantic. Just before the end of the war she was offered a job in the north of England as a sub-editor for the prestigious *Manchester Evening News*, where she found 'there was no discrimination in the allocation of work' (Stott 1989: 60). Freed from working in the narrow area of women's pages she felt like a 'real journalist'. None the less, she was sacked in 1950, by which time most men had returned from the armed forces, 'in order to protect the male succession to the post of chief sub-editor'. She spent the next seven years 'mainly in "domesticity"'. Once replaced by men, many women stayed out of journalism or even out of the workforce altogether. However exciting and satisfying their wartime work had been, many settled down to domesticity and homemaking.

Ironically, on the one hand, the likelihood that women would quit the newsroom in order to devote themselves to childrearing was often used as an excuse for not hiring women. On the other hand, women were fired upon announcing their pregnancies. For example, Betsy Wade, whose major legal suit against the *New York Times* is described in Chapter 6, was fired from the

Herald Tribune in 1953, when she became pregnant. In any case, most women journalists experienced the post-war period as a turning back of the clock. Through a series of redundancies and demotions, the majority of women were forced to leave the profession or go part-time to concentrate on home-making. Many of those who remained in journalism were confined, once again, to 'women's journalism': features and women's page work, fashion and society. The decade immediately after the war was therefore a difficult time for women journalists. Employment opportunities were limited because of the restricted size of newspapers, with men being given priority over women in recruitment. However, women were beginning to enter the new medium of radio. We argue that although women were confined to a restricted area of journalistic reporting, they brought about changes to print and broadcast journalism at least in the sense that they broadened the topics deemed newsworthy. Women were centrally involved in developing a style of reporting aimed less at delivering facts and more at evoking a response from the audience by showing how events affected them.

In both the United States and Britain, the late 1940s and early 1950s were a time of readjustment and recovery from the upheavals of the war. The Second World War had created a society hungry for news and that habit continued, with newspapers enjoying rising sales and profits. Although radio was a vital news medium during the war, in Britain it was limited to three BBC stations, so newspapers remained a key source of information for the population. Moreover, since radio was restricted to public service broadcasting within the non-commercial BBC, newspapers were the main mass advertising medium, even though newsprint rationing until 1955 restricted their size and number. In fact, this made newspapers more profitable than ever: government-imposed restrictions, keeping paper and printing costs low, and the limited size and number of pages led to great demand for advertising space.

This chapter examines how the post-war growth of the news media, and the resulting increased competition for audiences, allowed women journalists to become more established. Initially they were confined, in the main, to domains directly appealing to women as an audience, such as women's pages, domestic issues and celebrity interviews. But the need to attract the largest possible audience and to be more appealing to women forced editors to adapt their products. They did so by broadening the news agenda from the traditionally 'masculine topics' of politics and economics, and by including social issues of direct concern to women. This came at a price, however, especially for the women who edited the women's sections. Meanwhile, women were initially deemed to lack the authoritative voice assumed to be necessary for broadcasting. None the less, women were eventually hired in broadcast newsrooms, first to attract women to radio listening (and radio advertising) and then to attract male and female television audiences. As well as the tensions women faced when they demanded to be hired, promoted and respected for their professional skills rather than their appearance, this chapter emphasizes the conflicts women faced in undertaking careers in the face of family responsibilities and, sometimes, family opposition.

Women at British newspapers

In the immediate post-war period, the entry route into journalism remained as it had been for earlier women journalists. The majority began in sections traditionally reserved for women, especially fashion and society news. Marjorie Proops, who was credited by *Daily Mirror* editor, Hugh Cudlipp, in the 1960s as being the 'first British journalist to attain the Instant Recognition status previously enjoyed by film stars, exemplifies this (Vincenzi 1996: 16). Proops started out as a fashion illustrator in the 1930s for various London newspapers. During the Second World War she moved to the countryside with her young son while her husband served in the military, but she was asked by the editor of the woman's magazine *Good Taste* to write about life as a young mother in wartime Britain. This led to a regular column and commissions from other editors. In 1945 she went to the *Daily Herald* as fashion editor and became woman's editor five years later. In 1954 she joined the *Daily Mirror* as a columnist.

Although not pigeon-holed as 'women's pages', Proops's columns in the *Daily Mirror* had an 'unusually intimate tone'[1] that made them more accessible than other columns of the time, and they became instantly popular. Generally they featured interviews with Hollywood stars and celebrities but they also included features about politicians and church leaders. Her success was attributed by journalist Penny Vincenzi (1996: 16) to 'her ability to makes friends with, to get along with, the subjects of her column'. Proops was unusual in the 1950s in that although she wrote a column with a traditionally 'feminine and intimate' approach, it was directed at both men and women readers.

Women's pages

Except for the *Daily Mirror,* many 'serious' British papers of the 1950s ignored women altogether. The only women's pages in national newspapers were in the tabloid popular press.[2] These tended to be dominated by the latest Paris fashions and society news. The British journalist Katherine Whitehorn, who began her career in the 1950s and went on to become one of the best-known journalists in Britain, remarks:

> Grander papers didn't have women's pages at all; women journalists in the main paper were supposed to write in exactly the same way as men, and there weren't many of them . . . The very phrase 'women's journalism' was a term of disparagement.
>
> (Whitehorn 1997: 1)

By the late 1950s the situation was beginning to change, with the 'grander' papers, broadsheets like the *Guardian* and the *Observer*, launching women's pages.

Newspapers' intensified targeting of women readers was partly a result of the rising competition from commercial television, which was beginning to eat into the advertising market. By 1958 television had already passed the total advertising revenue of the national newspapers (Tunstall 1993: 80). But the change also reflects the structure of the British press in its distinction between 'quality' (broadsheet) and 'popular' (tabloid) newspapers. This distinction in style and content, originally based on class, income and education levels, can be traced back to the 1830s' competition between establishment papers like *The Times* and the populist radical press. Then, as now, the prestige press relied on an advertising revenue base that 'forces them "up market" . . . because advertisers are willing to pay several times as much to reach readers who are several times more wealthy' (Tunstall 1993: 77). Broadsheet papers followed the popular press by introducing women's pages from the late 1950s in order to attract advertisers wishing to target women consumers directly. Katherine Whitehorn said that during the early days of women's pages 'the function of women's journalism [was] to teach women how to be perfect' and the advertisements implied that 'they would be perfect if only they used the product' (Whitehorn 1997: 1).

The number of women journalists began to rise in the early 1960s. Once established, the woman's page expanded beyond fashion and household tips. By the mid-1960s, in response to the second wave of feminism, woman's pages were distinctly political, dealing with matters of serious social concern, as Katherine Whitehorn recalls:

> The women's pages . . . were airing a whole lot of personal concerns and discussing human problems like addiction or divorce. They emphasized everything that goes on in people's lives that isn't work, saying 'Human relationships, your life at home, your children, your garden, what you cook are just as important as anything in the working day'.
>
> (Whitehorn 1997: 1)

This form of women's journalism contrasted sharply with the fact-laden, detached and 'objective' style of other sections of the paper that dealt with institutions and (habitually male) figures of authority. Although often maligned and trivialized by male journalists at the time, women journalists of the 1960s were at the forefront of changes – in both the topics they covered and the approach they took to stories – towards the current newspaper practice of focusing on human-interest stories and evoking an emotional response, from anger to empathy, with readers.

One example is British journalist Mary Stott, who became editor of the *Guardian*'s women's pages, 'Mainly for Women', from 1957 until 1972. As mentioned in Chapter 1, Stott did not relish being sidelined to the low-status women's pages. On taking up her position at the *Guardian*, her response was to gradually change the nature of the pages away from garden parties and fashion tips towards social and political issues. Following Stott's death in September 2002, Fiona MacCarthy (2002), who was her women's page assistant in 1964, recalls that many of the issues raised on Stott's pages led to direct action. In 1961 the Housewives' Register was formed to help combat the social and intellectual isolation of women working in the home that the women's pages had highlighted. Other organizations, from the Pre-school Playgroups Association to the Invalids at Home Trust, were formed as a direct response to articles from and about women in the *Guardian* women's pages. As MacCarthy notes in her obituary for Stott, 'The 1960s women's page was an onslaught on old-time suburban female values from within' (2002: 20).

In particular, Stott built up a rapport with readers by featuring the lives of 'ordinary', working- and middle-class women. She deliberately included articles that might open up the possibilities for women to form supportive networks and create a sense of solidarity amongst women of all ages, classes and political persuasions to voice their stories: 'Such missives from the coal-face of female deprivation drew an enormous correspondence, and started a whole journalistic genre of personal unburdening. Mary's women were the first of the "Woman Who Told All"' (MacCarthy 2002: 20).

While women readers responded to this new approach, resistance still came from male journalists like Peter Preston, then features editor of the *Guardian*, who described it as 'entrail slashing':

> How does one reconcile Militant Mary, parading with lib' banners outside the *Punch* office, and the Mary who describes every last nuance of bitter, private grief? One Mary is rampaging to be treated on equal terms, another is making a personal livelihood . . . by exposing her soul in a way which . . . is womanly.
>
> (Chun 1992: 2)

The personal as political

The feminist aim of making the personal political, reflected in women's journalism at the time, was particularly evident in the work of journalist Jill Tweedie, who wrote for the *Daily Telegraph* and later the *Guardian*. Widely credited as providing the 'human face of feminism', Tweedie is most famous for her column entitled 'Letters from a Faint Hearted Feminist', which comically explored the everyday obstacles to putting feminist theory into practice. Thousands of women dealing with demanding men, small children and the dreariness of domesticity identified with her character because it was said to be so 'human' and realistic. But Tweedie also dealt with 'serious' political topics of importance to women. As one of her colleagues, Polly Toynbee, wrote following Tweedie's death in 1993:

> She was a campaigner on issues people had scarcely thought about. She was one of the first to campaign about how women were treated in maternity wards, shaved, drugged, legs strapped in stirrups, treated by doctors like vets with farrowing pigs. There was outrage when she wrote about rape within marriage, but now the law has been changed.
>
> (Toynbee 1993: 25)

Towards the end of the 1960s, Marjorie Proops also began to move away from celebrity interviews to tackle serious social issues including illegitimacy, contraceptives, drug addiction and abortion law. Many of Proops's topics were inspired by letters from readers to her 'Dear Marje' advice column, which ran from 1959 in the weekly magazine *Woman's Mirror*. Hugh Cudlipp, the editor of the *Daily Mirror*, noted the column's growing success and suggested that Proops do the same thing for his daily paper, and in 1971 she began the column she is best remembered for.[3] During the 1960s and early 1970s the *Daily Mirror* was the top-selling national newspaper in the UK and Proops's column had a tremendous impact on newspapers' content and approach.

> Proops became a campaigning journalist, changing people's perceptions to an extent now hard to imagine, so thoroughly did she break new moral ground. Never a militant feminist . . .she was nevertheless a huge champion of women's causes. She spoke out in favour of pre-marital sex, of contraception, of open, unequivocal sex education, of a more tolerant attitude towards homosexuality.
>
> (Vincenzi 1996: 16)

Her work was so highly regarded that in 1969 she was awarded an OBE (Order of the British Empire), and in the 1970s she served on two government committees, one on one-parent families and the other on the Gambling Commission, and was involved in campaigns to reform the laws on homosexuality and children's rights. In 1978 she was appointed the *Mirror*'s assistant editor.

Other women journalists at the time adopted different approaches. Journalist Jean Rook, for example, earned her reputation as 'The First Lady of Fleet Street' by playing up another stereotype – that of the straight-talking 'bitch'. Although trained as a reporter in the provincial press, her entry into Fleet Street and national newspapers was, like so many women of her time, as fashion editor on the *Sun* in 1964. She held a series of woman's editor positions on various papers before getting a column on the *Daily Express*. Regarded as a hard-hitting, no-nonsense writer, Rook earned the title of 'Britain's bitchiest, best-known, loved and loathed woman journalist'.

Rook wrote exactly what she thought about public figures. She was particularly scornful of those she perceived as left wing or feminist. She advised the Queen to pluck her eyebrows, dubbed Sarah Ferguson, then the Duchess of York, the 'Duchess of Pork' (quoted in Paton 1991: 26), and branded Prince Philip as a 'sponger' (quoted in Booth 2002: 5). Meanwhile, she never came to terms with what she called 'hairy-legged feminism' and referred to homosexual men as 'a limp-wristed army of insecure wicked fairies' (quoted in Booth 2002: 5)

Journalist Joan Smith, a respected columnist for the *Guardian*, says the way women are allowed to express themselves in columns echoes the politics of their publications, and far from freeing them, makes them conform to standard stereotypes.

> Right-wing editors favour female columnists who reflect the prejudices of their women readers, creating a spurious sisterhood of the 'wouldn't you like to knock their silly heads together' variety. Papers on the centre-left subscribe to a more complex model of sexual difference, employing women who espouse a wishy-washy brand of feminism
>
> (Smith 1994: 13)

Daily Mail special correspondent Ann Leslie, who has covered assignments in seventy-two different countries since the 1960s, admits that she often played on her femininity to gain access to people and places where male journalists have been excluded. She adopted the 1934 observation of adventurer Dame Freya Stark that 'being a woman . . . one can always pretend to be more stupid than one is, and no-one is surprised'. As Leslie (1999: 221) wrote:

> Even the most stunted, scrofulous and crotch-scratching example of local manhood believes, in his heart of hearts, that he is – compared to a mere woman – a Master of the Universe. The woman who conforms to his bird-brain stereotype is therefore no threat to him at all.

Leslie was unusual in being a high-profile, hard-news reporter at the time. Many of the women who went on to succeed in newspapers began their careers during the 1960s in magazines and established themselves as feature writers rather than news reporters. Eve Pollard, for example, who went on to be one of the first women to edit a British national newspaper, began her career as an assistant to the fashion editor on teenage magazine *Honey*. Similarly, Lynn Barber, dubbed one of the 'bitches of Fleet Street' for her assertive style of writing in the 1990s, began her career in the 1960s on *Penthouse* magazine, before specializing in celebrity interviews for British newspapers including the *Sunday Express* and, most famously, the *Independent on Sunday* (Dougary 1994: 127) in what has been described as an 'ultra-feminine, totally subjective' (quoted in Saunders 1993: 13) style.

Newspapers' financial problems intensified in the 1970s in competition with broadcasting and again they sought to attract more women readers to match the higher male readership. Many newspaper editors headhunted magazine writers to bring what was perceived in the trade to be a more 'feminine touch' to their product. As journalist Zoe Heller comments, 'Historically, the role of the female newspaper writer has been to leaven the serious (male) stuff of reportage and analysis with light dispatches – news from the realm of the domestic, the emotional, the personal' (1999: 10).

Women at US newspapers

Partly because American women had a long, if not altogether secure, history in journalism before the Second World War, a higher proportion of American than British women managed to retain their jobs as journalists after the war. Again, some left for family reasons, such as Margaret Dempsey, who talked her way into a job at the *Baltimore Evening Sun* but left when her fellow-reporter-husband (known on television as Jim McKay) took a job in New York (Mills 1988: 72). Yet many of the women journalists who were well established before mobilization were able to stay in journalism. More to the point, they broke out of the fashion and society ghetto to write about economics, science, crime, politics. Kay Mills's anecdotal account of how women struggled for *A Place in the News* (1988) mentions several women who obtained jobs during the war and kept them afterwards. These include Grace Darin, who in 1943 became the first woman on the copy desk at the *Baltimore Evening Sun*, where she stayed until her retirement in 1978; Ann Sullivan, who in 1942 began covering medicine and science at the *Portland Oregonian*, and stayed twenty years; Ann Holmes, who as military editor at the *Houston Chronicle* had to write the account of her brother's wartime death and then became the paper's arts critic; and Mildred Hamilton, who in 1944 signed on as a member of the nearly all-female news staff of the two papers in Baton Rouge and in 1958 moved to the *San Francisco Examiner.*

Two examples demonstrate a variety of career trajectories that underscore the range of ways that women developed to deal with domestic and family responsibilities while working – but also highlight the fact that women had both a sense of facing gender issues on the job and the primary responsibility for managing the work/home tension. Bess Furman (1894–1969), who, like her journalist-husband was the child of journalists, began her career in Omaha at the *Bee-News*. In 1929, after gaining attention with a prizewinning story about a presidential candidate's appearance, she accepted a job working for the Washington, DC bureau of Associated Press (AP), where she first covered various bureaus, including those for women, children and also for veterans and the census bureau. Then she went on to cover a number of political battles, political conventions and races and political figures, especially women. Furman did not, therefore, owe her job to Eleanor Roosevelt's requirement that only women reporters attend her press conferences. None the less, as with several others, she owed much of her visibility to Mrs Roosevelt, whom she described as the 'star' to which her journalistic wagon was hitched (Furman 1949: 153). First Lady Roosevelt even offered to write a story for Furman, when Roosevelt's dog bit Furman so badly that she had to go to a hospital to be stitched up. Furman quit the AP in order to have children, but, significantly, she noted that, having basked in the glamorous hot air of Washington, once she snipped off her AP title, she felt like a 'zombie' (Furman 1949: 258). As a result, she and her sister formed a quite profitable and successful partnership writing features. During the war she worked for the government, writing news and features. Anxious to return to newspaper work, and by now a much more serious journalist as opposed to the cocky girl reporter of her Nebraska days, in 1943 Furman became the White House correspondent for the *New York Times*, where she remained until 1961.

A different model emerges with Eileen Shanahan, who began her career with a newsletter covering the price and wage controls that had been imposed during the Korean War. Soon she moved to the *Journal of Commerce*, covering virtually all the federal government's major economic policy agencies, plus the federal budget. In 1961, she was hired as an economics writer by the *New York Times*, becoming the first female reporter in its Washington bureau to be hired for any assignment other than covering the First Ladies. She became the de-facto editor for the eight-page federal budget sections the paper carried in the 1960s and 1970s. She was also, for many years, the only woman among a dozen or so reporters for other publications whose full-time assignment was the national economic policy beat in Washington. She covered major tax legislation of the Securities and Exchange Commission during its most energetic period of increased regulation of the securities markets since the administration of Franklin Roosevelt. In the early 1970s, she added coverage of the economic aspects of the women's movement: job discrimination, primarily, and the struggle of union women for positions of leadership in unions. Before long, she was also covering the rocky journey of the ill-fated Equal Rights Amendment and virtually every other Washington-based women's movement story. These examples of continuing successes across a variety of beats helped defeat what otherwise could have been editors' prejudice that women could do little more than address women's interests.

Family connections in publishing

For all women's success in reporting, until recently few made it as top editors, and even fewer as publishers. Admission into management and ownership came through family connections, echoing the British experience. Many women in journalism are children of journalists, siblings of journalists and/or married to journalists, and this is particularly true of women editors and publishers who were regularly excluded from the family business and then brought back in when convenient. Even in the colonial era, some thirty American women were involved in the publishing and printing business, nearly all of them doing so in the context of helping out family members. The first woman to publish a newspaper (previously there were women printers) was Elizabeth Timothy, who ran the *South-Carolina Gazette* in Charleston from 1738, when her husband died, until 1746, when her son Peter took over. After emigrating from Europe, Lewis Timothy had borrowed money from Benjamin Franklin to set up a publishing and printing business. When he died, Elizabeth Timothy – pregnant and already the mother of six – managed to support her family by publishing the paper, as well as printing other kinds of material, including histories, poetry and religious writing (Beasley and Gibbons 2003: 8–9). When Peter died, his wife Ann Timothy took over.

Similarly, Sarah Updike Goodard and especially Mary Katherine Goodard picked up the slack when their son and brother, respectively, needed assistance in his publishing and printing business. When her brother needed to travel throughout the colonies to set up a mail delivery system, Mary Katherine Goodard moved to Baltimore to run the *Maryland Journal*. A keen judge of news, she built the paper into a vigorous advocate of the colonists and she even published 'extras' on significant events (Beasley and Gibbons 2003: 10–11). She also published a popular almanac in Baltimore, was the city postmistress, and ran a bookselling and book binding business. Most importantly, she was authorized in 1777 to print the first copy of the Declaration of Independence with the names of signers attached. In 1784, however, her brother resumed control of the paper, and in 1789, just as the job was beginning to become profitable, a new male postmaster replaced her.

Ellen Browning Scripps (1835–1932) is another early case in point of the family connection. Born in London, Ellen Scripps moved to Illinois with her family. She had started a teaching career but then agreed to help an older brother with his two Detroit newspapers. First she was an investor and copy-reader, but she also did some writing. When her half-brother E.W. Scripps launched the *Cleveland (OH) Penny Press* in 1878, she supplied money, advice and some writing. She was both surrogate mother and alter ego to 'EW', the youngest of her father's thirteen children (by three wives). EW credited her with significantly lightening his work and called the 'Miscellany' of items she sent his 'best stuff' (Preece 1990: 34). By 1900 she was a share-holder in six of his nine newspapers, a business which later became the Scripps–Howard chain; eventually she was using the profits from her shares in sixteen dailies to produce better, more attractive papers (Dillard and Schusky 1971: 251). She was particularly active in helping to set up enter-prising editors in smaller cities and promising them autonomy (Dillard and Schusky 1971: 251).

The Medill family is a more dramatic example, though one too complicated and melodramatic to explain here, of an intersecting publishing family that included a journalistic daughter who could run a paper on her own when called upon. Eleanor Medill Patterson (1881–1948) was the granddaughter of Joseph Medill, who in 1855 bought the fledgling *Chicago Tribune* and made it into a major paper. Male family members long continued to run the *Tribune*, although in the 1950s, the wife of then publisher Colonel McCormick, Maryland McCormick wrote a column, 'The Distaff Side'. Medill's daughter Elinor married a journalist Robert Patterson. Although the marriage was unhappy Patterson succeeded his father-in-law as editor (Hoge 1966). The Pattersons had two children, Eleanor and Joseph Medill Patterson. The latter worked on the *Tribune* and in 1919 founded the *New York Daily News*, the first successful tabloid in the US. Joseph Medill Patterson's daughter, Alicia Patterson (1906–1963) began reporting for the *Daily News* in 1927, although her father fired her when she married her third husband, a Jew, Harry Guggenheim (Smith 1997: 464). Guggenheim, a former ambassador to Cuba, encouraged her to take up some serious work, and in 1939, using money from her husband, Alicia Patterson founded *Newsday*, which took on her internationalist and liberal politics. With its intense local coverage, its courageous investigative journalism and lively style, *Newsday* became the largest suburban paper and remains a highly respected Pulitzer-prize winning newspaper.

In 1930, after the death of a second husband, the fabulously wealthy but apparently somewhat bored Eleanor 'Cissy' Patterson signed on as editor and publisher of the *Washington Herald*, then a rather dilapidated and unprofitable part of the Hearst chain. She worked hard, however, although not specifically on her writing. Her judgement was good with respect to layout and photography, and she personally helped promote advertising accounts. She even did some reform-oriented investigative reporting herself (Healy 1966). Patterson hired many women as long as they could produce 'sparkle' (Hoge 1966: 136), especially for her important society pages. Although she was known as temperamental and capricious, and again, her life was filled with melodrama, she could be quite generous with the women who worked for her. And, although her first front page attack-editorial caused such a stir that even one of her strongest supporters, Arthur Brisbane, warned her against turning the paper into 'a woman's paper' (Hoge 1966: 94), she did manage in her own writing to use a woman-to-woman tone that courted women readers without turning the entire paper into one only for women. In 1939, she purchased the *Herald* and the *Washington Times*, and merged them into the *Washington Times – Herald*. By 1943, Patterson, a supporter of Roosevelt but an isolationist, enjoyed profitability and the largest circulation in Washington (Denker 1971). While Collier's magazine called her 'the most powerful woman in America', *Time* called her 'the most hated woman in America' (Denker 1971: 28).

The intersecting story of Katharine Meyer Graham (1917–2001) is slightly less dramatic, but repeats some of the classic contours of the situation of a publishing family's daughters entering the business. Katharine Meyer was not terribly interested in journalism and did not know that her wealthy financier-father Eugene Meyer had bought the *Washington Post* at auction in 1933 until some time after the purchase. Eugene Meyer had known nothing about journalism, but did quite well with it, including winning a major battle with his rival Cissy Patterson over a group of comic strips. In any case, after graduating from the University of Chicago in 1938 and spending a year as a reporter for the *San Francisco News*, Katharine Meyer joined the editorial staff of the *Washington Post*; she also worked in the editorial and circulation departments of the *Sunday Post*. In 1940 she married Philip Graham, a law clerk, and soon abandoned journalism to raise her children. In 1946 her father turned publication of the *Post* over to her husband, and in 1948 the couple bought the voting stock of the corporation from her father. Eventually they also bought the *Times – Herald*, merging it with the *Post*; and Graham bought *Newsweek* magazine and several radio and television stations.

In 1963, after the death of her husband, Katharine Graham, at age forty-six, returned to work, as president of the Washington Post Company. From 1969 to 1979 she also held the title of publisher. Under her leadership, the *Washington Post* became known for its aggressive investigative reporting. The woman often known as an 'iron lady' decided to publish the Pentagon Papers, although a judge had halted their publication in the *New York Times*. She stood up to the Nixon administration during Watergate, at great risk to the paper's viability, since Nixon appointees threatened to challenge the *Post*'s TV licences. Circulation increased and the *Post* became one of the most powerful newspapers in the nation. From 1973 to 1991 Graham was chairman of the board and chief executive officer of the Washington Post Company. In 1999 she received the Pulitzer Prize for biography for her charmingly modest autobiography, *Personal History*, in which she admits her insecurities and self-doubts – many well placed, given her inexperience in publishing. Graham certainly was regarded as an exception, a rarity; and even she admits that she knew little about journalism when she took over the running of the paper, having had nothing to do with it for many years except to entertain her husband's business guests. Nor did she know much about feminism and the feminist movement then sweeping the country. Furthermore, not only her entrée into journalism but also, and especially, her role as publisher rested on her family connections; even her father had put the *Post* in the hands of her husband, not her. Yet, she is widely accepted as having been a strong and influential leader, both at the *Post*, and in journalism as a whole.

As successful as each of these women were, they did not inspire a stampede of women into leadership roles; not merely in the nineteenth but also through the end of the twentieth century, women were a rarity in publishing, and the exceptions came by the position through family connections.

The 'new' New Journalism

For all the enormous cultural changes in the United States in the 1960s – new forms of music and art, the wilder forms of dress and hair associated with hippies, political activism on behalf of the civil rights of African Americans and women and on behalf of farm workers – journalism was relatively slow to change. Ironically, a few women's careers indirectly may again have been boosted by the Vietnam War (see Chapter 10), not because of the protest against the war, although anti-war protests were a major theme in the late 1960s and early 1970s. Rather, as a couple of women told Kay Mills (1988), male journalism applicants with high draft numbers were told to come back later, presumably leaving these jobs available for women in the meantime.

Despite these changes, women were still treated like ladies, to their dismay and detriment. They were essentially confined to the ladies' room. Kay Mills (1988) tells of countless women – Sue Hobart of the *Portland Oregonian*, Elizabeth Rhodes of the *Seattle Times*, Marie Freivogel of the *St. Louis Post-Dispatch*, Jane Brody of the *Minneapolis Tribune* and now a well-known health writer at the *New York Times* – who not only in the 1960s, but also the 1970s were told that they could not or should not work in newsrooms. Either it was no place for a lady, since they would hear or see bad things, or they would have to work at night, or it was useless to hire them because they would have babies and quit or just plain quit. It is still difficult to guess how many women received such responses and gave up on journalism. Obviously, the women mentioned above persisted and not only got a job but kept it.

Several social and cultural changes brought the flowering of yet another 'New Journalism', at this time, referring to a kind of literary journalism that rejected the mythology of objectivity such that journalists might even become personas in their own stories. Literary journalists employ some conventional information-gathering methods – especially in-depth interviews and close, extended observation. Yet this New Journalism, associated with figures like Tom Wolfe, adopted the narrative technique conventions of fiction, including scene-setting, characterization and dialogue. Oddly enough, or typically, this long-form journalism is rarely practised by women, perhaps because women either are not allowed, or do not allow themselves, to enjoy the freedom and sense of literary experimentation that is permitted to, or claimed by, men. Thomas Connery's 1992 edited collection includes essays on thirty-five writers, of whom four are female: Dorothy Day, Lillian Ross, Jane Kramer and Joan Didion. Art Kaul's 1997 edited collection of essays about thirty-six contemporary literary journalists also includes four women, with Sara Davidson substituting for Dorothy Day. In some sense this is ironic, given that on the surface, both the narrative intentions and the novelistic writing style of literary journalism might seem to accommodate what women writers had long been expected to do.

The issue of the women's pages

Another support for hiring and promoting women in the newsroom during the 1940s had come from the evidence that women were reading the news, information that was of interest to publishers and advertisers. In a sense, some of the changes in the American newspaper that apparently seem to reflect a softer, more feminine approach were based on research data from men and women – although the scientific reliability and validity of the research has been controversial and vigorously challenged. Thomas Leonard's (1995) detailed history of newsreading and newsreaders notes the importance of one report, based on focus-group data, commissioned in response to the crisis in newspaper circulation in the 1970s. The 'Changing Needs, Changing Readers' report by Ruth Clark asserted that readers (or at least the 120 people she talked to in a dozen focus groups) wanted news relevant to their lives, and wanted an emotional bond with the newspaper. Clark said readers considered the 'self' to be a vital news beat and were interested in the importance of 'me' (quoted in Leonard 1995: 141).

The case of women's sections or women's pages continues to be controversial. In the 1970s and 1980s, several women's sections were revamped, becoming sections about style or lifestyle, about design and the home. Susan Miller, director of editorial research for the Scripps-Howard newspaper chain, wrote a 1987 article for the *Gannett Center Journal* saying that, thanks to market research and to the increased hiring and promotion of women, 'editors realize that women do not require a separate section of the paper filled with anything and everything that might interest members of their sex' (quoted in Leonard 1995: 142). Such decisions had some problematic consequences for women as journalists, and as news topics and therefore as readers.

Women in radio in Britain

Until 1967 there were only three radio services were legally available to the whole of the United Kingdom as had been the case since 1946 when the BBC restructured. The Home Service remained, but the Forces Programme became the Light Programme, providing, as its name suggests, a more entertaining mix of music and speech programmes than the staid Home Service. The third BBC station launched in 1946, unimaginatively called the Third Programme, catered to fans of serious music, literature and drama. The south of England was also able to pick up a populist music station, Radio Luxembourg, broadcast from the Duchy of Luxembourg between 1932 and 1992.

Commercial radio did not exist in the UK until 1973, with all airwaves controlled by the BBC until then. The BBC monopoly on British radio had far-reaching implications for women. As Chapter 1 explained, the organization was moulded by the ideas of its first Director General, Sir John Reith, and although he left in 1937, the Puritan principles, middle-class tastes and strict standards he established survived for decades after his departure. There was a complete ban at the BBC on women reading the news until as recently as 1974, although there were a few working as reporters. So although the organization employed women, those used on-air were restricted to a few programmes catering for children and housewives. Veteran BBC journalist Sue MacGregor, who made her name as one of the presenters on the prestigious Radio 4 news programme *Today*, says that when she first applied to the BBC in the late 1960s for a job as a continuity announcer on the Home Service she was turned down. 'Male voices, they said, in the end carried more authority. In the late 'sixties this was a widely held view' (MacGregor 2002: 116).

Such opportunities that existed for women journalists in the BBC were limited and often dependent on individual programme editors. Sue MacGregor recalls that, in the late 1960s, Andrew Boyle, the editor of the prestigious news programme, *The World at One*, was unusual in going out of his way to employ equal numbers of men and women. It was, says MacGregor, 'an even-handedness unprecedented at the time, and a far cry from the prevailing ethos within the BBC' (MacGregor 2002: 125). However, once employed, women faced widespread discrimination in terms of assignments.

> While . . . there was no gender discrimination in the BBC pay packets, I discovered that not all the most interesting reporting jobs were evenly distributed. Foreign assignments and anything involving possible physical danger were handed out to the men in the team: rioting students at home or abroad, or industrial unrest, were not considered the province of women.
>
> (MacGregor 2002: 122)

The original relationship between women and radio news was quite clear – women should listen but not be heard. Programmes like *Housewives' Choice* set the stereotype of daytime listeners being addressed as housewives who relied upon radio for companionship and relief from their domestic chores. This attitude prevailed in Britain even when commercial radio was introduced in 1973, as the franchise application for the London commercial station Capital Radio shows:

> In constructing programmes to appeal to women (and to a large extent women as housewives) two things have to be borne in mind . . . Women are sentimental . . . Women are fanatical . . . They are escapist, or they are not sufficiently cold-blooded to enjoy drama which, if taken seriously, would represent alarm and despondency. This is what gives them their bias towards stories about hospitals and against stories about guns; towards

local issues (where they can plainly see what is at stake) and away from foreign news (of dubious implication); towards happy endings, but happy
endings to sagas which are as grittily tough as they know real life usually is.
                                                        (quoted in Karpf 1980: 47)

One of the few mainstream programmes to resist this stereotype was the
BBC's *Woman's Hour*, now the BBC's longest-running radio programme.
Launched in the autumn of 1946 on the Light Programme, its magazine
format sought to help women recreate 'normal' home life after the ravages of
war. It offered 'earnest advice on how to knit your own stair carpet, how to
bleach your blackout curtains and how to deslime your flannel' (Feldman
2000: 66). Remarkably, this was all advice presented by the programme's
male presenter Alan Ivieson.

Yet *Woman's Hour* also explored other issues of interest to women such as,
for example, the 1946 Royal Commission on Equal Pay and the 1947 campaign for better wages for home workers (Feldman 2000). Following Ivieson's
short-lived reign as presenter, the programme was also presented by women
and began dealing with medical and sexual issues, as well as human relationships. Olive Shapley, the presenter in the early 1950s, admits that some of
these topics were barely mentioned even in private conversations at the time.

Indeed, the frankness of the programme occasionally shocked some of the
all-male BBC managers. For instance, a talk about the menopause in 1948
caused one Assistant Controller to write in a memo: 'it is acutely embarrass-
ing to hear about hot-flushes, diseases of the ovaries, the possibilities of
womb removal and so on being transmitted on 376 kilowatts at two o'clock
in the afternoon' (Feldman 2000: 67).

Although several programmes featured issues raised by feminists – including equal pay, contraception and legalized abortion – 'young grass-roots
feminists in Britain were virtually ignored' (MacGregor 2002: 157).
According to Sue MacGregor, who was the programme presenter at the time,
the producers did not want to alienate the majority of listeners, who were not
working outside the home. The producer, Wyn Knowles, was anxious not to
alienate what she thought were the programme's audience of 'contented
housewives' (MacGregor 2002: 159). The lack of connection with feminists
might also be attributed, in Sally Feldman's view (Feldman 2000), to the fact
that its producers were somewhat out of touch with emerging intellectual
ideas of the time.

In 1967, in response to losing audiences to pirate radio stations like Radio
Caroline, the BBC was revamped. Yet Britain still had a grand total of only
four national radio stations. In the same year the first BBC regional station
opened in the Midland's city of Leicester. However, the new stations did not
open the airwaves to women's voices. If anything, they, along with the first
commercial radio stations in the UK that went on air in 1973, stereotyped
women even more rigidly as listeners rather than producers and speakers. The

new stations set about wooing what was perceived to be an audience of largely housebound, isolated women. In line with the more liberal attitudes emerging at the time, however, there was a shift away from an emphasis on domestic chores towards sex.

The role of the radio DJ was to flirt with the female audience – a role that effectively debarred women from popular-music radio presentation.[4] However, in the early 1970s on speech-based stations like BBC Radio 4, women were beginning to be more acceptable in the newsroom, at least if they conformed to the established work practices. Julia Sommerville started her broadcasting career in the early 1970s as a newsroom sub-editor, writing copy for news bulletins. At the time very few women were employed as sub-editors, perhaps because the twenty-four-hour newsroom required unsocial working hours as well as after-hours networking. Sommerville says of those days, 'It was hard drinking but fun . . . As a woman you were accepted if you accepted that, and did a decent job'.[5] She became the first female BBC labour affairs correspondent in 1981.

The new BBC local radio stations provided many of the opportunities for women as reporters, newsreaders and managers, probably because they were regarded as of lower status than the national stations, especially in the 1970s when they were notoriously underresourced. Moreover, by the late 1970s, as women gained experience on air, management realised that a woman reading the news – especially on a male-DJ-dominated station – provided 'balance' and added 'texture' to the rest of the output (MacGregor 2002: 218).

Women in radio in the United States

Just as was the case in Britain, by the end of the Second World War most of the women who had been hired in US radio reporting, as with print, found themselves out of a job. Certainly many of the female print reporters in search of new posts could only find women's and society pages work. Women who had presented radio news were even more likely to lose their on-air jobs, although some found work as writers and producers. US Department of Labor data from 1946 suggests that while women were 28 per cent of all broadcast employees, few of them were announcing the news (cited in Sanders and Rock 1988: 8). As the men returned from the front, 'women faded out of these jobs except for a few who made an outstanding success and permanent place for themselves with the networks, radio stations, and advertising agencies' (Sanders and Rock 1988: 8).

Some of the women who attained success in radio created and established their own niche, similar to the women's departments at newspapers – but as such, they could become a top radio celebrity. As Bess Furman (1949: 81) described her in her own autobiography, in the late 1930s, Mary Margaret McBride (1899–1976) was on the verge of an illness 'brought on by disillusionment, wrecked hopes, futile labours, and seeing her own creative work go

up in political smoke'. But then McBride, a 1919 graduate of the University
of Missouri School of Journalism, began broadcasting as 'Martha Deane' for
WOR radio in New York in 1934, and attracted millions of listeners, mostly
women, with her personal folksy confessions and interviews with noted personalities. The fifteenth anniversary of her show was held in 1949 at Yankee
Stadium in order to seat her loyal fans. While she giggled in the fairly high-
pitched twang of her native Missouri she was, apparently, a penetrating and
insightful interviewer.

However, there was continuing concern over the suitability of women's
voices for radio. As late as the mid-1960s, the president for news at ABC,
Elmer Lower, said

> Many women may possess the knowledge and authority but they seldom
> can convey this through their voices . . . Her voice is naturally thinner,
> with less timbre and range. It's not as appropriate for reporting crucial
> events. For hard-core news, the depth and resonance of the male voice are
> indispensable.
>
>   (Hosley and Yamada 1987: 22)

Some audiences and producers accepted the notion that women's voices did
not carry well by microphone. Presumably, it was more a question of what
people were accustomed to, and not something inherent. None the less, the
notion that women lacked suitable vocal authority to deliver the news carried
over into their role within television news. In the 1960s and 1970s, some
reporters, including many who were aiming for television, obtained a start in
radio.

Beginning in the 1960s, most AM radio was devoted to music, although
this decade also saw the evolution of the talk show. Although radio had
some relatively important figures – that is, people who hosted their own talk
shows, including women – very rarely did journalists achieve major reputations and journalistic successes on the basis of radio. Not only has radio been
relegated by television to the margins, but the centralization of radio by the
radio networks means that there are few high-profile radio reporting jobs.
Again, there are plenty of women who are radio announcers, disc jockeys,
talk show hosts and reporters. To take but one example, for thirty years,
Irene Cornell has covered crime and the courts for WCBS, in New York City.
She apparently loves covering trials, saying in her official WCBS biography
that trials 'condense all of human emotion'. Perhaps the one site for important radio news is through National Public Radio, which, indeed, has several
women news anchors (including Susan Stamberg), specialist reporters (such
as Nina Totenberg) and talk show hosts (such as Diane Rehm).

Interestingly, radio has both its centralized network aspect and a suitability for narrowcasting, that is, niche marketing to special interests, such
as ethnic stations, urban/black-oriented stations. Even within the music

formats, radio is specialized – country & western, jazz, hard rock, oldies, Christian, Jewish, and so forth. It is therefore surprising that there are no radio stations now specifically for women despite the popularity of radio among women at home in the 1940s and 1950s, the current interest in segmentation in radio and given the success of magazines and, more to the point, cable systems, in gearing content specifically to women. In 1927 there was a very short-lived experiment with an all-female radio station. Only a few years earlier, the owner had refused to let a long-time employee at his WNAC, Bertha Mitchell, do anything but secretarial work or a woman's show; but he went on to hire many women for his WASN (All Shopping News) (Halper 2001: 46–7). Apparently the women were highly professional in running the station, but it failed for technical reasons (Halper 2001). A few women in the early days had their own small stations, most notably Ida McNeil, who single-handedly ran a folksy station in a small town in South Dakota, where KGFX and McNeil together were beloved as the 'Voice of the Prairie' (Halper 2001: 68–9). The all-girl radio gimmick was tried in 1955, when Sam Phillips – famous as the owner of Sun Records and the producer of Elvis Presley – bought a station in Memphis and made it into WHER. Now there are some radio programmes for women, but these are primarily on the non-commercial public radio stations, especially FM stations (see Chapter 9).

Women in television in Britain

The development of television in Britain was hindered by the Second World War in 1939, when all broadcasting stopped and was not resumed until June 1946. By 1954 the BBC was broadcasting about six hours of television a day (Crisell 1997: 73). However, the BBC hierarchy harboured an underlying suspicion of the new medium.

Both within and outside the BBC there was also a moral panic about television's effect on national culture. In particular there was growing concern about the influence of American popular culture on the British way of life through imported programmes and through the copying of American models for programmes (in addition to the wider cultural impact of Hollywood cinema and American popular music in Britain). As Janet Thumim (1998: 95) points out, critics in the 1950s described television's content in terms associated with the feminine. For example, television was seen to be 'frivolous, light, distracting, mindless'. The very act of 'passive viewing' has, in patriarchal discourse, certain feminine associations. Thumim (1998: 95) suggests that the fear of the feminizing potential of television contributed to the creation of a particularly masculine space in the new medium within news:

> Such anxieties about the consequences of television per se might also account for the perceived importance of maintaining the equation between

The News and 'the masculine', each term being called on to buttress the other, as it were, against the dangers of cultural degradation.

The development of a distinctive style of news presentation on British television was a slow and uphill struggle. Early post-war bulletins started in 1954 and were produced and read anonymously by the BBC radio news section over a picture of a clock. The newsreader was invariably a man, since the BBC ban on women reading the news on radio was extended to television. Asa Briggs (1975: 539) attributes the style of television news bulletins to the limited technology of the time. Stuart Allan (1999: 37), however, suggests that BBC management believed that in order to maintain the BBC's commitment to impartiality, newsreaders could not be seen in case their facial expressions betrayed their opinion on what was being read.

Although the potential for television news to build audiences was recognized in Britain as early as 1947 (Briggs 1995: 200), it was the advent of competition from commercial television in 1955 that spurred changes. Independent Television News (ITN) was established as a specialist subsidiary company in February 1955 by the Independent Television Association to provide news bulletins for the fledgling commercial television network. On 23 September 1955, Barbara Mandell became the first woman to read a bulletin on British television, albeit the lunchtime bulletin which not only had a very small audience but which was also read against a painted set of a domestic kitchen to highlight women news audiences' place in the home (Thumim 1998, Allan 1999). According to Aidan Cawley, the first editor of ITN, it was Mandell's 'pleasant good looks, open manner and mellifluous voice' (quoted in Allan 1999: 131) that made her suited to newsreading. Although the lunchtime news on ITV was scrapped after a year, Mandell returned to newsreading later in the decade, presenting the Sunday evening bulletin. As the second editor of ITN Geoffrey Cox recalls, 'to put a woman in charge of a main bulletin in those days, I fear, would be seen as a gimmick' (quoted in Allan 1999: 131).

The BBC evidently had a similar opinion. Its first female newsreader, Nan Winton, was also given the Sunday night bulletin to present for a short time in 1960. Despite this schedule being something of a television backwater, senior BBC manager Stuart Hood recalls that it was not popular.

> I thought it would be rather nice to have a woman newsreader on television. Now this was greeted with alarm and dismay and resistance by my editors. The thought that a woman could be the conveyor of truth and authority on the television screen was something they couldn't imagine, couldn't accept.
>
> (quoted in Thumin 1998: 97)

In fact the BBC's first regular female newsreader of a main bulletin was

Angela Rippon in 1975. Despite ITN's early experiment it was not until Anna Ford joined the *News at Ten* in 1978 that ITN had a *regular* main newswoman presenter. All women newsreaders were white and middle class. Their accents conformed to the uniform Received Pronunciation and were perceived to be non-regional, an accent which came to be known as 'BBC English'. No black female newsreader was recruited until the 1980s, reflecting the dominantly white, middle-class cultural environment of the institution.

Magazine programmes for women with a focus on fashion, cookery and childcare became a feature of the limited daytime schedules of the 1950s. Joy Leman (1987) points out that initially they were produced less to cater to women and more for economic and organizational reasons: 'Equipment and staff which would otherwise be "lying idle" could be used to produce cheap programmes to fill the screen during daytime transmission hours' (Leman 1987: 75). In 1955 a separate department for Women's Programmes was approved with Doreen Stephens as editor. This department survived until it was merged with Children's Programmes in 1964 to form the short-lived Family Programmes Department. As Leman (1987) details, the programmes produced for women by the BBC were distinctly middle class in flavour and home-focused, with offerings such as *Twice Twenty*, 'a magazine programme for older women' and *Your Own Time* and *Around and About* 'for the younger married woman'. *Pennywise* and *Look and Choose* were consumer advice programmes, chaired by Lady Isobel Barnett (Leman 1987: 84). In line with its more informal approach, ITV promised to cater more for women at its launch in 1955, but in fact it produced very similar consumer/family-oriented programmes, produced, directed and often introduced by men. As Leman notes, 'The prejudice . . . against women as broadcasters was not restricted to the BBC and neither was the related assumption that a male presence adds authority/sexual interest to women's programmes' (1987: 85).

Despite the absence of women on television in general and the news in particular, a great many women were employed by television off-screen, although as Janet Thumim points out they were most often found 'in the permeable boundary between news and current affairs . . . than that bastion of masculinity, the newsroom itself' (1998: 98). Grace Wyndham Goldie (1977), for example, who began her BBC career as a talks producer in 1948, was a considerable force in developing current affairs and political programming like the news magazine programme *Tonight* and the more serious weekly political programme *Panorama*. *Tonight* in particular, first broadcast in 1957, took a new approach to news that was to influence the content and approach taken by other news programmes. According to Briggs (1995: 162), '*Tonight* deliberately blurred traditional distinctions between entertainment, information, and even education'; while through its informal styles of presentation, it broke sharply with old BBC traditions of 'correctness' and 'dignity'. Although the programme was predominantly presented by men, the approach was more in line with what was to be labelled as a 'traditionally feminine' one of conceptualizing and explaining stories in everyday terms.

By the 1960s television in Britain had established itself as a part of national life but it was overwhelmingly male-dominated, especially in news and current affairs. As Tunstall (1993: 175) explains, the employment pattern of women in television was one of advance and retreat.

> In the Second World War many women were promoted during the BBC's huge wartime expansion. This forward march of women was, however, again followed by a retreat after the war. The big TV expansion of the 1950s also saw women pushed aside. A few women moved into high positions in television in the 1960s, but the great majority of new TV producers were thrusting young men. Film-industry craft unionism took over the main technical areas in ITV and helped to confirm the established BBC tradition of male dominance.

This dominance was particularly evident in news and current affairs, and Tunstall (1993: 174) quotes one senior BBC executive who said as late as 1968, 'To read the TV news, you need a pair of balls'. The first woman to be a regular reporter and presenter on national television was Joan Bakewell, who was part of the team of *Late Night Line Up* on BBC2 in 1964. Not only was this a mainly arts-based programme, traditionally a feminine field, it was also a programme on what was then a new national station aimed at 'minority interests'. In its first few years it had a limited audience because it required a new television set in order to be received.[6] Tunstall points out that the recruitment and promotion procedures of television were based on a civil service tradition that tended to work against women: 'The concept of selected young "leaders of men" entering through a special entry-gate excluded women' (Tunstall 1993: 174). But he also admits that the culture of long working hours and general animosity towards women in senior positions discouraged women from applying for promotion. This position remained the same until the late 1980s, when the BBC set up and implemented an equal opportunities policy (see Chapter 4).

However, Thumim argues that resistance to women in news and current affairs in the 1950s and 1960s was caused by the male domination of public affairs. She also links the lack of women in television to fears about the medium itself:

> As television's place in society became more secure and more central, its inherent dangers – frivolity, passivity, feminization – had to be overcome. It had to be masculinized in order to be tolerable as the hub of national life it was clearly becoming.
>
> (Thumin 1998: 103)

Women in television in the United States

Although television was further developed in the US than in the UK (in terms of size, number of stations, programming and audience sizes) it was also affected by the outbreak of war. The resources and technological developments intended for television were redirected toward military applications and very few of the thirty-two television stations that had been authorized actually made it on to the air (Beadle, Murray and Godfrey 2001: 7). Moreover, there was such chaos in television once the war was over that in 1948 the Federal Communications Commission stopped processing licence applications so that it could work out some sensible long-term solutions to the technological and policy problems. It might be noted that the FCC recruited its first woman commissioner, Frieda Hemlock, in 1948. Hemlock was known during her seven-year term for her support of educational television. A lawyer born in Poland, Hemlock was able to inspire and support non-commercial broadcasting. Beadle, Murray and Godfrey (2001: 7) note that this four-year moratorium created an opportunity for women to insert themselves in local television. In particular, women found opportunities to do weather reports for US television. Most of the early 'weathergirls', however, 'were hired for looks and had little to no training in meteorology' (Dick 2001: 229).

One of the United States' pioneering television journalists was Pauline Frederick, the first woman to find full-time employment on the air in network television news. She was primarily a print reporter who had done a few radio features on women's subjects. After the war ended, both NBC and CBS told her that women's voices lack authority (Sanders and Rock 1988: 8), so the best she was initially able to accomplish was some freelance radio features on 'women's' issues for ABC, her first story discussing how to find a husband. However, she was encouraged to sign up to report on the political conventions in 1948 – the first year these were covered on television (Sanders and Rock 1988: 10). She primarily covered the United Nations until 1974, when, at the compulsory age, Frederick retired. After her retirement, Frederick worked for National Public Radio, the non-commercial public system for the United States. Hosley and Yamada (1987: 65) list a number of accolades, awards and firsts that Frederick accrued during her career, such as the first woman elected president of the United Nations Correspondents Association. As exceptional as Frederick was, her case is representative in this sense: in the early years of television, nearly all television reporters had background and experience in print and/or radio.

A Washington bureau chief for CBS once wrote a musical comedy premised on 'the sidesplitting notion that the network had inexplicably hired a bunch of girls to deliver the news' (Blair 1988: 78). As Chapter 6 indicates, the Civil Rights Act of 1964 outlawed sex discrimination as a result of a last-minute addition to the Act. This opened the door to complaints from women in journalism. By 1971, for example, *NBC News* had six women – all powerful, highly visible professionals: Nancy Dickerson, who in 1963 became the first woman to have her own news broadcast, albeit for five minutes in the afternoon and was also perhaps the first to be promoted as an attractive woman (Blair 1988: 79), Liz Trotta, Barbara Walters, Pauline Frederick, Aline Saarinen and Betty Rollin. Liz Trotta, who had begun her journalism career at the Associated Press wire service and the *Chicago Tribune*, became the first woman foreign correspondent for NBC. As such she served three tours of duty in Vietnam (1968–1971); then spent two years as Singapore bureau chief, going on to serve as a London-based correspondent from 1973 to 1975. *CBS News* got its first woman foreign correspondent in 1974 when it hired Susan Peterson for its London bureau.

Jessica Savitch's story speaks volumes about the significance of women's physical appearance in the 1970s and 1980s. Savitch got her on-air reporting job with Houston television station, in the wake of an FCC ruling requiring more local news. There Savitch experienced a moment of truth about importance of appearance when her station got sixty calls from viewers afraid that she might be ill, having seen a cosmetics-less Savitch cover a raging storm. To this, Savitch, widely known as a very attractive blonde, said:

> Looks should neither attract nor distract. Ideally, a reporter's appearance should just be pleasant enough to be disregarded . . . I have decided to quit apologizing for my looks, which have played both a positive and negative role in my career. I have my own theory that attractive people in the industry are considered bad journalists; average looking reporters are automatically given more credence.
>
> (Savitch 1982: 72)

Savitch soon landed a bigger job, with even bigger celebrity status with KYW-TV in Philadelphia. In 1977, at her very first opportunity to move again, Savitch became NBC's Senate correspondent; within two years she was doing *Prime Time Sunday*, NBC's magazine show. *Newsweek* called her NBC's Golden Girl. One poll called her and Dan Rather the sexiest anchors in the US and she was said to be the fourth most trustworthy anchor in the US (Blair 1988: 15). Finally she got her wish and moved to the national NBC network in New York. The networks were clearly recruiting women for their looks, indeed, for a certain look. In 1981 *Life* magazine commissioned a story on the blonde women of television news. Besides Jessica Savitch, they pictured Lesley Stahl, Jane Pauly, Lynn Scherr, Sylvia Chase, Judy Woodruff, Betsy Aaron and Diana Sawyer (then co-anchor on CBS *Morning News*). Blair (1988) describes 'Savitch clones' sending tapes to talent scouts and the stations instructing younger women how to look like Savitch. Diane Allen, Savitch's replacement in Philadelphia, dyed her hair the same colour and was sent to the same speech coach.

But then the network standards changed and beauty and 'looking' smart were no longer enough. By the early 1980s, Savitch was essentially relegated to a journalistic backwater, although her two nightly NBC *News Digests* enjoyed huge popularity and credibility with audiences. Savitch's professional difficulties and anxieties were compounded by personal ones – in very quick succession, a marriage, separation, problems with drugs, an affair, a miscarriage, a divorce, a remarriage, another miscarriage, threats by a stalker, the suicide of her second husband, and not surprisingly, a nervous breakdown on camera. In 1983, she died in a car accident. While the story of the golden girl, or almost golden girl, is more melodramatic than was the case for the other blondes on network and local news, it illustrates the problem of hiring inexperienced women and promoting them too quickly, merely because of their good looks.

Racial discrimination

It was late before black women wrote for the mainstream press, although they continued to write for the black papers, which through the 1970s remained relatively healthy in the major cities across the United States. None the less, the black press remained male-dominated. For example, Marvel Cooke was first hired as secretary to the society editor at the *Amsterdam News*, a black daily paper in New York established in 1909. Only in the mid-1930s, was she rehired as both writer and secretary, thus becoming its first woman reporter (Mills 1988: 176). Cooke, a graduate of the University of Minnesota, had before worked a couple of years at the *Crisis*, a literary, news and opinion magazine founded and edited by W. E. B. DuBois for the National Association for the Advancement of Colored People.

Two years after the American Newspaper Guild was established, Cooke helped organize the first local newspaper guild at a black newspaper; the paper's (black) owner fired the founding members and they went on strike. Eventually the paper was sold, and the new owners had to rehire the workers at higher pay (Mills 1988: 91). Cooke herself continued to chafe at the sensationalistic crime stories that dominated the Amsterdam Press, so in 1942 switched to a weekly newly established by the Harlem political leader Adam Clayton Powell. In 1950, the *People's Voice* having died, she became the only African American and only woman at the *Daily Compass*, a leftist paper, and even at that, she accused her managing editor of some degree of sexism and racism (Mills 1988: 176). None the less, in her two years at the *Compass* until 1952 (when the paper closed), she produced some highly influential work, including an in-depth series on drug use among black children and a twelve-part investigation of prostitution. For her very first series, following a decades-long tradition (including the fact that it prompted reform) dating back to Elizabeth Banks, Cooke worked as a maid in order to expose exploitation of black domestics: 'I was part of the Bronx Slave Market long enough to experience all the viciousness and indignity of a system which forces women to the streets in search of work' (quoted in Streitmatter 1994: 92).

As a black woman who had made it into the mainstream white press in 1961, Dorothy Gilliam was the exception who proved the rule. After a couple of years of working for the black press, Gilliam realized she needed 'some white credentials' (Mills 1988: 179). Her Columbia Journalism School degree helped. She started writing for the *Washington Post*, covering welfare, homelessness and the Civil Rights movement. She says her experiences as a black woman, and her experiences with poverty and welfare, helped make interviewees feel comfortable: 'I am sure some of the stories I got, I was able to penetrate more deeply because I was a black woman . . . I was able to empathize' (quoted in Mills 1988: 179). In 1965 Gilliam left the paper because she was pregnant with her second child, although she did some part-time reporting for a local television talk show. In 1972 she returned to the *Post*, first as the assistant editor of the newly revamped Style section, then as a columnist. Since 1997 she has directed a programme at the paper to encourage minority students to journalism.

The situation for women, including women of colour, changed considerably with the impetus of several social and political movements in the 1960s, including the women's movement. The hiring of black and ethnic minority women in print and television news began in earnest during the 1970s in the United States especially in the wake of the 1968 publication of the report of a national commission headed by Illinois Governor Otto Kerner. Finding that less than 5 per cent of journalists in the US were black, and most of those were working for the black press, the Kerner Commission had excoriated journalism for failing to recruit, hire, train and promote African Americans. News media organizations realized that by employing a black woman they could satisfy two affirmative action policy quotas simultaneously. It was a number of years, however, before African American and Asian American women were seen on national television newscasts or on local newscasts serving cities in the United States without a substantial minority population.

Implications for the women's movement

The changes in employment practices for black women originated in part from the women's movement and from sustained advocacy by the few female women journalists. Minority training programmes, such as one established in 1968 at Columbia University with funding from the Ford Foundation, also helped recruit and train minority broadcasters, including Gloria Rojas, who was the first Puerto Rican reporter in New York City. The efforts of the National Organization for Women to challenge the licence renewal of WABC-TV in New York also spurred on the networks to hire women. By the 1970s, 45 per cent of TV newsrooms in the United States had women reporters (Hosley and Yamada 1987: 101). By the 1980s, even more women went overseas – usually one per US television network.

Nevertheless, the problems of sex discrimination had not been solved. Data for 1987 showed that of a total of 239 network reporters, none of the thirty-six women ranked among the top ten in airtime (Sanders and Rock 1988: 113). The top six men enjoyed more air time than all thirty-six women together. Moreover, resistance to women anchors was still evident in prime time (except on a substitute basis). Not only did television women need to juggle seemingly incompatible demands between personal and professional life, but they needed to deal with continuing resistance from male co-workers. That is, at least some co-workers. In particular, several women complained that anchors (anchor*men*) got to choose who would appear on their broadcasts (Sanders and Rock 1988: 70–3). If the male anchor preferred to use a man, a woman might remain underutilized . . . and frustrated. It is merely one more source of unease and risk that compounds the ongoing sources of workplace tension for all journalists.

As well as many women reporters admitting they agonized over family issues and life changes, one of the most consistently raised concerns about gender distinctions in television news has to do with age. Few old(er) women are anchoring broadcasts, while men are allowed to age – and get fat and bald as well. There are exceptions, of course. Dorothy Fuldheim was born in 1893 and, having been highly successful on the lecture circuit, became a radio commentator in 1944. In 1947 she was hired as a newscaster for a brand-new television station in Cleveland, Ohio, and became famous for her news commentary. She interviewed hundreds of famous people, from the Duke of Windsor to Albert Einstein (O'Dell 1997: 109). She remained active – and controversial, given her outspoken positions – in television for forty years, and just before her ninetieth birthday, signed a new three-year contract with WEWS. In 1984, having outlived her daughter and two husbands, she suffered a stroke and retired. And famously, of course, there is Barbara Walters, who began at CBS, then moved to NBC, and made headlines when she jumped to ABC News for $1 million a year, becoming a regular evening news anchor. She continues to be widely recognized for her 'specials', including one with Monica Lewinsky, the White House intern who was President Bill Clinton's undoing. The contemporary obsession of the public and management with women news anchors' appearance is developed again in Chapter 11 on postmodern journalism.

Conclusion

A striking feature of women's participation in journalism in the decades after the Second World War is not only the gender restrictions they faced in a male-dominated occupation across all media, old and new, but also the impact they had on journalism as a whole. The effect is most noticeable in

newspapers where topics previously confined to women's pages gradually
began to be used throughout the paper, until the need for a defined space for
women disappeared. It was also on those early women's pages that several
now-familiar practices began, such as involving readers by responding to
their letters and featuring the lives of 'ordinary' people as newsworthy.
Although there were fewer women in radio and television than their female
counterparts in the press, and they were less audible and visible since they
tended to work as producers rather than presenters, they nevertheless made
their mark in broadcasting by creating programmes that moved away from a
strict diet of 'hard' news and that contextualized stories by explaining how
reported events influence their audience. This is especially the case in broadcasting in the United States, where women were not constrained by the
puritan values of the BBC. Of course it must be acknowledged that changes
to the approach and content of the news were primarily made as a response
to market forces, but that should not detract from a realization of the fact
that women journalists in the 1950s and 1960s were recruited precisely to initiate the now-familiar changes in news values, as discussed in Chapter 5.

It is significant that women journalists in Britain made more progress in print
than in broadcasting, in those years. One reason for this is the BBC's domination
of British broadcasting which not only stifled competition but also formed a
template that was used by all broadcasters until the 1990 Broadcast Act liberal-
ized approaches through deregulation. In its early days, and some would argue
even now, the BBC reflected the establishment which was white, male and
(upper) middle class. This is evident in the civil-service-like structure of the corporation with its hierarchy, its strictly demarcated departments and its rules for
the conduct of its employees, all of which have tended to work against women.

While women were central to broadcasting even in the early post-war days,
their position continued to be defined as that of audience rather than producers and presenters of programmes. Indeed, when commercial television
was launched it emphasized the presence of men in programmes for women.
As the *Daily Herald* announced on 19 May 1955 'Men will be the main attrac-
tion of the morning programmes for women' (cited in Leman 1987: 85). One
reason women journalists were more successful in print than in broadcasting
might also be connected to the nature of the media. Compared to newspapers, broadcast news was relatively new and tended to be regarded as a
gimmick. So, as Thumim (1998) suggests, in order to provide sufficient
authority and gravitas broadcasters stressed the 'maleness' of their news and
current affairs programmes with male presenters and (mainly) male interviewees. While the 1960s marked a turning-point for women in journalism, as
in many other professions, it was their ability to communicate as women
rather than as professional journalists that was valued by the news media
industry. None the less, the efforts of women in journalism in those days
contributed to a change in news values still evident in the twenty-first century,
as the following chapters show.

3

The education and training of women journalists

As a profession, journalism exercises very few formal controls over itself. It does not require its practitioners to have specific training or education, and unlike medicine or law there are no licensing requirements. Indeed, one journalist said: 'You become a journalist when you declare you are one, and you remain a journalist as long as you keep declaring you are one' (Delano 2000: 264). That said, throughout the twentieth century in both the United States and in Britain, journalism became increasingly professionalized, although at different rates, and this is reflected in the different approaches to journalists' education and training. All of these factors have gendered implications.

In the United States, journalism education at undergraduate level started growing quickly at the beginning of the twentieth century, with the first journalism school founded at the University of Missouri in 1908. Not only did nearly all journalists soon have an undergraduate degree (already by the early 1970s, 60 per cent of all US journalists had college degrees), but by the early 1990s, 75 to 80 per cent of newly hired entry-level daily newspaper journalists were graduates of journalism programmes. In contrast, in Britain, a postgraduate diploma course in journalism was first offered in 1970 and it was the 1990s before undergraduate degrees began. The majority of journalists had no university education in any area up to the 1980s: in 1955/6, 25 per cent of British journalists had been educated to university level, although this rose to 69 per cent in 1995 (Delano and Henningham 1995: 13). This situation is particularly significant for women in journalism given that the increase in women studying journalism coincides with a rise in the proportion of women in the profession. For that reason this chapter compares how the training and education of journalists has developed in the United States and Britain and how it affects the position and status of women journalists. Moreover, because the kinds of presence that women have had, or not had, as faculty members in university-level journalism programmes has an impact on journalism students, this chapter also assesses the status of women who teach journalism.

Training and education in the United States

The first call for formal journalism education in the United States was issued in 1789 by John Ward Fenno, in his periodical, the *Gazette of the United States*. There was little response until after the Civil War, when General Robert E. Lee established a chair in journalism and fifty scholarships 'for young men proposing to make printing and journalism their life work and profession' (Sloan 1990). At that point Lee was president of an all-male school later re-named Washington and Lee. Editors and publishers were polarized in their responses to Lee's plan, however, and it was abandoned in 1878. Washington and Lee opened its journalism laboratory (learning by doing and observing on the job) only in 1925 (Sutton 1948). As such, the apprenticeship approach to journalism training continued into the twentieth century. Interestingly, those who opposed journalism schools and who ridiculed college-educated reporters more generally used highly gendered language. Book-learning, these critics said, was impractical, effete and 'womanish'. In contrast, journalism and the people who belonged in the occupation were vigorous and 'masculine'.

None the less, by the late nineteenth century, during an era when professions were demanding university qualifications, the notion of college education per se began to sound better to news workers and newspaper readers. The notion of journalism education sounded less and less absurd, especially as many universities began to expand their curricula beyond the traditional liberal arts areas. Accompanying these changes was the growth in the newspaper business and calls for professionalism in journalism akin to the professionalism of law and medicine. Some of these calls came from inside journalism. It is likely that editors and publishers regarded a university education as a way to assert their status – specifically the status of journalism as a profession, as opposed to a trade – and to acquire a reputation for professional ethics (Steiner 1992). In keeping with this growing support for 'practical' education, including journalism education, Cornell University offered a lecture series on journalism in the 1870s (Sutton 1948). By the 1890s, the Wharton School of Business at the University of Pennsylvania offered five journalism courses, taught by a former financial editor.

Journalism education at the college and university level took off after the turn of the century. The University of Illinois launched a four-year curriculum in 1904; and the University of Wisconsin began an undergraduate journalism programme in 1905. The University of Missouri had begun offering journalism courses through its English Department in 1878. After years of petitions from students and journalists, it established a fully-fledged journalism school in 1908 with eighty-four men and thirteen women taking journalism courses that year. After protracted wrangling with its benefactor Joseph Pulitzer, in 1912 Columbia University launched an undergraduate journalism programme which it later converted into a graduate school (Baker 1954). During the same decade journalism programmes began at the University of Minnesota and at Northwestern University, both with the financial support of a local newspaper.

The number of programmes ballooned, as did the number of majors they produced. While the four four-year programmes in 1910 produced twenty-five graduates, the fifty-four programmes with majors in 1927 produced 931 graduates. By the end of that decade, about 300 colleges or universities in the United States offered some undergraduate-level journalism courses (Williams 1929). Journalism programmes at master's and doctoral levels began in the 1930s and burgeoned in the 1950s. By the early 1990s the 400 programmes in the United States were producing over 35,000 degrees annually.

Early responses to women journalism students

The Board of Directors planning Columbia University's new journalism school opposed the admission of women (Baker 1954). However, women's exclusion was overruled and the inaugural class included several women. None the less, the Columbia Graduate School of Journalism maintained a 10 per cent quota on women students until 1968 (Beasley 1986: 39). Other schools did not anticipate women applying, and therefore very few of them had policies excluding women. Nevertheless, the male pronouns used to describe journalism students were more than a grammatical habit. Sara Williams's 1929 history of the Missouri programme quotes several texts and documents that refer to 'men' and 'newspapermen', including Missouri's mission statement asserting the school's interest in furnishing 'well-equipped men for leadership in journalism' (Williams 1929: 53).

With the benefit of hindsight, and given the relative glamour of journalism, it is no surprise that women did apply to join journalism programmes. Women were admitted from the beginning at Missouri. Notably, the same year that Missouri's journalism school began, the Missouri Press Association, which had vigorously pushed the university to establish the school and which had helped organize it, elected its first woman officer (Beasley and Theus 1988). Missouri's journalism student body included 1,398 men and 272 women in its first decade. Within twenty years, over one-third of the graduates of Missouri's journalism programme were female. Missouri's annual conferences for journalists from across the state often included a lecture on women and journalism. Nevertheless, the advice that women were offered at those lectures would not be considered feminist by today's standards. That is, women warned female students to expect work assignments quite different from those of their male colleagues.

The impact of journalism education on women in the profession is difficult to assess, but one interesting piece of information concerns salaries. For her doctoral dissertation published in 1938 Iona Logie surveyed 881 women journalists, including several women working in advertising and publishing: one-fifth of her respondents were not doing any kind of media-related work. Some 57 per cent were graduates of journalism programmes. Logie found that for women working five to ten years, journalism graduates were typically earning more than liberal arts graduates or non-college women working on newspapers. But for those who had been working between eleven and fifteen years, liberal arts graduates were earning more than journalism graduates. Logie's data suggest that excluding from journalism schools women who wanted to (and did) work as journalists hurt them, salary-wise.

Admissions policies aside, evidence abounds that in both trivial and significant ways, gender was an issue for students and teachers in journalism programmes. In 1909 a professional honorary sorority (i.e. one where membership was by invitation) for female college journalism students was formed at the University of Washington. Apparently the idea behind Theta Sigma Phi (the female sorority) was to match Sigma Delta Chi, an honorary fraternity for male students headed into journalism.

Theta Sigma Phi maintained a national register, essentially an employment bureau, and published the *Matrix* (first edited by Ruby Black, in Washington DC), a magazine carrying 'inspirational and practical guidance articles'. In 1971 Sigma Delta Chi became the Society of Professional Journalists and accepted women; in 1972 Theta Sigma Phi became Women in Communications.

Clearly, one of the issues for university administrators was whether women graduates really intended to go on to work as journalists. Sara Williams's 1929 history cites a survey showing that 85 per cent of graduates through 1920 were working in journalism and 'excluding the women graduates who had given up journalism for marriage, ninety per cent were actively in the profession' (Williams 1929: 35). Beasley and Theus (1988: 10) note that of the ten men who founded Sigma Delta Chi, eight initially went into journalism, while of the seven Theta Sigma Phi founders, only the one woman who remained single did well – at the *New York Herald Tribune*.

The last chapter of Baker's (1954) history, dealing with what Columbia's graduates did with their degrees, says:

> The biggest single loss to journalism is, to no one's surprise, the gain of the home. The largest group who are no longer employed in journalism are, of course, women graduates who have found their employment in the home a first responsibility and somewhat too time-consuming to permit their continuance in journalism. Some housewives have found time to toss off a book or continue their careers and take leadership in civic activities, but they admit that they find it hard. Despite this continuing counter attraction to a journalistic career, it must be said that some of the School's most distinguished alumni are women.
>
> (Baker 1954: 128)

Training and education in Britain

One reason for the lack of attention paid to British journalism training is that, historically, the occupation adopted a trade union model. Journalists regarded themselves as crafts*men*, who trained through an apprenticeship and developed their skills through emulation. As Delano (2000: 264) points out, the apprenticeship system that preceded university training in Britain 'was susceptible to "complex and subtle" connections with media ownership which ensured a "passive" media liable to uphold the status quo', and the status quo at the end of the 1800s was that the vast majority of journalists were male. Alongside this there was, and to some extent still is, a general belief that journalists are 'born', not 'made', thus rendering a high level of education unnecessary. As David English, a former editor of the *Daily Mail*, recently said, 'Journalism is a skill that can only be acquired on the job and at the end of the day it depends on whether someone has a burning individual talent' (Keeble 2001: 235).

The first moves to a recognized training route were introduced by the National Association of Journalists, founded in 1884, which became the Institute of Journalists under a Royal Charter in 1890. Its main aim was 'to achieve professional status for journalists by promoting the interests of journalists, raising their status and qualifications, supervising their professional duties and testing qualifications for membership' (Elliott 1978: 177). Thus, the main focus of the Association, and later the Institute, was to achieve professional status for journalism. While members recognized that this involved training and entrance qualifications, they disagreed over exactly what should be tested. Apart from the specialist skill of shorthand, 'there were few skills that could not be picked up in a short spell in a newspaper office, and to demand more than these, such as academic qualifications, or language skills, would have meant raising wage rates to a level unacceptable to the proprietors', as Lee (1976a: 35) points out. Their efforts to monitor standards within journalism were therefore carried out on a very informal basis. Women were admitted to the Association of Journalists in the nineteenth century, and in 1895 they formed a separate Society of Women Journalists with the aim of improving the status of women journalists. They were aware that in order to achieve status, they needed to set a standard for entry into the profession, making clear that 'we do not welcome the crowd, or endeavour to encourage the amateur' (Lee 1976a: 35).

In 1907 the National Union of Journalists (NUJ) became the world's first trade union for journalists. Much of its efforts were spent on improving conditions for members, with a focus on raising wages. Again, this demonstrates that the notion of a trade rather than a profession shaped ideas about journalistic training in Britain. The union's original rulebook specified equal treatment for both sexes in terms of employment and training practices. Nonetheless, this was not actually practised, so journalism continued to be a male profession deemed unsuitable for 'the fairer sex' (Sebba 1994: 235). Indeed, as late as 1972 Cecil King, a former Fleet Street editor and chairman of the International Publishing Corporation (IPC) claimed that 'ordinary news reporting is a hard life for anyone and perhaps too hard for women' (Sebba 1994: 235).

Moves by the NUJ and other trade organizations to articulate recognized standards of training were undertaken more to increase the status of the job of a reporter and so validate claims for better wages and conditions of work than to provide a formal education in journalism. In fact, not until 1949, when the Royal Commission on the Press drew attention to the need for better training, was any real effort invested in journalism education. A national advisory council formed in 1952 (Keeble 2001: 236) and three years later this became the National Council for the Training of Journalists. The NCTJ continues to be the main professional body concerned with journalist training standards throughout Britain. While the NCTJ did bring about a formal training route for journalists it was still largely a skill-based training carried out mainly 'on the job', that is: in the newsroom rather than at college, to standards set by those working in the profession. The minimum education requirement to enter the profession in 1965 was three General Certificates of Education (GCEs[1]), one of which had to be in English. This basic educational level was the only objective standard used in hiring journalists, the rest was down to the 'gut feeling' of the editor – who was usually male and tended to hire young men with whom he could identify. Women were obviously disadvantaged by this mode of hiring and training.

Routes into journalism in Britain

The traditional route into newspaper journalism has been through direct entry and on-the-job training. Typically, entrants join a local newspaper straight from school at the age of either sixteen or eighteen and become 'indentured' (apprenticed) to that paper. Within this system trainees are contractually tied to a specific newspaper for a set period and, in return for training, the paper benefits from cheap labour. After a few months of on-the-job training and experience, trainees are usually released from their newspapers to attend college for a twelve-week 'block release' course at NCTJ accredited centres, after which they return to their newspapers for continued on-the-job experience. The focus of these courses is on practical skills taught to all trainee journalists regardless of gender. No special training is given to women, who may or may not want to focus on feature writing (the so-called 'softer' news not pegged to immediate or breaking news). No specialization is offered in 'women's journalism'. At the end of the course, trainees sit seven NCTJ preliminary examinations, including in law, central and local government, and 100-words-per-minute shorthand.[2] After two more years of experience, they can sit for the NCTJ National Certificate Examination

(NCE) to be fully qualified. An alternative to direct entry into journalism is to take a one-year pre-entry NCTJ college course. This is a full-time college-based course that covers the same ground as block-release courses but also includes newspaper practice. Again, men and women get identical training. At the end of the year students take preliminary examinations, and seek a position on a newspaper. After eighteen months on the job in a newsroom they can sit the NCE to become fully qualified.

In addition, some of the larger newspaper groups run their own training schemes using National Vocational Qualifications (and Scottish Vocational Qualifications). These are work-based assessments made over one to three years, based on nationally agreed standards set by the Newspaper Society and monitored by the training organization Skillset. The main reason for the distinction between NVQs that cover England and Wales, and SVQs in Scotland is that Scotland has its own legal and public administration system, separate from the rest of the UK. Otherwise, the training is identical.

Until the 1970s there were no training courses for broadcast journalists. Radio and television stations usually recruited from the print sector and provided in-house, on-the-job, technical training. Postgraduate diploma courses in radio journalism began from the middle of the 1970s, and a decade later similar courses became available in television journalism.

However, journalism in Britain has increasingly become a graduate profession over the last decade. In 1965 only 6 per cent of those entering local newspapers had a university degree while a further 33 per cent had one or more A levels[3] (Keeble 2001: 236). Sixty-nine per cent[4] of all British journalists had attended university or college in 1992, and A levels in varying number were held by 83 per cent (Delano and Henningham 1995: 13). According to Delano and Henningham's (1995) survey of British journalists, more women journalists are degree holders than men: 55 per cent to 45 per cent, with the majority of graduate journalists holding an arts degree (47.9 per cent). Of the specialist subjects studied by graduate journalists 11.3 per cent studied economics, 5.1 per cent science; even smaller percentages took business/commerce, engineering, law, and fine art. They found that only 2 per cent of graduates had a bachelors degree in journalism, while 13 per cent had taken a postgraduate diploma in journalism and 4 per cent a postgraduate diploma in radio journalism (1995: 14). The increase in the number of graduates entering journalism in the UK has to be considered against a fifteen-fold increase in the national university population as a whole, from 50,000 in 1938 to 750,000 in 1992 (Delano and Henningham 1995: 20). The low number of journalists with graduate qualifications from journalism programmes reflects the fact that such programmes are relatively new in Britain.

The first university journalism programme in Britain was a postgraduate degree launched in 1970 at University College, Cardiff, followed by a similar one-year postgraduate diploma course at City University, London in 1976. A diploma course had run at Kings College, London, between 1922 and 1939 but this was not restarted after the war (Keeble 2001: 236). Undergraduate degrees in journalism did not appear in Britain until the early 1990s but their popularity ensured a rapid growth. In addition, by 2001 several of the 331 undergraduate programmes in such areas as communication studies and media and cultural studies contained a substantial element of journalism (Hann 2001).

The training and education of journalists in Britain has never taken account of gender issues. This has had both positive and negative implications for women. On the positive side, women gained the same skills as men and therefore had the potential to do the same work and follow the same career pattern: they were not 'tracked' in the same way as women journalists in the United States. Moreover, the emergence of a higher education qualification as a de-facto prerequisite has helped to level the playing field for women. On the negative side, because there were few objective criteria for hiring trainees until relatively recently, the subjective criteria of personal connections and other attributes of the 'old boys' network' came into play. This clearly worked against women being hired.

Both the formal training of journalists and research into their training and education in Britain continues to lag behind that of the United States. As yet there is no data available on the gender structuring of journalism courses in Britain as there is in the US. For that reason the following section examines journalism programmes in the United States and the links between the status of women as journalists, journalism students and journalism educators. This involves an analysis of how welcoming journalism programmes have been to women students and how women have been treated when they were admitted to those programmes. It is a matter of how or whether women have been mentored, how (or what) they are taught and which specific careers within journalism they are encouraged to pursue.

In this context, then, the status of women journalism students is also closely linked to the status of women journalism faculty members (or lecturers as they are called in Britain) – whether women are hired to teach in journalism schools, what they are allowed or encouraged to teach, whether they achieve tenure, whether they achieve policy-making (that is, administrative) positions, how they are rewarded and promoted. Universities produce changes in students, not merely in their knowledge but also in values, as exemplified by a standard mandating diversity among the accreditation requirements for journalism programmes in the United States. So-called Standard 12 of the Accrediting Council on Education in Journalism and Mass Communication (ACEJMC) (2001: 59–60) insists: 'Units should demonstrate a commitment to increased diversity and inclusivity in their student populations and faculties and to the creation of a learning environment that exposes students to a broad spectrum of voices and views.'

Early efforts of women to teach journalism in the United States

US journalism programmes hired women almost from the beginning of university training. Yet, women have generally found it much harder to get positions teaching journalism, and have often been essentially confined to teaching female students. There is a link here: most of the women who were first hired to teach journalism had been 'tracked' as women in the newsroom, and they apparently tried to encourage women students to avoid sex discrimination by entering the women's market, by writing for the women's pages or society pages. From 1886 to 1900, parlaying her experience at the *Chicago Tribune* and the *Detroit Free Press*, Martha Louise Rayne operated her own journalism institute for women, in Detroit. Four women were among the 107 journalism faculty members attending a national convention of journalism teachers in 1916. Already by 1921, 12 per cent of the members attending the convention of the American Association of Teachers of Journalism were women (Henry 2004).

Women were well aware of their lower pay and their token and secondary status. After her retirement in 1967, for example, Frances Grinstead said that 'one woman to a faculty total of 15 or 20 men is female underemployment, sure enough!' (Henry 2004: 5). Presumably when they hired women the schools chose carefully – often selecting their own graduates. Moreover, the fact that some schools hired a few women to teach does not mean that women had an easy time obtaining faculty positions. In 1916 Walter Williams, the founding Dean at Missouri, wrote to the Dean at the University of Washington, who was looking for someone to teach advertising: 'The best man among our journalism graduates this year for the place you have in mind is a woman'. Adding that 'Her sex is her only drawback', Williams admitted that he would not himself have the nerve to hire Merze Marvin. Sure enough, the University of Washington declined to hire her (Henry 2004). Missouri did hire women to assist in teaching copy reading and reporting. Indeed, this job seemed to be exclusively in the hands of women. No wonder, then, that women were not seen as making much of a contribution to journalism education, in both the very early and the more modern history of the field. Of the thirty-eight people described in *Makers of the Media Mind: Journalism Educators and Their Ideas* (Sloan 1990) only one woman was mentioned, and she was part of a three-person team.

Tracks for women in US journalism education

Women and men students have typically been tracked quite differently, with women encouraged to study (and prepare for) feature writing and writing for and about women. Having designed and taught 'Writing for Homemakers', Helen Patterson said, 'Speaking for myself, I have little interest in cooking and such, but I recognize the enormous market for articles on the home and think it offers a wide opportunity for women writers' (Beasley 1986: 15). Helen Hostetter's course on 'Journalism for Women' trained women to write for women's and 'home' pages. Indeed, when Hostetter, who had begun as a society editor, took her five-year break from Kansas State, it was in order to become editor of the *Journal of Home Economics*. By 1940 several other universities across the country offered courses for women in writing for women's pages or women's magazines.

The fact that it was women teaching the courses designed for women students can be interpreted as creating opportunities for women faculty. Alternatively, this could be seen as tracking the women's faculty in the same way students were tracked. Baker's history of Columbia's journalism school described Eleanor Carroll as having been hired in 1937 in order to 'add the woman's touch, teach a sequence of studies in the magazine, and lend wise counsel' (Baker 1954: 107). Just as the creation of women's pages or women's beats required hiring a certain number of women reporters, so establishing courses for women required hiring a small number of women to teach those courses. In both cases, the women so hired were restricted to a women's track that was quite far from, and regarded as inferior to, the main track. Significantly, men had no wish to derail their own careers by following the women's track. This demonstrates clearly that 'women's journalism' was considered inferior to other forms of mainstream journalism. The tracking is also seen in their assignments, or at least in what gets preserved of course assignments. Beasley and Theus (1988) note that a woman wrote only one of the sixteen editorials published by the University of Missouri in 1927 (the said collection was edited by Sara Lockwood Williams); of the fourteen news stories in the collection, two were written by women: one on wedding vows and one on a student hike.

Precisely for this reason, the courses for women could be controversial. Jean James asserted in a 1932 *Matrix* article that journalism schools should teach women and men the same things, even including printing, stereotyping and engraving. She acknowledged that 'One frequently hears the remark that since women do a different type of work from men on newspapers, it is foolish for them to take the same courses' (quoted in Beasley 1986: 24). James called this 'fallacious' reasoning and noted that, at the very least, women might need to substitute for men, in emergencies or because of illness or vacation (Beasley 1986).

The representation of women in journalism textbooks

The earliest printed resources for would-be journalists in the United States were manuals written by men and for men. Certainly, only men – and gentlemen – are mentioned in manuals and booklets such as Benjamin Drew's 1874 *Pens and Types: Or, Hints and Helps for Those Who Write, Print, or Read*; Thomas Campbell-Copeland's 1889 *The Ladder of Journalism. How to Climb* it. *A Primer for Beginners in Newspaper Work*; and Robert Luce's *Writing for the Press* (1889). The few early textbooks that mentioned women were not encouraging. Edwin Shuman, the literary editor of the *Chicago Record-Herald*, wrote a handbook in 1894, which he expanded in *The Art and Practice of Journalism: How to Become a Successful Writer*. In that 1899 textbook, Shuman predicted that the dailies would continue to be dominated by men. Articles from a woman's point of view, he said, are 'naturally superficial and frothy'. In his view, women who were hired would find the sacrifice not worth the gain: 'Women will swiftly lose many of their high ideals and sweet and tender ways, as inevitably as if they had been run through a machine for the purpose. And what is the use?' (Shuman 1899: 156). His 1903 assessment was even more negative. In *Practical Journalism: A Complete Manual of the Best Newspaper Methods*, Shuman admitted that 'Yellow Journalism' (referred to in Chapter 1) provided opportunities for women but claimed it was difficult, risky, unpleasant and defeminizing. More generally, he said, newsgathering is 'too rude and exacting' for women. Not surprisingly, the only early manual that really encouraged women to take up general reporting was written by a woman. In her 1900 guide *What a Reporter Must Be: Helps to Success in Newspaper Work*, Nevada Davis Hitchcock said that 'sex makes practically no difference in the requirements of a reporter'. Women were clearly being typecast and treated with contempt within practical guides on journalism and by faculty as a whole.

A snapshot of the status of women in journalism emerges from the discussions of women in journalism textbooks by journalism professors in the early and mid-twentieth century:

- 1911 Charles Ross, University of Missouri, acknowledges women only as readers;
- 1913 Willard Grosvenor Bleyer, founding director at the University of Wisconsin, says no more about women than that the society editor is 'almost invariably a woman' (the same is true of the 1923 and 1932 editions);
- 1917 Lyle Spencer, journalism school director of the University of Washington, departs from masculine nouns and pronouns only in the chapter on society news;
- 1924 Phil Bing, faculty member at University of Minnesota, never mentions women;
- 1926 Gerald W. Johnson, teaching at University of North Carolina, makes no mention of women.

Not surprisingly, the textbooks specifically for women were usually written by women. And most of the textbooks by women were for women. Over the entire twentieth century, including during periods marked by greater gender equity, women have produced relatively few journalism textbooks. Most of the ones women have single-authored were published in the early to mid-twentieth century, when courses for women were first developed, and most of these written for such courses. For example, in 1926 Wisconsin professor Genevieve Boughner published a textbook, *Women in Journalism: A Guide to the Opportunities and a Manual of the Technique of Women's Work for Newspapers and Magazines.* Boughner, who taught feature writing for women (i.e. for women readers, for women students), vigorously underscored in her foreword 'the desirability of specialization on the part of the woman beginner in some branch of magazine or newspaper work, that demands the distinctly feminine background and experience' (Boughner 1926: viii). One of the few men to write a textbook aimed at women was the novelist Arnold Bennett. His 1898 *Journalism for Women: A Practical Guide* steered women to the spheres men disdain, such as fashion and cooking. Even in that limited arena, Bennett complained that much of the reporting for women, and therefore by women, was slipshod and careless.

Contemporary opportunities in journalism education in the United States

As Chapter 1 indicates, the Second World War expanded opportunities for women workers everywhere while men went to war. Not only did editors of United States newspapers move society editors into city rooms, but they began begging journalism schools to train more women – with formal programmes, accelerated programmes and crash courses, in writing and in mechanical areas. An April 1943 *Matrix* article, for example, described a special training programme for women who were not journalism majors that ranged from public affairs programmes to typography and printing press operations. This opening was clearly a response to the wartime shortage of men. After the war, as Chapter 2 shows, women were booted out of the city rooms, and they returned to the secondary status in universities as well.

All of this should be placed in the context of the century-long gradual increase in the importance of a college degree and a journalism degree. In 1971, about two-thirds of American journalists had college degrees. By 1982/3 some 40 per cent of US journalists had majored in journalism (Weaver and Willhoit 1996). It is a popular major: if journalism is defined as including broadcasting, telecommunications and communication, the percentage of journalists who graduated from college with majors in these areas increased from 41 per cent to 56 per cent between 1971 and 1992.

Although the majority of journalism undergraduates were women by the late 1960s, the percentage of women teaching journalism at the college level remained very small throughout the 1970s. Many journalism schools had one (token) woman lecturer, but the percentage of women had not increased, given increases in the overall size of journalism faculties over the century. The percentages of women teaching journalism was 7 per cent in the mid-1960s and 11 per cent in 1970 – less than in 1921. More strikingly, 81 per cent of journalism schools had either one or no women faculty members by 1970. Women faculty members were not studied much (or thought about) as a group until three women teaching at Kansas State presented a paper at the 1972 national convention of journalism professors. Among other findings, Ramona Rush, Carol Oukrop and Sandra Ernst reported that for 1970/1, women were 8 per cent of the journalism faculties nationally, most of them in the lowest ranks (see appendix to Rush, Oukrop and Creedon, 2004). Moreover, no women were then officials of the national organization of journalism educators, the Association for Education in Journalism (AEJ, with the term 'and Mass Communication' added later) or members of its executive committee, advisory board or standing committees. No woman was voted president of AEJ until 1978. The 1972 report lit a fuse. It immediately precipitated several other studies and some attitudinal as well as policy changes, both in the organization and in schools, many of whom became more serious about hiring women faculty. The female membership of AEJMC and/or journalism faculties increased to 17–19 per cent by 1983 and to 28 per cent by 1992 (Viswanath, Kosicki and Creedon 1993). In the early 1990s, AEJMC members passed a resolution calling for gender parity by 2000, but data from 2000 indicate that across all faculty ranks, women were 31 per cent of the journalism and mass communication faculties in the US (Oukrop and Rush 2003).

Of course, part of the problem of women's lack of recruitment into faculty positions was initially the relatively low number of women applying for and being awarded terminal degrees (Ph.D.) in relevant disciplines – and later, the perception that women with doctorates were a rare commodity. Women earned only 10 per cent of the doctorates granted in communication between 1968 and 1972, but that percentage doubled quickly, and by 1983, they were 40 per cent of the Ph.D. students. And pay (in)equity continues to be a problem across all ranks. A 2000 survey found that 62 per cent of women journalism faculty members put salary inequity at the top of their list of discrimination concerns (Oukrop and Rush 2003).

A census of AEJMC journalism faculty undertaken in 1992 found that, on average, women teaching in journalism are younger than men (forty-three versus forty-eight years) and a greater percentage of them had started teaching after 1975 (as opposed to earlier). This is echoed by the age differences between men and women journalists in the profession as a whole, with women being younger. This indicates that women are finding it difficult to sustain a career both as lecturers and practitioners of journalism for a number of reasons including sexism, barriers to promotion, inflexible work practices and lack of childcare support. Furthermore, while a larger percentage of women than men held a terminal master's degree, a somewhat smaller percentage (62 per cent versus 73 per cent) held a doctoral degree, which many colleges and universities regard as crucial for tenure, if not hiring. The male faculty members had about nine years of professional experience, yet the female faculty had about eight years (Oukrop and Rush 2003). These differences, especially in age, may (or may not) explain some of the other data from that study:

- About 13 per cent of women and 40 per cent of men are full professors (the national averages for all disciplines are that about 17 per cent of women and 44 per cent of men are full professors). This is up from 1985, when 4 per cent of women were full professors and, altogether, the number of tenured women saw very sharp increases;
- Women seemed, on average, to spend less time 'in rank' (that is, at the same rank without being promoted) than men;
- The teaching load of women and men is comparable.

Sex discrimination in journalism has not necessarily discouraged women from attending journalism schools, as shown by the statistics published in the annual enrolment survey (collected at Ohio State University and published by AEJMC). In 1977, and for the first time, women were statistically the majority of the undergraduates studying journalism.[5] In 1978 they were about 53 per cent, in 1984 about 59 per cent and in 1992 about 61 per cent. At the same time, the total journalism enrolments were growing, but also the total number of women college students. It should be noted that these percentages are approximate, and many of the women – disproportionately to men – were entering the advertising and public relations options that journalism schools offer, thus reflecting gender segregation in various fields of journalism (see Chapter 4). Moreover, the percentages grew smaller at higher levels of study – in 1983, women were 52 per cent of the masters'-level enrolments and 36 per cent of the doctoral candidates in journalism and mass media.

Ironically, during the 1980s, journalism employers were apparently beginning to grow concerned about the declining percentage of male journalism graduates. A 1983 report published by the American Newspaper Publishers Association Foundation underscored the difficulty of finding male – especially black male – journalists (Beasley and Theus 1988). Fears of a 'pink ghetto' – which would mean the feminization and therefore devaluing of journalism – also spread to the academy. This is seen in the transcripts of two roundtables convened by the University of Maryland in 1984 to discuss, as Maurine Beasley put it:

Do we risk flooding the market with an influx of women fighting for the same job and further depressing salaries? . . . Are we turning out an increasing number of women students who are going to be fighting for the same jobs and thus the pay will be depressed.

(Beasley and Theus 1988: 98)

Reese Cleghorn, Dean of Maryland's College of Journalism, whose student body at that point was 69 per cent female, said:

> I have to confess my nightmare, which is that journalism will become even more female and all of our students will go off and marry male engineering students and have to have a break in their career and never get back to it.
>
> (Beasley and Theus 1988: 115)

Ironically, at least one survey (Becker, Fruit and Caudill 1987: 51) of graduating students (seniors) strongly suggests that women and non-white students were more professionally oriented than males and non-white students. Comparing an interest in job security (interest in journalism because it is a good 'fall-back' major and the perception of available jobs) to a professional orientation (linked to an interest in journalism because it is seen as exciting and involves politics, having pride in one's profession), women and black students scored higher on professional values while men and white students scored higher on the security index.

Diversity in the curriculum

Principles and standards for journalism education in the United States were first formulated in 1924, and, since the 1940s, an accrediting council has set standards for journalism programmes and has served as the sanctioned accrediting organization. The Accrediting Council on Education for Journalism and Mass Communication (ACEJMC) recently added a requirement that journalism programmes articulate their goals regarding diversity and inclusivity and demonstrate their success in achieving these goals. In explaining the new Standard 12, the Council explicitly linked journalism's special role in supporting free expression and access to information to journalists' responsibility to disseminate diverse opinions and serve diverse audiences, with race and gender being of crucial import. Notably, the major evidence that journalism programmes are serving such responsibilities is the diversity of the student body and faculty. The Council now assesses how journalism programmes recruit, advise and retain both minority students and minority and female faculty members.

One reason to be concerned with the presence – in sheer numbers or percentages, and specifically in the tenured and upper reaches of academia – of women in journalism education is their direct impact on women students. As Larissa Grunig (1993: 277) notes: 'Today's undergraduate is tomorrow's practitioner; today's graduate student is tomorrow's professor.' Survey data for 1999/2000 suggest that while women are 31 per cent of the journalism and mass communication faculty, they are 18 per cent of the full professors (the highest rung in the professoriate) and they are 25 per cent of the top administrators (Oukrop and Rush 2003). Grunig (1993: 277) points out how a glass ceiling within academia that keeps women journalism and mass communication professors at the lower rungs of universities also sends a 'forceful and negative message to female students' hindering recruitment of women and discouraging them from entering the field.

Presumably, Standard 12 implies that creating a learning environment that exposes students to a broad spectrum of voices and views requires social diversity among faculty, administration, guest speakers and part-time faculty members. Promoting diversity is also a curricular matter, although we argue that a curriculum that promotes diversity probably requires, or at least is highly linked to, a diverse faculty. Luckily, several tightly interrelated factors have led to the emergence of free-standing courses on women and media (or women and minorities in journalism and media) and the incorporation of units dealing with these topics into existing courses:

- the women's movement, feminism, representations of women;
- the hiring of women faculty members with relevant skills;
- publication of popular press articles, scholarly articles and books, and textbooks and other curricular material (and eventually of entire journals) on related issues;
- sharing and critique of relevant syllabi, materials and documents for such courses;
- mutual support and encouragement at conventions, especially the establishment of divisions, commissions and committees to support relevant research within existing faculty organizations, especially at the national level;
- increasing attention to diversity training, and demand by journalism organizations for this. (For example, the Code of Ethics of the Society of Professional Journalists asserts that journalists should show the diversity of the human experience and give voice to the voiceless; likewise, the code of ethics asks journalists to examine their own cultural values and to avoid stereotyping by race, gender, age, religion, ethnicity, geography, sexual orientation, disability, physical appearance or social status.)

Developments in British education and training

As mentioned earlier, the craft rather than professional approach to training and education of journalists in Britain, and the late development of the country's university programmes in journalism, has compounded the lack of research on the subject. Instead, the focus of the debate in Britain is on whether or not journalism is a suitable subject for academic study, and what approach should be taken to improve journalism education. Given that the British training of journalists was entirely 'on the job' until the 1970s, there was little need for textbooks.

None the less, books were written to guide would-be journalists into the profession and, predictably, these tended to be written by men, with few references to women who might wish to enter the profession. For example, the 1963 book entitled *Freelance Journalism* by A. K. Astbury typically makes no reference to women journalists at all, and refers to 'men' and 'newspapermen', using masculine pronouns throughout. In the same year, a book on journalism by Neil Stephens that was part of a series to provide 'all those in public, secondary grammar, secondary modern and secondary technical schools a better idea of the opportunities that await them in many absorbing careers' made just one reference to women aiming to work as journalists. Writing about 'a young man's, or girl's, prospects of a career in journalism', Stephens (1963: 55–6) notes that there is 'no system of recruitment: youngsters simply present themselves to the editor and ask for a job'. He then goes on to note that the whole process is a 'question of luck', although 'once the applicant is appointed, his immediate future is well-defined'. No mention is made regarding what a 'girl' might do, and specialist reporters such as lobby correspondents, court reporters and industrial and science correspondents are described entirely as men.

Since 1970, when the first British postgraduate diploma in journalism was established, the relationship between academia and the industry has been strained. Academics in the humanities and social sciences, where journalism courses tend to reside, claim journalism degrees are too vocational and that they amount to little more than training courses. This belief is further fuelled by the fact that those degrees accredited by the industry are taught by former journalists rather than traditional academics. Although there are no statistics on the gender of those teaching journalism in British universities, a telephone survey we undertook of university courses in the UK in 2002 showed only slightly more men than women teaching journalism.[6]

The history of journalism training in the UK is described by Ian Hargreaves as 'a professional wild west' (quoted in Hann 2001: 4). Just like the real Wild West, women did not feature prominently in its early days, and those who did were often believed to have got there regardless of ability. Veteran writer and broadcaster Olga Franklin stirred up a storm of protest when she suggested this in the *Spectator* in 1972.

> She [the woman journalist] may make a quick killing and marry the editor; she may land Gregory Peck like the French girl reporter, or President Kennedy like Jacqueline Onassis, or end up with Anthony Crossland like Susan Barnes . . . Or perhaps, most unfair of all, she may rise straight from the top editor's bed into Fleet Street, with hardly any qualifications at all, as I did myself, and as I know some of my colleagues also did (but I do not want to libel anybody).
>
> (cited in Sebba 1994: 236)

While this suggestion was hotly refuted by the Women in Media group (who have surveyed and promoted the position of women in journalism in Britain), it is indicative of the way women entering journalism were regarded until very recently. Indeed, barriers to women entering journalism were even recognized by those teaching on NCTJ courses in the 1970s, when the standard advice to female students (by the predominantly male tutors) was to sign letters of application with their last name and an initial to avoid their gender being disclosed.

By the 1990s the majority of trainee journalists were women. 'Whereas in 1981/2 forty-one per cent of all entrants into newspapers were women, ten years later this figure had risen to fifty-two per cent' (Sebba 1994: 247). It is no coincidence that during this time the training of journalists in Britain began to move away from the industry into colleges and universities. The adoption of more formal and objective criteria used by academic institutions has given women a better chance of gaining access to training, although not necessarily on an equal footing given the differing treatment of male and female students by the teaching profession. However, Britain is still a long way from providing a unified and recognized approach to journalism training, as Ian Hargreaves acknowledges: 'We have a large agenda ahead of us, including the effects of technology changes and the proper demands of the equality agenda', he says (quoted in Butcher 2001: 18–19). This means that objective criteria for entry into the industry and a clear career path still need to be established. For most of the last century, journalism in Britain has been a matter of 'jobs for the boys' with women relegated to 'pink ghettos'. As more women enter the profession this situation is changing. Anthony Delano (2003: 277–8) notes that, in the twenty-first century, 75 per cent of the students in British postgraduate broadcast journalism courses are women, 'which has elicited some concern' that broadcast news may become dominated by women.

Conclusion

The United States and Britain have very different histories in their systems of education and training. This has implications for women's recruitment and advancement within the profession. Formal training and the recognition of entry standards began much earlier in the United States than in Britain, which has meant that women gained more ground and did so earlier in the US. Formal training for journalists in Britain was hampered because journalists have, until recently, regarded the occupation as a trade rather than a profession. This perpetuated the belief that the only way to learn to be a journalist was to be trained 'on the job'. Women in Britain have been barred from the newsroom by an aggressively masculine apprenticeship system of on-the-job training which encouraged male editors to employ young clones of themselves. While no distinctions were made between the training of men and women as journalists in Britain, women were less likely to be taken on by male editors, who perpetuated the myth that journalism was a 'man's job'.

American female university students received journalism education, but of a kind quite different from that of their male counterparts. For many years women were trained within a specific, narrow category of 'women's journalism', configured by the curriculum, textbooks and the attitudes of lecturers as marginal, if not subordinated. The fact that women were taught to write specifically *as* women and *for* women perpetuated the myth that to be a 'real' journalist, dealing in hard news, you had to be male. In both countries, then, the training of journalists has historically been unsuccessful in transcending the stereotypical figure of a journalist as inherently male with the male attributes of being tough, hard-hitting and ruthless in the pursuit of a story. The patterns in the journalism classroom are certainly not unconnected to the patterns in the university, which in turn are linked to larger social and workplace issues. Male journalists and teachers imported rather than invented the variety of ways for devaluing and limiting women writers and women's writings (Steiner 1993: 314). Professional mythology created initial opposition to formal university education for journalists, which was deemed 'effeminate'. The privileging of a masculine set of occupational values begins at the level of training and is echoed in the newsrooms.

In the United States, who teaches journalists and whether the profession is becoming a 'pink ghetto', are issues that continue to be areas of concern. In Britain, the issue of journalism as a suitable topic for university education, and how it should be taught, is being debated, not least by the organization of journalism teachers, the Association for Journalism Education, <http://www.ajeuk.org>, established in 1997. In both countries anxieties linger about the number of women able to pursue and sustain a successful career in journalism after graduation. These questions are addressed in the next chapter on recruitment into and promotion within the profession of journalism.

4

'One of the boys'?

WOMEN'S EXPERIENCES OF THE GLASS CEILING

In May 2002 discussions began to circulate publicly in the United States about who would succeed Tom Brokaw as NBC's lead television network news anchor. Since Peter Jennings at ABC and Dan Rather at CBS were both nearing retirement age, speculation immediately emerged as to their likely successors. A feature common to each of the names mentioned to succeed these three men was that they were all male. The fact that the maleness of the evening news was even publicly raised as an issue is perhaps a sign of progress, along with the question about whether men or women would notice (or complain about) the assumption that evening news anchors must be patriarchs. Although women journalists are quite visible on television, the sense of the evening news as a male bastion raises the spectre of the glass ceiling, or a cathode-ray ceiling, as a *New York Times* story put it after Brian Williams was officially named as the heir to Brokaw's 'throne' (Rutenberg 2002). Jim Rutenberg described an anchor as someone who is not merely the face of a network but also someone who 'at crucial moments is the kind of single combat warrior who carries his company's reputation in the steadiness of his hands and eyes, conveys strength and order and helps calm a nation' (Rutenberg 2002: C1). So, while the highly popular morning programmes are very profitable – for both the networks and for the women who co-anchor them – the highest-status evening newscasts remain out of reach for women.

The power of the patriarch is not limited to broadcasting. According to figures from the American Society of Newspaper Editors (ASNE), in 1998 women ran thirteen of the 103 US daily newspapers with circulations over 100,000 (Thompson 1998), although women were 17 per cent of the members of ASNE. In 2002, women ran eight of the thirty largest-circulation daily papers in the US (Strupp 2002). And a major survey of 137 papers with circulations over 85,000 found that women held 26 per cent of the executive jobs and they were 14 per cent of the CEOs, presidents and publishers (Hemlinger and Linton 2002: 11). In the UK's newspaper sector, a survey of the whole decade of the 1990s shows 14 per cent of women journalists became editor or deputy editor compared to 20 per cent of men. In periodicals and broadcasting the difference was more pronounced with 27 per cent of women becoming editors or deputy editors compared to 40 per cent of men; and 12 per cent of women became section editors or heads compared to 16 per cent of men. However, within these two latter sectors, 12 per cent of women became a senior executive, assistant editor, news director or chief sub compared to 4 per cent of men (Delano 2003: 278). This suggests that women have been making gains in some fields of journalism faster than in others, but have been underrepresented in many high-prestige areas such as the national daily newspapers and overrepresented in what are regarded as the lower-status sectors of commercial television and radio.

Although some women have achieved management positions in journalism, over the last few years the rate of increase has been slow and comes nowhere close to matching women's overall presence in the profession. This chapter assesses the recruitment, status and level of success of women in decision-making positions in journalism. Among the stubborn barriers discussed here that prevent women from entering top management are the male culture in the newsrooms, family–workplace conflicts, a weakening economy (which means, among other things, fewer jobs) and male chauvinism among the very top executives – owners, presidents, publishers. We chart some of the distinctive ways that sexism and gender segregation operate in particular fields of journalism, and in the work routines of the newsroom more generally. We examine some of the strategies that women have used to overcome the sexism (and racism) that continue to be a problem at the apprenticeship levels and as people move through and up the pipeline.

Setting the scene: problems and issues raised about women's career progression

The term 'glass ceiling' was first coined in a 1986 column in the *Wall Street Journal*, referring to an invisible but seemingly unbreakable barrier preventing women from breaking through to the top echelons of industry and business. The concept refers to distinctive forms of sexism that limit success at top echelons of management and that therefore require distinctive kinds of protections or policies. The U.S. Department of Labor defines the glass ceiling as artificial barriers based on attitudinal or organizational biases preventing qualified women or ethnic minorities from advancing into upper management positions and obstructing them from getting assignments that can lead to developing expertise and credibility and, in turn, to promotion. By the early 1990s, only one in twenty of the very top executive positions across all corporations in the US was held by a woman.

Not surprisingly, journalism's glass ceiling is a global phenomenon. In June 2001, the International Federation of Journalists (IFJ) meeting in Seoul,

Korea, heard that while women comprise 30 to 40 per cent of the workforce in the developed countries (somewhat less in Asia and in most of Africa), they hold less than 1 per cent of the executive posts in the news media transnationally. More than 1,000 media organizations from fifty-six countries responded to a call from UNESCO on International Women's Day in 2001 to appoint women journalists to management positions, a call echoed in the UNESCO (2001) report 'Women Make the News: A Crack in the Glass Ceiling'. As a result, the IFJ launched a seven-point world-wide action plan to encourage and reinforce union efforts to crack the glass ceiling. The plan called for improvements in working conditions, among other items, to meet the needs of women and to promote women to higher jobs in unions as well as campaigning for equal pay.[1]

Some women fail to shatter the glass ceiling because they quit their jobs. A report entitled 'The Great Divide: Female Leadership in U.S. Newsrooms' jointly commissioned and released in 2002 by the American Press Institute (API) and the Pew Center for Civic Journalism[2] involved a survey by the API and Pew of 202 men and seventy-one women editors, managing editors and assistant managing editors. According to the report, about half the women editors but only one-third of the male editors expected to leave their current newsroom or exit the news business altogether. Just one in five women definitely wanted to obtain promotion; only one in three predicted that it would actually happen. This compares to 36 per cent of men who definitely want to be promoted and 42 per cent who expect promotion.

But why women quit is an issue. It is generally assumed that women abandon the executive track in order to spend more time with their families. Certainly, most chief executive officers of news organizations attribute the loss of women to family commitments. Hemlinger and Linton (2002) interviewed fifteen chief executive officers of media companies or presidents of newspaper divisions, mainly male, responsible for more than 400 daily papers across the United States. Their views about the status of women executives ran the gamut from 'there's no problem' to 'the problem can't be solved' to 'we're working on it' to 'we've solved it'. These executives generally agreed, however, that women faced discrimination, that more needed to be done to address it, and that eventually gender disparity would be solved.

Career patterns in journalism in the United States

The US journalism workforce in 2002 was about one-third female, as it has been since 1982, although more women than ever are graduating from journalism schools (Weaver et al. 2003: 4). This was better than several other professions such as college faculty (27 per cent female), law (22 per cent), physicians (18 per cent) and dentists (9 per cent) (Weaver and Wilhoit 1996: 9). On the other hand, journalists are less likely to be female compared to the total civilian labour force in the US, which was about 45 per cent female in 1991, and a decade later about 46.5 per cent (US Bureau of the Census 1991: 392, Weaver et al. 2003). Weaver and Wilhoit's 1992 and 2002 data indicate that the average US journalist is getting slightly older, perhaps reflecting the ageing of the baby boom generation (Weaver et al. 2003).

According to recent newsroom censuses (the American Society of Newspaper Editors 2000, Weaver et al. 2003: 4)[3] women are approximately 37 per cent of all newspaper and television journalists; these percentages have also not changed over the last decade. According to Vernon Stone's (1997) 'Women Break Glass Ceiling in TV News',[4] 36.2 per cent of the TV workforce was female by 1994. Stone noted that when male-dominated positions in the areas of sports, weather and photography are excluded then the rest of the news staff is roughly half women. Among all journalists, the largest proportion of women work for news magazines (43.5 per cent) and the smallest for the major wire services (20.3 per cent) (Weaver et al. 2003: 4).

Forty-six per cent of men and only 32 per cent of women had fifteen or more years of experience of journalism (Weaver and Wilhoit 1996), suggesting that women generally do not stay in journalism as long as men. Retention is a greater problem for women. Men and women did not differ much with respect to education, religious background, membership in journalism organizations (Weaver and Wilhoit 1996: 9). Data from the recently updated study by Weaver and Wilhoit suggests that overall, full-time journalists of colour (working for conventional, not ethnic presses) are 9.5 per cent of all journalists; this represents an increase since 1992 but not to an extent proportional to the overall percentage in the population, or even in comparison with the percentage of college degree holders who are people of colour. On the other hand, perhaps testifying to the success of recruitment efforts, nearly 20 per cent of the journalists with less than five years experience are people of colour (Weaver et al. 2003: 5).

In terms of ethnic representation, Weaver and Wilhoit (1996: 11) found that Jewish journalists, as 5 per cent of the journalism workforce, continued to be overrepresented in US journalism. Otherwise they found minorities to be underrepresented, as seen in Table 4.1.

Table 4.1 *Ethnic groups as percentage of US journalists and total US population*

	% of journalists	% of total US population
African American	3.7	12.1
Hispanic	2.2	9.0
Asian American	1.0	2.9
Native American	0.6	0.8
Jewish	5.4	2.4
Other/Caucasian	87.1	72.8

Notably, in 2002, journalists of colour are more likely to be women (50 per cent). While 34 per cent of all journalists were women, Weaver and Wilhoit (1996: 179) found that 52.5 per cent of Asian American journalists were women. This figure was 53.2 per cent for African Americans, 48.1 per cent for Hispanics and 42.9 per cent for Native Americans. Such statistics seem consistent with the 'two-fer' phenomenon ('two for one'), that is, organizations receiving 'credits' under equal opportunity law for hiring both a racial minority and a female in a single hire. But Weaver and Wilhoit (1996: 179) note that among racial minorities and especially African Americans, women are more likely to complete their college training than men and more likely to major in journalism. Indeed, African American scholar Paula Giddings (1984) noted that, because of sexism and racism, African American women were more likely than African American men to obtain a college degree to prepare for paid work. This continues to be the case decades later. Moreover, in the US, African American women are more likely than Caucasian women to be employed at all, as they are often the principal wage earner for their family.

Some news media were more successful than others in recruiting non-Caucasian journalists, as seen in Table 4.2 from Weaver and Willhoit (1996: 13).

Table 4.2 *Percentage of non-Caucasian journalists employed, by media type*

Media Type	Non-Caucasians as % of journalists
Radio	14.3
Television	11.8
Wire services	5.2
Daily papers	7.6
Weekly papers	1.9
News magazines	5.1

Stone's (2001)[5] survey on 'Minorities and Women in Television News' found that minorities 'held their own' in the television workforce, constituting about 18 per cent of the broadcast workforce (but holding only 8 per cent of the news directorships). The same was true of radio. His survey of 47 per cent of the 900 non-satellite commercial television stations found that white men were 54 per cent of the news personnel, white women were 28 per cent, minority women were 10 per cent and minority men were 8 per cent. The overall minority share was twice as great at Fox and independent stations (especially since this category includes Spanish-language stations, where much of the staff is Hispanic) than at ABC, NBC and CBS affiliates.

One case in which women are doing significantly better than men is among Asian American anchors. The USC/Annenberg study[6] presented at the Asian American Journalism Association convention in August 2002 found that the top twenty-five television markets had hired eighty-five Asian women on air and only nineteen Asian men. Indeed, television stations' interest in Asian anchorwomen is widely known as 'the Connie Chung phenomenon'. The theory is that an 'exotic' woman will attract white male audiences without threatening white male management.[7] In any case, it has led to other Asian American women being hired as anchors, and then being asked to look as much like Connie Chung as possible. The Asian woman anchor is such a popular cultural 'type' that Hamamoto (1994: 246) sees it as a direct outcome of imperialist, sexist and racist attitudes, adding: 'Once subdued and wrested from her male defenders, the fantasy-ideal of the Asian woman can then take her rightful place at the side of the Euro-American conqueror as war bride, mail-order wife, as whore, as TV news anchor.'

According to Stone's (2001) study, sponsored by the Freedom Forum,[8] black television journalists were more likely than Hispanics to see their minority status as a career barrier and to say that racial discrimination may drive them from the field. Thirty-seven per cent of the black journalists said they suffered racial discrimination. Notably, when asked about long-term career goals, 16 per cent of the black, 16 per cent of the Hispanic but only 9 per cent of the white journalists said they hoped to become station general managers or network executives. But ethnic minorities are having a harder time cracking the glass ceiling.

Women account for 20.2 per cent of television news directors and 22 per cent of radio news directors in the United States, according to the 2001 Women and Minorities Survey conducted by the Radio-Television News Directors Association and Foundation. Minorities are 5.7 per cent of radio general managers and 4.4 per cent of radio news directors (Papper and Gerhard 2001). Women comprised 12.6 per cent of the general managers of television stations that cover news (and 8.7 per cent are minorities). To the person who sees the glass 'half-empty', this statistic may be dismaying. On the other hand, when Vernon Stone first surveyed news directors in 1972, during the period when the Federal Communications Commission (FCC) extended its affirmative action rule to women, only 12.8 per cent of the entire television news workforce was female and women held 0.5 per cent of the television news director spots. By 1996, according to a survey by Lee Becker and Jerry Kosicki (1997), 24.1 per cent of the news directors were women. Furthermore, the percentage of female TV news directors apparently peaked at 24 per cent in 2000, but at least women news directors were as likely to be found in major markets as in the small ones (Papper and Gerhard 2001).

As in Britain (detailed below) women journalists continue to earn less than men in the United States, although the discrepancy narrowed from 64 per cent of men's earnings in 1971 to 81 per cent in 1992 (Weaver and Wilhoit 1996). Weaver and Wilhoit (1996: 179) do point out, though, that women were less likely to be married (48 per cent) than men (65 per cent) and also that women were less likely (28 per cent) to have children living with them than their male counterparts (44 per cent) in 1992, with little change from the previous ten years. They note that although the proportions of both married women and men declined significantly in the United States during the 1970s, these increased slightly in the 1980s.

Career patterns in journalism in Britain

A national survey of 726 full-time British journalists in England, Scotland and Wales conducted by Henningham and Delano (1998) in 1995[9] found that the provincial press is a crucial recruiting arena for journalists, with 65 per cent starting their career in regional newspapers. Only 6 per cent began their career in journalism with a national daily. Another 6 per cent began their career with the BBC, one-third of whom were in BBC television. As few as 4 per cent of journalists began in independent commercial broadcasting.

The favouring of male full-time journalists reflects the British average: women constituted only 25 per cent of *full-time* employed journalists in 1993 compared to 28 per cent of women employed full-time (aged twenty to sixty-five) across the whole British workforce (Central Statistical Office 1993 quoted in Henningham and Delano 1998).

Reflecting the pattern in the US, women working full-time in British journalism are notably much younger and more likely to be single compared to their male counterparts.[10] A far higher percentage of women working full time in the profession are single compared to the national average. While 31 per cent of male journalists are single, reflecting the total male population of single men at 29 per cent, 53 per cent of full-time women journalists are single, which is significantly more than the overall female population of single women at 21 per cent (Henningham and Delano 1998: 148). But British newspaper journalists, especially at the national papers, are typically older than broadcast journalists. The youngest group are working in independent radio, with nearly 60 per cent under the age of thirty, followed by regional weeklies with 42 per cent aged under thirty. These figures suggest that the lack of provision of childcare facilities or flexible work schedules creates difficulties for women trying to balance work and family commitments (Ross 2000). Not surprisingly, women are concentrated in the part-time sector.

Data collected in Britain in the 1990s reveals a continuing discrepancy between men's and women's earnings (Delano 2003). Women earn on average 83 per cent of men's salaries. The discrepancy is widest at the age of forty-six to fifty, when women earn only 59 per cent of men's income, and this is typically the crucial age for managerial promotions. Women have found the long hours as well as the atmosphere in newspaper newsrooms prohibitive, as Christmas (1997) and Ross (2000) report. As one journalist commented (Ross 2000: 533): 'Although I am not a mother, I see juggling home and family as the single most important issue affecting women journalists today. In my office, there are very few working mothers. The long hours culture must be stopped.'

As in the United States, young women are being employed in Britain in increasing numbers as national and regional television newscasters and as journalists in local radio (Fleming 2000, Howarth 2000). While women have a significant on-screen presence, this trend does not guarantee women's increased promotion and entrance into decision-making position in media organizations (Gallagher 1995). Women remain underrepresented in positions of authority compared to men, as we detail below.

Journalism in Britain is dominated by white, Anglo-Saxon Protestants. Only 1 per cent of the sample were of Indian and Pakistani origin in 1995 (the major origin of Asian immigrants in the UK), and only 1 per cent were black African or Caribbean (Henningham and Delano 1998: 148–9). The dearth of ethnic minority journalists in mainstream media was highlighted in 2001 when the Director General of the BBC, Greg Dyke, described his organization as 'hideously white' and pledged to raise the number of ethnic minority employees to 10 per cent of the workforce by 2003. A study of British black and Asian journalists (Ainley 1998: 60) showed that broadcasting employed the highest number of black journalists from African Caribbean and Asian (Indian subcontinent) communities during the 1980s and 1990s, showing that the broadcasting industry's equal opportunities policy operates more effectively than the print media. Beulah Ainley found fewer than fifty black journalists in mainstream print media as a whole out of 3,000 journalists, and only between twelve and twenty across all national newspapers. Joy Francis, the co-founder of a collective providing internships in newspapers for ethnic minority students, laments the white male culture of newspaper newsrooms (Ainley 1998).

While provincial newspapers provide a crucial training context, they have a poor record for employing black journalists. None of the provincial newspapers that Ainley (1998) studied intended to introduce ethnic monitoring, nor did they see the need for it. Over half of all black journalists in Britain work in the black print media – (such as the *Caribbean Times* (begun in 1977), the *Voice* (1982), the *Journal* (1992) and *New Nation* (1997) – and in approximately thirty black community vernacular papers. These publications provide an important training ground and increase black journalists' chances of working in the mainstream (Ainley 1998: 67). Television and radio programmes for black audiences, such as *Ebony*, *Eastern Eye* and *Black on Black* employ black journalists exclusively, apart from the usually white director.

Echoing the US situation, including the 'two-fer' policy of many US organizations, black women journalists tend to be employed in larger numbers than their male counterparts in Britain. Ainley (1998: 84) found that 56 per cent of black journalists were women. As Ainley suggests, 'I think the reason there are more black women than men in the media is that employers feel they are killing two birds with one stone; they're covering themselves on race and gender issues in one go'.[11] While some black male journalists argue that black women are 'more attractive to white males' and employed in television for their looks, Ainley (1994) found that black women are better educated and journalism-trained than their male counterparts. More than 90 per cent of black female journalists have a degree compared to 60 per cent of black male journalists.

One of Britain's highest-profile black female journalists is the broadcaster Moira Stewart, who has inspired many young journalists. When she joined BBC Television News in 1981, Stewart was the only female black news presenter on national television in Britain, and like the male black presenter Trevor MacDonald on ITV news, she developed something of a cult following. Rianna Scipio, a journalist on the BBC's London News Network, says Stewart's success has contributed to the trend of employing more ethnic minority women than men. This echoes the comments Ainley heard from black men journalists: 'It's true that black women are having it easier than men on screen, mostly because the media power brokers are white males and black women are a more attractive proposition than black men.'[12]

The position of ethnic minority journalists in Britain has improved since 2000 with several initiatives aimed at encouraging ethnic minority participation in the media, including the Greenwich Fellowships in International Journalism launched by the then Secretary of State for Culture, Media and Sport, Chris Smith, in October 1999. The Fellowships offer experienced American ethnic minority journalists the opportunity to work for a British news organization while acting as a mentor to young British ethnic minority journalists. In this way, young black British journalists can have an experienced role model and mentor. Nevertheless, effective change will ultimately be driven by commercial forces, as Gary Younge, a *Guardian* columnist, explained:

> It's exactly the same as the gender issue we went through a few years ago, when the media realized they needed more women journalists, because they had more women readers with money to spend. There is a rapidly growing black and particularly Asian middle class that is relatively affluent, and advertisers want to reach them.[13]

Professional and union organizations

British occupational organizations in journalism have not been particularly effective in advancing women's employment conditions. Although equal pay law has been enforced in Britain since the Sex Discrimination Act of 1975, the traditions of past discrimination against women continue more covertly. Many female journalists find they have been employed on lower pay scales than men with equivalent qualifications and experience.

As well as being blocked from promotion, women are often given different job titles to justify lower pay than men earn for identical tasks (Creedon 1993, Dougary 1994, Gallagher 1995, Christmas 1997, Sieghart and Henry 1998). The lack of union support for women's equal employment is not surprising given the turbulent history of the British journalism unions. Until the 1970s, British journalism involved intense union activity including union engagement in industrial conflict. The National Union of Journalists reflected other trade unions by seeking collective ends such as the raising of minimum rates of pay. Following the curtailment of union power by Britain's Conservative government between 1979 and 1997, by the 1990s the membership of the NUJ was reduced to half its former numbers and employers took the opportunity to side-step the union in wage negotiations.

As a result, the workforce was fragmented by the management offer of individual contracts to journalists. The shift to individual contracts has had a detrimental effect on women, who can be particularly vulnerable to negotiating poor individual contracts with employers. For example, journalists situated at the lower rungs of the national press hierarchy experience great insecurity with three- and six-months trials followed by short contracts, while others work as 'regular casuals' for a few days a week. This contrasts with senior journalists at the higher levels of the profession in the London system who command full superannuation pension benefits and may also generate other incomes from freelancing in addition to their main employment (Tunstall 1996: 55). Women have therefore been recruited in larger numbers by newspapers since the collapse of the 'closed shop', but many are on poor contracts with low salaries.[14] The fact that there has been a strong union tradition in British journalism, rather than a professional association tradition, may well explain why many journalists are ambivalent about the professional status of their occupation.[15]

Conversely, professionals and, indeed, most white-collar workers in the United States have historically been reluctant to organize, much less unionize. Journalists, who have historically been individualistic and often caught up in the mystique and romance of journalism, were similarly disinterested in trade unionism. There were various kinds of journalism 'associations' or clubs on a geographical basis (for a city) or for specialities (such as editorial writers). After the turn of the twentieth century, and especially after the First World War, journalists did try to organize, presaging management's response to organization in the 1930s. As Leab puts it (1970: 20): 'the publishers cried "Red" and clamoured about threats to freedom of the press'. Most of the attempts to organize a union petered out.

Perhaps reflecting its more ambiguous origins in a liminal state between middle-class profession and trade, the American Newspaper Guild (ANG) was launched in 1933 during a period of a more general upsurge in unionism (Leab 1970). Money was the main reason for their collectivizing, given extraordinary disparities in salaries; and pay interests continues to be at the forefront of the Guild's concerns. Its mission statement begins by saying that the Guild's purpose is to 'advance the economic interests and to improve the working conditions of its members'. That said, in the 1970s, when its name changed to the Newspaper Guild, it began to confront sex discrimination; and its second aim is to 'guarantee, as far as it is able, equal employment and advancement opportunity in the newspaper industry and constant honesty in news, editorials, advertising, and business practices'.

Under the charismatic leadership of its first president, Heywood Broun, a highly popular (and highly paid) syndicated columnist, the Guild began with a rather hostile attitude toward trade unions (Leab 1970). Yet within a few years it moved to make peace with organized labour, and became a formal union. The Guild affiliated with the American Federation of Labor in 1936 and expanded its membership to include commercial departments with the Congress of Industrial Unions in 1937. It later came under the umbrella of the Communication Workers of America (CWA). The Guild therefore includes not only journalists, but also sales people, artists, photographers, editors, paginators, editorial artists, among others, as well as more technical labourers who work in business and customer service departments, maintenance, mailroom, pressroom, and drivers and distribution. Each local chapter, however, conducts its own bargaining with individual news organizations and develops its own goals for the employment contract.

The New York founders of ANG did not appear to pay particular attention to the distinctive problems of women in journalism, and Leab's (1970) history ignores what may have been issues important to women. However, they initially planned to name their group, 'Guild of New York Newspaper Men and Women'. A few women were among its founding members, most notably Doris Fleeson (1901–1970), then writing for the *New York Daily News*. Fleeson was among the Guild members who argued before the Depression-era National Recovery Board for a minimum wage for reporters (and argued against publishers' claim that reporters, as professionals, should be exempt from the minimum).

Again, since the 1970s, the Guild is more interested in advocating for contracts that include family-friendly benefits and in opposing sexism in the workplace. Media executives are not themselves part of the Guild, but some women who make it into executive positions affirm their Guild ties. For example, Margaret Sullivan, the first woman to be managing editor and then editor at the *Buffalo (NY) News* (from 1999), made sure to remind people that she and her husband, also a journalist, were part of a Guild 'family'.

Gender segregation in specific fields of journalism

The presence of distinctive male and female ghettos of employment is not only an established feature of journalism in both Britain and the US but also the basis of discrimination, with women being discouraged either from entering the hard news arena or from progressing within it, through lack of promotion prospects for women. Women experience the strongest hostility in areas dominated by men, such as political and sports journalism. Political (or 'editorial') cartooning has remained a male bastion, although there are notable exceptions. The 'bunching' of women in distinctive areas of journalism creates feminine and inherently less prestigious 'ghettos' (van Zoonen 1994, Skidmore 1998).

Evidence is emerging that many women take the freelance route so that they can combine it with family/childcare commitments (Franklin 1997, Ross 2000). According to the Women in Journalism survey of 2001,[16] two-thirds of women with young children are choosing to do freelance work rather than bid for senior executive jobs that require a fifty-hour working week including routinely working evenings or weekends. Freelance journalists benefit from flexibility but are vulnerable in that they lose out on company benefits such as maternity leave and pay, and are forced to rely on state provision. Their salaries are often deemed secondary within a continuing 'male breadwinner' ethos. Over half the freelancers said that their caring responsibilities determined their decision to go freelance. The rates of pay are lower for freelance journalists and, as an 'invisible group', they can be easily exploited. Moreover, part-time working is discouraged and frowned on in the news industry. One journalist on a regional newspaper who attempted to set up a crèche (childcare centre) was ridiculed (Ross 2000).

Young, qualified women are now sought after as television newscasters and war reporters, and their skills in feature writing are used for national newspapers. There are indications that women are becoming established in the field of British local radio and local newsrooms, with a rise in the proportion of women being recruited into this field (Fleming 2000). However, like advertising and PR, local radio is not as prestigious as national radio or other areas of 'serious news' journalism.[17] So although women are faring well in the profession as a whole, they pay the price of remaining in a backwater, with little prospect of progressing to more prestigious fields of the profession.

In the UK, periodicals contain the highest number of active women journalists, followed by television and radio broadcasting. The newspaper sector (including dailies, weeklies and Sunday newspapers) employs the smallest number of women according to a study undertaken by the London College of Printing throughout the 1990s (cited in Delano 2003), as shown in Table 4.3.

Table 4.3 *Percentage of women employed as journalists, by media sector*

Media sector	Women as % of journalists
Broadcast	40.8
Periodicals	55.6
Newspapers	22.6
All sectors	39.6

Women in decision-making positions

United States

Weaver and Wilhoit's (1996: 9) survey indicates that women gained responsibility in journalism over the previous decade:

- 41 per cent of women journalists supervised news or editorial employees (compared with 43 per cent of men);
- 18 per cent of women journalists (compared with 22 per cent of men) were owners, publishers or upper-level managers (city editor, news director or higher);
- 32 per cent of women journalists (compared with 30 per cent of men) were desk editors, assignment editors or assistant editors.

One of the most interesting findings in Weaver and Wilhoit's (1996: 184) study is that although women were not as likely as men to perceive themselves as having much managerial influence, they seemed to at least equal men in the amount of editorial control they exercised. Asked about their influence on hiring decisions, nearly 40 per cent of men and 35 per cent of women in print, and 40.5 per cent of men but only 21 per cent of women in broadcasting said they had 'a great deal of influence'. But asked whether they could select the stories they worked on, 47 per cent of men and 46 per cent of women in print, and nearly 45 per cent of men and 54 per cent of women in broadcasting said 'almost always'. Asked how much editing they do, 39 per cent of men and 43 per cent of women in print, and nearly 21 per cent of men and nearly 40 per cent of women in broadcasting said 'they do "a great deal"'. These are only perceptions, of course. Indeed, network anchor Diane Sawyer apparently laughed at a description of her as having 'unrivalled influence over network decisions' (Rutenberg 2002).

Data regarding the glass ceiling comes from the 2002 version of a biennial study of US newspapers with circulation over 85,000. Hemlinger and Linton (2002: 14) found huge variation in gender parity (or lack thereof) by position. For example, women were 14 per cent of the presidents, publishers and chief executive officers (CEOs) (this was up from 8 per cent in 2000) and 21 per cent of the general managers or executive vice presidents. However, women were 100 per cent of the assistant or associate publishers of 137 papers in both 2000 and 2002; and about 39 per cent of the managing editors in both 2000 and 2002. Women were half of the senior vice presidents for legal counsel, and 44 per cent of the senior vice presidents for personnel (down from 62 per cent in 2000), neither of which have historically led to the very highest positions; they held far fewer of the posts controlling production and finance.

Importantly, Hemlinger and Linton (2002: 16) demonstrated that – for all the criticism directed against newspaper chains – the largest newspaper groups tended to have the highest percentages of women at assistant vice-president level or above, although few in the very top corporate executive ranks. Women held nearly a third of such positions at A. H. Belo, 27 per cent of such positions at Dow and Cox Newspapers, and above 20 per cent at the New York Times Company, Community Newspaper Holdings, Knight Ridder, Gannett and the Washington Post Company. With respect to who were the named publishers of newspapers within these groups, they found that in terms of sheer numbers, Gannett and Community Newspaper Holdings had the most female publishers (eighty-seven and a hundred, respectively). The highest percentage was McClatchy; of its eleven papers, six have a female publisher (Hemlinger and Linton 2002: 17). Furthermore, Hemlinger and Linton (2002: 18) noted the importance of who sits on the board of directors of these companies, since boards establish policy and hire the CEO. Gannett's board was 38 per cent female, and seven of the other newspaper companies they surveyed had boards that were between 20 per cent and 33 per cent female. Allen Neuharth (who otherwise boldly cultivated a bad-guy image) became Gannett's CEO and within two years had appointed two women publishers.

Neuharth and Gannett have been commended by many for consistently hiring white women as well as women and men of colour as publishers, editors and other executives at both the level of individual papers and at corporate headquarters. Gannett not only recruited and promoted women and minorities, but also based promotions and bonuses on affirmative action performance. As Mills (1988: 300) comments: 'Gannett is unarguably the industry leader in finding talented women and absorbing their ideas . . . If other news organizations had Neuharth's commitment, the glass ceiling would long ago have been shattered.' Gannett claimed Neuharth had been concerned that too many men were editing the newspapers for themselves or their male associates and were ignoring a major segment of the readership.

Many journalists and journalism critics complain about newspaper chains, especially their obsession with cost cutting and profit maximizing, and their power to drive out independent newspapers. Gannett, known for having papers in many smaller-size cities, has also been criticized for moving people in and out of towns with its minor league system, so that they barely know a community before they are moved again. This has been true for men and for women, certainly; but it speaks to two issues important in the analysis of women in journalism. First, Neuharth's acknowledged interest in profitability and in boosting circulation and advertising revenue, makes clear this notion that women have often been hired to appeal to women audiences. This may mean that they are in some sense confined to a gendered role no matter how they define the news. Second, the fact that so many women in the US who have broken through the glass ceiling have done so in the context of large chains (albeit often working for smaller papers) may explain why women may not have been able to change newsroom culture. When relatively few

women enjoyed such rare heights, one explanation for women's lack of significant impact and for the newsrooms' failure to implement women-friendly
policies was that women had not yet formed a critical mass. Segregated and
isolated, women were unable to make an impact on recruitment and promotion practices. Arguably, there are enough women in the media in the United
States, including in prominent positions, to see whether women actually do
produce a 'multiplier effect'. Hypothetically, if women were so inclined, they
could hire other women, put women on their boards of directors, and conduct their work in new ways. But the point is that women – especially at
chains such as Gannett – operate under severe and often frustrating organizational constraints. They are obliged to be loyal to the company and
shareholders rather than to their professional principles.

A Federal Communications Commission law against discrimination in
news broadcasting has ensured that television has a better track record of
hiring African American, Asian American and Latina anchorwomen (Mills
1997: 55). A series of leadership workshops organized by the International
Women's Media Foundation held across the United States have provided
women in mid-level management positions with practical skills that they can
use to work within the newsroom culture and change that culture.[18] The
training sessions dealt with conflict resolution, career mapping, communication skills and risk-taking.

Britain

In Britain women began to be promoted into decision-making roles at newspapers during a crisis in sales in the late 1980s, when newspapers' dependence
on advertising revenue (itself based on circulation) dictated a renewed appeal
to women. This explanation seems to be borne out by the fact that the first
newspapers to recruit women editors were those with the most rapid falls in
circulation.[19] Those daily national newspapers that boasted stable or buoyant
circulations were not in a hurry to recruit women editors. With their emphasis on the male domain of 'serious news' and politics (discussed in Chapter 5),
broadsheet newspapers in Britain continue to have a reputation for marginalizing women within a form of cronyism known as the 'old boy's network'.

Independent television organizations do not keep records on gender breakdowns in recruitment and promotion. However, the BBC, the largest (and
public) broadcasting organization, has a policy of affirmative action for
women and ethnic minorities which has been improving the recruitment and
promotion practices of the organization. Although in 1985 only six women
were in the top 165 executive and editorial posts at the BBC (Baehr 1996: 15,
Skidmore 1998), by 1992 women held 10 per cent of its senior positions
(Dougary 1994: 19). More recently, the BBC has set targets for women in
management positions and come close to meeting them. Over a third of
senior executive and senior management positions are now filled by women,

and 40 per cent in middle management and senior professional positions. The BBC 2003 target for senior executives is 30 per cent, for senior managers it is 40 per cent, and for middle managers and senior professionals it is also 40 per cent.[20] BBC employment targets for ethnic minorities were also raised to 10 per cent for 2003 (the time of writing), achieving a rise from 8.4 per cent to 8.9 per cent by March 2002. Within senior staff, the percentage of ethnic minorities rose to 3.2 per cent by 2002 and the target for 2003 is 4 per cent.

Dougary (1994: 71) found that the independent ITV network reflected a similar picture to the BBC in the early 1990s. For example, Channel Four's top-grade positions were held by twenty-nine men and eight women in 1994. Although a significant expansion of the independent sector allowed women to gain entry into the British media during the 1990s, with 56 per cent men and 44 per cent women in a survey of fifty-two companies (Baehr 1996: 40), in fact 63 per cent of executive producers and 76 per cent of directors were men in the 1990s while a massive 88 per cent of the low-grade positions were occupied by women (cited in Skidmore 1998: 206). Men continue, then, to command the senior levels of the news media but the BBCs affirmative action policy is an important indicator of future trends in the industry.

Women were beginning to be recruited into British newspapers in more than superficial numbers from the 1960s. But it was not until 1987 that the first female editors were appointed on Sunday newspapers, with Wendy Henry at *The News of the World* and Eve Pollard at the *Sunday Mirror*. It was their expertise in magazine and feature skills that was sought after, since Sunday newspapers are characterized by feature articles with a focus on entertainment as well as traditional news (Christmas 1997). The drop in newspaper sales in Britain from the 1960s, which led to the commercial need to attract women readers and consumers, provided opportunities for women to gain promotion to managerial positions below the level of editor, including deputy editor, feature editor and news editor. This also led to the hiring of eight women editors of national newspapers and five women editors of the regional press. Data collected by Dougary in 1994 found that across twelve tabloids then being published in Britain, the highest editorial positions were held by sixty-four men and eleven women, and within the ten broadsheets, sixty-one men and just two women were in equivalent positions (Dougary 1994). By the mid-1990s, female decision-makers in British national newspapers rose to 20 per cent (Christmas 1997: 8). But without a critical mass of women staff and majority of male readers, they faced great challenges. The less prestigious *weekly* regional newspapers, whose readers tend to be female, have had women editors for the last thirty-five years.

Women experience similar difficulties in gaining promotion in British *daily* regional newspapers as they do in nationals (Christmas 1997). Out of ninety-four regional daily newspapers, five have women editors, the first female editor having been appointed as late as 1990. It is likely that these difficulties result from the fact that 'news' remains the highest priority in the daily regional newspapers. Their editors are typically promoted from the ranks of news, sub-editing and production, which are the most male-dominated areas of newspapers. It is no accident, then, that women have had more success as editors of Sunday national newspapers, which aim to attract women readers. Editors traditionally succeed through the magazine and feature route, the fields in which women dominate.

Interestingly, women have made progress in terms of recruitment into decision-making positions in local radio in Britain. Carole Fleming's (2000) study of women in local radio and television in the East Midland city of Nottingham found that, of the five newsrooms, four of them are now headed by women: almost equal number of male and female journalists work at those stations. However, as mentioned above, local news has lower prestige than national news. The difficulties that women have in combining career with family commitments are further exacerbated by the continuing 'informal male socialisation' or 'old boy network' which acts to marginalize women (van Zoonen 1994, Skidmore 1998). Some women journalists have also identified the after-hours culture of male journalists as a barrier to women's integration into the newsroom culture (Ross 2000).

A survey of 200 senior women journalists from national and provincial media by the British lobbying group, Women in Journalism in 2001,[21] concluded that many highly experienced women journalists in television, newspapers and magazines are forced to quit senior positions because their employers fail to provide flexible working hours or to invest in childcare and child support. Chair of Women in Journalism, Rebekah Wade stated, 'Clearly, brilliant women are falling by the wayside and employers are halving their pool of talent by cutting it off early. Newspaper executives are disproportionately male.'[22] Women continue to suffer at the hand of unsympathetic bosses and unrealistically long hours. The survey referred to a 'culture of presenteeism' whereby journalists feel obliged to be at the office for long hours, making it difficult to juggle motherhood and a career. Of those women in the sample who had taken maternity leave, under half took less than the statutory minimum because they needed the money or because they were concerned that their career would be at risk. Out of seventy-five who had taken maternity leave, twenty-two did not or could not return to their jobs. In Britain there are still significant variations in maternity leave provision: the majority interviewed were not allowed to take twenty-six weeks off work at full pay. Most women admitted that they felt guilty or anxious about taking time off for the children. One woman stated: 'I am worried about starting a family. There are rumours here that women are dismissed if they become pregnant.' Another woman in the Women in Journalism survey said:

I asked to go part time but was refused because I was an executive. I fought for a year, was ignored and sidelined by management as a result. I finally had to accept demotion, and even then, when my baby was in an accident and I had to leave work early, I was sacked.

The woman won financial compensation in an out-of-court settlement but her career suffered.[23] The survey found that combining motherhood and childcare actually gets more difficult as children get older, in contrast to policymakers' assumptions. With few women able to cope with the pace during early motherhood, top management positions are being populated mainly by men and a small minority of women with no dependent children – and these are the people who make key editorial decisions. Although 75 per cent of the women interviewed said that media employers should introduce more family-friendly policies, a significant minority were resentful of the privileges of motherhood and believed that they were forced to take on more work to cover for absent mothers. Moreover, some managing editors are reluctant to extend family-friendly working practices because they believe such practices have already gone far enough, while others are aware that such an environment can boost morale and productivity.

With over three-quarters of women journalists stating that they would be influenced by the provision of family-friendly working in deciding to take a job, there is enough evidence to show that women want a culture change to get rid of the long-hours convention and allow employees to balance family and work needs.

Sexism in the newsroom

Eve Pollard was one of the first generation of women newspaper editors in Britain as editor of the tabloid newspaper the *Sunday Mirror* in 1988 and of the *Sunday Express* from 1991 to 1994. She began her career working on teenage magazines, then presented on *TV am* and thereafter launched the US version of *Elle* magazine. Pollard was labelled the 'killer bimbo' by her male colleagues when she became a newspaper editor. Pollard complained about 'the depths of misogyny that runs through Fleet Street' (quoted in McCann 2000: 19) that she faced, as did Janet Street-Porter when she was appointed editor of British broadsheet, the *Independent on Sunday* in July 1999. Pollard remarks:

> It was horrible, just horrendous, how she [Janet Street-Porter] was greeted. I and the other first female tabloid editors were called 'killer bimbos' at the time. Look at how Tina Brown and Rosie [Boycott] have been slated. But if you work like an editor it means you are a complex, demanding person having to deal with volatile situations, speedily – it isn't calm and it isn't always logical, but when a male editor looks at the front page and says this is a disaster, he is decisive and is determined. When a woman does it she is a cow – a demanding, irritating bitch.
>
> (quoted in McCann 2000: 19)

A major problem is male innuendo, or worse, explicit sexual objectification used to undermine women's confidence and discredit their professionalism. Even women who have reached senior positions and achieved high levels of career success have been subjected to misogynistic comments and implications that they offered sex, flirted or flaunted themselves in order to obtain a story to compromise their expertise. Senior news reporter for the BBC, Kate Adie, notes not only that television constrains talented women from reaching senior positions, but also that the scarcity of women at the top invites male innuendo: 'I've been in and out of Libya several times and I know that every single sniggering remark about Colonel Gaddafi has got to do with, "Has he tried it on with you?".' Like Goodman, Kate Adie says that she had to work twice as hard as male journalists when she joined the BBC news team, 'because as a woman you never give up on a story. You go the extra mile, especially when you're younger, you feel you have to prove yourself because THEY are waiting for you to fail' (quoted in Sebba 1994: 264).

Recent studies indicate that the sexism Goodman and Adie mention continues in both the US and Britain. Weaver (1992) found that between 40 and 60 per cent of the US women journalists surveyed had experienced harassment. A study of Indiana newsrooms shows that almost 70 per cent of women journalists said they have been harassed while working (Flatlow 1994). A study of Washington women journalists by McAdams and Beasley (1994) found that 60 per cent of women surveyed who worked in the Capitol press gallery had experienced sexual harassment and 80 per cent said that they thought sexual harassment was a problem for women journalists generally. In another US study by Walsh Childers, Chance and Herzog (1996), more than 60 per cent of women journalists regarded sexual harassment to be a general problem and one-third claimed that it had been a problem for them personally. Two-thirds had experienced non-physical sexual harassment, and 17 per cent had experienced physical harassment. In a British study, twice as many women as men 'believe that it is more difficult for capable women to get ahead in their careers' (Henningham and Delano 1998: 148). Sixty per cent of women in the survey indicated that they either had experienced being the victim of prejudice in the newsroom or had knowledge of it, while 31 per cent of men had witnessed such prejudice. Sieghart and Henry's (1998) British study shows that over 50 per cent of women and over 25 per cent of men in journalism claimed to have experienced or witnessed discrimination against women and 17 per cent of women experienced sexual harassment, ranging from degrading comments to physical sexual assault. They also found that newspaper organizations were more likely contexts for sex discrimination against women than magazines, where there is more likely to be a critical mass of women journalists. More recently, Ross (2000) found that the majority of women said they had experienced discrimination in the newsroom, and many said it was the price one has to pay for working in a 'male ordered' context.

Conclusion

Sociological analyses of the glass ceiling point to a vicious circle of cultural barriers. As Newman (1995: 24) states, a senior management culture based on male work patterns and ethos results in the expectation that women appointed to senior management will be nonconformist and fail to 'fit in' and that they will therefore exit rapidly, resulting in few positive female role models at the top. Accordingly, senior roles may be unattractive to women who are then reluctant to apply for open posts. This leaves management unchanged and predominantly male. Newman notes that breaking this vicious circle requires multiple points of intervention. Indeed, a single intervention may make a situation worse. For example, an individual leader may not be able to change the work culture, even the culture of a single organization. Instead, the elimination of sexism in organizational culture requires attention to the symbolic level of organizational practices, values and norms of behaviour.

The argument has been made that women's presence makes a difference to journalism practices and products and at all levels including in news media management. For example, Kay Mills, a former *Los Angeles Times* reporter, asserts that women *have* made a difference:

In some cases, it has been a matter of perseverance by individual women; in some cases, it's been a matter of organization and sustained protest; in some cases, it's a matter of critical mass. Glenda Holse, an editor writer for the Pioneer Press in St. Paul, Minnesota, says: "You have to have 'the rule of three' functioning before there will consistently be impact. If there is just one woman in a story, conference or editorial page meeting, you have to blend in. If there are two, you compete for attention. When there are three women, you reach a critical mass.

(quoted in Mills 1997)

Progress has been made in terms of achieving gender parity in overall numbers of jobs, particularly in the United States. Moreover, women are increasingly being hired in executive positions, especially over the last thirty years. Some newspapers have even extended their openness to women to include women managers. For example, the *Sarasota* (Florida) *Herald-Tribune*, founded over a century ago by a married couple and published (and later edited) by Rose Wilson after the death of her husband in 1910, employed women in all three top spots from 1999 to 2000, until the managing editor Rosemary Armao resigned rather than be fired by executive editor Janet Weaver. The current publisher of the Sarasota newspaper is Diane McFarlin, who began working for the paper after college and worked her way up the ranks. Yet evidence suggests that, like many other professions, there is not only ongoing horizontal gender segregation (the notion that some work is for women and other work for men) but also vertical segregation, with women concentrated in lower-status media management positions.

In neither the United States nor Britain has the glass ceiling been wholly shattered in journalism, even though women fare better in decision-making positions in the US. Yet many women editors and publishers themselves say that demands for women to constitute 50 per cent of newsroom bosses are unrealistic, especially in a weakened economy, and 'that equal-rights activists should instead seek the slow growth they claim is happening, at least among larger papers' (Strupp 2002). Certain spaces have been opened up for women, allowing women to make important inroads into feature forms of newspaper journalism, and they have established themselves on regional radio. Moreover, young female newscasters are now in high demand within television broadcasting.

In both countries, the fact that women journalists are disproportionately younger than their male counterparts suggests that they are often pressured into quitting their jobs as a result of difficulties in juggling childcare and work responsibilities. More women tend to take the freelance route as a way of attempting to solve a cluster of problems that they experience in the profession as a whole: male-dominated newsrooms, the long-hours culture, lack of childcare facilities, inflexible hours, sexism and barriers to promotion. Yet, as we have noted, freelancing breeds its own problems of isolation and lower rates of pay, as well as lack of entitlement to such employee benefits as maternity leave, holiday pay and company pension schemes. A key question raised by the increase in numbers of women journalists and the gradual rise in decision-makers in newsrooms is the effect on news media content. This is explored, together with women journalists' views of newsroom culture, in the following chapter.

5

Gendered newsroom cultures and values

Although the conventional view of journalism is that it involves and requires 'objectivity', some feminist scholars and women journalists argue that news values would be transformed if women formed a critical mass in the profession (van Zoonen 1998: 34). Some activists and scholars have long claimed that women are likely to have distinct values and perspectives but that the experiences and demands of white men are privileged over those of women, people of colour and political dissenters within mainstream journalism. Can we argue that women journalists are challenging the mainstream worldview? This chapter considers the extent to which the professional culture has changed women's working practices and, conversely, whether women have changed the newsroom or the news agenda.

From the outset it should be conceded that US and British data on gender differences in professional values is unclear and contradictory. Large-scale surveys in the United States (for example, Weaver and Wilhoit 1986, 1996, Weaver 1997) and in Britain (Henningham and Delano 1998) indicate that gender is an unreliable predictor of differences in professional values and journalistic practices. Yet these same studies, and others, suggest that women have brought new perspectives and styles of news presentation (Weaver 1997). Marzolf (1993), for example, found that 84 per cent of the managing editors of the 100 largest daily US newspapers claimed women had redefined the news and extended the scope of topics deemed newsworthy. As a result of pressure by women journalists, news topics were broadened to include women's health, family and childcare, sexual harassment and discrimination, rape and battering, homeless mothers, quality of life and other social issues. Women are more likely than men to say that they research and write differently than their male colleagues. Van Zoonen describes women's journalistic style as less formal and states that their work 'feminizes' the news (1998). A 2000 survey by the International Women's Media Foundation[1] reported that many women believe female journalists offer a different, 'more human perspective' to the news and that women's presence in newsrooms makes a difference in how news is selected and presented. However, some women journalists believe that women simply take their lead from male journalists who set the newsrooms' standards; in particular, women who want to cover politics or economics believe they must do what male colleagues do, or risk being assigned to soft news. 'Often, women are conditioned to respond to news in a "male" pattern. It's how many of us avoid being labeled "too soft" and get the positions we have', one editor told the IWMF survey.

With respect to professional values and principles, however, there is no consensus that women as such have distinctive journalistic approaches. Furthermore, identifying cause and effect is difficult. Ross (2001: 539) states:

> If more women than men are assigned the fashion, lifestyle, cookery, education or health beats, then it is hardly surprising that women journalists come to be seen (including by themselves) to be good at and interested in lifestyle, background and soft politics – the classic chicken-and-egg dilemma.

Some women try to 'beat the boys at their own game' by adopting assertive and macho styles. But as we discuss below, women have attempted to challenge masculine newsroom cultures that masquerade as neutral professionalism in a number of ways, including by inventing alternative journalistic practices and by developing professional links with alternative organizations, such as those representing journalists of colour, gay and lesbian journalism groups, and feminist organizations.

Gender and professional values

Liesbet van Zoonen suggests that women have a 'womanview': women tend to be more interested in their audience, more concerned about the background and context of stories, more enquiring about experiences than end results, and tend to cite more female sources than male journalists do. She argues that women are somewhat dismissive of male journalists' detachment and indifference and believe that men use objectivity as a shield to distance themselves against the kind of sensitivity and sympathy that journalism requires. However, socio-economic background and political values better predict journalists' attitudes and values than gender, according to British and US data (Weaver and Wilhoit 1986, 1996, Weaver 1997, Henningham and Delano 1998). More significant differences occurred according to news media (daily and weekly newspapers, news magazines, radio, television, and wire service) and by race and ethnicity than by gender (Weaver 1997: 36–7). Likewise, newsroom and community environments appear to have more impact on the professional values of American journalists than gender (Weaver and Wilhoit 1996: 185). When provided with a list of potential roles for news media (investigating government, getting information to the public quickly, discussing national policy, analysing complex problems), men and women rated these dimensions in fairly similar ways (Weaver and Wilhoit 1996, Weaver 1997). Men and women journalists did not significantly differ in terms of the acceptability of controversial reporting methods, such as unauthorized use of confidential documents, getting employed to gain inside information, using hidden microphones or cameras, or disclosing names of rape victims, according to Weaver and Wilhoit (1996: 188). Family background and journalistic training had greater influence on journalists' ethical and news values than gender.

Surveys do show some gender differences regarding journalists' perceptions of their work and why they work. US women, who did more editing work in 1992 than a decade before, particularly in broadcast media, claimed almost total freedom over stories, unlike men (Weaver 1997). Moreover, nearly 68 per cent of women journalists, compared to 57 per cent of men, said that 'the chance to help people' was very important to them (Weaver and Wilhoit 1996: 185).

The question remains whether news content changes when women's presence in the newsroom and especially in decision-making positions increases. Some media may be resistant to change, even with the emergence of a critical mass. The increasing popularity of tabloid-style reporting, for example, compounds the problem of ignoring feminist sources and discourages more substantial and fully contextualized reportage of sex crimes, sexual violence, sexual harassment and domestic violence.[2] But, analysing 180 stories sent to them by respondents in 1992, Weaver and Wilhoit (1996) found that women journalists were more likely than their male counterparts to include women as news sources. Second, women were more likely to write about social problems and protests as part of a wider shift from traditional government and crime news stories towards human-interest and personality-based news stories from the 1960s to the early 1990s. Third, they suggest that journalists, especially women, may be stepping out of more conventional newsbeat systems and tapping ordinary people as sources more often. The increase in features in 1992 seems consistent with the shift in news sources found in this group of stories (Weaver 1997: 39). Thus, survey research indicates that women articulate attitudes and views about professional ethics and roles similar to those of their male colleagues, perhaps in part because women must adopt male-dominated newsroom values and practices in order to be regarded as professional. On the other hand, some empirical evidence suggests women do their work somewhat differently.

A majority of women journalists who responded to an informal International Women's Media Foundation (IWMF) survey (2000)[3] said the news would be different if more women held leadership positions in media companies. Over 90 per cent of respondents to a small-scale survey of a specific group of international journalists said that women bring a different, more human perspective to the news, at least some of the time. In addition, some 60 per cent of respondents to a 1997 IWMF survey[4] said that women approach international news differently compared to men, both in the way they select topics and the angles from which they choose to cover those topics. At the same time, many women journalists asserted that the news is not defined by gender, that 'the news is the news'. They argued that standards of accuracy, fairness and ethics apply equally to all journalists, regardless of gender.

Interviews, personal statements and anecdotal data present contradictory evidence on this question. Again, many women adamantly deny that they practise journalism differently than men, except perhaps with respect to their greater interest in reporting on issues that specifically concern women. Candy Crowley, a political reporter for CNN, says, for one, 'The bottom line is that journalists think alike; having journalism in common is a stronger bond than the differences that result from gender' (quoted in Woodruff 1997: 157). A study of editors and publishers of weekly papers in Mississippi in 1964 (of which 18 per cent were published or edited by women), found that gender made little difference with respect to coverage of the civil rights movement during that 'Freedom Summer' (Weill 2000).

Linda Christmas (1997) suggests that women give prominence to news topics traditionally consigned to the women's pages (on women's health, children and childcare, family issues, education and health). But her study of British women decision-makers found that some women downplayed gender difference while others claimed that, as women, they were able to attract a female readership, a central objective of the newspaper industry. Karen Ross's (2001) small-scale British study likewise found that women journalists strongly disagreed about whether women report women's issues differently, whether changes in the news agenda (such as the introduction of more 'human interest' or 'women's news') mean much for women journalists. Most of the women told Ross that having more women in senior positions help other women's career prospects. But women disagreed about whether women and men have equal changes for success or whether an 'after-hours' pub culture hinders acceptance of women by male colleagues.

Likewise, Ross (2001) found that while a quarter of women said that the sex of the person in a story made no difference to the way they covered the story, the majority of the sample claimed a general empathy with women's causes. Many women said that they react differently from male colleagues to stories about women because they have more sympathy for women interviewees. In particular, some said they tried to emphasize the more personal and emotional side of stories. Yet many women claimed that they did not approach male or female interviewees differently – although some of their examples demonstrated otherwise. For example, they suggested that men talk less 'and often need prompting'. Half of Ross's (2001: 543) sample agreed strongly that women and men bring different perspectives to their work. But three-quarters disagreed strongly with the statement that 'I try to do journalism from a feminist perspective', and only 40 per cent agreed strongly that 'More women in journalism would make media output more woman-friendly'. This lack of consensus among women journalists thereby challenges the assumption that a 'critical mass' of women in the news industry will transform the workplace.

Broadening the definition of news

One of the first scholars to suggest that women journalists might have a different approach to writing news was Cathy Covert, an American historian who noted already in 1981 that journalism history celebrated independence and individual autonomy and that journalism itself was written in the language of conflict, controversy and winning or losing. Covert took this to be specifically masculine language, reflecting men's interest in winning. Covert (1981: 4) suggested that women's values were 'concord, harmony, affiliation and community'. Her concern was that historians ignored the influences on journalists of family and friendship networks, and ignored small-town news media that did not define their role in adversarial terms. But her suggestion has been taken to explain women journalists' preferences for human interest stories rather than the conflict-driven formulas seen on the front pages. For example, women's coverage of the war in Bosnia shows that women can transform the conventional news agendas they inherit, especially if they achieve 'critical mass' but also how the coverage of women's stories is still left largely to women journalists. Margaret Gallagher (1995: 59) emphasizes that the fact that an unusually large number of women covered the war in the former Yugoslavia compelled news media to report the systematic rape of women as a weapon of war. Gallagher (1995: 60) quotes journalist Penny Marshall, a British Independent Television News (ITN) reporter:

As soon as I saw the men (in the camps), partly because of their physical appearance, I wanted to know if they had been tortured. It didn't strike me that the women's story was as urgent as the men's, and I think that is because I had inherited a news agenda that had subsequently changed. It has occurred to me since that the next generation of reporters may well put rape on the agenda much higher, and much earlier in the war, because of this experience.)

Studies of content suggest that women have helped transform news pages by changing and broadening the definitions of news to include coverage of subjects of interest to women such as childcare, women's health education and women in the workforce. Mills (1997) compared front pages of the *New York Times* in 1964 and 1994. Of the stories on the January and February 1994 front pages, she found that nineteen could be considered of special interest to women, of which eight were written by women. The topics under this category included research on fertility, the popularity of women's colleges, sex education for young people, developments in amniocentesis, the care of the elderly at home, a lesbian harassment case and the abuse of women world-wide. By contrast, while one front page from 1964 described Senator Margaret Chase Smith's presidential candidacy, most articles about women from 1964 were framed as 'society' topics; that is, women figured as wives of VIPs, especially as wives of major political figures. The entrance of more women into newsrooms is also said to affect editorial policy, assignments, story decisions and hiring decisions. Mills (1997) provides anecdotes to back up her claim that women tend to interview women more often as sources for their articles than do men. For example, as assistant national editor at the *Los Angeles Times* in the mid-1980s, Linda Matthews, when she was pregnant with her third child, lobbied for a series of ten front-page reports on the changes and problems for women in the workforce.[5]

Journalism awards

Pulitzer Prizes in the US

The fact that women now report on different, or additional, issues is not necessarily an indication that they are transforming the nature of news since women have long been assigned to write about different things from men, and to write about them in different ways. However, Pulitzer Prizes, the major prizes in US print journalism and letters, offer an indication of what kinds of stories are most highly valued (see Brennan and Clarage 1999). Not only are more women winning major prizes in journalism but they are also winning them for stories that in an earlier era might not have reached the front pages (if they were published at all). This may offer strong evidence of women's slow but eventual success in broadening definitions of what is considered newsworthy. In 1917, the year when Pulitzer Prizes were first awarded, three women won prizes in autobiography and biography categories, and for many years women did extremely well in the novel and poetry categories. But no women's names appeared as journalism award-winners for twenty years.[6] The first woman to win in journalism was *New York Times* foreign correspondent Anne O'Hare McCormick (1880–1954), who won a Pulitzer in correspondence in 1937 (the category had been established in 1929).

After a long gap, in 1954 Virginia Schau was the first woman and the second amateur to win a Pulitzer in news photography. Schau, a homemaker with one son, was on a fishing trip with her husband when she photographed the rescue of two men whose truck was dangling dangerously from a bridge. In 1955 Caro Brown, who had been a reporter for a small Texas paper called the *Alice Daily Echo*, won a Pulitzer in the local reporting category, for her stories exposing a history of corruption among county officials. In 1959 the Washington, DC *Evening Star*'s Mary Lou Werner won in the same category for her coverage of school integration. Werner went on to edit the *Evening*

Star and later to write commentary for the *Washington* (DC) *Times.* In 1960, one of Werner's *Evening Star* colleagues Miriam Ottenberg (1914–1982) won a Pulitzer for her expose of the techniques of used car dealers, a series that apparently led to legislation to curb such practices.

By the 1970s, however, the tide had turned, especially in some of the newer award categories. In 1991, the first year a prize was awarded in beat reporting, Natalie Angier, a *New York Times* science writer with degrees in English and Physics, won. The very next year, Deborah Blum won for a four-part *Sacramento Bee* series about the ethics of conducting scientific experiments on primates; Blum later turned 'The Monkey Wars' into a book. And in 1998 Linda Greenhouse won a Pulitzer for beat reporting for her *New York Times* coverage of the US Supreme Court.

Women have been under-represented in certain categories. But they have done well in photography and various reporting categories. Margo Huston won under general local reporting in 1977 for her influential week-long series for the *Milwaukee Journal* about services for the elderly. Well-known *Miami Herald* crime reporter Edna Buchanan (who also writes novels featuring a police reporter) won in 1986. *Washington Post* journalist Loretta Tofani won in the special local reporting category in 1983. By the 1980s women were frequently members of reporting pairs or teams that won Pulitzers in the special local reporting, investigative reporting and national reporting categories. Suggesting the breadth of women's concerns, women were involved in the teams that won Pulitzers for national reporting (a category created in 1948) on the following issues:

* 1971: a United Press International story about a member of Students for a Democratic Society who died in a bomb factory in Greenwich village
* 1980: a 14-part series in the *St. Petersburg Times*, about the move into Florida of the Church of Scientology
* 1990: coverage of the Exxon Valdez Oil spill
* 1991: a series for the Gannett newspaper chain about child abuse
* 1994: an *Albuquerque Tribune* investigation of experimental injections of plutonium by the US government
* 1996: a *Wall Street Journal* story exposing how tobacco companies used ammonia to spur delivery of nicotine.

More women are winning Pulitzer Prizes, then, and they are winning them for stories that in an earlier era would either not have reached the front pages or would not have been reported on. Pulitzers in categories traditionally dominated by women – such as feature writing, commentary and criticism – continue to be dominated by women.[7] But some women have indeed taken up issues and problems that men are unlikely to have considered worthwhile. For their prize-winning series for Gannett about child abuse, Marjie Lundstrom and Rochelle Sharpe analysed the deaths in 1989 of every child under nine years old. Over time, then, there has been a broadening – and humanizing – of the topics that professional journalists will accept as legitimate and that their editors, as well as Pulitzer Prize juries and the Pulitzer board, will recognize as praiseworthy.

A study (Voss 1991) of Pulitzer Prize winners across twenty-two years confirmed this. In 1991, nine women received Pulitzer awards. According to Voss, although five won for 'typically hard-news subjects', the other four wrote reports about the everyday lives of women and their families on subjects that would not have been considered appropriate prize-winning material in previous decades such as deaths from child abuse and rape. A series on 'violence against women' around the globe won the *Dallas Morning News* the Pulitzer Prize for international reporting. The series offered personal stories of women in rural and urban environments who had been beaten, tortured, mutilated and forced into prostitution. One of the Dallas journalists, Pam Maples, said the series would have been unlikely without women of status in the newsroom. Moreover, certain issues that women spearheaded as newsworthy are also being reported on by men and women in teams and individually.

British journalism awards

An analysis of the Regional Press Awards, which is much newer than the Pulitzers, reveals a gender imbalance in those award categories typically perceived as male-dominated sectors of journalism that matches the gender imbalance in those sectors of news. Reflecting the fields in which women journalists are poorly represented, no woman has ever won the Regional Press Awards,[8] the Sports Journalist of the Year or Photographer of the Year (both awarded since 1992) or the Business and Financial Journalist of the Year (awarded since 1998). Women have fared only a little better in Columnist of the Year, which women have won twice in eleven years. However, five women have won the Young Journalist of the Year in the last eleven years, indicating the younger age of women journalists. Women have out-performed men only as Specialist Writer of the Year (awarded only eight times since 1992), with five prizes to women and three to men.

Regarding the more prestigious national British Press Awards,[9] again, women have never won in several categories: Financial Journalist of the Year (awarded since 1998), Business Journalist of the Year (awarded from 1996), Sports Reporter of the Year (awarded since 1992), Sports Photographer of the Year (awarded since 1997), Sports Writer of the Year (awarded since 1997) and Photographer of the Year (awarded since 1992). These are precisely the categories of news that are poorly populated by women. Women are not being recognized as much as their male counterparts for Scoop of the Year (six men to one woman since 1994) or Foreign Correspondent of the Year (ten men to one woman since 1992), where the proportion of women is higher and growing but where they are still in a minority. Women are, however, excelling in the category of Interviewer of the Year, with five prizes to women and one to a man (awarded since 1994). Not surprisingly, women are also being recognized for their work in feature writing (six men and six women since 1992 have won Feature Writer of the Year) and as Young Journalist of the Year (seven men and five women since 1992), indicating fields in which women journalists have become well established.

Women in the UK are being recognized more frequently for their excellence in news and current affairs journalism by the journalism sections of British television and radio journalism awards within BAFTA, Sony Radio Academy Awards and EMMA awards (the first ever Ethnic Multicultural Media Awards, since 1998). Women appear most often as part of male/female teams, but usually as presenters rather than editors or producers. For the BAFTA Television Awards between 1991 and 2000, women have never been awarded prizes individually in the category of 'specialist factual award' (the Huw Wheldon Award) while men have been awarded individually four times; women have been awarded jointly as part of a male/female team once, and part of an all-women team once. Women have never won a prize in the sports award. In the news/current affairs category no women have won individually while men have done so three times, although women have won joint awards as part of a male/female team twice. So gender segregation in the various sectors of news journalism is reflected in the British awards, revealing the fields in which women are in a minority. The issue of critical mass is, indeed, critical when it comes to public recognition of professional excellence.

'Humanizing' the news?

Linda Christmas (1997) says that women consistently personalize or humanize news in order that readers can identify with it and regard as relevant. This humanization of news brings 'women's style' closer to feature presentation. Moreover, the movement of women into newsrooms means that newspapers are providing more context in news stories, and more content for women than television and radio news, according to Christmas. Christmas (1997: 3) argues that her research on UK women journalists demonstrates that:

* women journalists tend to put readers' needs above those of policy-makers
* women are inclined to be more people-oriented rather than issue-oriented
* women emphasize news in context rather than in isolation
* women prefer to clarify the consequences of events.

Sports journalism

Sports news is home to one of the most intense and most historically enduring gender divisions in journalism, in terms of who is permitted to cover which sports as journalists, how athletes are covered as well as in terms of which genders are served as audiences. Accordingly, sports journalism offers a site for examining a variety of issues involving gender differences in writing, in newsroom treatment, and in status. This gender divide is complicated and intensified by the enormous, and still increasing, amounts of money on the line and amount of space and time allocated to sports coverage in both print and broadcasting. Whatever the national or global meanings and importance of sports, sports coverage has been an important way of attracting and retaining audiences for well over a century. Mass-media organizations are very protective of their sports sections and sports segments, given that sports commands a dependably loyal audience that dependably attracts lucrative advertising contracts. Ironically, some of these issues were already apparent in the early 1800s, at least in the US to Mary Russell Mitford, who provided regular discussions of cricket in *The Lady's Magazine*. Mitford criticized the professionalism of cricket, at one point prophetically noting, 'Everything is spoilt when money puts its ugly nose in' (Boyle and Haynes 2000: 25).

The enormous imbalance in the representation of sportsmen and women is not unconnected to sexual imbalances in the newsroom. Moreover, the general notion that women reporters should be confined to writing about women for women has carried over into sports. Not surprisingly, the secondary status of women's sports results in secondary status for those who report on them – invariably women. Men's sports enjoys massively more print coverage than women's. In the US, print stories exclusively about men's sports outnumbered those about women's sports by 23:1, with 92 per cent of photographs of athletes showing men (Duncan and Messner 1998). Similarly, in the UK between a half per cent and 5 per cent of the total sports space in national papers concerned women's sports in 1992 (Hargreaves 1994). In 1995, around 3 per cent of the sports pages in both national and Sunday newspapers dealt with women's sports (Boyle and Haynes 2000: 131). In both countries, the explanation for the concentration on a few men's professional sports is that these are the major, big money sports, as well as the fact that men are the consumers of sports news and men are not interested in women's sports. Nor are they interested in serious sports news produced by women.

The reportage of the athletes themselves is highly gendered, playing up particular and essentialized notions of masculinity and femininity. Coverage of women athletes consistently plays up their femininity or their 'heterosexy' image, often by playing up their adornments, their roles as girlfriends and/or wives and mothers, and going to enormous lengths to avoid the implication that the women are lesbian (Griffin 1992). Journalists often refer to women athletes as girls, young ladies, ladies or by their first names. They are infantilized. During the 1992 Winter Games skater Bonnie Blair was called America's little sister and America's favourite girl next door; Cathleen Turner was a 'pixie', a 29-year-old 'Tinkerbell' (Daddario 1994). In contrast, men are rarely described as boys or gentlemen, or by their first names.

If these patterns are gradually shifting, at least partly, this represents the cumulative effect of protest and resistance by women reporters. The improving landscape in sports journalism may also reflect a gradually increasing appreciation of female audiences. Television coverage of recent Olympic competitions showed more interviews with women athletes and women sports commentators. US television executives are coming to understand the financial advantage of supporting women's sports. Similarly, in the UK, more women are watching sport on television, and Sky Sport 1, a dedicated subscriber sports channel, obtained a 30 per cent female audience in 1998.[10]

Nevertheless, much of the homophobic, hyper-heterosexual, masculinist and often racist coverage of athletes can be attributed to the continuing domination of sports journalism by men. In 1990, the 1,800 dailies in the US employed a total of 400 women sports writers and only twenty women and ethnic minority copy editors (Shapiro 1990). In the early 1990s, the Association of Women in Sports Media (AWSM) estimated that only 3 per cent of the 10,000 print and broadcast sports journalists in the US were women. So even with an increasing number of women since the 1970s entering sports journalism, this increase is not nearly as dramatic as the increase in women's participation in sports (Creedon 1994: 100). Women and people of colour are similarly significantly under-represented in editorial ranks, at sports news magazines and in television, including sports channels such as ESPN. As late as 1988, only one black woman was reporting on sports for a major New York daily: Karen Hunter-Hodge, of the *Daily News*. Pam Creedon (1994: 95) calls the number of African American women covering sports 'minuscule'. In the 1990s, some national organizations of publishers and editors developed projects to increase minority sportswriters and sports copy editors. Although in the 1920s through the 1940s women were covering sports for some of the black papers, few women are now doing so (Creedon 1994: 96). Sports reporters in the UK are also 'overwhelmingly' white and male (Rowe 1999: 43).

The case of Phyllis George is instructive regarding the peculiar place of the female body in sports reporting and the problem of hiring a female body for the sake of that body. An undeniably attractive woman who was a former Miss America, George was one of the first women to land a job as national sportscaster. In her autobiography, George (2003) notes that she had no female role models in sports reporting to emulate, a comment suggesting that she never imagined she would emulate 'a sports reporter', a male sports reporter. More importantly, George was simply not prepared for the job. In any case, at the time, both male and female sports reporters were aghast that someone who was neither athlete nor expert would be interviewing professional athletes for national television. In 1975, when George became a co-host (or 'hostess') for *The NFL Today*, on CBS, the station already employed Jane Chastain, who by then had spent over a decade of television sportscasting in three Southern US cities before moving to CBS – first as an analyst for women's bowling, and then as a colour commentator for football.

It took even longer for women to get a foothold in British sports reporting, but there was growth in the 1990s, especially – as with the US – in broadcasting. According to Boyle and Haynes (2000: 133), BBC Scotland is at the forefront in promoting women sports journalists and presenters. In 1999 it had four high-profile women reporting radio and TV sports. In 1999, presumably in deference to its female audience, Channel 4 used Sybil Ruscoe to present cricket. Meanwhile, noting that the ratio of male to female listeners shifted from 75:25 to 60:40, the BBC radio station devoted to news and sports, Five Live, has hired more women for sports reporting (Boyle and Haynes 2000: 133).

Women sports journalists in the UK have had a tougher time in print, especially in the broadsheets, despite the recent growth in sports in the broadsheets. Some 1992 statistics from the Sports Council showed that of the 513 members of the Sports Writers Association of Great Britain, only twenty-four were women; no women were sports editors of national daily or Sunday papers; and of the ninety writers and photojournalists accredited at the 1990 Commonwealth Games, only two were women (Hargreaves 1994: 198). Boyle and Haynes (2000: 134) note how women journalists have reproduced a conventionally 'gendered' (that is, sexist) approach. They quote a 1997 *Sunday Times* feature by a woman about BBC Scotland's Jill Douglass, the first woman to present rugby on British television. While the article examined the difficulties women face in covering male prejudice, the *Times* reporter focused on Douglass's physical appearance, referred to her as 'girl,' and speculated on whether she would marry. At a minimum, it remains to be seen how different this 'innovation' is from, as one critic put it, 'honey shots' of scantily clad young female spectators, used to keep heterosexual male viewers from switching television channels (Barnett 1990: 169).

Informal strategies that women journalists use to challenge the hyper-macho world of sport range from persistent attempts to subtle digs. Reporter Susan Fornoff (1993: 68) said that she occasionally inserted in a post-game story a statement – really intended at her editors – noting that a player 'was unavailable for comment to women sportswriters'. A fuller explanation of the efforts of several women to challenge the hyper-macho world of sports is offered in Chapter 6 on organized resistance to sexism in journalism. But it is worth saying here how the harassment of women reporters in the 1980s, but also continuing into the 1990s, exposes male athletes' attempts to sexualize the locker room as a way to reinforce power inequality within sexual politics.

For example, as a *Boston Globe* sports reporter, Lesley Visser was ejected from several male locker rooms across several sports; members of the Cleveland Indians players harassed Jane Gross, of the *New York Times*; Melody Simmons of the *Baltimore Evening Sun* was verbally harassed in the Orioles' locker room. A Green Bay Packer 'vigorously fondled' himself while being interviewed by Rachel Shuster, of *USA Today*. A Detroit Tiger dumped ice water on a woman. Dave Kingman of Oakland A's sent Fornoff a live rat because he didn't want her interviewing players in the locker room. In 1989, when the issue was allegedly settled, Melanie Hauser, who covered football for the *Houston Post*, commented acidly: 'Sometimes their idea of equal access is women standing outside while men go in' (quoted in Miller and Miller 1995: 883). Often the excuse is that women who conduct locker room interviews really want to 'peek', something that women journalists dismiss as derisory. As a woman who covered the Oakland A's for five seasons for the *Sacramento Bee* put it: 'No, not even those slow Luther Vandross tunes . . . could turn this grown-up version of a tree-house into a love shack' (Fornoff 1993: 34).

Fornoff worked hard to fit into the world of 'muscle and machismo' but she also admits that she was willing to be 'opportunistic', sometimes even 'flirtatious' and to take advantage of her femininity (Fornoff 1993: 12). Other women have also conceded that they used their feminine charms to convince a sports world source to talk and even to scoop a rival male reporter. Confronted by the contempt of the male sports community, the pressure has forced this response from women professionals. To the extent that sports reporters need to become 'mates' or 'pals' with athletes, especially during road tours, the double standard for women presents considerable tensions. Notably, Fornoff (1993: 227) said that she did not want to be 'one of the guys'. Still, she concluded her book by noting that eventually the 'big locker room' – the entire system of sexual politics in sports, enforced by team management – drove her away from sports journalism. Black women sports reporters may suffer the most – this seemed to be the case for Claire Smith of the *New York Times* (Turner 1991). Fornoff (1993: 109) suggested, nevertheless, that African American athletes were the most sympathetic and courteous to women sportswriters: 'They know what it's like to qualify for insider status yet be stuck on the outside looking in.'

Locker room access and treatment, however, are not the only issues. A national survey in 1993 of the 408 members of the Association of Women in Sports Media (AWSM) found that the majority of women sports journalists rejected the proposition that there is equal opportunity for women to enter the sector of sports reporting (59 per cent disagreed), in obtaining promotions (56 per cent disagreed) or getting coveted beats (63 per cent disagreed) (Miller and Miller 1995: 885). Nearly 60 per cent agreed that men expected them to know less about sports. Only 18 per cent of them agreed that more errors are expected of women journalists, but the issue clearly uncovered a hot subject, and several women took the opportunity to comment that women are more closely scrutinized than men.

Notwithstanding the difficulties women sports reporters face, some three-quarters of the AWSM respondents described themselves as very satisfied or fairly satisfied with their jobs – very high compared with women and men in non-sports news journalism. Whatever the sexism including barriers to promotion, women liked the freedom they had as sports reporters, and presumably most of them liked sports (Miller and Miller 1995).

The under-representation of women in political news

The under-representation of women as journalists in the most 'serious' and highly respected areas of the news, especially politics, may well be linked to their under-representation as primary sources, experts and spokespeople. A study by the White House Project (Cook Lauer 2002) in the US in 2000 and 2001 found that women were only 11 per cent of all guests on Sunday talk shows, programmes which tend to be hosted by men. If presidential and vice-presidential candidates were included, women accounted for only 10 per cent. Once invited on the talk show, women spoke 10 per cent fewer words, and were much less likely to be called back as a repeat guest. In fact, women accounted for only 7 per cent of repeat guests. The situation significantly worsened after the September 11th terrorist attacks, according to the study. From 11 September to 28 October 2001, guest appearances by American women dropped 39 per cent. Together with foreign officials the drop was 12 per cent (Cook Lauer 2002). 'When there are only one or two women on these shows, people think there aren't any women authorities out there', said Marie C. Wilson, president of the Ms. Foundation for Women and the White House Project.

> People don't know their women leaders. The Sunday shows have the potential to allow women to be seen in intimate settings as trustworthy authority figures, debaters, leaders, communicators and experts. Conversely, they have the potential to maintain traditional gender roles and to perpetuate existing notions that women lack the credibility, expertise and authority to address our nation's most significant problems.
>
> (Cook Lauer 2002)

Similarly, Christmas (1997: 28) refers to political news as the most 'unre-formed' section of British newspapers. In Britain there are no women political editors at the time of writing, though they are junior members of political teams. A field relying on intimate conversations with senior politicians, polit-ical writing relies on an 'old boy' style of networking and often on the covert 'leaking' of information by political figures for personal gain rather than public good. Readers' needs are secondary to the newspaper, which is 'engaged in a blinkered symbiotic relationship with the powerful' (Christmas (1997: 31). The writing style in editorials is often perceived to be aggressive and posturing, as one that foregrounds contention and polarization – which may be off-putting to both women readers and writers.

A two-week study of the television reportage of the 1997 British General Election confirms that only 10 per cent of journalists involved were women; 16 per cent of TV appearances were women; and eight out of 135 politicians appearing on the news were women. Out of twenty-six government spokes-people and seventeen academics who were interviewed, all were men (Coles

1997 quoted in Skidmore 1998: 209). This marginalization of women in 'serious news' and their overrepresentation in what is considered to be 'trivial' news results from a continuing male-biased culture. Moreover, most women readers are unimpressed with this gladiatorial style of journalism. Neither this style nor the political agenda – including that of elections – appeals to women audiences whose most pressing concerns are all-too frequently childcare, equal pay, health care and so on. Mills (1997: 50) argues optimistically that women journalists' participation in political reporting improved political coverage in the United States, initially by women reporters by bringing women candidates into the mainstream spotlight.

Strategies for dealing with masculine newsroom cultures

Sexist language in newsrooms

In the late nineteenth and early twentieth centuries, men reporters and editors often complained that women's entrance into newsrooms would have a constraining impact in the newsroom and that a feminine sensibility would require men to be careful about their personal habits and language. A male *Washington Post* reporter said he was happy when Mary McGrory joined the travelling campaign press corps in the 1960s, because the 'boys on the bus' were getting sloppy; 'now that you're here, we've spruced up a lot,' he told McGrory (quoted in Woodruff 1997: 157). But few men wanted to be careful and even fewer actually changed their behaviour, according to autobiographical and biographical accounts. Moreover, although many of the early women journalists apparently noticed some masculine crudity, they do not seem to have been particularly bothered by it.

Oddly, perhaps, the 1993 national survey of the membership of the Association of Women in Sports Media found that 43 per cent of the 215 respondents agreed or strongly agreed with the assertion that women face more sexist language from co-workers in sports than do women who work in news, while 33 per cent disagreed (Miller and Miller 1995: 885). The respondents were essentially split when asked whether women faced more condescension in sports news than non-sports news. But this comparison does not measure actual problems, or even perceptions of how pervasive the problem is. Phyllis Miller and Randy Miller (1995), who conducted the survey, add that the women who were the oldest and earned the highest salaries reported enduring the least sexist language. This could be because older women were treated with more respect, or because older women no longer notice sexist language.

Moreover, there is little evidence that women have invested much energy in removing sexual banter from the newsroom. Several journalists, both male and female, have mentioned – without complaint – newsroom flirtations. Memoirs, autobiographies, biographies and newsroom histories treat this as,

at best, part of the territory. Likewise, few women discussed sexual harassment in their autobiographies – perhaps for the same reasons that women
tended not to complain about sexual harassment – although, as one might
expect, the evidence leaks out in interviews. Long-time *New York Times* executive editor Abe Rosenthal was once quoted saying that if being a womanizer
were a disqualification for working for the *Times*, the 'place would be empty'
(quoted in Gates 1996: 72). Gay Talese (1970: 218) came close to judgemen-
tal language in his history of the *New York Times* with the comment 'Sex has
been the traditional excess of so many of the paper's most prominent
reporters, editors, executives, and shrine keepers'.

Women journalists' acceptance of sexual innuendo and womanizing may
have changed with increasing attention in recent years to the issue of sexual
harassment in the workplace (Steiner 1999). For example, some women at the
Washington Post accused *Post* columnist Juan Williams of sexual harassment – ironically, at around the same time as Williams was defending
Supreme Court nominee Clarence Thomas against accusations of sexually
harassing Anita Hill. More to the point, the *Post* ombudsman ultimately dismissed the allegations against Williams as 'surprising' in view of the
newsroom's 'laid-back,' 'sexually tolerant' environment (Harwood 1991: C6).

Sexist writing styles

In the 1970s, feminist activists and scholars started to become very visible and
assertive in offering up critiques of the news media and suggestions for overcoming persistent negative portrayals of women. Guidelines were produced,
sometimes with the assistance of feminist organizations, to improve the news
coverage of women – the most extensive composed in 1975 by a US commission on the observance of International Women's Year. The 1975 guidelines
called for more coverage of women's activities at local, national and international levels, and locating news 'by subject matter, not sex' – signalling the
opposition to women's pages (Beasley 1997: 238). Feminists condemned journalistic treatment of women as sex objects and the use of irrelevant personal
details about women. They called for avoiding the use of a male pronoun or
the word 'man' to stand for all humanity. Gender-free terms were recommended over gender-specific ones: 'firefighter' instead of 'fireman',
'letter-carrier' instead of 'mailman'. Reporters were advised to treat women's
organizations with the same respect as men's. Women were to be called
'women' rather than 'girls' or 'chicks' or 'broads', and should be allowed to
choose their own courtesy titles (Miss, Mrs, Ms). As a result, many newspapers eliminated courtesy titles altogether; other papers and wire services
began to insist on parallel uses of courtesy titles. As late as the 1990s, a few
papers continued to refer to men by professional titles but to women with
courtesy titles that indicated their marital status and that added 'female' endings to words to mark the person as female: store 'manageress' or

'stewardess', for example. But several US journalism stylebooks, such as that of the Associated Press, were amended to discourage sexism and to provide guidelines on avoiding stereotypical phrases such as 'petite blonde'.

The Associated Press Stylebook continues to assert: 'Women should receive the same treatment as men in all areas of coverage. Physical descriptions, sexist references, demeaning stereotypes and condescending phrases should not be used' (Associated Press 1994: 219). With counter-examples that suggest how things were formerly phrased, The *AP Stylebook* insists, 'Copy should not assume maleness when both sexes are involved', and 'Copy should not express surprise that an attractive women can be professionally accomplished, as in: "Mary Smith doesn't look the part, but she's an authority on . . .".' And it says 'Copy should not gratuitously mention family relationship when there is no relevance to the subject, as in: Golda Meir, a doughty grandmother, told the Egyptians today . . .' (Associated Press 1994: 219).

None the less, 'mistakes' get made and the guidelines are violated – and not merely in sports reporting. For example, a 1992 *Washington Post* story about Lynn Yeakel, then challenging Arlen Specter, referred to her as 'feisty and feminine 50-year old with the unmistakable Dorothy Hamill wedge of gray hair and the dazzling silk suit of lime, tangerine and blue', 'a congressman's daughter . . . and unlikely standard-bearer with a wardrobe befitting a first Lady', 'married to a once-Republican stockbroker . . . a former full-time mother'. The *Post's* profile of Specter described him as former 'crime-busting district attorney' without describing his hair or clothes. Similarly, a 1992 *New York Times* article used highly gendered language to compare Carol Mosley-Braun, the first African American woman to be elected to the US Senate, to her opponent. Although Mosley-Braun was a former federal prosecutor and state representative, the *Times* wrote: 'The two cut strikingly different images on the campaign trail: she is commanding and ebullient, a den mother with a cheerleader's smile; he, by comparison, is all business, like the corporate lawyer he is' (both quoted in Witt, Paget and Matthews 1994).

Arguing that improved coverage of women is necessary if women are to become 'full participants in the democratic political process', Maurine Beasley (1997: 244) calls on journalists to recognize their history of differential and unequal treatment of women candidates in political campaigns. Women politicians' dress, voice, hairstyle are judged by different standards than those of men. Women candidates with young children often get criticized for being bad mothers. News accounts, she says, emphasize disagreements among women. Given this history of harsher criticism, she recommends that journalists focus on women's areas of strength. Beasley would allow individual women candidates to speak for themselves, to put their own case forward as far as possible to ensure accuracy and avoid stereotypes. She also recommends that some foundation should finance and promote the improved coverage of women's political participation, for example, through annual prizes.

Strategies used by women to challenge masculine newsroom cultures

Among the strategies women have used to challenge newsroom cultures are monitoring of content, language, photographs and patterns in coverage. For example, FAIR (Fairness and Accuracy in Reporting) maintains a women's desk to monitor mainstream media for sexism, racism and homophobia, and it issues 'action alerts'. After a gang-groping of women at parade in Central Park in New York City in June 2000, FAIR exposed how some news coverage (especially NBC Dateline) seemed repeatedly to run exploitative images of women being stripped and groped.

In addition, individual women have addressed the masculinist newsroom culture. Byerly and Warren (1996) interviewed seventy-two journalists at nineteen large urban papers in the United States who had either been activists themselves or who had an interest in newsroom activism. Although race and ethnicity were perceived as negative factors, interestingly, 46 per cent of the respondents (three-quarters of whom were female) said gender did not adversely affect their careers or those of others. Yet, they described engaging in a variety of change-oriented activities, as well as in systematic and ongoing efforts. Nearly half of them said that in-house women's organizations had improved working conditions for women journalists and only a few said their activism had not affected them personally. Many said they were better informed about gender or sex issues and some even thought that their work had deepened their conviction to work for change (Byerly and Warren 1996: 11–16).

In a Scottish study, Melin-Higgins and Djerf Pierre (1998) say women cope with sexism in the newsroom through incorporation, feminist action and retreat. *Incorporation* functions when women try to become included as 'one of the boys', by adopting masculine values and practices, including the appeal to 'objectivity'. A *feminist* approach operates when women deliberately choose to produce an alternative style of reporting, by writing on issues such as sexual violence and child abuse. *Retreat* occurs when women decide to become freelancers and work from home to avoid the workplace problems. Melin-Higgins and Djerf Pierre (1998) found that women whose intention was to make a difference either chose subjects that allowed them to work in ways that interested them or worked in media dominated by women, such as women's magazines or women's television and radio programmes. However, as Ross (2001) points out, how much choice women really have was not established in the study, given that the history of journalism is rife with examples of news assignments being offered or denied to women because of their gender.

Many of the women Ross (2000) and Christmas (1997) interviewed normalize the masculine news culture and engage in self-deception, refusing to recognize the kinds of disadvantages that women as a group struggle against. Some women blamed women for their own subordination. One woman journalist said: 'I feel strongly that women these days often blame their lack of initiative on "discrimination". The time for whinging [sic] has passed and it is up to us to fend for ourselves' (quoted in Ross 2000: 534). Such views may reflect women editors' fear that they will be accused of having benefited from positive discrimination (since affirmative action for women is not allowed under equal opportunities principles in Britain) when offered their editorships. They are concerned to be seen as the best for the job. Some women are professionally insulted by the suggestion that a woman has been appointed editor to boost the number of female readers to attract advertising revenue. Many women say 'being a woman should not be an issue' and that they would prefer to be treated as a professional first and woman second (Ross 2001). Moreover, Melin-Higgins and Djerf Pierre (1998: 10) found that adopting masculine values and styles of doing journalism as a way to avoid colleagues' sexism can expose women to other forms of sexist, derogatory remarks. They quoted several men interviewees, and even some women, saying of successful women 'so-and-so is a hard-bitten old hag' or 'so-and-so slept her way to her job with different editors'.

Women's management styles

Whether women media executives can or do enact their leadership responsibilities differently from men, or even want to, is a controversial question. The evidence is not strong or consistent in either direction. Some women editors of British regional newspapers or sub-editors at national papers assert that women and men have different management styles, while others argue that gender makes no difference to management. There may be some national differences regarding the extent to which women have introduced new styles of management. With respect to editors, a national survey of 1,151 journalists in 2000 conducted by the American Society of Newspaper Editors (2000: 35) apparently found 'very little difference' in leadership by gender, ethnicity or age.

There does seem to be broad agreement that as editors and publishers, women journalists support a redefinition of 'news'. Most women editors are committed to ensuring that stories of interest to women are prominently displayed. In the UK, Rosie Boycott, formerly editor of the *Independent on Sunday,* agreed (Christmas 1997: 22):

> I want women to feel that the things that concern them are not trivial. I certainly try to get more stories of interest to women in the paper, issues to do with health, children, work. For instance, I pulled an anorexia story on to the front page recently because it interests me. I doubt if a man would do that.

In the recent past, a macho style of management involving bullying and ritual humiliation was typical of Fleet Street, the home of British national newspapers (Christmas 1997). Some women decision-makers in newspapers told Christmas (1997) that they shared the same professional values as men, having been forced to adopt a 'macho process of story getting' in order to reach the top level of the organization. However, others claim that they experienced difficulties in proving themselves to be ruthless and 'hard-boiled' journalists like their male colleagues, particularly in the 'serious news' fields. A third group of women editors argued that women are less likely to be concerned with hierarchy, are more likely to foster team work and regard the macho style as outmoded. Victoria Britain, foreign news editor of a department of the *Guardian* employing more women than men, comments:

> There is no doubt about it, in my view, that the kind of harmoniousness and ease in problem solving that we now have is quite different. Women tend to be just a bit easier to work with. They are good at working in teams, they are good at listening to other people. Nobody is throwing their weight around saying: 'Do it like this'. Instead they are saying: 'What do you think?' On the whole this tends to produce a more creative mix, in the way stories are laid out and how they are chosen in the first place.
>
> (quoted in Christmas 1997: 39)

Conclusion

News agendas and priorities have clearly changed with the increasing number of women journalists, and men and women seem to adopt distinctly different approaches to reporting. But assertions about these differences must be qualified. The evidence regarding the impact of gender on newsroom culture and news agendas is contradictory and ambiguous and may be related to whether the data has been generated through news content analysis or interviews with journalists. Moreover, there is little consensus about the extent to which gender matters in the way reporters access and write stories. Journalists are increasingly subjected to the demands of their news organizations to accommodate organizational, occupational, economic and audience needs. However, as seen in Weaver and Wilhoit (1996) women journalists are more likely to draw on women and also on ordinary people as news sources than are men, are more interested in social problems and protests, and have provoked a shift in news values from conventional government and crime news to human interest news.

Key characteristics of emergent forms of news in which women journalists are heavily involved include the increased emphasis on the personalization of issues, the foregrounding of a personal standpoint over a professional one, and the increased use of women as sources, including feminist sources. Rape and sex crimes, including as instruments of war and genocide, are now taken more seriously. The shift to a 'magazine style' of news which has given women an important entrance into the profession was not, however, initiated by women journalists. It was prompted by the need for newspapers to attract women readers and by a host of wider social and political changes leading to a recognition that coverage of women's experiences and issues was economically and culturally essential. In turn, these changes in news agendas and ways of writing stories associated with women's increasing presence in journalism expose and challenge the traditional dominance of masculine professional values and techniques of gathering news. Thus, newsrooms continue to be dominated by male editors, but they are now more open to stories about women's issues because news organizations are desperately seeking female audiences and male editors are more receptive to issues affecting women.

Despite these changes, the gendered nature of the newsroom persists. The male-ordered newsroom culture operates throughout macro structures, micro routines and interpersonal relations. '[N]ewsroom culture that masquerades as a neutral "professional journalism ethos" is, for all practical (and ideological) purposes, actually organized around a man-as-norm and woman-as-interloper structure', as Ross states (2001: 533). Yet newspapers, for example, have paid a high price for their desire not to upset male readers, male editors and publishers, and male sources. Perhaps in the future, male-dominated decision-making editorial teams and masculinist perspectives will be regarded as a liability by readers, editors and publishers, and by official and unofficial experts and sources – in government and business – all of whom include women in their ranks.

Judy Woodruff, a senior correspondent and anchor for CNN, is among that faction sceptical of the claim that women and men practise journalism differently, although as the parent of three children, she grants legitimacy to the observation that far fewer female political reporters (at least those who travel) have young children at home. She notes the number of women – or at least young mothers – who turned down plum assignments on the political beat because of their family responsibilities (Woodruff 1997: 158). She quotes Candy Crowley: 'Things have changed less on the home front than on the work front.'

Notwithstanding a changing climate at newspapers, many scholars worry that women journalists are continuing to be typecast by the persistent allocation of the traditionally feminine 'softer' and less prestigious categories of lifestyle, education or health beats to women (Mills 1997), thereby sustaining a feminine ghetto. Certainly women do not inevitably practise either a feminine or feminist form of journalism. Nor are gender or feminism necessarily their main form of personal or political identification. The movement towards a style of reporting that is more personal, human-interest-oriented and more informal, (i.e. 'soft' journalism), does not constitute a 'feminization' of news. Women reporters have professional reasons for distancing themselves from the notion that they 'do' journalism differently from men. They are particularly sensitive to what they would regard as an 'accusation' that they advocate on women's behalf. Many deny that they report differently, if only to protect themselves professionally against the accusation that they push a women's agenda. Some women journalists have voiced concern that one of the reasons why women are being promoted more frequently today is because they are cheaper, not necessarily because they are better leaders (Christmas 1997). Indeed, economics may constrain women executives from acting in a markedly different way from men, especially if they are executives at publicly owned companies with obligations both to shareholders and to larger corporate entities. Principles of cost-cutting and maximizing profit often compel executives to believe they have little flexibility when it comes to implementing policies or offering expensive services and facilities (from child-care to weight-rooms).

The dilemma for women journalists, then, is that the notion that they have redefined, 'taken over' and feminized journalism may undermine the status and credibility of journalism and journalists, making it less prestigious as an institution and less desirable as a profession. Although the recent declines in job satisfaction and in entry-level salaries in journalism have not been attributed to the rise in the recruitment of women into the occupation, an insistence that women have radically transformed journalism may, indeed, drive out male job candidates and depress salaries. Thus, ironically, while equal opportunities policies aim to protect women from sex discrimination in the workplace, these do not protect them from the downgrading of those professions that they dominate numerically.

6

Challenges to sexism and discrimination

Women have pushed for a variety of changes in journalism and in news organizations: they have demanded more news about women, different kinds of news about women and even different ways of writing about women. Women journalists have argued for the recruitment of more women, for pay equity and for greater access to the upper reaches of news organizations' hierarchies, as well as for better treatment of women in journalism education and training programmes. Some of the issues are relatively minor but symbolic. For example, May Craig, the Washington correspondent and panellist on the TV programme, *Meet the Press*, led a protracted battle in 1945 to get a women's restroom near the Congressional press galleries. One of the more dramatic 'extra-legal' challenges in the United States came on 19 March 1970, when representatives of feminist groups invaded the offices of John Mack Carter, editor of the *Ladies Home Journal*. The organizations represented that day were the National Organization for Women, the major liberal feminist organization in the US; Media Women's Association, a group of media professionals; Older Women's Liberation (OWL); as well as two more radical groups, Redstockings, and New York Radical Feminists. Armed with a dummy of an alternative version of the magazine, 150 women took over Carter's office for eleven hours, demanding that he hire women and people of colour among the editorial and advertising staffs. Finally Carter promised them they could edit a section; their eight-page section appeared in August 1970, with feminist 'takes' on childbirth, marriage and sex.

Other issues are, however, substantial and far-reaching. This chapter provides a history of the broad range of strategies women journalists have deployed to advocate, promote and sustain these changes. They have worked through unions, especially in the United Kingdom, and through professional organizations, including, with even greater effect, sex-specific organizations, especially in the United States. Having advocated changes in federal legislation, they have sought redress and remedy through regulatory bodies and other governmental organizations as well as through civil suits.

Early challenges

Not surprisingly, most of the earliest efforts to use the system to challenge the marginalization of women journalists were undertaken by individuals. One of the earliest heroines of US journalism may be Mary Katherine Goddard, who was a colonial-era printer and newspaper publisher. As the postmistress of Baltimore, Goddard was the first woman appointed to federal office (Beasley and Gibbons 1997: 52). After fourteen years as a postmistress, however, she was replaced by a man. Goddard did not take her discharge lightly; just when the position was finally starting to be profitable, she said, she had been 'discharged without the smallest imputation of any Fault, and without any previous notice whatever' (Beasley and Gibbons 2003: 53). She filed a petition to President George Washington and the US Senate complaining: 'And now to deprive her of this Office, to which She has a more meritorious and just claim than any other person, is a circumstance, pregnant with that species of aggravation, which a Sense of Ingratitude inspires' (Beasley and Gibbons 1997: 54). Her appeals, however, were to no avail.

Women begin to organize

Beginning in the 1880s, there were enough women journalists to come together in press clubs that served both specific professional causes (helping to develop their journalism skills and find work) as well as social and networking purposes. Indeed, in this sense they were parallel to the male-only press organizations which helped shore up men's sense of having professional prestige and status and provided camaraderie. The first such women's press club was formed in 1881 by 'lady correspondents' in Washington, DC who, out of 'Necessity and Ambition', formed the Ladies Press Club (Burt 2000a: xviii). In 1885 women from around the country formed the National Woman's Press Association, soon renamed the International Woman's Press Association. Their founding document stated: 'Innumerable benefits will arise from mutual help and encouragement. One aim of the association is to forward the interests of working women in every possible way by combined action of newspaper women' (quoted in Burt 2000a: xviii). This group also hoped to spark city and state organizations around the country and, sure enough, within ten years there were some two dozen women's press organizations, including several national and international groups as well as city and state-wide groups (the original Women's National Press Club essentially died by the end of the First World War, however). In 1889, Jane Cunningham Croly founded the Women's Press Club of New York City, and served as its president until her death in 1901. Well before then Croly was already a highly successful and popular syndicated writer about women's topics under the byline Jennie June. When women journalists were banned from an all-male press club's reception for Charles Dickens in 1868, Croly and a few other writers founded Sorois, a women's club.

Some of these organizations were linked to specific women's rights movements, particularly the suffrage movement and as such published periodicals. The pro-suffrage *Woman's Exponent* became the official organ of the Utah Woman's Press Club; and the *Justitia*, published 1887/8, became the organ of the Illinois Woman's Press Association. After socialist Charlotte Perkins Stetson (Gilman) became president of the Pacific Coast Woman's Press Association, she edited its official journal, the *Impress*, which she described as a uniquely non-sectarian woman's paper not dedicated to one particular reform but instead motivated by the objectives of 'thinking women' (Yamane 2000: 192). Some of these organisations grew quickly – in numbers of branches. For example, the National League of American Pen Women, one of the few nineteenth-century organizations (its name was changed) to continue into the twenty-first, was organized by seventeen women who resented their exclusion from the all-male press groups. By the end of its first year it had fifty members from many states; by 1921, it had thirty-five branches and 300 women attended its first convention. It now has over 200 branches in the US and the Panama Canal Zone (Gottlieb 2000: 147–50).

The early women's press organizations were usually allied to the woman's club movement, with its charitable, philanthropic and reform-minded interests. For example, the New England Woman's Press Association was formed in 1885 'For the purpose of promoting acquaintance and good fellowship among newspaper women; elevating the work and the workers; and forwarding by concerted action through the Press such good objects in social, philanthropic and reformatory lines as may from time to time present themselves' (quoted in Burt 2000b: 153).

None the less, these organizations promoted the legitimacy of women journalists, in part by distinguishing professionals from amateurs. Several, although not all, late-nineteenth-century organizations created different levels of membership to distinguish women who earned their living through reporting from occasional correspondents. The Women's National Press Club (WNPC), which was founded in 1919 as a social and professional club for women, who were excluded from the National Press Club, limited its members to reputable journalists 'actively engaged in Washington on well established newspapers, press associations or periodicals including government publications, and deriving there from all or the greater part of their income' (Beasley 1988: 115). The WNPC founders included three women who wrote for newspapers, including Cora Rigby, who headed the Washington bureau of the *Christian Science Monitor*, as well as three publicists for the National Woman's Party, one of the more militant groups of the American women's suffrage movement. It also admitted some women doing public relations, but they could not serve as president. Indeed, although rules were bent to admit Eleanor Roosevelt, her membership was controversial. As Beasley (1988: 112) remarks, the Women's National Press Club, which lasted until 1971, 'facilitated a sense of solidarity that allowed members to enhance their self-images and advance the idea that they were true professionals'.

The WNPC looked for ways to exercise its muscle, including by sending letters to foreign leaders, such as Soviet Premier Nikita Khrushchev, who then demanded that women be allowed to cover his 1959 speech at the National Press Club (NPC). WNPC also sent cables to women in Parliament who were members of the British Labour Party, asking them to pressure Prime Minister Harold Wilson not to speak at the NCP when he was in the US. The strategy worked: Wilson rescheduled his speech for the British Embassy.

In Britain, the very small number of women working in this male-dominated profession formed the Society of Women Journalists in 1894 to defend their interests and identity. However, the society was not successful in advancing women's interests, as indicated by the fact that while the 1891 national census listed 661 women as authors, editors and journalists, by 1900 the Society only had sixty-nine members (Sebba 1994: 32). Reporters of both sexes were at the mercy of editors and proprietors, since even the Institute of Journalists, which had formed under a Royal Charter in 1890, had no control over standards of entry into the occupation or over salaries. In 1907 reporters (of both sexes) formed their own National Union of Journalists. As much a male domain as the Institute of Journalists, this union also failed to advance women's interests. None the less, in 1894 the London district of the Institute did appoint two women on to its committee: Catherine Drew, who was Irish and assistant editor of the *Irish Builder* and then wrote a women's interest column in 1871 for the *Belfast News Letter* called the 'Ladies' Letter', and Grace Benedicta Stuart, who wrote for a range of magazines and was sent to Germany by the *Daily News* as a special correspondent (Sebba 1994: 38).

By the turn of the twentieth century, a few women's press groups in the United States were affiliated with press organizations that were for men. A few organizations began to admit women, and in a very few cases, men and women together formed press organizations. Eventually, even the most stubborn of the male-only press organizations agreed to admit women. Meanwhile, by the 1930s a number of these organizations had disbanded or ceased activity – given the passage of the constitutional amendment enfranchising women, the death of some of the pioneers of the press clubs, the end of the Progressive era, and the onset of the Depression (Burt 2000a: xxiii–xxiv). These days, the most prominent activity of women's press clubs is, as it always has been, providing scholarships (or internships or mentoring programmes) for women studying journalism at colleges or universities. Moreover, more recently – in the wake of more recent waves of feminism – some women's press clubs have recruited men and so dropped the name 'women' from their titles.

Transatlantic allies at press conferences

Sometimes women journalists received help in challenging journalism conventions from unexpected allies, including from several United States Presidents and several First Ladies. Most famously, from 1933 to 1945, while her husband Franklin was US President, Eleanor Roosevelt excluded men from her weekly press conferences. Roosevelt had a number of close friendships with women in the journalism profession. Moreover, on the basis of the fact that for two years Eleanor Roosevelt had written a syndicated daily column, in 1938 she was elected to the WNPC. More importantly, by providing occasional scoops for the women who attended her press conference, Roosevelt's policy placed pressure on news organizations to keep some women on staff and even to hire women (Roosevelt 1949: 102). The United Press, for example, hired Ruby Black as a result of the First Lady's decision; otherwise it would have been unable to obtain news from those press conferences.

Eleanor Roosevelt's 1943 visit to England inspired the establishment of the Women's Press Club there, after women in Fleet Street were denied access to Mrs Roosevelt. Women journalists' anger turned to protest, with Phyllis Deakin of *The Times* insisting that women should set up their own club. Some sixty women journalists set up the lobbying organization, in part to support women in their attempts to get accreditation as war correspondents (Sebba 1994: 169). But the War Office opposed requests until 1944, forcing women to find ingenious ways of overcoming the barriers against them.

The issue of whether to allow women journalists to cover speeches and press conferences was, perhaps surprisingly, not trivial. It was not merely a question of adequate access to bathrooms. In 1954 the WNPC unanimously adopted a resolution urging the male-only National Press Club to let accredited newspaperwomen cover its events. The WNCP also complained to government officials about women's exclusion (Mills 1988: 95). The following year the NPC decided to let women into the balcony to cover luncheon speeches. Still, this left women unable to ask questions (or even hear well). A *Washington Post* reporter was apparently taken off a story because she could not cover a 1963 NPC press conference by leaders of a major civil rights march. WNPC leadership continued to complain, reminding the civil rights men that 'the balcony as well as the back of the bus should have special meaning to civil rights leaders' (Mills 1988: 101).

Then, in 1964 Elizabeth Carpenter, who had been a WNPC president as a *Houston Post* reporter, became press secretary to Lady Bird Johnson. At Carpenter's prompting, President Johnson had the US State Department threaten the NPC that visiting dignitaries could not speak there unless women could cover the speeches on an equitable basis (Mills 1988: 102). At that point, the NPC agreed to let women cover the speeches 'from the floor'. Six years later, both organizations voted to admit both sexes, and in 1985 the two groups merged.

Meanwhile, other organizations in the US such as male-only country clubs retained male-only policies that excluded women, including women journalists. Even *Washington Post* publisher, Katharine Graham who concedes in her autobiography (1997: 422, 427) that she was initially put off by pioneering feminists and 'bra-burning symbolism' and that her consciousness was slow to emerge, noted that there were in the early 1970s 'many unenlightened, regressive sanctuaries of male supremacy'.

Storming the locker room and stadium press box

Sparking far greater publicity and controversy than other areas of news journalism have been cases of women sports reporters who, in addition to the problems generally faced by women reporters, were harassed and ridiculed when they tried to gain access to locker rooms which were frequently the sites for 'up-close' interviews with athletes right before or immediately after competition (see Chapter 4). Women denied access to such information-giving forums because of decisions made by team management or individual coaches are clearly at a disadvantage, at least if male reporters were able to obtain the 'fresh-off-the-field' interviews. Furthermore, the exclusion of women from the locker room could and was used to justify not hiring them as sports reporters in the first place.

The history of the particular marginalization of women sports reporters is suggested by a series of incidents in the US in the 1940s, when a number of women were barred from the press box. The Associated Press's Doris Blackmer was barred in 1943 from a Denver University stadium press box at the insistence of a *Denver Post* sports editor. The editor said:

> The press box is exclusively for male sports writers. It's a tradition of the newspaper game – and the war is no excuse to change it. Sports writers have the privilege of using their own kind of language in their own domain – and it's no language for a girl to hear, even if she purports to be a sportswriter.
>
> (quoted in Creedon 1994: 81)

The following year, Marie Williams, also reporting for the Denver AP bureau, was ejected from a press box, again at the editor's insistence. And Beth Hightower, a well-known golf writer, wrote her first sports story in 1942 for the *Sports News*, about the exclusion of women from baseball press boxes of the Pacific Coast League. She obtained her first full-time sports writing job, at the *Sacramento Union*, however, at a point when most people retire.

In the 1970s the number of women sports writers ballooned across the country. A couple of coaches did allow women into the locker rooms, including Bud Grant, who granted Betty Cuniberti access to the Minnesota Vikings in 1977. Cuniberti had been the first woman sports reporter at the *San*

Francisco Chronicle before moving to the *Washington Post*. These women were usually treated as oddities, however. And many teams blocked women from doing their work. Time, Inc. sued the Commissioner of Baseball and the New York Yankees in 1977 for barring *Sports Illustrated* writer Melissa Ludtke from a World Series locker room. Ludtke noted in her suit that half of *Sports Illustrated*'s reporters were women, and the magazine wanted to assign its reporters to cover the 1978 baseball season on the basis of their expertise without regard to sex (Creedon 1994: 88). For their part, the defendants claimed they excluded women to protect the privacy of players, to protect the image of baseball as a family sport and to preserve 'traditional notions of decency and propriety'. Federal court judge Constance Baker Motley ultimately rejected Baseball Commissioner Bowie Kuhn's appeal that allowing women in the locker room would 'undermine the basic dignity of the game' and ruled that all reporters, regardless of sex, should have equal access to the athletes, including the locker room if necessary.[1] As important as this case was, the ruling did not bind other baseball clubs or sports, or even the Yankees when playing outside New York. Reporters continued to mock and even vilify Ludtke.

The publicity led to some formal rules changes. The National Hockey League established equal access rules in 1982. In 1985 such rules were ordered for football and major league baseball. But, the issue was still raging in 1987, when, after a couple of years of discussion and recruiting, women journalists organized the Association for Women in Sports Media. AWSM (pronounced 'awesome') had 'for' in its name to indicate the organization's openness to men to join. AWSM immediately undertook action on the locker-room issue, calling and complaining whenever they heard that someone was denied access, according to Christine Brennan, a *Washington Post* sports reporter who was elected president at the inaugural convention (Hall 2000: 22). Eventually, AWSM persuaded all professional sports leagues to establish equal access policies to post-game interviews (Hall 2000: 23). AWSM continues to run a scholarship and internship programme, a job bank and a mentoring programme.

None the less, in 1990 Lisa Olson, a *Boston Herald* sports reporter who had twice requested permission to interview a New England Patriot in the media room, was sent to interview the player in the locker room. During the interview, a naked Patriots team member taunted Olson verbally and with body language, daring her to touch him, and accused Olson of 'looking, not writing'. Eventually, three Patriots players were fined and team owner Victor Kiam, who had initially appeared to side with the players, apologized to Olson publicly. The National Football League also fined the coach of the Cincinnati Bengals for barring *USA Today* reporter Denise Tom from the locker room. Unfortunately, Olson continued to be harassed. She was jeered at games and received threatening phone calls. In 1991 Olson sued the Patriots management and the three players for sexual harassment, intentional infliction of emotional distress, and damage to her professional reputation. Olson eventually fled to Australia, but the Patriots settled. Susan Fornoff (1993), who quit sports writing after thirteen years, admits that she and several colleagues only reluctantly and belatedly realized the necessity of challenging sexism, rather than trying to laugh it off, as many of them tried to do.

Laws and legislative action in the United States

One of the most important events in the US, having enormous implications for American women journalists as well as women across many professions and occupations, was the passage of Title VII as part of the Civil Rights Act of 1964. That extension of protections to women was, as the head of the Equal Economic Opportunities Commission (EEOC) put it, a 'fluke'. Congressman Howard W. Smith, a conservative from the South, had added the word 'sex' to the list of bases, which originally included race, colour, religion, or national origin, by which the Act would outlaw employment discrimination. By adding the reference to sex, Smith apparently hoped to ridicule the civil rights legislation. Indeed, liberal/Democratic supporters of the legislation first opposed Smith's amendment, fearing that adding 'sex' would doom the bill's passage. But then Senator Hubert Humphrey, a powerful Democrat, decided to support the amendment, and it was passed.

Using Title VII, women filed sex discrimination suits against *Newsday*, the *Detroit News*, the *Washington Post*, the *Baltimore Sun*, *Reader's Digest*, *Newsweek* and NBC. Most importantly, there were suits against the Associated Press (AP) and the *New York Times*. In the case of the AP, in 1973 women reporters filed a complaint with the EEOC, which finally ruled in 1978 in favour of the women, giving them the go-ahead to sue the AP. The women's class action suit charged that the AP discriminated against women in hiring and promotions, as well as in merit increases and retirement benefits. In 1983 the AP settled, giving over $83,000 to the seven women named in the suit, plus $800,000 in back pay to women who had worked for the AP in the previous ten years. The AP also agreed to an affirmative action plan for women, African Americans and Latinos; and it promised to help women formally prepare for promotion to decision-making positions. Mills (1988) found that the AP came through, hiring and promoting a far greater percentage of women, including as national and foreign bureau chiefs – and not unimportantly, setting a good example for other wire services by doing so.

Yet, as Kay Mills's (1988) discussion of the case highlights, several people who were active in the case say they were punished by AP management for their participation. This even includes men who were visible in the Wire Service Guild, which backed the women's class action suit. Ken Freed, the AP State Department correspondent who was active in the Wire Service Guild, was one of those punished (Mills 1988). When Freed returned from a Nieman

Fellowship, the State Department beat had been given to someone else.

Meanwhile, at about the same time, women working in a range of jobs for the *New York Times* formed a Women's Caucus in 1972 in order to organize their cause. Their suit, first filed in 1973 against the *New York Times*, functioned as a wake-up call for the entire newspaper industry, both because of the elite status of the *New York Times* and because the named members of the suit included an accountant, a telephone solicitor in the advertising department and an African American staff member. Of the four journalists who were named, the best known was Eileen Shanahan, a top economics reporter from the Washington bureau. The first named and most senior woman of the named plaintiffs was Betsy Wade Boylan, then the head of the foreign copy desk. Wade had worked for the *Herald Tribune* until 1953, when she was fired for becoming pregnant; she began working for the *Times* in 1956.

The *Times* women enjoyed limited success, at best. The *Times* was not found guilty of sex discrimination. Nor was the *Times* management forced to admit that they had treated women unfairly. It was, however, forced to provide back pay to some 550 women. The newspaper also had to promise to promote women to some top corporate and editorial positions, but its record on this was patchy. In the wake of the Boylan decision, LeAnne Schreiber, for example, who had covered the Olympics for *Time* and spent a year as editor of *womenSports* before going to the *New York Times* as an assistant sports editor, became the first woman sports editor at the *Times*. But two years later, in 1980, she moved to the book review section. Certainly the named plaintiffs did not do particularly well. After the suit Wade was again sidelined to lesser beats, although she stayed with the *Times*, and only recently did she retire from travel writing for the *Times*. Grace Glueck, another named plaintiff, continues with arts and cultural writing.

Some people accuse the Caucus of not sufficiently monitoring compliance on the part of the *Times*. As late as the 1990s, however, the Women's Caucus of the *New York Times* had come together at various moments to criticize the sexism and insensitivity on the part of *Times*'s management. For example, the Caucus led a protest in 1991 when the *Times* ran a profile of a woman who had accused a man from a politically prominent family of raping her. The profile named the woman and essentially portrayed her as a slut. Betsy Wade says, 'The Caucus always needs to be there . . . for the next time things go haywire'.[2]

Given that the US Federal Communication Commission's regulatory authority encompasses broadcast media, but not print, legal action against employment discrimination in broadcasting was better routed through the FCC. In 1969 the FCC adopted a rule prohibiting discrimination based on race, colour, religion and national origin. That is, it threatened to withhold licences to stations engaging in employment discrimination. Under pressure, it amended its rule in 1971 and required stations to apply affirmative action standards to women. As Linda Ellerbee (1986: 100–1) put it, the FCC policy 'was met with less than raging enthusiasm' by the networks, who feared 'putting the broads in broadcasting would flat out ruin the party'. A number of stations did hire white women, black men and black women as reporters. The 'class of 1971' included a number of women who went on to enjoy great success, including Jane Pauley, Carole Simpson, Lesley Stahl and Diane Sawyer, most of them initially drawn from the staffs of newspapers and wire services. Sometimes the affirmative action policy backfired, however. In 1998 the US Court of Appeals struck down the EEO affirmative action rules of the FCC, although this does not seem to have hurt women.

British initiatives for gender equality

In the UK, the 1919 Sex Disqualification (Removal) Act aimed to ensure that 'no person was to be disqualified on grounds of sex or marital status from exercising any public function, holding any civil or judicial office, entering any civil profession or vocation, or being admitted to any incorporated society'. Yet despite the Act, women could be and were routinely paid less than half of the wages paid to men for carrying out similar work. This discrimination was justified on the grounds that men were likely to have dependants (Horn 1995, Carter 1988). The informal prejudices against women were suspended during the Second World War by organizations such as the BBC, the police and other public services, but when men returned, the barriers were re-erected.

The legal protection of women from employment discrimination has been slow and recent in the UK. Until the 1975 Sex Discrimination Act women journalists had difficulty mounting legal challenges against employers for lower pay, unfair dismissal or sexual harassment. In addition, the UK is characterized by a less litigious culture than in the US, resulting in fewer cases resorting to the courts. By the early 1970s, influenced by the rise of second-wave feminism, women journalists began to bring to public attention their experiences of sex discrimination through the press (Sebba 1994). Yet discrimination cases that were brought to court have not been well documented in studies of the British media.

The National Council of Women gave evidence to the Lords Select Committee on the Anti-Discrimination Bill of 1972 and noted that there was 'hostility shown to women at almost every level of the newspaper industry and that the National Union of Journalists Training Scheme operated a de-facto quota of 25 per cent of places for women'; they cited evidence that women trained in journalism and photography found it harder to get jobs after their training than men (Carter 1988: 33). For example, women were barred from the occupation of compositing despite having undertaken this job during both world wars while the men were away fighting.

Women journalists in the UK were not ensured equal pay until 1975 when the Equal Pay Act, passed in 1970 to secure equal pay and conditions for the same kind of work, finally began to be enforced. The Sex Discrimination Act of 1975 barred discrimination on the grounds of sex and the Equal Opportunity Commission was set up the following year to investigate discriminatory practices. However, in contrast to the United States, there was no British legislation of affirmative action within the Act, so companies were not directed to produce targets or quotas for women employees. Moreover, as mentioned in Chapter 4, the National Union of Journalists, which should have advanced the interests of women journalists, and identified the equal treatment of both sexes in its rulebook from 1907, suffered from the weakening of the British trade unions by legislation during the 1970s (Sebba 1994: 235). Yet this crisis galvanized journalists into developing a set of strategies for media reform which included an important focus on the needs of women in the industry (Loach 1987). Women's challenges to the television industry were supported by the effective women's movement from the mid-1970s to the 1980s. For example, the Campaign for Press and Broadcast Freedom was a trade union organization established in 1979 aimed at campaigning on the industrial right of reply and involving people who were mistreated or misrepresented by the media.

In the UK, women have had to face both sexist media management as well as the male domination of the trade unions. Women were forced to campaign both with and against the unions. A further difficulty has been the lack of effectiveness of the laws against unequal pay and sex discrimination, because media organizations were not obliged to take positive action to eradicate the work structures and practices that had contributed to past discrimination and marginalization of women which, in turn, dissuaded women from applying for promotion or positions dominated by men. The principle of affirmative action was recognized for a long time in the United States. Indeed the National Organization for Women led the way in urging employers to meet quotas of jobs for women. US organizations that fail to fulfil quotas are barred from government contracts (Coote and Campbell 1982: 131 quoted in Loach 1987). While positive discrimination is unlawful in the UK, 'positive action' is not. Thus, the Trade Union Congress introduced a resolution for 'positive action in favour of women' to raise women's pay levels and end gender segregation in employment.

A report by the BBC in 1973 revealed prevalent sex discrimination with a lack of women in middle or senior management. Women's groups such as the Women's Film, Television and Video Network and Women in Media emerged during the 1970s to advance women's interests in radio and television. They urged for women to be employed as news announcers and in current affairs programmes (Sebba 1994: 205). Women in Media had more than 300 members by 1975, and thus was able to help advance reform. It set up an information resource and writers' co-operative initiative. The organization worked with women's rights organizations to set up a women's advisory centre and produce news reports. Yet by the mid-1980s, London's Fleet Street was still a male sanctuary. As Sebba (1994: 237) points out, during this period only nine of the thirty-five general news reporters at the *Guardian* were women and at the *Daily Mirror*, three of the thirty-two general news reporters were women. None of the nine general news reporters on the *Sunday Times* were female, and out of forty general news reporters at the *Sun*, only three were women.

An expansion in television during the early 1980s, with the introduction of a fourth channel and changes in independent television franchises, prompted a feminist engagement in positive action plans. A women's committee aimed at advising unions and management was set up at London's biggest contractor, Thames Television, after a positive action scheme was piloted. The piloted scheme was initiated by a group of professional women called the Women's Broadcasting and Film Lobby (WBFL), established in 1979 to find ways to improve women's career prospects in the industry and challenge sexist images of women. There were no women in senior management at Thames Television when the Robarts (1981) report (instigated by the National Council for Civil Liberties) was written. The report recommended strategies for eliminating barriers to women's progress, including the development of better training schemes, a code of practice on conducting interviews for managers, improved childcare facilities and an equal opportunities committee. Thames Television made several changes in 1981 as a result of the report, creating a seconded personnel post of Women's Equality Officer which was extended to include race as well as sex discrimination two years later. Yet, as Loretta Loach (1987: 58) points out, no extra funds were provided for the operation of the scheme. A code of practice for recruitment and equal opportunity appeals procedures were adopted and a technical and training course was offered to women to allow movement from secretarial and clerical positions to camera and sound. Yet four years later no women were in senior management, demonstrating the difficulty of dislodging sex discrimination in recruitment and promotion practices (Loach 1987).

In the BBC, no action was taken after the 1973 report summarized changes required to better women's employment opportunities. There was therefore no improvement during a ten-year period with 159 men and only six women in senior management grades of the BBC, as detailed in the 1985 Sims report for the BBC (Sims 1985). During this time head hunting was the usual way of recruiting, rather than advertising deputy editor posts. This exacerbated the 'old-boy' networking system. In the mid-1980s, maternity agreements and job-sharing schemes were union initiatives set up in the BBC along with procedures to deal with sexual harassment. However, Loach (1987) points out that at times when the principles of public service broadcasting have been under threat, much of the union efforts have been concentrated in defending jobs and the editorial independence of the BBC rather than working pro-actively to support positive strategies. The neglect of women's employment opportunity issues during periods of economic or political crisis is characteristic of the labour movement, prompting Loach to call for a more woman-centred trade union movement. Indeed, the gains made by women journalists during the following decades were initiated as much by the commercial imperatives of attracting female audiences and the shift in emphasis to 'soft news' and human-interest stories as it was by equal opportunity principles.

The 1985 Sims report was criticized for its weak conclusions, especially in the area of recruitment and training, and it made no recommendations to extend childcare facilities. An Equality Officer was appointed but only as a two-year post seconded from another position which, as Loach (1987) points out, is an inadequate response in an organization with then 30,000 staff members of whom more than half were women. During this whole period, legislation in the United States already outlawed sex discrimination; companies were directed to take affirmative action to eliminate it, guided by targets and quotas. As mentioned above, affirmative action objectives have not been implemented in the UK. However, the Sims report did provoke the establishment of a BBC Equality Network in 1986 and the BBC introduced clearly defined equal opportunities principles and guidelines in the late 1980s, which have benefited women and ethnic minorities alike.

Loach (1987) points out that the strategy of positive action has been crucial for precipitating changes to improve women's and ethnic minorities' employment conditions in the media industry, but its effectiveness relies heavily on men's goodwill. A further weakness of positive action programmes is that they offer opportunities for individual women to gain promotion but can leave women feeling isolated when they reach grades populated by few women and find their identities swamped, rather than being able to challenge the values of a competitive masculine working culture. A BBC Crèche Campaign grew in the 1970s in response to strong resistance by the Corporation and was revitalized in the mid-1980s by the BBC Equality Network. The provision of childcare facilities is now recognized as a critical element among positive action strategies.

By the 1990s the National Union of Journalists boasted an equality council but had not produced any figures on women's promotion prospects since 1984 (Dougary 1994: 115 and 238). However, the organization Women in Journalism was set up during the mid-1990s, according to the WIJ mission statement, to [3]

increase the power and visibility of women in journalism, to advance their professional interests . . . to collate and analyse information about women in journalism and make such information widely available, to assist and encourage women journalists to improve their professional competence, position and profile.

(quoted in Ross 2001: 543)

Women in Journalism sponsored important studies of barriers against and progress of women journalists, including Linda Christmas's (1997) *Chaps of*

Both Sexes? Women Decision-makers in Newspapers: Do They Make a Difference? and Mary Anne Sieghart and Georgina Henry's (1998) *The Cheaper Sex: How Women Lose Out in Journalism*. In 1994, Sally Gilbert, the legal officer of the National Union of Journalists, reported that difficulties in obtaining maternity leave intensified from 1991 onwards during the economic recession. She told Dougary (1994: 155):

> Women on magazines and newspapers who go on maternity leave find that their jobs have been miraculously reorganized or disappear. We're treating a lot of the cases as sex discrimination, as well as unfair dismissals. These days, if someone is pregnant, problems seem to be inevitable.

Examples of challenges in the United States

Black women's law suits

Many of the organizations of women journalists have a long history of being mostly or even entirely concerned with white women's interests. For example, although individual members may have objected to employment discrimination, the Women's National Press Club (WNPC) did not object as an organization to blatant racial prejudice during the Second World War (Beasley and Gibbons 1993: 15) and some members declined to protest, on the basis that protests were un-lady-like. And it admitted its first African American member – Alice A. Dunnigan of the Associated Negro Press – only in the mid-1950s.

Analogously, in 1960 the Colorado Press Women, a group founded in 1941 that had often joined with others in promoting social and political reform, refused to admit an African American woman from Denver who was the associate editor for the *Call* (a black weekly published in Kansas City) (Whitt 2000: 43). By-laws for the Colorado Press Women apparently stipulated that an applicant for membership could get no more than three 'no' votes and five members had voted against Betty Wilkins. After two members resigned and Wilkins was the subject of considerable publicity, the by-laws were changed so that candidates required merely a simple majority (Whitt 2000). But Wilkins did not reapply. Analogously, African Americans often formed their own organizations and caucuses.

Referring to the 1970s, Pamela Newkirk (2000: 81) describes:

> the requirement for African Americans to mimic whites not only in their behaviour and attitudes, but also in appearance. As such, the African Americans [reporters] on television spoke in the same clipped diction as their white counterparts and bore no traces of African American culture in their mannerisms or appearance. These became, for some black viewers, a

source of contention and alienation, although most accepted the affections of black television journalists as prerequisites for middle-class achievement.

Some black women resisted the requirement, such as Melba Tolliver – who was originally hired at ABC as a secretary and soon after found herself filling in for Marlene Sanders during a strike. Tolliver was sporting an Afro hairdo when she showed up to cover the 1971 White House Rose Garden wedding of Tricia Nixon (Newkirk 2000: 81). In doing so, she was disobeying a WABC-TV news director, who had already seen her with her hair in the 'natural style' associated with black power movement and had ordered Tolliver to straighten her hair (Newkirk 2000: 82). ABC management took her off the air, relenting only when her story was reported in *New York Post*. Ironically, later, she did a programme about African influences on American style for the station; and, when she switched to the NBC affiliate, NBC wanted her to wear an Afro (Newkirk 2000: 83).

Yet, as late as 1981, Dorothy Reed, a co-anchor for ABC television affiliate in San Francisco, was suspended for wearing her hair in cornrows (Newkirk 2000: 83). Some of her black colleagues advised her to avoid being 'blackballed', but she decided not to back down. She went public, telling reporters that this was 'a case of white male-dominated management deciding how I should look as an acceptable black woman' (Newkirk 2000: 85). With the support of the NAACP, she filed a grievance, won back pay and returned to the newsroom wearing the braids, albeit without beads. It may, however, have been a pyrrhic victory. When Reed's contract expired, it was not renewed. But today viewers do see many black women who wear twists, cornrows and Afros, including Farai Chideya, who was formerly with ABC-TV and now does political commentary for BET News, CNN, MSNBC and FOX.

The National Association of Black Journalists was formed in 1975 but very few of its forty-four founding members were female. A notable exception was Marcia Gillespie, then *Essence* editor but who later became editor of *Ms.* In late 1986, several black women reporters at the *Washington Post* formed a black women's caucus to address both individual concerns and overall pay inequities, since black women earned less than white women. Among the leaders of this caucus was Jill Nelson, who had once been president of New York City chapter of the National Association of Black Journalists and then, when she moved to the *Post*, became the elected unit chair of the *Post*'s local Guild unit. Caucus members met with managing editor Len Downie, but according to Nelson, Downie listened but made no promises. Eventually, the *Post* managing editor did promote some black women and 'the Group' 'faded away from lack of interest, commitment, and nerve' (Nelson 1993: 138).

Much more successful were the four black journalists who sued the *New York Daily News* in 1980. Notably, both members of the National Association of Black Journalists (NABJ) and Bob Herbert at the *News* refused to support the four. One of the four, Joan Shepard, specifically complained that the *News* refused to let her work on consumer and fashion stories, that her editor Dick Blood made racist and sexist remarks against her, and that for a time she was reassigned to writing captions when she complained about all of this (Newkirk 2000: 105). For its part, the *Daily News* said Shepard was a mediocre journalist. The case dragged on for seven years, but ultimately in 1987, a federal jury decided that the *New York Daily News* had discriminated against the four black journalists on the basis of race. It agreed to pay $3.1 million in damages and to implement an affirmative action plan. Shepard's career went into a steady decline, however; she died at age fifty-six in 1998.

It might be said that Jill Nelson's (1993) autobiography *Volunteer Slavery* is itself an extended form of resistance, given that she pulls no punches in telling of her unhappy four years at the *Washington Post*, which, she said, needed her 'black and breasted' (Nelson 1993: 9). She became the only black reporter on the staff of the *Post*'s weekly magazine section. At the time, Dorothy Gilliam was the only black female columnist at the *Post*. Nelson (1993: 10), who had attended Columbia University's prestigious journalism school and had written for *Essence*, likened her job interview to an interrogation by white men, while she performed 'the standard Negro balancing act'. Later, she suggested that they regarded her as 'a happy darkie'. It's worth noting that Nelson also bitterly criticized her black male colleagues, as a group and by name. And among her criticisms of the NABJ was its sexism.

Meanwhile, a woman could be powerful enough to be challenged. In 1991 a black woman who had been fired, along with eighteen other part-time staff members, sued Patricia Wente, the general manager of KWMU, a public radio station licensed to the University of Missouri at St. Louis. However, US District Judge Jean C. Hamilton ruled that news announcer Winifred Sullivan had not proved that Wente's actions were motivated by racial bias (Wilner 1993). Wente said that Sullivan was dismissed as part of an overall reform of KWMU to create a state-of-the-art public radio station in the 1990s and that accusations of racism were retribution from former employees who were disgruntled that they'd lost their jobs (Wilner 1993). Wente noted that consultants had advised her to fire some of the part-time and student workers in order to hire full-time staffers.

'Too old, too unattractive, and not sufficiently deferential'

One of the most well-known legal controversies in the United States involved Christine Craft, who fought a protracted court battle after she was fired as a news anchor for a Kansas City television station. As had many television stations, KMBC had hired a consulting firm to help it improve audience ratings. The consultants advised the station to hire a female co-anchor to work with its male veteran. Following the advice, in January 1981 the station hired Craft, who had begun her broadcast journalism career as a weathergirl in California, where she also spent a fair amount of time surfing. Apparently indicating that she was not naturally litigious, she noted in her book that when her general manager asked her to do the weather in a bikini to cheer up the farmers, she showed up in a turn-of-the century bathing costume, complete with bloomers and ruffles (Craft 1988: 17). She quickly moved up, even hosting a new, albeit short-lived 'Women in Sports' segment for CBS. She apparently warned KMBC before she auditioned: 'I am a thirty-six-year-old woman with lines, bags, wrinkles, the signs of my experience. I am not a fixture, a beauty queen, or a token' (Craft 1988: 30). Complaints were expressed from the very beginning about Craft's performance and appearance, so, among other things, Craft was coached on make-up and clothing; she was given a highly specific 'clothing calendar'.

On the basis of focus group data collected six months later, Craft was reassigned. According to Craft, the news director told her the audience didn't like her because she was 'too old, too unattractive, and not sufficiently deferential to men'. Apparently the audience did not like that she did not hide her intelligence 'to make the guys look smarter' (Craft 1988: 66). Craft returned to her anchor position in Santa Barbara although not before telling local reporters that 'men could be balding, jowly, bespectacled, even fat and encased in double-knit, yet the women had to be flawless' (Craft 1988: 10). The EEOC granted Craft permission to sue, which she did. Agreeing that there had been sex discrimination and hiring fraud, the trial jury awarded her $500,000.

Craft enjoyed huge support from feminists, media critics and reporters, including Dorothy Fuldheim, at ninety, the oldest – by far – anchorwoman in the country. But an appellate judge reversed the lower court's ruling, in part because the co-anchor, the one witness to Craft's removal as anchor, recanted his testimony and said he did not recall the news director saying she was 'too old, too unattractive, and not sufficiently deferential'. Expert witness testimony on the value of the consultants' research was also key. The judge found that consultants' reports and ratings routinely serve as the basis for personnel changes, including with male anchors. Ultimately, a Circuit Court in 1985 ruled unanimously for Metromedia and the Supreme Court refused to reconsider the case, with only Justice Sandra Day O'Connor, then the only woman on the bench, wanting to hear the case.

Craig Allen (1999) concedes that Craft's case continues to be significant because the media owners and managers who employ TV journalists were given a legal licence to go on doing what Craft showed they had done. Essentially, station management across the US as well as in Britain and elsewhere in Europe and Asia are using consultants and are hiring and retaining (or firing) anchors and reporters on the basis of market research. None the less, Allen argues that Craft's case was weak and he is not convinced by Craft's claim that she helped correct what she called 'the bigoted mindset that would keep me and other female colleagues in a state of perpetual second-class citizenship' (Craft 1986: 219). He notes that in 1991, both to raise money for Vietnam veterans and to generate publicity for her radio talk show (which fired her after three years), she appeared nude in a pin-up photograph – a decision widely condemned. Allen claims several women declined to pursue legal action because of what happened to Craft. For example, some time after Craft's case was decided, a Duluth weather reporter said she was fired because she refused to arrange her microphone cords in a way that would highlight her bosom. She withdrew her $8 million discrimination suit. Moreover, Allen notes, since Craft's failed suit, not one similar case has been successfully tried. *Craft vs. Metromedia* was cited when an Albuquerque anchor lost her discrimination case against a television station. Ironically, Craft's own successor Brenda Williams filed a discrimination case against Metromedia, but settled for $100,000.

Subsequent lawsuits confirm that Craft failed to reverse the power of market researchers or the importance of appearance for women newscasters. On the other hand, as Craft's 1988 book predicted, that failure did not prevent several women from challenging very similar cases of sex discrimination and sexual harassment. Some of these suits were successful and others settled out of court. In 1999, for example, Janet Peckinpaugh won a major and widely reported sex discrimination suit against WFSB-TV in Hartford, Connecticut, where for eight years she had been one of the highest-rated television anchors. Peckinpaugh said she had turned down higher-paying jobs in other cities because she had been promised she could grow old at the Hartford station. Separately, Peckinpaugh complained that her former co-anchor tried to fondle and kiss her in a hotel room late one night following a telethon. The man, who was not fired, said he was merely giving her a friendly gesture.

While rejecting her age discrimination claim (she was forty-four when she was fired), the jury agreed on the sex discrimination charge. Her lawyer noted: 'A newspaper could never say: we're hiring a reporter, we already have a woman, so we want a man.'[4] Eventually, Peckinpaugh was hired by a lower-rated station in Hartford, but for the early morning shift and for $40,000 a year, rather than $250,000. Explaining the grounds for their appeal, the president of Post-Newsweek Stations, which had owned the station, defended firing Peckinpaugh because of her ratings: 'Viewers and research saw her as polarising, that she was silly. Whereas other women were seen as much more professional.'[5] CNN's story about the case quoted the head of Geller Media Management: 'There are many members of management all over the country who do indeed let women go because they are no longer in their 20s and have lost their sex appeal', said Alfred Geller.[6]

TV news insiders said the verdict would make stations think twice before promising anchors and reporters anything resembling a lifetime position, and Peckinpaugh herself claimed the verdict was a blow to the male–female dogma. But her $8.3 million award aside, the verdict has not undone the power of market research, which may be both methodologically flawed as well as journalistically irrelevant, to dictate hiring decisions. And even the lawyer predicted that the issue would eventually get litigated as a class action.[7]

Another reporter who charged her television station with race, sex and age discrimination was Beverly Williams, an African American reporter who has worked for KYW-TV in Philadelphia on and off for about twenty years. At one point she was one of the station's top-evening anchors, earning $350,000 a year (Smith 2002). In 1992, when Williams was forty-five, she was demoted to weekend anchor with some backup anchor work during the week. Her salary was cut to $216,000. Her replacement on the nightly weekday news was a white female in her thirties. Five years later, her backup work was given to a white male in his forties. A year later, she was again demoted, to general assignments, and her pay cut again. According to her lawyer, KYW said it 'based its decisions upon market-share ratings' (Smith 2002).

Although the commercial basis of media outlets and especially of television makes women – especially black women and older women – vulnerable, not all sex discrimination suits involved market shares. In 1995 Katie Davis settled a sex discrimination suit against the non-commercial radio network National Public Radio, where she had worked for fifteen years, as a reporter, producer and host of *Weekend All Things Considered*. Davis alleged that NPR paid her less than men and that it consistently refused to give her a permanent correspondent's position, although it gave such posts to less qualified men (Conciatore 1995, 1996).

According to one story about Davis's case, NPR often used temporary reporters without giving them permanent work and at least one a female employee said women were more vulnerable to that condition (Conciatore 1995). The story noted that many reporters at NPR celebrated the number of women given plum assignments. Health-policy correspondent Patricia Neighmond, said: 'There isn't a lack of female reportorial voices on the air. Just listen. We've got them all over the world and all over the country' (Conciatore 1995). But another woman said:

> I think years ago NPR lulled itself into thinking it did well by women, because it had some very visible, very prominent women. But underneath that, women were having a very difficult time . . . Today there is still the feeling that NPR treats men well because they're married and have families to support, while women can fend for themselves.
>
> (Conciatore 1995)

Ironically, but not surprisingly, the fact that many news organizations hired women in order to achieve some diversity, and perhaps the fact that some women succeeded in their sex discrimination suits, led to some men suing for sex (as well as age and race) discrimination. In 1999, a male sportswriter settled his sex discrimination lawsuit after a jury announced it was unable to agree. Bud Withers, now a *Seattle Times* reporter, claimed the *Seattle Post-Intelligencer* had discriminated against him and hired a woman as a sports columnist solely because of her sex. *Post-Intelligencer* managers said they hired Laura Vecsey because they liked her fresh, off-beat approach (Porterfield 1999).

Conclusion

In her memoir recalling her up-and-down, in-and-out career in radio and tele-vision news, Linda Ellerbee (1986: 17) asserted, 'Never trust anyone in this business who hasn't been fired at least once'. Ellerbee did not sue. And in recent years, few class action suits have been filed, although in 2000 the US federal government paid $508 million to settle a class action sex discrimina-tion case involving 1,100 women who said they had been denied promotions at the US Information Agency and the Voice of America. Carolee Brady had filed suit twenty-three years earlier after she applied for a job as a *USIA* magazine editor, only to be told that managers were seeking a man for the position. Her suit later was broadened into a class action suit including reporters, editors, announcers, producers and technicians. But plenty of women are continuing to bring suits on charges of sex discrimination.

Complaints brought through the EEOC have been won, some lost. Some have been settled. In any case, many women have won redress under Title VII, a section of the legislation that forbids discrimination on the basis of sex, age, race or religion; and into the twenty-first century, women are continuing to go to the EEOC and suing under Title VII. Meanwhile, to those who might have been unapologetic about sexism (that is, compared to racism, which is more difficult to defend in public), the federal prohibition of discrimination on the basis of sex/gender is an important symbolic statement.

Many of the changes over the last century in the status of women in jour-nalism – as subjects and as professionals – can be largely attributed to the courage, dedication, commitment, perseverance and patience (and anger) of women journalists. In some cases, the changes have resulted from individual actions. More often, it was a case of collective action. When their monitoring efforts turn up evidence of systematic problems, women have organized visi-bly – and loudly – to protest and demonstrate. Even more effective have been press clubs, organizations and guilds or unions of and for women journalists. Furthermore, for the most part, women have been strategic in how they helped one another. That said, even collective actions have been fairly nar-rowly focused, episodic or sporadic, rather than broadly defined, consistent and sustained. As a result, certain problems remain.

7

The 'first wave' of women's alternative journalism

In both the United States and the United Kingdom, news media produced by, for and about women have long been crucial mechanisms by which women can define alternative visions of womanhood and cultivate new socio-political landscapes. Alternative news media advocated versions of women's political, social and cultural roles that were quite different from those proposed by or imposed by mainstream media. Such media have enabled women to exchange and share news unlikely to find a home in mainstream media institutions, and to develop journalistic and media skills. Relative to the mainstream media, these alternative journalism institutions have had very small audiences. They were and are rarely profitable. Many of them have lasted only a few years, if that. None the less, as news organizations, they are important, as we demonstrate in the following three chapters.

Moreover, women have long understood the role of their own media in promoting and sustaining women's social movements. With reference to women's enfranchisement, for example, a few mainstream magazines, including some of the women's magazines, were mildly sympathetic to the suffrage movement. But most newspapers of the time either ridiculed suffragists and suffrage activities or ignored them altogether. As suffragist Susan B. Anthony asserted:

> Just as long as newspapers and magazines are controlled by men, every woman upon them must write articles which are reflections of men's ideas. As long as that continues, women's ideas and deepest convictions will never go before the public.
>
> (cited in Endres 1996: xii)

Furthermore, women's alternative news media have contributed to the evolution of press theory, sometimes by enacting new principles and sometimes even explicitly articulating new, and even feminist, press principles. In general, the women who established news organizations on behalf of feminism, the women's movement or other women's social movements never intended them to be profitable businesses. These organizations have been a forum in which to experiment with alternative journalistic tools. Finally, although several of these institutions appreciated participation by male volunteers, their concern for nurturing the talents and skills of women means that they have a specific import in the history of women as journalists, as reporters, editors, publishers, directors, producers.

Here we offer an overview of women's 'alternative' journalism, defined loosely as the news organizations operating outside the mainstream, and certainly outside the conception of news as a profit-earning business, and as substantially directed and produced by women. The story of underground and radical papers devoted to various causes that happened to involve substantial contributions by women writers and editors is much larger, and so is not included here. The story of what 'counts' here as alternative women's journalism begins with the path-breaking newspapers and magazines established and produced by American and British women on behalf of moral reform, female mill workers and the Abolition movement, all three quickly sketched here. This chapter describes news organs advocating other reforms to benefit women, including health and dress reforms, birth control and especially women's suffrage. The experimentation and innovation in journalism of the twentieth century is discussed in the next chapter.

The American moral reform and suffrage press

In the early nineteenth century in the United States, several women published news of various reforms that had distinctly gendered interests. In 1828 Frances Wright began editing the *Free Enquirer*, a paper established by a socialist commune. Two years later, the *Amulet and Ladies' Literary and Religious Chronicle* was established to fight 'intemperance and infidelity' (Stearns 1932). The *Female Advocate* (1832) took on vice and prostitution, while the *American Woman* (1845) took on 'masculine failings'.

Early periodicals by 'mill girls', young textile workers, such as *The Lowell Offering*, published between 1840 and 1845 (and with a somewhat different title from 1847 to 1850) are perhaps the first consistent efforts by women to produce their own news. The *Offering* received considerable attention at the time, including from Charles Dickens, who said, having visited Lowell:

> Of the merits of *The Lowell Offering*, as a literary production, I will only observe – putting out of sight the fact of the articles having been written by these girls after the arduous hours of the day – that it will compare advantageously with a great many English annuals.
>
> (quoted in Cronin 1996: 186)

The *Offering* was produced by an 'improvement circle' of local factory women determined to better themselves. This periodical was not only a forum through which the workers could defend their work and their status, but also a literary outlet. A number of contributors to the *Offering* went on to fame as writers, editors, novelists, teachers and artists (Cronin 1996). It also inspired several other magazines by factory operatives in Massachusetts and New Hampshire, some of which were much more critical of the New England textile mill owners and the factory conditions. Among them were the *Operatives' Magazine*, the *Olive Leaf*, *Factory Girl's Repository*, the *Wampanoag and Operatives' Journal*, the *Factory Girl*, the *Factory Girls' Garland*, the *Factory Girl's Album* and *Operative's Advocate*.

More important, of course, was the movement to abolish slavery. Many of the women active in alternative journalism projects (again, as defined here) began their activism in the movements to abolish slavery and to promote temperance, although eventually the limitations on women's participation in both of those movements inspired female abolitionists to shift their loyalties to more specifically women's periodicals. Lydia Maria Child, for example, wrote a number of novels and non-fiction books – about early American history, housekeeping and especially about abolition – and edited *Juvenile Miscellany*, published 1826 to 1834, the first American periodical for children. Beginning in 1841, she edited the *National Anti-Slavery Standard* on behalf of the American Anti-Slavery Society, of which she was a board member. Ironically, although her earlier writing had been highly controversial, she resigned in 1843 when she was criticized as too genteel, as was her husband, who followed her briefly as editor.

Other pre-Civil War papers by women included Elizabeth Aldrich's *Genius of Liberty*, an Ohio paper 'Devoted to the Interests of American Women', published from 1851 to 1853. Aldrich called for the 'enlargement of the sphere of women' such that women were included in all aspects of society that seemed to reflect 'the Right, the Beautiful and True'. In 1852 Anna Spencer published the *Pioneer and Woman's Advocate* on behalf, as its motto stated, of 'Liberty, Truth, Temperance, Quality'. This Providence, Rhode Island paper also advocated expanding women's education and work opportunities. And for nearly three years, beginning in 1853, Paulina Kellogg Wright Davis published the *Una*, 'A Paper Devoted to the Elevation of Women'. Davis (1854a: 4) declared that 'Women have been too well and too long satisfied with Ladies' Books, Ladies' Magazines, and Miscellaneous; it is time they should have stronger nourishment'. As a result, she promised to speak not to the sentimentalized 'true' woman, but a real woman: 'We ask to be regarded, respected, and treated as human beings, of full age and natural abilities, as equal sinners, and not as infants or beautiful angels, to whom the rules of civil and social justice do not apply' (Davis 1854b: 73).

As was the case for later women's rights and feminist editors, Davis's problem was money. Davis had sent early issues to non-subscribers, hoping thereby to pick up regular readers who would support her financially, in the name of 'honesty and decency'. Unfortunately, many women could not afford even the dollar subscription fee. In some cases their husbands refused to hand over the cash. Davis tried to convince one of the national suffrage associations to take over the *Una* as its official organ, 'which could give to the future a correct history of this revolution and which would be a true and just exponent of our views and principles of action'. Her proposal was rejected; although a patron kept *Una* going for a few more months, the paper then died.

Often their gender precluded women from many forms of public activity, the male-dominated reform organizations often being more interested in women's financial contributions than their oratorial or expressive ones. The husband of Julia Ward Howe allowed her to assist him in 1853 when he edited *Commonwealth*, 'a Free Soil journal', but she was long frustrated in her reform efforts; and Samuel Howe apparently despised her poetry and dramatic works, which alluded quite strenuously to their marital unhappiness. Julia Ward Howe, best known for writing the 'Battle Hymn of the Republic', eventually found satisfaction in suffrage activities. She helped found the weekly *Woman's Journal*, and wrote for it for some two decades.

Even more notably, in Seneca Falls, New York, which had hosted the first suffrage convention in 1848, a committee of the Ladies Temperance Society decided to publish their own journal, in part out of frustration with their marginalization in the temperance movement. As it turns out, the Society's committee members lost interest, but Amelia Jenks Bloomer, conveniently married to a newspaper editor, decided to carry on as publisher, editor, writer and business manager of the *Lily*, which first appeared 1 January 1849. Although originally conceived as a temperance journal, the *Lily* described itself by 1850 as 'devoted to the interests of women',[1] and by 1852 its interests were explicitly said to be 'Emancipation of Woman from Intemperance, Injustice, Prejudice, and Bigotry'. Bloomer did not invent the 'bifurcated trowsers' that bore her name but she promoted and advocated 'bloomers' in the pages of the *Lily* as crucial to women's health and safety, given the hazards of climbing stairs with a baby in one hand and a lit candle in the other. The paper carried instructions for sewing bloomers and heroic tales of women who wore them. A statement of mission promised in July 1853 that *Lily* would labour for the emancipation of women not only from 'unjust laws' but also 'from the destructive influences of Custom and Fashion'.

Bloomer received help from many reform-minded women, and thus established a tradition – very unlike the routines of the mainstream press – of activist female editors helping one another. For example, a contributor to *Lily* was Jane Grey Swisshelm, who had written for several commercial and abolitionist papers. Swisshelm also had published her own highly outspoken journal, *The Pittsburgh Saturday Visiter* from 1847 to 1854, sometimes with the help of another Pittsburgh male editor and sometimes with the support of her husband. Elizabeth Cady Stanton was probably most responsible for *Lily*'s shift from temperance to concerns for suffrage and women's rights. Although her columns were explicitly addressed to mothers, she did not define mothers narrowly in the tradition of 'true womanhood'. Instead, she cast mothers as responsible for the broader education of their sons, including their sons' political and legal education. Over time, *Lily* insisted that the problem of women's vulnerability to drunken husbands required larger structural and legal changes; the solution was not merely temperance but legal and voting rights.

Perhaps the best-known of the suffrage papers, although it lasted only two years, was the *Revolution*, whose publishing genealogy suggests the support community that emerged among suffrage journalists and at their connections to other reform movements. The *Revolution*'s editors were Elizabeth Cady Stanton and Parker Pillsbury, the latter a former editor of the *National Anti-Slavery Standard*. Elizabeth Cady Stanton and Susan B. Anthony, who was the *Revolution*'s publisher, had regularly written for the *Lily*. Originally, the paper also had the backing of George Francis Train, an advocate of the Irish rebellion and of greenbacks and other monetary movements. Soon after the *Revolution* first appeared, in 1868, Train went to Ireland, where he ended up in jail. The *Revolution* continued to run letters from Train and especially to run columns on finance from his friend, David Meliss, the financial editor of the *New York World*. Meliss supported the *Revolution* and edited its financial page until January 1869, when Cady Stanton appointed a woman for that page, which was at best irregular. In the summer of 1869 Parker Pillsbury gave up his editorial title; in January 1870 Paulina Davis was named corresponding editor. The *Revolution* reprinted articles from other suffrage papers (and even from those hostile to women's rights). It also carried essays and reports from regular correspondents from suffrage leaders, including Matilda Joslyn Gage, who went on to edit another major suffrage newspaper, the *National Citizen and Ballot Box*.

The *Revolution* took on highly controversial ideas – did so aggressively, assertively and acerbically, as its name had promised. To the dismay of the more responsible-minded suffragists, the *Revolution* expressed sympathy for prostitutes and other women who were victimized or abused by men, and Stanton advocated changes in marriage and divorce law.

Meanwhile, since Anthony was particularly concerned to expand the readership and the movement to working women, much of the content, including 'The Working Woman' column, was addressed to bring them into the fold. She also kept the subscription rate low ($2 a year, for a weekly), so that it would remain affordable. When Anthony gave up the paper in May 1870, she assumed a $10,000 debt. Laura Bullard, a much more moderate suffragist, toned down the paper considerably, but it died two years later.

The most widely distributed and longest-running women's alternative organ was the *Woman's Journal*, which debuted on 8 January 1870 and carried on with its task until 1920, when the Nineteenth Amendment to the Constitution enfranchising women was ratified. The last three years it published under the name *Woman Citizen*, with which it had merged. It was published in Boston, also the home to the more conservative or genteel suffrage organization, at least compared to Stanton's more radical one in New York. The masthead declared that the *Journal* was 'devoted to the interests of Woman, to her educational, industrial, legal and political equality, and especially to her right of Suffrage'. It lacked the abrasive, sarcastic tone of the *Revolution*. However, it was clearly feminist, not feminine. It carried news for women, not ladies.

Lucy Stone received financial help. She received $10,000 from the same wealthy woman's rights sympathizer who gave Susan B. Anthony $10,000 to publish *The History of Woman Suffrage*. Two businessmen also helped set up a joint-stock company, and shares were sold to members of Stone's organization. Suffrage bazaars and other fund-raising devices, a large subscription base and advertising (but, unlike *Revolution*, not for liquor, tobacco or medicinal products) sustained it over time. Furthermore, Stone had enlisted the help of several others, including her husband Henry Blackwell who, among other chores, managed the paper's finances. For the first two years, the *Journal*'s editor-in-chief was Mary Ashton Livermore, a former Civil War nurse and moral reformer who had edited the *Agitator*, a suffrage organ in Chicago. The various assistant editors all had distinguished reputations in the anti-slavery movement, such as Julia Ward Howe and also Colonel Thomas Wentworth Higginson, who served for several years, until he resigned to write for *Harper's Bazaar*. William Lloyd Garrison was known for his founding of the abolitionist weekly, the *Liberator*, but as a long-time women's rights advocate, he was also active in the *Journal*'s production.

Lucy and Henry's daughter, Alice Stone Blackwell, became increasingly involved and eventually she essentially took over the *Journal*. Meanwhile, in 1882 some 100 to 200 newspapers accepted an offer from Henry Blackwell to use a weekly column of news items from the *Journal*. In 1888 this free mailing became a weekly four-page journal called the *Woman's Column*, a supplement to the *Journal*. Since subscriptions to the *Column* cost far less than other suffrage journals, some suffragists even paid for subscriptions for other people, who would therefore learn about suffrage arguments, women's working conditions, the club movement and other women's reform movements, as well as professional organizations. Moreover, in order to carry out its missionary work it was sent free of charge, until it ended in 1904, to politicians and the clergy and was also distributed free during special expositions and campaigns.

Suffrage news was not merely an East Coast phenomenon. In January 1869, a young teacher bought a half interest in a San Francisco weekly. Emily Pitts (later Emily Pitts Stevens) changed its name to the *Pioneer* and changed its focus from literature to women's suffrage. It lasted until 1873. From 1871 to 1887, with only the help of family members, the crotchety Abigail Scott Duniway published the *New Northwest* in Portland, Oregon. Duniway was in the Stanton–Anthony camp and used the same assertive language, with the *New Northwest* declaring its right to use 'whatever policy may be necessary to reduce the greatest good to the greatest number'. The weekly's slogan was 'A Journal for the People Devoted to the Interests of Humanity Independent in Politics and Religion, Alive to all Live Issues and Thoroughly Radical in Opposing and Exposing the Wrongs of the Masses'. In 1879 Caroline Nichols Churchill began a monthly in Denver, the *Colorado Antelope*, which she called 'the most original . . . wittiest, spiciest, most radical little sheet published in the United States'. Renamed *The Queen Bee* it lasted until 1895. *Our Herald* and *Woman's Own* both came from Indiana. Several state and regional suffrage organizations had their own suffrage periodicals.

Clara Bewick Colby published the *Woman's Tribune* from 1883 to 1909. With the initial support of the Nebraska Woman Suffrage Association, she began publishing in Beatrice, Nebraska. But at times she also published from Washington, DC, for a month offering it as the daily organ of the International Council of Women. Later she moved the paper to DC, where her husband had been appointed assistant attorney general for President Harrison. For its last five years, it was produced in Portland, Oregon, where Bewick Colby – perhaps wrongly – thought the suffrage movement would enjoy greater success. Bewick Colby had also staked her reputation to the Stanton–Anthony faction, which certainly gave her access to writing and appreciation of Stanton and Anthony, but which perhaps in the long run did not help her personal or political cause.

The *Farmer's Wife* was edited and published in Kansas by Emma and Ira Pack, from 1891 until 1894, when the People's Party and the woman suffrage amendment were soundly rejected by Kansas voters. Very unlike most suffrage editors or publishers, the Packs did have mainstream journalism experience, Ira having published a Topeka paper about real estate, while Emma had edited *Villa Range: Ladies Home Journal*, which carried more traditional news and advice for women. With their salaries as superintendent and assistant superintendent of the state's insane infirmary paying their bills, the Packs's paper was an organ of Kansas populism and woman's rights; the *Farmer's Wife* also advocated prohibition, veterans' benefits, and protection for industries and farmers.

Anti-suffragist periodicals also appeared in the United States; since papers and magazines such as the *Reply* (published 1913 to 1915) were usually led by women, these also 'count' as women's alternative publications. New York anti-suffragists began the *Anti-Suffragist* in 1908; this became the *Woman's Protest* in 1912, when a national organization took over, and it was renamed *Woman Patriot* when the organization moved to Washington, DC. The *Remonstrance* was published 1890 to 1920, when the anti-suffragists' hopes of repealing the federal amendment were finally crushed. Perhaps in keeping with its advocacy of separate spheres, women's sphere being in the home, the Boston anti-suffrage women who founded *Remonstrance* hired a male journalist as editor, and the positions they advocated were attributed to 'average' women or the 'majority' of women, rather than to bylined individuals.

The British suffrage press

In Britain, periodicals played a vital role during the women's suffrage movement, a movement largely dominated by well-educated middle-class and upper-class women who were adept at using journalism skills and practices to spread the cause. By 1903 Emmeline Pankhurst founded and led the militant movement called the Women's Social and Political Union of Women Suffragettes (WSPU). All men over twenty-one and only women over the age of thirty were granted suffrage in 1918 (with some exceptions). Voting rights were extended to women over twenty-one in 1928. During the period of the campaign, between 1903 and 1928, a number of suffrage periodicals were launched. Some continued beyond the extension of the franchise, including *Vote* and the *Common Cause*, which was renamed the *Woman's Leader*, and lasted until 1933 (DiCenzo 2000).

In 1870 Lydia Becker, who served as secretary of the Manchester Society for Women's Suffrage, founded the *Women's Suffrage Journal*, one of the first British suffrage journals. Becker, who edited the paper until she died in 1890, was a member of the Married Women's Property Committee and the parliamentary secretary for the National Society for Women's Suffrage, for which the journal was the official publication. Becker used the *Women's Suffrage Journal* on behalf of the parliamentary campaign. To emphasize that the movement appealed to working-class women as well as the middle classes, the paper used anecdotal evidence to document the level of demand for women's suffrage among the wider population. It quoted ordinary women who were approached by canvassers in the streets stating: 'Why should not a woman vote as well as a man, 'specially if she pays rates and taxes?' and another saying: 'I am not so particular about it for myself, because I have a good husband, but I will sign it, because I know many who have none, and who wish for it.'[2]

The immediate aim of the WSPU was to pressure the Liberal government to draft a bill enfranchising women. Their tactics included not only heckling politicians at meetings, holding public debates and organizing demonstrations and marches but also launching feminist periodicals to spread the word. Suffragists also wrote letters to mainstream newspapers, published articles and printed thousands of pamphlets to circulate the suffrage cause and undermine the opposition (Van Wingerden 1999). The socialist press such as the *Workman's Times* supported women's suffrage although it declared that a woman's place was in the home. The mainstream press, however, ignored the suffrage movement until the illegal activities of the WSPU (such as disrupting meetings and organizing demonstrations that also aimed to be disruptive) provided headline news (Bartley 1998: 80). When they did cover the movement, the mainstream press was generally hostile, either objecting to the entire concept or objecting to the suffragettes' militant tactics. In 1912 *The Times* referred to the suffragettes as 'regrettable by-products of our civilisation, out with their hammers and their bags full of stones because of dreary, empty lives and high-strung, over-excitable natures' (Harrison 1978: 33). So suffrage organizations used their own periodicals for the dual purposes of publicising their cause to the popular press and overcoming bad publicity (Harrison 1982).

As in the US, the women who established suffrage organizations and wrote for the suffrage press were not political novices. Many had taken part in the anti-slavery campaign or been active in the Anti-Corn Law League.[3] Skills and experiences gained in these pressure groups were used to establish the suffrage movement across political party lines (Smith 1998). Annie Besant wrote about the social ills of the time from a feminist perspective. She was a member of the Social Democratic Foundation and launched her own campaigning newspaper, the *Link*, having gained experience writing articles on subjects ranging from marriage and women's rights for the *National Reformer.*

As well as Besant's famous articles, such as 'White Slavery in London', which exposed the working conditions of women workers at the Bryant and May match factory (see Chapter 1), her 1874 feminist work *The Political Status of Women*[4] was highly effective in reaching and informing a large number of women. The text was produced by the Women's Press, which by 1910 became an important part of the WSPU, publishing penny pamphlets as well as feminist journals such as *Votes for Women* (published 1907 to 1918) (Morley and Stanley 1988).

Votes for Women was edited by Emmeline Pankhurst and Frederick Pethick-Lawrence, who were arrested in 1912 along with other WSPU leaders, and charged with conspiracy for producing what was regarded as 'inflammatory matter', indicating the radical nature of the material published in the paper. *Votes for Women* stressed that women's disenfranchisement was merely one element of women's subordination and that the vote was just one hurdle on the road to equality. Inferior housing, low pay, sweated labour, inadequate medical provision for childbirth and the sexual slavery of women and children were among the social injustices it tackled (Morley and Stanley 1988). Despite its radicalism, it reached a national circulation of 40,000 and was able to attract advertising revenue, in part, due to a strong sales campaign with a large number of women involved in promoting and selling the paper. Thus, *Votes for Women* is an example of a periodical that managed to combine a commercial strategy with radical political objectives (DiCenzo 2000). DiCenzo (2000: 116) argues that these suffrage periodicals force a reconsideration of what is generally accepted as the decline of a radical press by the end of the nineteenth century, due to the increased costs of newspaper ownership and the subsequent reliance on advertising.

A split occurred in 1912 between the Pankhursts, who espoused violence, and the Pethick-Lawrences about the degree of violence in the campaign. As a result, the Pethick-Lawrences were expelled from the Women's Social and Political Union and *Votes for Women* was no longer its official voice. The Votes for Women Fellowship was formed to gain support for their cause, but the paper was losing money. The Pethick-Lawrences offered their services for free and were able to produce a paper with more variable views. It supported George Lansbury who ran as an independent MP supporting the suffrage cause and who wrote about wider issues concerning women such as white slave traffic, prison reform and so on (DiCenzo 2000: 124). In 1914 *Votes for Women* became the official organ of the United Suffragists. Regarded as a vital organ for persuading people to join the cause, *Votes for Women* played a central role in contesting the strategy of suppressing of the 'public press'. Schemes were devised to increase circulation such as asking volunteers to sell the papers outside theatres and at public meetings, and donating copies to libraries. Street banners and colourful posters were used to sell the paper on urban streets (DiCenzo 2000: 122).

A surprisingly large number of advertisements in *Votes for Women* promoted women's fashions but this practice was criticized by a number of people, including Sylvia Pankhurst (daughter of Emmeline) for revealing the middle-class nature of the movement. The dependence on advertising, which brought in profits to support the campaign, raises questions about whether it was justified to use women models in advertisements in relation to the periodicals' politics (DiCenzo 2000). While advertisements emphasized women's decorative features, the suffrage movement was calling for women to be taken seriously to obtain citizenship (Bentham 1996). However, DiCenzo reminds us that the suffragettes were keen to encourage readers to dress in feminine clothes to counter the raft of caricatures of masculine-looking suffragettes so that 'dressing fashionably became a political act' (Kaplan and Stowell 1994 quoted in DiCenzo 2000). The WSPU was looked upon as a union that addressed and attracted educated, privileged women, prompting Sylvia Pankhurst to go to work for the East End Federation of Suffragettes (DiCenzo 2000: 122). It was difficult to promote *Votes for Women* when the First World War started, and membership of the organization waned. The paper folded in 1918 when the Representation of the People Bill gained royal approval.

From 1914 to 1924 the Women's Social and Political Union of Women Suffragettes published the *Women's Dreadnought* (the title changed to the *Workers' Dreadnought* in 1917), edited by Sylvia Pankhurst. It was also the mouthpiece of the East London Federation of the Suffragettes (ELFS), a radical, working-class and feminist organization led by Sylvia Pankhurst that used militant tactics in trying to expose women's exploitation and oppression. After the outbreak of the Second World War it became a national weekly, and achieved a readership of about 8,000. Indeed, eighteen-year-old Patricia Lynch accomplished a remarkable journalistic coup for the *Dreadnought* during the abortive rising against the British government on Easter Sunday 1916 by the Irish socialists and nationalists. Insistent on obtaining a first-hand account, she evaded the British Army barricade around the city of Dublin by posing as the sister of a sympathetic army officer whom she met on the train to Ireland. Lynch's report was so highly sought after that the *Dreadnought* sold out and the story had to be reissued as a pamphlet (Winslow 1996: 102). The weekly was then banned in Ireland. The *Dreadnought* became one of the most prominent anti-war newspapers in England during the Second World War and increased Sylvia Pankhurst's reputation as an anti-war militant.

The British suffrage movement and its feminist press went beyond campaigning for enfranchisement for women. Alliances between the suffragettes and male workers, such as dockers, demonstrated the shared experience of struggle between feminists and working-class men. *Dreadnought* was one of the most effective socialist newspapers and had strong links with the Communist Party. Over time, its articles about strikes and conflicts in Britain and events in the trade union movement were replaced by poetry and literary criticism, indicating that contributors' links with workers' struggles were diminishing. However, *Dreadnought* maintained effective international links. It reported on the oppressive conditions of women workers, including first-person accounts of women who worked twelve-hour days. In particular, the paper dramatized the stories of women who went on strike, who struggled against both their factory bosses and the local police.

Turn-of-the century efforts and lessons

Although the fervour for alternative women's and feminist publishing subsided after the turn of the twentieth century in both the United States and United Kingdom, a few publications continued and some new ones were established. For example, in the United States the *Woman Voter* was launched in 1910 as the organ of New York City suffragists. In 1917 it merged with the *Woman's Journal* and the *National Suffrage News* into a new weekly, the *Woman Citizen*, as the official organ of the national suffrage organization, (well) funded by the Leslie Woman Suffrage Commission. One of the more lively and graphically innovative suffrage periodicals was the *Suffragist*, launched in 1913 as the organ for the Congressional Union and later the National Woman's Party (NWP). It was edited by Rheta Childe Dorr, already a famous journalist (mentioned in Chapter 10). The paper was best known for its advocacy of the NWP's controversial political tactic: members jailed for picketing the White House, including CU chair Alice Paul and the *Suffragist*'s advertising manager, underwent a hunger strike in jail. The tabloid-style weekly represented the hunger strikers in the mould of Revolutionary War patriots. It published photographs of police harassing suffrage picketers and clever political cartoons by Nina Allende – regularly featured on the cover – satirized President Wilson. A year after the picketing began, Wilson publicly endorsed the suffrage amendment, which was almost immediately approved in the House of Representatives. It ceased publication in 1921, but was superseded by the *Equal Rights*, a paper devoted to an Equal Rights Amendment, published 1923 to 1954.

Women were also involved in other kinds of alternative newspapers around the turn of the twentieth century. There were several labour papers in the United States. For example, *Far and Near* represented a loose-knit coalition of working girls' clubs, its name suggesting the goal of spreading ideas from near to far and unifying the cause of working women. Published 1890 to 1894, a farewell editorial commented: 'There is no such thing as absolute failure for any conscientious effort. Some boundaries we have shown to be impassable, some limitations we have helped to define, some questions we have settled by the things we have eliminated' (quoted in Davies 1996: 80–1). Some publications were devoted to peace and many concerned broad political causes. For example, there was the *Socialist Woman*, started in 1907, retitled in 1909 the *Progressive Woman*, and again retitled the *Coming Nation* under which name it was published from 1913 to 1914.

What, then, is the lesson of these 'first-wave' periodicals? First, they show that women could and would produce these periodicals, with a fair degree of technical quality. However, because of exhaustion of volunteers and lack of financial and intellectual assistance, they usually did not last long. Editors and publishers coped with relocations, bad career and backfiring business decisions of husbands; they coped with children, domestic responsibilities and career changes. That said, some periodicals were successful, especially those underwritten by large, well-financed national women's organizations. The *Woman's Journal* published with absolute regularity for fifty years, despite financial difficulties, a fire and several changes of editorial boards. Obviously, all these periodicals were partisan to a degree not seen or admitted among the mainstream news media described in other chapters in this book. But the fact is, these efforts sustained and nurtured the community of new women that these periodicals dramatized. The extent to which they actually gained new converts is unclear. But they circulated the news to women who were geographically isolated, thereby motivating and encouraging them, and keeping the movement and its ideas alive.

The suffrage and early women's rights editors formed a community among themselves – writing, reprinting and borrowing from one another – and a community of new women in the nineteenth century. For example, Abigail Duniway wrote for Bloomer's *Lily* and for the *San Francisco Pioneer*, whose publisher she met at an 1871 suffrage convention; and she also knew Myra Bradwell, the editor of the *Chicago Legal News*. The periodicals provided training for women. These newspapers and magazines also offered a heroic model for later feminists. *Chrysalis*, for example, a high-quality feminist magazine published from 1977 to 1980 took to publishing selections from the 'first wave,' such as pieces by Susan B. Anthony and Amelia Bloomer. The feminist collective that published *New Women's Times* from 1975 to 1984 in Rochester, New York, the hometown of Susan B. Anthony, often invoked Anthony's name.

Many of the women were highly courageous, their dedication to social and political change signifying even more than sacrificing time with family. Ida B. Wells-Barnett stands out here. Born a slave in 1862, she was forced off a train in 1884 when she refused to move to the smoking car, where black passengers were required to sit. She sued the railroad company and won, although later the Tennessee Supreme Court overturned the decision. Wells was hired as a school teacher in Memphis in 1884, and wrote for a number of black newspapers across the country until in 1889 she purchased a one-third interest in *Free Speech and Headlight*, founded by and still co-owned by a Memphis Baptist minister. As editor, Wells immediately took on the poor quality of public schools serving blacks – and when her teaching contract came up in 1891, it was not renewed. More importantly, she wrote about lynching. The Reverend Nightingale suffered first: he had to sell his third of the *Free Speech* and leave the state as a result. But Wells and her partner expanded the paper and continued to cover the issue. Indeed, when Wells called on Memphis black citizens to leave the city, given the continuing racial injustice and power of white lynch mobs there, some 6,000 black citizens did indeed leave, thus hurting the businesses that relied on their patronage. In 1892 while Wells was out of town, a mob ransacked the *Free Speech* offices, destroying its presses. A note left behind threatened death to anyone trying to publish the paper again. Wells did not return. She moved to New York and bought an interest in the *New York Age*, a black paper. Later she wrote for other white newspapers as well as black newspapers, including the *Chicago Conservator*, whose owner she married and which she edited for two years.

Margaret Sanger, an obstetrics nurse whose own mother died at age forty-eight after having eleven children, knew well the health dangers to women from lack of information about pregnancy and contraception. She wrote a column for the *Call*, a well-known socialist paper for which Dorothy Day, who established the *Catholic Worker* in 1933, also wrote. Sanger's series for girls ran successfully until one Sunday it was replaced by a box reading 'WHAT EVERY GIRL SHOULD KNOW – NOTHING – BY ORDER OF THE POST-OFFICE DEPARTMENT'. The post office threatened to suppress the entire paper because of her article on venereal disease. Sanger decided to publish her own monthly, the *Woman Rebel*, with the slogans 'No God, No Masters' and 'A Monthly Paper of Militant Thought'.

Yet from the start, the *Woman Rebel* also ran up against the Comstock Law, named for a Civil War soldier and grocer who was obsessed with pornography and had lobbied for a law prohibiting mail distribution of obscene materials. Once the law passed in 1873, Comstock himself decided what was obscene. The Post Office confiscated several issues of Sanger's periodical. She was handed a federal subpoena after the July 1914 issue carried a defence of political assassination. After seven issues and shortly before Sanger's trial was to begin, she fled the country, leaving her husband and children behind. Comstock then prosecuted her husband for distributing Margaret Sanger's pamphlet, 'Family Limitation', and William Sanger spent a month in jail. She spent a year in Europe, returning a month after Comstock's death in 1915. Not wanting to make her into a martyr, the government dropped the charges in February 1916 (Cronin 1996: 452). None the less, when she opened the first birth-control clinic, in October 1916, she was arrested for dispensing birth-control information.

Conclusion

Suffrage publications and other women-run alternative newspapers and magazines constructed new conceptions of womanhood – in some cases, we might even say forms of a specifically feminist identity. Different editors articulated and promoted somewhat different versions of new womanhood (Steiner 1991). Some claimed women had a unique moral sensibility and sense of responsibility that would lead them to make distinct political contributions. A more radical argument was that women were fully and equally human – and, like men, flawed. In either case, the papers had a crucial journalistic mission: to teach women how to take up their lives as 'new women'. The papers carried news of how these new women might dress themselves, name themselves, and judge themselves and others.

Little research has been conducted on the newspapers and periodicals produced by British suffrage organizations in the early twentieth century. These publications were even excluded from the history of the radical, popular and political presses, since most British press historians have focused on class rather than gender politics (DiCenzo 2000). Yet reform and activist groups invested heavily in periodicals to disseminate their ideas, especially when access to existing mainstream publications was blocked. Some recent scholarship has turned to the suffrage press as an example of women's activism in the public sphere, the sphere that allows ordinary people to debate and deliberate on issues of concern to them, and distinguished from the domestic, commercial and government spheres. Ironically, Jürgen Habermas's (1989) classic work on the public sphere, a book that largely ignores both women and the alternative media, dates the decline of public life to precisely that period when women succeeded in articulating their political concerns. Mary Ryan (1992) emphasizes that women's political history subverts Habermas's notion of decline of public life, since women succeeded in being heard in public quarters. More specifically, DiCenzo (2000) asserts that the suffrage press in Britain is important for having advanced women's access to the public.

The suffrage press offers important evidence to support feminist critiques of the gender-blindness of Habermas's theory of the public sphere. Rita Felski (1989: 155–82) formulates a model of the feminist public sphere to examine an oppositional discursive space for gender politics in today's society. She refers to the feminist public sphere as a 'counterpublic' that is not universally representative but provides a critique of cultural values from the perspective of women as a subordinated group. This sphere is 'public' in the sense that its ideas are directed to wider society. Fraser (1992) refers to 'subaltern counterpublics' who, because they are marginalized, produce 'counterdiscourses' and thereby expand the topics of public discourse by forcing public debate on issues otherwise ignored. Women, whose access to the public sphere was systematically obstructed, were brought together and developed a sense of feminist identity by the act of reading suffrage periodicals and pamphlets. Thus, running their own presses, writing and publishing their own literary and political works, and setting up their own libraries were important ways of networking among the various professional, political and labour/trade organizations. They promoted a sense of community among women readers, readers who often would have felt emotionally, if not geographically, isolated (Steiner 1983). And these periodicals helped women learn how to argue for their cause. Not only the government sphere but also the public sphere was dominated by white men of the middle and upper classes. Women's access to political clout was contingent on these men granting women the franchise. But men were unlikely to read most of these periodicals. Therefore, together the editors, writers and readers of these periodicals developed, critiqued and taught one another the tactics that could be deployed on behalf of their various movements. Finally, these papers provided women with an opportunity to experiment with alternative mechanisms for organizing, producing and distributing the news (Steiner 1993). Some of these innovations in 'doing' journalism and these alternative conceptions of 'being' a journalist were further elaborated in more recent alternative news media described in the following chapter.

8

Women's alternative print journalism of the 'second' and 'third' waves

Liberation politics during the counter-cultural period of the 1960s emphasized 'personal liberation' from the repressive structures of society and therefore produced at best an ambiguous and unfocused politics around femininity and women's issues. Likewise, much of the so-called alternative or counter-cultural journalism in the 1960s in the UK and the US ignored women as such. British periodicals like *It*, *Oz* and *Frendz*, and US publications such as the *Rat* and the *Village Voice* rarely addressed women. Often, radical leaders – and their publications – were conspicuously sexist. This was a particular problem for the lesbian community, which established its own periodicals after being marginalized by the organizations and periodicals of the radical left, the gay liberation movement and the women's liberation movement. More generally, this context gave rise to a new wave of feminism highlighting the issue of women's interests, this time in a form that questioned the automatic association of women with the domestic sphere and assumption of their lack of interest in participating in the public sphere, and that underscored how a variety of social issues affected men and women differently.

Feminists called for mainstream journalists to take seriously women's viewpoints on health, fertility, childcare, work, housing, marriage and divorce. But, as with the 'first wave' of the women's movement a century before, women interested in 'alternative' versions of womanhood realized that they required alternative platforms for defining and producing news. In particular, the shift to a more sharply defined feminist politics during the late 1960s and 1970s and continuing into the 1980s gave many women a collective voice with which to express their anger and to implement the politics of the 'second wave' of the women's movement. The women's liberation movement of the 1960s and 1970s stimulated a thriving feminist news media during which a number of feminist publishers, local and national women's liberation newsletters, magazines and journals emerged as part of the women's alternative press.

Consistent with a feminism inspiring many women to question their work-ing relationships with men and to make a bid for autonomy by gaining financial control over their work in developing feminist enterprises, feminist ways of working became central objectives of women's alternative news media. For most feminists who have been engaged in writing and broadcast-ing, developing collective and non-hierarchical ways of working, both as a feminist principle and for the joy of working with like-minded sisters, has been crucial. Many feminist groups did not wish to be perceived as 'profes-sionals', since this smacked of hierarchy and elitism, but they did want to control 'their' news and to be centrally involved in the production process. They wanted to publicize political and ideological issues rather than to earn profit for the owners, whether printers, publishers or authors. On the one hand, their independent enterprises typically require less financial outlay and perhaps even fewer skills than the technologically specialized processes dom-inating the mainstream commercial sector, especially in print. On the other, these projects were unlikely to earn a profit; indeed, they were rarely out of the red. This chapter begins by examining the print media that, for a variety of reasons, continue to be the mainstay of women's alternative journalism, showing how women made distinctive contributions not only to the definition of news but also to how it was produced and distributed.

We highlight the unusual success of *Spare Rib* in the UK and *Ms. Magazine* in the US, but it is worth noting from the outset the flood of fem-inist newsletters, newspapers and magazines in the US and UK in the 1970s. In the US, literally hundreds of journals were published, some only for a year or two, some even only for an issue or two, when the economic, physical and time burdens of production outweighed passion and zeal for exchanging information. Archives at the University of Southern California hold issues of more than 300 lesbian and feminist periodicals published in the US since the early 1970s, and its holdings are incomplete. There were Christian feminist publications (*Daughters of Sarah*, a Chicago-based publication begun in 1974); Jewish magazines (*Lilith*, established in 1976 and named for Adam's first companion, who, since she was not taken from his bone, was his equal); ecofeminist periodicals; and magazines for feminist witches or 'goddess-minded wimmin' (such as *Thesmophoria*). There were publications for and about (and therefore also produced by) members of various professions – nurses, lawyers, sociologists, clerical workers, teachers, business executives. The National Association of Working Women, 9to5, published *9to5 Newsline*, beginning in 1973. *Prime Time* (published 1971 to 1977), origi-nally subtitled *For the Liberation of Women in the Prime of Life*, reached older women. *La Wisp* discussed peace. *Union Wage* advocated labour issues. *Red Star* (originally called *Hammer Sickle Rifle*) was the newsletter of the Red Women's Detachment of the Marxist-Leninist Party, published 1970 to 1971. *Coyote Howls* was a highly sophisticated San Francisco-based newspa-per in the late 1970s published for and by prostitutes, while *The Celibate*

Woman Journal (published 1982 to 1988) provided moral support and information for women contemplating or practising celibacy, on a long- or
short-term basis.

Similarly, British women's liberation periodicals of the 1970s, including
local newsletters such as the *Revolutionary and Radical Feminist Newsletter*,
provided information, support and consciousness-raising for working-class,
black, young and old women. Some newsletters attempted to transcend political labels, such as *Catcall* and *WIRES* (the official title of the British
national women's liberation newsletter) and others that served particular
campaigns on issues such as abortion and sexual violence. Some of these
publications emphasized news and information while others offered more
academic analysis. For example, intellectual and theoretical journals such as
the British *m/f* were more interested in extended and even esoteric analysis of
feminist ideas and debate. The *Manchester Women's Paper*, on the other hand,
tried to attract readers of mainstream women's magazines, and so adopted a
style that was lively but 'discreetly feminist' (Cadman, Chester and Pivot
1981: 73).

This newer interest in individuality and personal style is reflected in contemporary alternative journalism, both that of feminists per se, and that
specifically for lesbians. As a result, if the definition of 'alternative' was historically blurred, what now counts as 'alternative' is even more ambiguous.
Part of this has to do with changes in the women's movements, and part
with the economics of publishing. Many periodicals that now claim to be
alternative, feminist or even radical do not seem to live up to this claim.
Indeed, today, not only have most of the newspapers and magazines for gays
and lesbians lost their political edge and adopted a focus on consumption and
entertainment, but they also continue to be addressed much more to men
than women. In very recent years, women sometimes have taken charge of
newspapers jointly serving the gay and lesbian community (including the
Philadelphia Gay News, the *Bay Times* in San Francisco and *Frontiers* in Los
Angeles) but the general move has been to a glossy consumer orientation.

Second-wave American periodicals

One of the best-known and longest-running of the second-wave periodicals in
the United States is *off our backs*, begun in 1970 in Washington, DC, and still
published by a collective and one staff member, with an emphasis on national
and especially international news of women. Marilyn Webb, one of the co-
founders of *off our backs* (known as *oob* and not to be confused with the
lesbian sex periodical *On Our Backs*), had been a reporter for the *New York
Guardian*, which, she said, had blacked out feminist news.

Webb called *oob* the 'quintessential child of the sixties – born of naïve
enthusiasm, a pinch of planning and a little bit of dope' (Webb 1980: 5). It
would be a paper 'for *all* women' who are fighting for liberation – by which

the collective signalled its commitment to expanding beyond middle-class women. Moreover, the *oob* collective made no commitment to conventional journalistic principles: 'We intend to be just; but we do not intend to be impartial. Our paper is part of a movement; we ourselves are committed to a struggle and we will take stands to further the cause of that struggle', it said in 1970.

Endres (1996) notes that sound business practices and reliance on volunteer labour significantly contributed to *oob*'s longevity. Ironically, perhaps, *oob* nearly folded in 1980, when in a virtually unique experience for women's news media, a member of the collective embezzled $5,000 from the paper. But the periodical never avoided major controversies, including the relative scarcity of women in editorial positions at top television and print organizations and in the radical press, and ruptures within and across women's groups. Indeed, some criticized it for focusing on 'intra-movement factionalism, from what appears to be a predominantly male-left perspective' (quoted in Endres 1996: 269).

New Directions for Women began in 1972 as a mimeographed publication for New Jersey women, produced, edited and published by Paula Kassell in her home. Its serious feminist fare was enlivened by humour, such as the recipe from the third issue published in Spring 1973 cited by Kassell and Beasley (1996: 228). The recipe called for mixing together, among other things, '1 crushed ego, 1 teaspoon job discrimination, 1 well-beaten path to the washing machine, one-half teaspoon grated nerves, 1 dash from the dentist to the babysitter'. The recipe continued: 'Cook until you feel a slow burn and then add one last straw. Serves 51 per cent of the population.' *New Directions for Women* eventually went national. It was awarded several grants under the Comprehensive Employment and Training Act to provide training in the business of publishing to minority women and displaced homemakers – all of whom subsequently found jobs, including at *New Directions for Women* itself. Other feminist papers, including *Plainswoman*, published 1977 to 1989 in Grand Forks, North Dakota, also used CETA grants to fund part-time staffs. In 1981 *New Directions for Women* won a substantial Ford Foundation grant for increasing subscriptions among minority women. The grant allowed the tabloid to be sent free to women in prisons and mental hospitals, and to university women's centres (Kassell and Beasley 1996). Other small grants allowed it to pay writers and to hire professional, albeit part-time, staff. The newspaper folded in 1993, in the wake of rising production costs that could not be offset by equivalent increases in subscriptions or advertising.

Almost none of the editors or publishers of feminist periodicals had mainstream experience when they started their alternative journalism projects. Most of these periodicals accepted some advertising. But few of them were able to get as many advertising accounts as they wanted and needed, especially since many of those that carried advertising limited the kind of advertising they were willing to carry. A few accepted no advertising, such as

No More Fun and Games, organized and published irregularly between 1968 and 1973 by a radical 'cell' in Boston that also questioned 'all phallic social structures' including heterosexual sex and the nuclear family. *No More* involved Dana Densmore, the daughter of Donna Allen, founder of *Media Report to Women*, and sister of Martha Allen, who published the *Celibate Woman*. *No More Fun and Games* looked to non-traditional schemes to support itself, including film showings and sales of posters.

Alternative periodicals almost invariably have died because of financial problems. In some cases, the women involved grew more committed to other causes, took on new jobs or had children. In many cases, personality or political rifts dealt fatal blows, especially with the presses organized by relatively large collectives. Early in its history, for example, lesbian volunteers for *off our backs* split to form their own newspaper, *Furies.* But the major problem as well as the final straw was nearly always that producing and distributing the periodical cost more than it brought in through subscriptions. This continues to be the case in the new feminist movement and in the new millennium. As will be elaborated below, while third-wave producers of alternative publications intend to create a product that will find a profitable niche, the alternative journalists in the 1970s and 1980s rarely expected to make money and were single-minded about feminism and alternative journalism.

British feminist periodicals

British women's liberation newsletters of the 1970s included the *Revolutionary and Radical Feminist Newsletter* and the *Cambridge Women's Liberation Newsletter*, both providing local information, support and consciousness-raising for working-class, black, young and old women. The newsletters constituted the 'internal organ' of the women's liberation movement, as Cadman, Chester and Pivot (1981) point out. The *Cambridge Women's Liberation Newsletter's* policy was to avoid editing, which smacked of censorship. Like the other local newsletters including *WIRES*, it published everything submitted, whatever its length or style, as long as it did not contradict the demands of the women's liberation movement. As a result, content in the *Cambridge* newsletter, distributed by subscription and sold at the women's centre, included opinions, reports, poems, a calendar of events, lists of local contacts, reports on conferences and minutes from meetings. By contrast, the majority of feminist newspapers preferred to commission stories on important topics, although most could not afford to finance such an initiative.

In stark contrast to the glossy women's magazines and the newspapers of the day, whose aim was to make a profit through advertising revenue, most of the women's movement publications of the 1970s and early 1980s were shoestring enterprises financed initially by donations, jumble sales and then subscriptions. The national analytical periodical, *Feminist Review*, raised money by charging a fee for its lecture series. Unlike commercial magazines and newspapers, women's liberation periodicals did not depend on high circulation figures. Nevertheless most periodicals struggled financially and were short-lived. A further difficulty for women's alternative media in Britain has been distribution, given that the commercial distribution networks cater to publishers with rapid turnovers and so were not useful to feminist news media. Radical distribution networks were available in the United States to distribute women's alternative media to bookstores, but these did not exist in the UK.

Feminist magazine Spare Rib

What has arguably been Britain's leading women's liberation monthly magazine, *Spare Rib,* was launched on the modest sum of £2,000 in 1972, the same year that the National Magazine Company spent £127,000 launching the British version of the glossy magazine, *Cosmopolitan. Cosmopolitan* represented a new and explicit sexual self-assertiveness based on a consumerist ideology of feminine competitiveness and individual success. By contrast, *Spare Rib* conveyed a critical dissatisfaction about women's experiences. Its monthly print run was only 20,000 to 25,000 copies at a time when *Cosmopolitan* had 483,000.[1] Yet *Spare Rib* influenced an entire generation of women, overturning taken-for-granted patriarchal assumptions about femininity and women's daily experiences of motherhood, family life, heterosexuality, feminine sexual images, division of labour and women's emotional dependence in marriage. The large newsagents and stationers chain in the UK, WH Smith, refused to stock the first issue, even though the launch issue contained a page on skin care, a recipe for chicken casserole and an interview with a famous British footballer, George Best. However, it also published stories on women's equality, women's role in history and an article by Patricia Hewitt – now secretary of state for trade and industry – who at twenty-three called readers' attention to the pension poverty trap (Lawson 2002: 5). During its hey-day in the 1980s, *Spare Rib*'s political tendencies were radically feminist: it defined men as universal oppressors and emphasized socialist feminism and a concern for class differences.

Spare Rib operated a collective with ten full-time and five part-time workers, several of whom already had experience in producing underground papers such as *Oz* and *Ink* (Cadman, Chester and Pivot 1981); its founders included Rosie Boycott, who moved on to become editor of the mainstream publications *Esquire* and the *Daily Express*. These women intended to 'put women's liberation on the newsstands' by targeting a mass readership of feminists and not-yet-feminists alike. *Spare Rib*'s intention to compete with the glossy magazines meant that it had to be very thoughtful about the 'politics of appearance' (Cadman, Chester and Pivot 1981: 77). On the other hand, Winship (1987: 123) says of *Spare Rib*:

To compare *Spare Rib* with commercial magazines is like evaluating the appeal of a spartan whole-food diet by reference to the rich diet of junk food. It is found, inevitably, to be lacking: no layers of sugary icing between the editorial cake and no thick milk chocolate as palliative to the 'hard nuts'. Instead a heavy textured pudding, dingy in colour, and somewhat hard work on the jaws. Or as Brian Braithwaite and Joan Barrell dismissively describe *Spare Rib*, 'It appears drab and colourless, a bit like a political tract . . . not the kind of magazine one could recommend for a jolly good read'.

Compared to feminist periodicals such as *Feminist Review* and *m/f*, *Spare Rib* was positively colourful, since it contained a large number of illustrations; and in contrast to mainstream newspapers and magazines, its fifty-six pages were filled with articles about women's rights, sexual violence and nuclear armament. The most provocative articles in *Spare Rib* approached politically sensitive and complex issues by blending historical information with personal experience and social analysis. This kind of feminist news media could be intimidating, as the magazine represented an opposition to patriarchal institutions and modes of femininity dependent on consumer culture, heterosexuality and marriage, including even women's desire to have children. The magazine's vision was often 'revolutionary' and much of its rhetoric militant and anti-reformist (Winship 1987: 130).

But as the quote above suggests, women accustomed to the glitzy and lustrous images of the then unique *Cosmopolitan* or the two most popular women's magazines on the British market at the time (*Women's Weekly* and *Women's Own*) found *Spare Rib* to be 'something of a cultural shock'.

Spare Rib's anti-capitalist, anti-consumer approach was highlighted in its design, layout and even its non-glossy advertising. The magazine also relied on donations and a grant from the left-wing Greater London Council, as well as paid advertising, although finding sufficient non-sexist advertising during the 1970s and 1980s was a significant challenge. All advertisements, apart from those for books and records, were for items produced co-operatively or by craft production. This contributed to the look of a periodical rejecting capitalist consumption, which in turn allowed *Spare Rib* to refuse to pander to a specific segment of the advertising market. The policy also meant that *Spare Rib* continually suffered financial crises.

Spare Rib focused carefully on ways of distributing the magazine and this approach contributed to its success. Like many feminist periodicals of the 1970s and early 1980s, it relied on the Publications Distribution Co-op (PDC), the major radical distribution network, to distribute the magazine, as well as alternative bookshops and mainstream newsagents.

Spare Rib never insisted on a rigid house style but instead encouraged a direct and personal style of language. Unlike many other feminist periodicals, however, it did not draw on a new language for women. It did not, for example, refuse to use male pronouns or substitute 'herstory' for 'history'. Initially *Spare Rib* paid its contributing writers; it dropped this practice to avert financial collapse. But the fact that anyone could submit writing to the collective (all decisions about content reflected group consensus) meant that its writers included women who were not part of the women's movement. This led to a dilemma about who its readers really were and about its political objectives, and arguments often arose over what to publish. The collective continuously reviewed its policy about whether the magazine should represent the varied politics of the women's movement and whether it should get involved in debates about the movement or concentrate on being a magazine aimed at women who were new to feminism. Differences in views between lesbian and straight women and between the objectives of black women's groups and those of white feminists led to fervent debate.

In 1983 after months of heated discussion within its collective, *Spare Rib* announced it was no longer a white woman's magazine aimed at white readers, but would now take on the challenge of dealing with issues related to women of colour, including the wealth and poverty associated with imperialism and the developing world. The collective transformed from an all-white one to one which was half 'Women of Colour'.[2] It also represented the concerns of lesbians, working-class and older women.

Like women's magazines and contemporary news journalism styles today, the articles began with women's individual experience but they emphasized political issues with the slogan, the 'personal is political' and critiqued the individualism and codes of femininity conventionally represented in mainstream news media. The wider structures of patriarchal power that shape personal experiences were carefully analysed in order to identify and publicize women's subordination and its social causes. It provided the means for a wider politics of engagement to change the key ideologies of society and the institutions that reproduced them (Winship 1987).

Spare Rib kept going during the 1980s by redesigning the magazine to appeal to a younger readership. The softer and more friendly look was accused by some of a cosmetic facelift and falling prey to the vacuous 'style' that became the hallmark of the 1980s. In 1983 the collective reached a crisis about its editorial role that had been brewing since a 1980 disagreement about whether to publish an article examining women's separatism, which the author regarded as a governing idea in the women's movement. While *Spare Rib* initially determined to publish 'Feminism for Her Own Good', members of the collective then blocked it as anti-lesbian.[3] Eventually, the collective told the readers about the crisis. While readers were disappointed that the collective failed to share their editorial problems in order that the women's movement could learn from them, the collective felt guilty about exposing internal disagreements to women new to feminism. The magazine went into liquidation in 1993.

The lesbian press and status of lesbian journalists

A major category of publications relevant here is the lesbian press which has a particularly rich history, in two key ways. First, changes in the lesbian press encapsulate much of the trajectory of women's alternative journalism, from marginalization to a highly provocative, if sectarian, experimentation with different ways of doing journalism, to the emphasis on style. Second – and this would not be surprising given the enduring stigmatization of homosexuality that predicts an intense reliance on periodicals – it is an active history, with one 1990 international directory of lesbian and gay periodicals published over the century listing 2,678 periodicals in the US (Miller 1990). The story can begin with *Vice Versa*, typed and mimeographed once a month from June 1947 to February 1948 by a secretary then working at RKO Studios who later used the pseudonym 'Lisa Ben' (an anagram for 'lesbian'). Edythe Eyde hated her job, but at least it gave her time to type each issue manually, and her boss at the time even wanted her to look busier than she was (Gershick 1998). *Vice Versa* lasted until she obtained a job that required all of her time. Subtitled 'America's Gayest Magazine', Eyde's own name did not appear in *Vice Versa* and she ran no bylines.

Perhaps the first formal publication for (and by and about) lesbians was the *Ladder*, published 1956 to 1972 by the Daughters of Bilitis, a national organization of predominantly white, middle-class women who promoted 'integration' of lesbians by taking on behaviour and dress acceptable to society. Del Martin and Phyllis Lyon had both studied journalism and been employed as journalists before founding the *Ladder*; indeed, they met while working for a trade journal. But they took on non-journalism jobs to support themselves while editing and producing the *Ladder*. *Ladder* volunteers asserted – in the context of unsuccessfully begging for subscribers in the April/May 1971 issue – that: 'We are the only magazine in the country that deals honestly with the needs of the Lesbian, and the only women's liberation publication that deals honestly with all women.'[4] Certainly it succeeded in providing a safe, open forum for the views of the community, including readers who were encouraged to submit their writing. Echoing almost to a word language heard by the suffrage editors about their geographically isolated readers a century before, Phyllis Lyon explained her commitment to keep the *Ladder* going 'for all those lonely women who wrote us, saying the only bright spot in their whole month was the arrival of our little magazine' (quoted in Streitmatter 1995: 49).

Ironically, although the two major publications for gay men of the period were larger and better funded, Streitmatter (1995) notes that *Mattachine Review* lost its energy and then its readership in part because their editors refused to adapt to changes within the gay community. In contrast, the editors of the *Ladder* were willing to pass their baton to the much younger Barbara Gittings, who could help the publication express the growing militancy and openness of the lesbian community, a frankness signalled by the addition of a subtitle 'A Lesbian Review'. In 1966 Lyon and Martin were so outraged by Gittings's decision to remove the disclaimer 'For Adults Only' that had appeared on the cover that they removed her from office and resumed their control, although eventually they lost control of the magazine. Still, over the years it continued both to push cultural and sexual boundaries and to bring together a community of sentiment across geography.

Immediately following the 1969 so-called Stonewall Rebellion (riots and demonstrations sparked off by a police raid on the Stonewall Inn in Greenwich Village) a great number of radical local and regional publications serving lesbian readers flourished. The most radical papers begun in 1970 were those of gay men, or for gay men and lesbians, such as *Come Out!* and *Gay Liberator*, both of which argued for revolution and anarchy. Still, as its title asserts, the *Killer Dyke*, for example, a post-Stonewall tabloid published in Chicago from 1970 to 1972, used a new vocabulary to celebrate lesbians and violence in both text and artwork.

In the mid-1970s, the radical flame having burnt out, dozens of lesbian magazines began, most of them separatist (that is, anti-male). Their names hint at their strident spirit and political independence: *Amazon, Dyke, Lesbian Feminist, The Furies, So's Your Old Lady*, and, one of the largest, *Amazon Quarterly*. There was the *Lavendar* [sic] *Morning* in Kalamazoo; *Lavendar* [sic] *Wave* in Long Beach, California; *Lavender Reader* in Santa Cruz, California; *Lavender Woman* in Chicago; and *Lavender Vision*, in Boston, which advocated gay nationalism and separatism. One editor typical of the era, apparently named Elana Dykewomon, of *Sinister Wisdom* (published from 1976 to 1994) wrote in 1987: '*Sinister Wisdom* is a place. A country. To which lesbians add their own villages, their own geography, issue by issue' (Dykewomon 1987: 3). They experimented with all kinds of schemes for attracting attention, for defining their mission, for language and even for pricing. Several used the words 'wimmin' or 'wymyn' to avoid using the word 'men', while *Lavender Woman* simply replaced the word with 'pricks' (Streitmatter 1995: 161). *Lesbian Tide* (published from 1971 to 1980) not only elected to offer only news, and only news about lesbians, but also rejected information from straight people or gay men (Streitmatter 1995: 161). *Focus: A Journal for Lesbians*, a Boston-based paper published from 1971 to 1983, at one point charged $3.50 a year, but $4.50 if delivered in a brown wrapper. *Tribad*, based in New York City, was subtitled 'A Lesbian Separatist Newsjournal' and stated on its cover 'TO BE SOLD TO AND SHARED BY LESBIANS ONLY'. Many of them were published by collectives, such as *Albatross*, which was produced by a women's collective in East Orange, New Jersey. The *Furies* was begun in 1972 by a collective of twelve women who lived in three houses in Washington, DC and who pooled their incomes from their side jobs. After ten issues they ran out of money – or things to say – but members of the collective later became involved in Diana

Press, a major lesbian publishing company, and Olivia Records, an all-woman record company (Streitmatter 1995: 160).

All these magazines inspired membership, addressed organizational issues and problems, announced events (whether celebratory or protest) and sports (as well as sponsoring their own athletic contests), and explained services for lesbians. That is, they carried news of specific interest to lesbians, very little of which was available in mainstream media. This silence partly reflected the explicit antipathy by mainstream news editors toward homosexuality and it was partly because of the corollary resistance of editors of mainstream papers to hire lesbians (and gay men) if they were 'out of the closet'.

Edward Alwood (1996) describes a number of reporters who expressed both personal and professional antagonism toward homosexuals (primarily men) at newspapers like the *New York Times* that affected both news coverage (or lack thereof) and personnel. Loretta Lotman told journalists in 1974: 'I couldn't even get an interview for a decent journalism job because I'm a known lesbian. If you're well-established, OK, but if you're on the lower levels, management will cut you quick' (quoted in Alwood 1996: 154). Few journalists were fired for their homosexuality, although this sometimes happened, such as in the case of Christine Madsen, fired in 1972 from the *Christian Science Monitor* after seven years (Alwood 1996). Not until 1992, when the *Detroit News* began running a column by Deb Price, was there a regular column in a mainstream newspaper by someone who was openly gay (Alwood 1996: 304). The *News* was then edited by Robert Giles, who went on to teach in journalism education, and it was published by Gannett, which, as noted in Chapter 2, continues to be respected for its commitment to inclusiveness and diversity. Indeed, Price's column occasionally ran in *USA Today*, Gannett's one national paper. Some gays and lesbians began their careers at gay publications when they could not get mainstream jobs (foremost among them, Randy Shilts, who began at the *Advocate*), and of course the gay community has organized to offer critiques of mainstream news, to teach mainstream news personnel how to do better, and to help gay and lesbian organizations get their news into the mainstream news.

And now, in the new millennium, there is much better coverage of the gay men and lesbian community, and considerable support and defence when the occasion calls for it, of gay and lesbian reporters. When the National Lesbian and Gay Journalists Association (NLGJA) held its first annual convention in 1992, it attracted 300 journalists and it was able to list fifteen news organizations that officially barred discrimination, including some very large metro dailies. By the next year, NLGJA had a dozen chapters with 800 members and nearly 600 attended its convention. Beginning in the 1990s, many newspapers began covering gay issues on a regular basis and even published announcements of same-sex commitment ceremonies on the wedding and engagement pages. Alwood considers it a measure of progress that news organizations were also allowing openly gay and lesbian journalists to cover news of their community, rather than taking the position that this would represent a conflict of interest.

Although news organizations are increasingly employing openly gay and lesbian journalists, many lesbians have stayed with the lesbian press. According to one source, in 1992 there were approximately 160 publications in the US for gay and lesbian readers. Many of the publications for both gay men and women have tended to be dominated by men and men's issues, primarily because the majority of the readers are male.

The *Advocate*, for example, began as a small newsletter for Pride in Los Angeles, much like *Vice Versa*, but for gay men: typed on a typewriter, and printed on cheap paper. It went on to become a commodity itself, to be bought and sold as a corporation for profit. It is slick and glossy, carrying articles for consumers and ads that are targeted at high-income consumers who are attractive to advertisers such as DINKS (double income, no kids) or GUPPIES (gay, upwardly mobile, urban professionals) (Streitmatter 1995: 309).

There are fewer magazines specifically for lesbians, but the national ones themselves are also consumer-oriented and slick, emphasizing lifestyles and entertainment. *Curves*, for example, advertises its interests by billing itself as 'the best-selling lesbian magazine' and its version of involving readers is to post polls on its website asking women what they wear to the Pride parade. *Curves* was launched in 1991 as *Deneuve*, and then renamed *Curve* after a trademark dispute with the actress Catherine Deneuve; and when it says it profiles women 'who really are making a difference', it refers to Rosie O'Donnell, Melissa Etheridge and Ellen DeGeneres. Alcohol companies such as Absolut, Beefeater and Budweiser are prominent among their advertisers. *Girlfriends*, subtitled 'Lesbian Culture, Politics, and Entertainment', features celebrity interviews. Its covers could be the covers for *Vogue*, with the models' 'come hither' looks, and the questions addressed to readers on its on-line message board ask for feedback on who should be their 'Girlfriend of the Month', who should be on the cover and who should be included in their annual 'Men We Love' feature. Even the oldest of the national lesbian magazines, the Los Angeles-based *Lesbian News*, features lesbian arts and entertainment, love advice and astrological predictions from the magazine's 'professional astrologer'.

In Britain, most periodicals aimed at lesbian readers are not aimed exclusively at this group. The narrower range of magazines reflects the smaller population and market in Britain compared to the US. The glossy monthly magazine *DIVA* is one which does serve a lesbian audience. Regarded as a 'positive, vibrant look at lesbian life in the UK',[5] it is a successful contemporary magazine launched in 1994 reporting on lesbian life and style and serving audiences across Europe. Its articles focus on such issues as lesbian parenting, forms of discrimination against lesbians and lesbian activism, and it contains photo features. For example, in the July 2003 issue number 87, *DIVA* contained articles on the following topics: the British government proposals to introduce civil registration of same-sex partnerships, reporting that lesbian and gay couples in England and Wales will benefit from the same rights enjoyed by married people over pension, inheritance tax, property and social security; and a school teacher who was forced out of her job by a campaign of harassment by pupils and found that the Sex Discrimination Act does not protect lesbian, gay or bisexual employees from abuse or dismissal on the grounds of sexuality, and so lost her case in the House of Lords. As well as classifieds, *DIVA* offers information on lesbian-authored or lesbian-themed books, videos and CDs. *G3* is a free independent glossy monthly for 'gay, urban women', distributed through gay venues; it provides features and reviews as well as information on arts, culture, community, sport, Internet, music, bars and clubs. Other magazines aimed at both gay and lesbian readers include *Attitude*, a monthly glossy magazine mainly but not exclusively for gay men, with features, interviews, fashion and lifestyle sections, and reviews ranging from the arts to books, films, nightlife, food and grooming products; *Fluid*, a gay club and culture glossy monthly magazine; *qx international*, a free weekly glossy magazine which covers the London gay scene with a pull-out classified advertisement section, referred to as 'interesting, popular and perhaps lewd';[6] *DNA magazine*, a free monthly student-style satirical magazine. There are a number of regional magazines for gay and lesbian readers in the UK such as *Uncover*, a free monthly glossy, gay lifestyle magazine catering for the south east of England, and *Midlands Zone* magazine, the biggest monthly glossy gay magazine in the Midlands.

Women's alternative news periodicals from 1980 to the present

The women's movement became dispersed during the mid-1980s in Margaret Thatcher's Britain and, within a celebration of individualism and consumerism, the mainstream news media began to talk about something called 'post-feminism'. Yet in 1985, *Everywoman* and *Women's Review* were launched in Britain to join *Spare Rib*'s mission. It was said that feminism had been so successful in its hey-day that many of its oppositional ideas had shifted to become mainstream. 'Post-feminism' came to signify feminism's broader and multiple components and it became increasingly difficult to identify the distinctive features that set it apart from non-feminist discourses. As Janet Winship (1987: 154) suggests, mainstream women's magazines and news media began to draw on a self-parodying humour aimed at the discontented and at post-feminism. Women could now laugh at images that made them look like a 'piece of meat' or a 'tart' by hyping up these styles and using them for their shock value, as the punk movement did. It was during this period that the Sunday newspapers were pursuing women readers with colour supplements promoting consumer lifestyles along with the more traditional women's magazines. And men's magazines were beginning to enter the market, opening up fashion products for men and exploring new modes of masculinity. However, as two members of the *Spare Rib* collective remarked, '"post feminism" is feminism without the politics' (quoted in Winship 1987: 150).

In the meantime, in the United States both popular culture institutions and mainstream news media began to promote the idea of the superwoman, a 'new woman' who was independent and totally in control, who enjoyed a successful career without stinting on her domestic and maternal responsibilities. The notion of the superwoman was a congratulatory one but depoliticized, reflecting the steady rise in married middle-class women's employment during the 1980s. It conveyed the idea that self-confidence, self-motivation and personal assertiveness would miraculously overcome all structural gender inequalities. A more diluted version existed in Britain during the recession period of the 1980s, portrayed in such magazines as *Working Woman*, which was imported from the States. Women's careers were taken very seriously in this periodical, in stark contrast to the raft of conventional women's magazines that emphasized cosy domesticity and fashion.

Everywoman was set up by a small collective as a feminist periodical in 1985 in reaction to the 'superwoman' phenomenon, as Winship (1987) argues. Yet during the advent of post-feminism in the 1980s, which made *Spare Rib* seem militant and puritan, at least until its redesign, *Everywoman* and *Women's Review* had to counter the idea that feminism was dated. During this period the feminist periodicals were expanding and becoming more varied. Unlike conventional magazines that used a personalized style, *Everywoman* was a news and current affairs magazine aimed at feminists and non-feminists alike – 'real women' – with a plain black-and-white documentary appearance rather than a glossy look. It was informational and liberal in approach with articles on a wide range of subjects aimed at improving women's lives through campaigns and pressure groups as well as containing a 'style' section on food and fashion (Winship 1987).

The objective of *Women's Review* was more focused: to offer a woman's approach to the arts and culture, especially 'high' culture, rather than popular culture. Nevertheless, it covered diverse issues including romantic fiction, Madonna and bodybuilding – topics that *Spare Rib* could not handle as a result of its strong political stance (Winship 1987). With a small readership, *Women's Review* was burdened by financial difficulties. Like *Spare Rib* and many other feminist alternative media groups, *Women's Review* relied on subsidy from the Greater London Council, which was dissolved under the prime ministership of Margaret Thatcher along with many other sources of funding. Other feminist magazines of the period included *Outwrite*, *Trouble and Strife*, *Wsafiri* and *Gossip*.

Ms. Magazine

In the United States, the exception to the rule that distinguishes mainstream and alternative sources of news is *Ms. Magazine*, the one example of a hybrid. Some people highlight its attempt to popularize feminism from within the Madison Avenue publishing context: that is, with the glossy high production values of a mass-market periodical. But it can also be legitimately regarded as alternative, as putting readers' interests above profit even before it dispensed with all advertising. Certainly, with a circulation of 400,000–500,000 (and a readership of 3 million) it is the largest feminist periodical. As one early critic noted, 'There is a female mind-set on those glossy pages slipping into American homes concealed in bags of groceries like tarantulas on banana boats' (quoted in Farrell 1998).

Ms. Magazine's preview issue appeared in December 1971 as an insert in 300,000 copies of *New York* magazine. It was co-founded by Gloria Steinem, who started working as a journalist in New York City in 1960, gaining particular attention for her article about working as a waitress at Hugh Hefner's Playboy Club, and then writing a political column for *New York* magazine. Steinem was a feminist. In the spirit of a grandmother who had been president of a state suffrage organization in the early 1900s, in 1981 Steinem, along with famous feminists Betty Friedan, Bella Abzug and Shirley Chisholm, founded the National Women's Political Caucus. After *Ms.* first appeared some 85,000 subscription cards were returned; and the preview alone drew 20,000 letters when, as Farrell (1998) notes, most quarterly magazines receive 400 letters per issue. Over time, *Ms.* received 200 letters per month, a huge number, given its circulation. *Ms.* cannot print all letters, of course, but consistent with its reader-centred philosophy, it publishes more letters than do mainstream periodicals. In any case, readers write to *Ms.* as if to a sister, lover or comrade who they imagine listening to their stories, being supportive – somewhat like a mass consciousness-raising group.

Ms. is an inherently contradictory text, although the precise nature of the contradiction has changed over time. First was the tension between feminism and capitalism: the contradictory responsibilities to readers and to advertisers/founders. Readers were not very sympathetic to the position of advertisers. Moreover, the audience itself has been divided, with each faction always sure that its position is the valid one. Some readers complain there is too much about lesbians and others have demanded more news about lesbians. Some readers demand more news about domesticity and others want no news about homemakers. Moreover, the magazine has held multiple and even contradictory intentions – to serve activists, to attract converts (i.e. by being easy to read, visually pleasing), to raise money for the movement, to support the advancement of women in the hierarchy of the publishing industry so that they can reform women's magazines and their market. Gloria Steinem famously described in a widely reprinted article how the magazine's refusal to let itself be co-opted meant the loss of many potential accounts (Steinem 1994). Revlon killed plans to advertise in *Ms.* after four Russian women, exiled for publishing underground material or *samizdat,*[7] appeared on a *Ms.* cover without make-up. When *Ms.* not only refused to provide complementary copy but reported that hair dyes at the time might be carcinogenic, Clairol stopped advertising with them. *Ms. Magazine*'s exposé did not stop the influence of advertising and advertisers on journalism, and particularly their clout among women's magazines, but it can take the credit for blowing the whistle on this.

Indeed, *Ms.* appeared for over a decade as an 'adless' magazine, supported entirely by subscriptions and magazine rack sales. Presumably during those years it suffered no compulsion to attract a mass audience or merely the readers desirable to advertisers. Ironically, Farrell (1998) says that the new adless *Ms.* lost its popularity, its ability to speak to and mobilize a wide range of people. She claims that the elitism of the 'alternative' rather than the censorship of the 'commercial' came to constrain *Ms.* Several critics attributed the failures of *Ms.* to its wrong-headed or impossible 'liberal feminist' notion of a universal womanhood, of a unified version of women. In any case, in 2002 the magazine reorganized once again, going into partnership with the Feminist Majority Foundation. The new bi-monthly accepts limited advertising (in number of pages per issue) for like-minded organizations, but it does not accept the kinds of advertising that have bedevilled conventional women's magazines.

Like many magazines, *Ms.* maintains a website – one that is particularly well-designed, and enables interactive continuation of its politics. The site has a calendar section, updated news and a poll. Besides sponsoring live on-line chats, the site has plenty of space for readers to register their opinions on issues of the day and to respond to one another. Presumably this new design did not solve all its problems or ease all tensions, but we would argue that *Ms.* deserves credit for continuing to struggle to bring feminist news and alternative perspectives to a mass audience. With a grant from the Ford Foundation, it has established a world reporting desk – at a time when many mainstream papers are reducing their commitment to international news – and thus can legitimately boast of having the most extensive coverage of international women's issues of any US magazine.

Recent trends in alternative and feminist print journalism

Additional print outlets for alternative and feminist journalism continue to come and go. Most of the developments within feminist journalism in the new millennium seem to emphasize sassiness, edginess, or at least humour, even at the same time that they aim to create and sustain a global network of women and claim to be provocative, fierce, challenging and visionary. They tend, however, to be more 'cutting edge' with respect to funkiness than political vision. *BUST*, for example, has adopted the slogan 'for women with something to get off their chests' and describes itself as the 'Voice of the New Girl Order'. Unlike feminists of the second wave, who refused to answer to 'girls', these third-wave feminists are apparently defined as, to quote *BUST*'s own self-advertising, 'today's sassy girls who know that *Vogue* is vapid, *Glamour* is garbage, and *Cosmo* is clueless'. These magazines avoid the to-do lists, how-to advice and pop psychology quizzes of *Vogue* and *Cosmopolitan*.

Similarly, *Bitch*, whose slogan is 'Feminist Response to Pop Culture', carries critiques of television, movies, magazines and advertising with a focus on 'cool', smart women. Lisa Jervis, its editor and publisher, notes that on one hand feminism has made gains in the last thirty years that have brought changes in women's lives. The bad news, however, is that feminism is routinely ridiculed and misrepresented, often by intention, in the news and entertainment media. Among other things, 'girl power' and 'girl culture' are more about fashion and marketing than politics or social change. *Bitch*, which is based in Oakland, California, not only critically examines images of femininity and feminism available in media by analysing the agendas of the makers and commercial sponsors of socio-cultural messages, but also publicizes 'girl-friendly' media.

One of the funnier outlets is *Hip Mama*, which began as a forum for young mothers and single parents but takes on all kinds of parenting issues for 'progressive families'. The quarterly magazine, based in Portland, Oregon, discusses legislative reform, raising a draft dodger, guerrilla mothering and other 'true challenges and rewards' of creating a family. *Hip Mama* is the 1993 brainchild of Ariel Gore, who is mother of a teenager and remains the editor and publisher. Bee Lavender launched and edits the on-line version, as well as new projects like *Girl-Mom*, a site for teen parents; *Mamaphonic*, an arts resource site; and *Yo Mama Says*, with activist news. The two women have both written and co-written other books. Bee says 'I was radicalized by my experience of being a parent, yet never saw my story or any honest stories in the media'. *Hip Mama* is the only parenting publication whose objective is to explores the real experience of parenthood, not just the superficial aspects. But Bee notes that the websites actively incubate real-life communities; women can find each other on the *Hip Mama* sites and organize in cities across the continent.[8]

Several periodicals have emerged, but then folded, which aimed to serve large and obese women, including *Radiance*, published from 1984 to 2000, as part of what it called the 'worldwide size acceptance movement'. It then sought a new publisher, although to date does not seem to have found one. A publication that came and went even more quickly is *Said It*, which emphasized feminist perspectives on news of the day, including national and especially international politics. In 2003 it stopped appearing in print, but is still available on-line. It had carried articles about global sex traffic and slavery, international violence, Afghanistan, Iran, Canada and feminist activism in Thailand. Clearly these feminist publications had their loyalists, such as 'I.B.', who posted the following message on the *Said It* website:

I just ran into Said It yesterday and have been up late for two nights in a row unable to stop reading it. I LOVE IT! Reading this infused me with a stronger commitment towards fighting the good fight, not just in my own mind but in real time as well, I am trying to become a stronger woman and it's good to see I am not alone. I'm sad to see that there will be no more publications but I am sure that I am not the only woman who has been moved and energized by reading Said It. So you can probably expect a huge donation one day (like ten or twenty dollars – wish I could donate a million) because regardless of future publications what I am reading now on the web is good enough for me to get up off my ass and actually contribute some sort of money towards.

(<http://www.saidit.org>)

Conclusion

While several groups experimented with non-hierarchical structures for producing their newspapers and magazines or cable news shows, most of them tended to be led by one or two women, with help from family or a small core of volunteers. Few of them had professional staff either in Britain or the United States; at best, they were printed by professional printers. Most of them did accept fairly professional values in terms of their writing per se (although not in terms of their choice of topics). In this sense, one of the 'radical' exceptions in the United States was *Notes from the First Year*, which was initially conceived as an annual summing up – unedited – of the discussions from 'rap' sessions and consciousness-raising, as well as positions papers by some radical feminists in New York.

Print media continue to be relatively easy and inexpensive to produce. Relative to television or radio broadcasting, or film, they require little capital investment, few technical skills and little access to complex, expensive technologies. These can be, and usually are, produced by a few people without professional media backgrounds. Feminist newsletters, pamphlets, journals and magazines are typically produced on low budgets and therefore – or, as a matter of principle – with primitive production values. Moreover, because politically alternative print media require little money to produce or operate, and do not need to charge much (especially since the goal is not making a profit), people are free to work for the sake of the project, without worrying about appeasing advertisers. Producers and readers of the feminist press have enjoyed a sense of community, a literal and spiritual identity; on one hand, knowing their definite, if small, mailing list, and on the other, receiving and sharing readers' submissions, including, of course, letters to editors (as well as exchanges from other editors). Second-wave feminist periodicals devote considerably more space to readers' letters and commentary than did traditional women's magazines. Some of them dedicate a great deal of space to community access and invite readers' submissions. In particular, the second-wave feminists produced their alternative journalism in alternative formats and with innovative organizations, often non-hierarchical collectivities. In some cases jobs and titles were rotated, or some collectives made all decisions as a body and dispensed altogether with titles and bylines.

Among the noteworthy limitations of print materials, distribution can rarely be free. As a result, feminists have experimented with many ways of subsidizing and pricing their publications to make them accessible. They have often encouraged their 'converts' to buy additional subscriptions for others, to enlarge and broaden the readership.

Meanwhile, not only are non-subscribers unlikely to flip through such a periodical on the news stand, availability is increasingly unlikely. The major bookstore chains and supermarkets may offer *Ms.* among the dozens of conventional consumer magazines. The others can only be found at small independent bookshops, which are themselves a dying breed. The *Feminist Bookstore News* ceased publication in 2000, after twenty-four years, given what for its publisher Carol Seajay were the brutal economics of the book industry; meanwhile, according to the Feminist Bookstore Network, between 1997 and 2001 the number of women's bookstores in the US and Canada dropped from 120 to 74 (Gibbons 2003). As a result, non-subscribers will not 'happen' to see a magazine's contents in the way that people flipping through their home television set's daily offerings might happen upon a cable access show.

Even if women's alternative print journalism continues to serve primarily the already converted, and if most publications continue to last only a few years, the medium itself will not die. Phyllis Holman Weisbard, a women's studies librarian at the University of Wisconsin-Madison who also co-edits *Feminist Collections*, a journal of women's studies resources, was recently quoted as saying that this ebb and flow is natural and inevitable: 'They come and go. I think over time, people lose steam; they move into other endeavors' (quoted in Gibbons 2003). Holman said that every issue of her quarterly reports some new periodical (although especially on-line titles). Holman conceded, however, that they may have 'a hard time pulling in new blood'.

9

Women's alternative media in broadcasting and the Internet

This chapter shows that a major aim in women's professional and amateur experiments in radio, terrestrial and cable television, and the Internet as alternative ways of disseminating news has often been the development and sharing of skills in using new technologies. Echoing the themes of the previous two chapters, however, women have experienced various organizational, technical and financial difficulties in sustaining these initiatives. British and American radio and television offer somewhat different opportunities for journalistic experimentation. The use of the Internet as a potentially global tool for producing and disseminating women's alternative news raises questions about women's role in new media technology, the rise of virtual communities and democratic participation in the public sphere. Internet radio specifically is still at an emergent stage, but is becoming an important forum for women's programming.

Producing feminist television is particularly difficult for several reasons. First, the enormous costs of establishing/operating a television station make owning their own television station virtually impossible for small feminist organizations (or even fairly large national ones). Given the role of advertising on commercial TV, producing a feminist series for a single city, much less for a national audience, is almost as unlikely. Dramas or situation comedies with feminist subtexts are possible, and many popular culture scholars find such subtexts; talk shows may have hosts who are self-identified as feminist. But an 'explicitly' feminist public affairs programme is a different story. Second, television's complex technical demands essentially require that some, if not all, of the producers of television programming have technical training. They need not all be professionals but they need to learn basic broadcasting skills. Even producing a fairly primitive programme necessitates a core mass of people; this job cannot be done on the spur of the moment, at home or alone. The very structure of television mitigates against this, and especially in commercial television. Efforts to create feminist and non-hierarchical working practices to counter male-dominated professional routines have, therefore, been difficult, since it is virtually impossible to establish such practices in mainstream television broadcasting. Finally, the dependence of commercial television on advertising revenue necessitates mass audiences of consumers to whom products and services are targeted. Alternative audiences are not so likely to be avid consumers. Moreover, advertisers will demand highly sophisticated, professional production values.

Women's alternative radio

Compared to television women have had more successes, but also their fair share of challenges, in the less expensive and more flexible medium of radio. In many countries, pirate radio and short wave have been used to open up access to alternative formats or alternative programming. In the United States, a low-power television (LPTV) station, which can broadcast a radius of twenty to thirty miles, can be set up for about $80,000 (which is relatively little); and the Federal Communications Commission (FCC), which began issuing licences for LPTV in 1982, still has thousands of licences available.

Some grassroots and oppositional radio stations also operate at very low power illegally. Black Liberation Radio, which has operated since 1987 from a housing project in Springfield, Illinois, has inspired a radio resistance movement exploiting unused parts of the FM spectrum in the name of democracy. However, in the United States, free-market rhetoric and commercial power have managed to crush these kinds of possibilities such that politically and culturally minority voices are virtually excluded. In the 1960s, Jerome Barron and others proposed that the US First Amendment[1] itself implied right of access to the mass media. None the less, not only did Supreme Court decisions end this hopeful idea with respect to print (Pember 1987), but also the Federal Communications Commission has not recognized rights of access to the airwaves by citizens without broadcast licences (Engelman 1990).

US experiments in feminist radio have been relatively sparse, although the left-wing 'progressive' network WBAI has aired feminist programmes, as have assorted college and university radio stations. Many of these have emphasized music and poetry rather than news, and so, strictly speaking, these are not key to the history of journalism we discuss here. Several radio shows have served gay, lesbian, bisexual and transsexual (GLBT) audiences, including *This Way Out*, which first aired in 1988 on twenty-six stations across the US, and lasted thirteen years. Like the magazines, these radio shows have been particularly important in reaching gay youth and adults who are in the closet and/or live in rural areas. For over ten years a commercial radio station in Boston has run a show for the gay and lesbian community. *One in Ten* is named after the statistic widely held among gays and lesbians about their percentage in the overall population and is a news and talk show with a lesbian co-host; it includes discussion and phone-in opportunities. In 2001 GAYBC.com, an Internet broadcasting company closed down, but its founders immediately began planning an on-line and digital gay radio network.

The Women's International News Gathering Service, WINGS,[2] is an all-woman independent radio production company that makes and distributes specifically feminist news and current affairs programmes for women across the world. Its programmes are used by non-commercial radio stations as well as by the National Women's Studies Association and individuals. These programmes can be heard on local radio stations, short-wave radios and cassettes as well as over the Internet. WINGS founder Frieda Werden also began a feminist cable access programme, also based in Texas (Werden 1996).

Women's radio stations in Britain

Until 1973 the BBC controlled *all* airwaves, so it was not until the mid-1970s that any experimentation outside the strict BBC ethos emerged. The so-called 'community radio' that emerged in the 1980s was actually a wholly commercial initiative established by Margaret Thatcher's Conservative government to erode the BBC's monopoly. In fact, community radio was regarded by many feminists and socialists to be part of the British Conservative party's attempt to deregulate and commercialize all radio, and so undermine not only the public service ethos of the BBC but also the quality of British broadcasting in general. Furthermore, notwithstanding the support – in principle – for equal opportunities, community radio's track record was as bad as mainstream radio for its male dominance and sexual stereotyping both in staffing and programme content. The first women's radio station in the UK was Fem FM, which began broadcasting in 1992. This Bristol station was followed by six more women's radio stations.

Women's alternative journalism in British radio began in a small way in 1979, with a radio collective called Women's Radio Workshop, later renamed Women's Airwaves (WAW), and funded by local arts and the Equal Opportunities Commission. WAW's objective was to publicize feminist issues to mass audiences on established, mainstream local stations. Around the same time, the Black Women's Radio Group was set up. These collectives produced feminist radio programmes on such issues as women and work, young black women, violence against women, housing and lesbian lifestyles. Such issues are now regarded as fairly mainstream but were then considered very radical (Mitchell 2000: 95).

Pirate radio stations that sprang up around London during the early 1980s allowed small groups and individuals to participate in radio. For example, a programme called *Gaywaves* had been intended to include lesbian producers, but the programme remained dominated by gay men (Hooligan 1987 quoted in Mitchell 2000: 96). *Women on the Waves* was a feminist programme featuring updates about Greenham Common Women Peace campaigners as well as music. Pirate radio was, however, subject to government raids and hampered by financial difficulties. In mainstream local radio, women were engaged in alternative projects such as the establishment of the post of woman's radio producer within the Cardiff Broadcasting Company, a Welsh commercial radio station owned in part by a community trust. The position was funded by the Equal Opportunities Commission and developed a range of programmes on women's health. Interestingly, this project developed guidelines for advancing women's issues in commercial radio (Baehr and Ryan 1984). There was some talk of transforming Radio London into a woman's station to be run by women for women and for an ethnically and generationally diverse audience, but the BBC could not cope with the idea. As a result, despite its commercial frame, the community radio sector in the UK was to be the only opportunity for women to experiment in radio.

During the late 1980s, when the Independent Broadcasting Authority awarded ten licences to community radio stations, women's programmes and women presenters were given a chance to develop but only on an ad-hoc basis. For example, a magazine programme entitled *Woman to Woman* was broadcast on Bristol's For the People radio station (Mitchell 2000: 97). During this period, feminist radio activists endorsed the training of women to use broadcasting to communicate their views. Women's Airwaves changed its name to Women's Radio Group (WRG) and extended its activities to encompass the training of women for mainstream and community radio. Members of the group were involved in Celebration Radio and Viva! Radio (Mitchell 2000). The black community in London was represented by the Black Women's Radio Group (BWRG). Given the BBC's lack of black reporters and producers, black women's issues were sidelined, aired at off-peak times on the BBC.

In the 1990s, UK broadcasting legislation and policy continued to lump commercial and community broadcasting structures together, with only small numbers of stations running under a community charter. However, feminist activists were able to launch all-women short-term stations for women audiences by drawing on a Restricted Service Licence (RSL). This supported groups in the setting up, running and financing of a community station, thus enabling women to experiment on a variety of levels (Mitchell 2000: 97). Fem FM inspired the emergence of several other women's stations, including Elle FM, based in Merseyside, Radio Venus in Bradford, 107 The Bridge on Wearside Celebration Radio, and Brazen Radio in London. Most of these enterprises were aimed at challenging mainstream portrayals of women; they also provided access to community-oriented training and airtime, so that women could have their voices heard (Mitchell 2000). Elle FM, for example, offered programmes about health, employment, arts and cultural activities. During the era of 'post-feminism', exemplified in the 1990s in mainstream popular and news media (with market-led representations of fictitious superwomen who found time to juggle successful careers, a family and a sexy image), 'feminism' confronted increasing hostility. Yet, some exciting and novel programmes were aired including Brazen's *Men's Minute* – in response to the veteran *Woman's Hour* on BBC Radio 4 – dealing with important issues about men's experiences of male sexuality. Fem FM's success in women's alternative news journalism has been demonstrated by the placement of many of its news items on the satellite channel Sky News, BBC Radio 4 and in national newspapers (Mitchell 2000).

Radio stations such as Fem FM and Elle FM relied on volunteers to develop the stations, raise money and provide training. Venus depended on a small number of paid workers. While none of the women's radio stations made a profit, some had commercials and sponsored programmes. Charity organizations and foundations funded certain initiatives, and others relied on grants from local community, education and arts ventures. Music figured prominently and the weekend programmes were wide-ranging to attract a broad audience; yet ethnic minority and immigrant community audiences were also served. Fem FM had no specific lesbian programmes, although lesbian and straight women developed a strong partnership on the production side. The main feature of these radio stations was the absence of male pre-senters, but otherwise they had the same wall-to-wall advertising and unrelenting chart music of conventional commercial stations.

Viva! Radio was Britain's first full-time women's commercial radio station to receive a licence. Established in 1994, it was run by a group of highly experi-enced women. Viva! divided its airtime equally between music and speech – consisting of news, current affairs and family issues from a feminist perspective.

Women's alternative television programmes

Television programming in the UK has always been structured according to implicit assumptions about cultural differences between men and women. Yet, as Rosalind Coward (1987: 97) points out, policy makers have persis-tently discouraged production of programmes designed for women audiences only, arguing that it would exacerbate gender inequalities. Roger Laughton, who became the BBC's Head of Daytime Television in 1986, told Coward (1987: 98) in a personal interview in the same year:

> We've got *Woman's Hour* on the radio and I don't think that we need to recreate that on television. It's the same argument that applies to women's pages in newspapers. We shouldn't need them. I'd argue that we're in a post-revolutionary situation. Far more people are now affected by a femi-nine (as opposed to a woman's) viewpoint and this should be incorporated into the mainstream of TV.

Such views and the policies supporting them not only blocked general pro-gramming for women but also explain why feminist programming never flourished. Standard television newscasts do, however, provide some attention to gender issues and debates, often by using feminist or other non-mainstream sources and experts. Broadcast news shows and documentaries have dealt with abortion and other issues of particular import to women, including childcare, health, poverty, divorce, as previous chapters about the role of women journalists indicated. That said, there is virtually no 'alternative' broadcast television in the United States or in Britain.

Examples of current affairs programmes produced for and by women in British mainstream television demonstrate the kinds of difficulties feminist production teams encounter in their attempts to develop alternative ways of working. The 1981 Broadcasting Act directed Channel 4 to transmit programmes to serve those minority interests not catered for by the first commercial channel, ITV, and to 'innovate and experiment' in programme style and composition. Beginning in 1982, Channel 4 was the obvious platform for women in the independent sector because, unlike the existing three national channels at the time, it was expected to buy at least some of its programming from independent companies.

Despite its commitment to experiment and innovate, and the fact that Channel 4 had acknowledged that most television served men's interests, even Channel 4 displayed a reluctance to develop programmes aimed at women. In a radical move, Channel 4 commissioned women's production companies, with notable women teams producing current affairs series such as *20/20 Vision* and *Broadside*. However, they were all short-lived, demonstrating a lack of commitment by the channel to the success of women's programmes. Coward (1987) claims that these women-centred initiatives were 'allowed to fail' and were treated by Channel 4 simply as 'interesting experiments'. Two key examples of attempts to address women's needs discussed below are a current affairs programme produced by all-woman teams and a magazine-style programme launched in 1985.

The lack of television news and current affairs programmes from women's standpoint was being raised in a number of quarters by the early 1980s. The idea of handing over Channel 4's weekly current affairs series to an all-women production team was initiated by the Women's Broadcasting and Film Lobby (WBFL) in 1980 and taken up by Channel 4 in 1982. A Channel 4 press release denied that its 'journalistic experiment' was related to 'positive discrimination or social justice' (Baehr and Spindler-Brown 1987). Stating that it wanted to incorporate new ideas and viewpoints, Channel 4 turned over production of its new series to two new production companies: a two-woman team experienced in television production, which produced a series called *20/20 Vision*, and a twelve-member feminist team for *Broadside*, composed of women with expertise as producers, directors, researchers and camera operators. Yet within a year of their first programmes, the initiative had been terminated. As Baehr and Spindler-Brown (1987) point out, these two companies were under great pressure and treated as exemplars of all women's television work. It is not clear why the series were axed. Similar problems were confronted by other independent production companies. It is significant, however, that during this period Channel 4 was competing for higher audience ratings and therefore was in the process of appraising its commissioning and programming strategy. As part of this process its documentary programmes were reduced in order to make way for an expansion in entertainment programming.

According to Baehr and Spindler-Brown (1987), the feminist standpoint of *Broadside*'s team shaped not only its content but also its ways of working. The team members were shareholders who had been working together since 1979 and were committed to advancing opportunities for women in the media industry. While feminist approaches had succeeded in alternative publishing and filmmaking, alternative forms of production, distribution and consumption in broadcasting had been severely restricted. The members of the *Broadside* team had already worked in mainstream television, where they were hindered in their attempts to produce programmes that reflected women's interests and views (Baehr and Spindler-Brown 1987: 120). Typically, 'women's interests' were regarded by senior male colleagues as 'minority interests'. *Broadside* sought editorial control and wanted to develop an alternative set of 'professional' values, but their aim was not simply to appeal to other feminists and the metropolitan avant garde. The *Broadside* team's aim was to create programmes that would be accessible to a wider group of women: mainstream television viewers.

Sixteen *Broadside* programmes were made despite severe economic constraints; it had half the budget of established programmes such as *TV Eye* or *World in Action*. Economic pressures and the need to fulfil 'professional' norms led to constraints on experimentation. Nevertheless, in terms of programme topics and perspectives, *Broadside* was highly successful, managing to develop programmes reported from a woman's standpoint. The team delivered a 'scoop' on the rise in cancer following British and Australian atom bomb tests in South Australia in the 1950s (Baehr and Spindler-Brown 1987: 124). The documentary on alternative treatments for breast cancer was told from the viewpoint of cancer survivors rather than that of the medical profession. And women's viewpoints and experiences were foregrounded in discussions of the women's peace movement and the Irish referendum on abortion. However, the trend towards using freelance production teams hired on short-term contracts meant that the *Broadside* team had little time to assess its programmes after transmission or to learn from its achievements and weaknesses. According to Baehr and Spindler-Brown (1987) Channel 4 terminated its contract with *Broadside* because Channel 4 decided that women's viewing needs were being well represented by existing commissioning editors and producers.

As one of the first companies commissioned by Channel 4 to produce a series of programmes, the *Broadside* team's experiences are instructive. Since

then Channel 4 has been obliged to change its terms of trade to add procedures for ending long-standing series. While *Broadside* tried to challenge the
principles and customs of the television industry, it ended up actually taking
on board its professional practices and objectives. *Broadside*'s experience
demonstrates the difficulties in transcending hierarchical professional conventions in the industry.

Watch the Woman further exemplifies Channel 4's lack of commitment to
women's programmes. Planned as an evening magazine programme for
women, *Watch the Woman* was unusual in having moved away from the convention of appealing to women audiences in the daytime. But, as Coward
(1987: 100) says, its relationship to feminism was 'ambiguous'. On the one
hand it attempted to develop a magazine-style programme with a focus on
fashion, domestic and personal issues, and on the other it echoed some of the
themes of BBC Radio 4's *Women's Hour* by providing a women's perspective
on current affairs and issues. Yet, as with previous women's productions, it
was not given the time needed to establish itself.

The evidence suggests that *Watch the Woman* had an inappropriate brief to
start with and Channel 4 brought it to a close. As Coward indicates, other
programmes enjoyed far more time to establish themselves. During the mid-
1980s Channel 4 gave the impression that the feminist struggle to ensure
equal representation of women's needs and views had been accomplished.
Consistent with a post-feminist ideology, broadcast decision-makers apparently assumed that women's needs were being met because women now
figured prominently in television broadcasting. While Channel 4 has certainly tried to recruit and attract audiences from ethnic minorities, it seems to
fear being accused of ghettoizing women's interests. Without a formal and
standard way of measuring the coverage of women's issues on television,
Channel 4 was able to convey that 'all was well'. Meanwhile, although
Channel 4 certainly had a better track record in employing women's broadcasting companies during the 1980s than other channels and even had a
woman at the top as its commissioning editor, women journalists and television producers did not find equal employment opportunities (WFTVN 1986
quoted in Coward 1987: 101).

The implementation of equal employment opportunity principles by
Channel 4 was misconstrued both as proof of women's strong presence in
production and across senior levels, which clearly was not the case, and proof
that women's issues were being fully aired within television contents. While
more documentaries were transmitted about issues that affect women, including health, hygiene and childbirth, mainstream television entertainment did
not change much during the 1980s. The programming continued to favour
sport and men's other interests. News and current affairs programmes have
endeavoured to cater to women by employing women newsreaders rather
than introducing issues of interest to women. Television companies such as
Channel 4 are eloquent in identifying the range of minority audience groups

who need to be catered for and recognize that there is no unified dominant audience identities. However, experimentation against the grain tends to be discouraged. Coward (1987: 104–5) calls for a more radical critique of mainstream television that recognizes that women may have distinct interests and priorities that require distinct programming.

The US cable experiment

We might hope that cable television, now even carried by satellite, would open up a counter-hegemonic public sphere, given the larger number of channels that can be carried. In 2002 Showtime and MTV Networks apparently planned to inaugurate the first twenty-four-hour gay and lesbian channel in mid-2003, to be called 'Outlet'. It was to carry entertainment (movies) as well as news. Thus far, the cable television channel has not yet begun. The idea certainly sounds plausible, given that gay and lesbian news is not significantly covered in television news. Entertainment shows on television (including broadcast television) now include large numbers of gay and lesbian characters of varying degrees of 'outness' and sexual assertiveness, numbers that reflect both the symbolic clout of national organizations like Gay and Lesbian Alliance Against Defamation (GLAAD) and the economic clout of lesbians and especially gay men. But even this is fairly commercial, and while it may be controversial, this experiment in gay and lesbian news and entertainment is intended to make money, and will continue only if it secures a profit.

The original idea of cable and the initial enthusiasm for it, however, was as a dramatically new public sphere. There have been some explicitly feminist attempts to use cable in this way, which have enjoyed limited success. Video artists, media activists and counter-culture activists of the 1960s and 1970s experimented with video as a politically emancipatory art form. The cofounder of the controversial Raindance media collective (Shamberg 1972) advocated video technology as a participatory, decentralized, emancipatory form of communication.[3] The characteristics of video 'camcorders' – low cost, the possibility of instant playback, portability and other features that made for easy use – rendered this technology available for grassroots nonprofessionals. Today, many local governments require cable companies, as a condition of obtaining or retaining franchises, to set aside public, educational or governmental (PEG) channels and provide training, equipment and facilities for producing programmes, usually for free. Cable TV is not free but PEG channels are free in the sense that they come bundled into the basic cable package. Indeed, once highly capitalized multi-system operators began to compete for domination in the cable industry, public access gained importance as a bargaining chip.

Although in 1984 only 10 per cent of US cable systems had dedicated public access channels (Moss and Warren 1984), in 1997 nearly two-thirds of the cable systems with non-automatic origination (i.e. not merely time, weather, bulletin boards) offered public access (*Television and Cable Factbook* 1997: F-1). Activist analysts who have been personally involved in public access projects are particularly optimistic about this as a tool for democracy, if not revolutionary social change (Kellner 1990, Goldberg 1990). Many people look to Paper Tiger TV as a model. Having received a grant in 1985 to distribute programming to public access centres via satellite technology, the fledgling guerrilla television collective expanded into its Deep Dish project, the first national public access satellite network, by collating and packaging the work of some 100 grassroots video producers into hour-long programmes that it then uplinked through satellite transmission (Drew 1995, Lucas and Wallner 1993).

New directions in cable TV for women in the US

Feminist groups have tried to use cable in ways consistent with feminist principles to reach a larger audience and mobilize that audience on behalf of social transformation. Under the aegis of the National Organization for Women (NOW), one such collective produces what it calls 'feminist television programs'. Since 1994, over two dozen NOW members, nearly all of them members of the same NOW chapter in New Jersey, have worked on a cable television show whose name became *New Directions for Women* (*NDW*) after the series began to be cablecast more broadly. The name change coincided with the death of a nationally distributed feminist newspaper *New Directions for Women*, which a member of the local chapter had established in 1972. The programmes are taped 'talks' – interviews with a single expert or conversations among two or three people. The group uses local feminist scholars, often from nearby universities.

Several members argue – presumably implying that this is important – that the *NDW* programming is relevant to males, that men are interested in the topics selected by *NDW*, and that people don't want 'women's shows'. They want to be effective and therefore to have topics that 'resonate'. *NDW*'s first programme dealt with sexual harassment experienced by female high school students. Since then, *NDW* has dealt with, inter alia, myths about older women, legislation mandating the public school teaching of abstinence, pay equity, female athletes, women in the music business, male feminists, 'non-traditional' jobs, the economic impact of divorce, spirituality, feminist ethics, date rape and sex crimes. Several shows focused on specific women's organizations, with an emphasis on political groups and coalitions. Several shows discussed reproductive rights, the debate over late-term abortion, and so forth. Several shows have also dealt in one way or another with homosexuality, including same-sex marriage. Within *NDW*, questions continue regarding how to choose topics, how much argumentation per se should be highlighted, and whether or how to present opposing or anti-feminist viewpoints. In general, however, members agree that it is a waste of a valuable resource to present anti-feminist content.

Once a month (with some exceptions), the crew tapes the shows, each of which ultimately runs for half an hour. The show is usually produced at the facilities of the sponsoring cable system. At least six members are needed to produce each show; and the producer usually tries to recruit one or two people more than necessary, so that someone is free to learn something new. Little or no editing is done. The cable system operator provides no production assistance. Typically, on the Saturdays when the show is taped, the only company employees in the building are clerical staff, who cannot answer technical questions. This is a source of concern for the NOW group: if equipment breaks down, no one is available to find a replacement part or fix the malfunctioning equipment. Indeed, the crew members agree that the disasters have been technical or equipment-related. That said, the tapings seem quite professional, or at least calm. While setting up, which can take an hour or more, people offer and accept sisterly, friendly advice. When mistakes are made (for example, requiring the introduction to be re-taped), no shouting or personal criticism is made.

The collective unquestionably expresses the voice of the middle-class liberal feminist; and the suburban towns where most of them live are among the wealthier ones in the state. It is a white woman who volunteers, with a bit of embarrassment, how few African American members have been active in *NDW*. Furthermore, no less predictably, the group is fairly middle-aged or older, although at any point in time one or two college students are always active.

For *NDW* to collect information on its audience size or its audience response would be extremely difficult and costly. But the point is that *NDW* does not really want to measure its size – and probably does not want to guess at its impact. For the members of the *NDW* production team, the satisfaction is in mastering the high-status journalistic and technical skills necessary to create and sustain the series, and to know that *NDW* is, in its collective work, challenging the silence about feminist issues on television. Comparisons to other feminist projects show that something is lost in activity that is both literally and spiritually anonymous. The rather thin sense of community at *NDW* may seem surprising, since people are necessarily working together, until one considers just how the structured setting of the cable station forces concentration on technique and technology. Although the collective can be commended for its conception of an active audience with which it is in conversation, the producers cannot 'commune' with its audience, which remains abstract and highly distinct. Furthermore, concerned for getting things done, members rarely question who is doing the work and how it is to be done (or what is to be done). They do not take the time to experiment with alternative modes of interaction.

Women's Internet news and information groups

One of the most exciting developments in women's alternative news media is the emergence of independent news networks and 'webzines' on the Internet. Independent information distribution media projects on the Internet are quickly growing in both number and sophistication, spurred on both by dissatisfaction with the mainstream news media and increasingly easier access to new media technology. The Internet allows women individually and in groups to produce their own information and control their networks of distribution in ways that echo the women's suffrage press in the nineteenth and early twentieth centuries. Yet it goes far beyond them in terms of their geographical scope, that is, their international reach. Importantly, several of these Internet news and information networks challenge mainstream definitions of news by overtly advancing feminist initiatives regarding women's human rights, the exposure of violence against women across the globe, the expansion of women's civic participation in new democracies, the training of women to use new media technologies for networking and the encouragement of activism among women to change policy nationally and internationally. Some women's information networks also challenge the boundaries between professional journalism and non-professional writing: many either strongly encourage feedback, dialogue and participation or provide a space for women to speak for themselves directly rather than having their concerns voiced secondhand, filtered through the lens of a journalist. Webzines tend to express more of an individual writer's personality, so even when taking on major political issues, these 'zines disdain the objective or neutral voice of the professional journalist. As Angela Richardson (1996: 10) noted:

> Like their punk rock predecessors of the 1970s, today's 'zine publishers are usually individuals who see little of their lives reflected in the pages of *Time* and *Newsweek*. The realm of modern-day 'zines exists as an arena for many marginalized populations, but perhaps for no one more fittingly than feminists. Particularly in today's backlash climate, 'zines provide an alternative to, as well as an oasis from, the mainstream press's (mis)representations of our experiences as women.

In this section we give examples of some of the largest and more relevant sites of women's organizations providing web-based news for and about women, mainly originating in the US and UK yet global in range.[4] Nearly all of them maintain links to each other, or at least to other alternative and independent media resources. Our examples aside, the array changes on a daily basis, and nothing substitutes for surfing the Internet to find new sites.

Aviva, a monthly webzine run by an international group of feminists based in London, covers women's news globally (<http: //www.aviva.org/>). It obtains news from both mainstream news organizations such as Reuters, the *Guardian* and the BBC World Service, and also non-governmental organizations such as the European Organization for Human Rights, Feminist PeaceNet, Lawyers for Human Rights and Legal Aid, Amnesty International and the World Organization Against Torture. It also obtains information from other women's news networks, such as the Feminist International Radio Endeavour (FIRE) (<http: //www.fire.or.cr>) based in Costa Rica, and provides links to other relevant organizations such as the US-based International Planned Parenthood Federation (<http: //www.ippf.org/>). It 'hosts' other women's groups and services. As much as it explicitly encourages readers' submissions, however, its design is both sophisticated yet easy to navigate. As have other feminist media organizations, *Aviva* trains women in Internet design and publishing. It relies for funding on sponsorship and donations and also on revenue from advertising. It has a substantial management team, including a managing editor who also serves as its European editor, and editors for Africa, Asia, Australasia, the Middle East, North America, Latin America, as well as a children's editor. The African pages of *Aviva* provide a British ethnic minority directory and a directory of African businesses in Britain.

Aviva emphasizes women's human rights, women's and children's poverty, violence against women and children, and peace initiatives. For example, in September 2002, 'Action Alert' news came from Iran about a woman sentenced to blinding by acid and from Sudan concerning children who were sentenced to death. The international news consisted of a report on the Earth Summit. African news during the same press release was from the Democratic Republic of the Congo about the violation of women's rights and Rwanda about the abuse of women witnesses at war crimes tribunals.

International Women's Word (<http: //www.womensword.net/>), an American network of independent producers and organizations, is aimed at promoting women's participation in traditional and new media initiatives including media arts, public media spaces such as community radio, public television and on-line networks. Women's Word debuted on International Women's Day 2002. The organization is funded by the City of Austin, Texas, Women's Radio Fund, *Ms. Magazine*, Austin Free-net and Austin businesses, but its partners include the Women's International News Gathering Service (WINGS), the independent media group in Austin, Indymedia and River City Youth. Women's Word's on-line media archive is an interactive compendium of audio programming produced by independent women journalists, artists and activists. The network is producing material for the archive to be used as a universally accessible resource for academics, journalists and community activists.

A more global initiative is Indymedia Centres (<http://www.indymedia. org/>), which brings together over fifty collectively managed independent media centres across twenty-one countries. These Indymedia Centres were initiated by a range of alternative media activists to supply grassroots reportage on the 1999 World Trade Organization protests. The Seattle Independent Media Centre acted as a clearing house for journalists, and provided up-to-the-minute reports, photos, audio and video footage through its website. It has produced five documentaries, distributed to public access stations via satellite. It also produced its own newspaper, as well as hundreds of audio segments, transmitted through the Web and Studio X, a twenty-four-hour micro and Internet radio station based in Seattle (<http://www.womensword.net/resources/>). Similarly, Internews (<http://www.internews.org/activities/gender_issues/gender_issues.htm) promotes open media across the world by advancing independent media in nations with developing democracies. It advocates using the media as a tool for diminishing conflict.

Set up in 1995 by women in law, television, activism, journalism, music, marketing and communications, Feminist.com (<http: //www.feminist.com/>) is a grassroots, interactive community by, for and about women. It promotes women's business development, supports women-friendly organizations, tries to extend civic participation and to foster women's self-sufficiency. Feminist.com provides current feminist news stories, especially regarding activism; it also carries activist advice, a directory of women-owned businesses, classified ads and job postings. More to the point, its section on speaking out against global violence (by Equality Now) highlights abuses of women across the world and provides statistics on violence against women.

WomensNet, launched in 1995, is an on-line international community of people and organizations using computer technology to advance women's interests. For example, it took on a major role in circulating information at the World Conference on Women in Beijing. WomensNet is part of the Institute for Global Communications (IGC) Internet which was formed in the US in 1987. Thus it is linked to a number of like-minded organizations including PeaceNet (providing on-line services to organizations and activists working for peace, economic and social justice, human rights, labour issues and conflict resolution, etc.), EcoNet (dedicated to environmental preservation and sustainability), Anti-racism Net and LaborNet.

Linked to groups such as WomensNet via IGC are trans-national initiatives that aim to connect women across nations such as Network for East–West Women. This organization promotes communication and activism for Western women concerned about the situation of women in Eastern and Central Europe and the former Soviet Union. Instead of relying on professional journalists to report women's experiences, Network for East–West Women gives a voice to women in Eastern and Central Europe to 'tell their own stories and connect with women in the west' (<http://www.igc.org/igc/gt/Women'sNet/>).

Several feminist webzines emphasize wider debates about women. For example, the Chicago-based *Merge* calls itself a feminist 'zine (<http://www.mergemag.org>), whose aim is to increase awareness and encourage action about the way in which the media represents women and sexuality though images. Its motto is 'Back-to-Basics Feminism is the Future'. Topics of discussion in *Merge* have included the meanings of masculinity and femininity, motherhood, and the influence of media images and music lyrics on ideas about sexuality.

The Women's Institute for Freedom of the Press (WIFP) is an important research, education and publishing organization founded in 1972 to increase communication among women. It now has its own website (<http://www.wifp.org/>). It is a non-profit organization based in Washington, DC, which publishes the Directory of Women's Media, and its Associates Newsletter, *Voices of Media Democracy*.

As with magazines and newspapers, there are both lesbian-specific websites, including some linked to lesbian periodicals as well as for gay men and women. The two largest websites for the gay community (PlanetOut.com and Gay.com) have news about women and have at times been headed by women.

The Internet also offers some alternatives to the expense of buying, producing and distributing paper hard copies. In 2002 *Sojourner: The Women's Forum* suspended publication for the third time, but, as have several similar news organizations, it maintains a Web presence. Likewise, Fran Hosken, who for thirty years produced WIN (Women's International Network News) as a kind of feminist wire service, announced that she would no longer publish a paper version of WIN News after 2003, but would produce an electronic version if she could find funding.

In fact, the growth of women's Internet news and activism groups raises important questions about the democratization of the public sphere and the technological potential for individuals and groups to communicate directly with one another on an equal footing. However, women's access to this new media technology is dependent on access to a number of resources, from electricity and computers to knowledge of Internet use and website production, as well as basic reading and writing skills. Women in poor nations and poor women in rich nations continue to be divided from one another and cut off from women's organizations by unequal access to these kinds of informational and educational resources. Notwithstanding these barriers of media access, the Internet is seriously challenging traditional power relations, not only patriarchal ones but also those of mass communication. The conventional means of disseminating news from a central source for individual consumption with restricted feedback is being disrupted. Indeed, these efforts work to broaden the very definitions of news and journalism. This is not an unadulterated good. Not all Internet sites offer completely and entirely useful and credible information, and even those able to access these computer services may not have the kind of literacy that helps them determine source credibility. By mobilizing groups of women in all walks of life to participate in civic action through training in Internet use, publicizing women's issues, and active engagement in policy change via the Internet, however, the 'professional' and 'mass' media control of the public sphere is being challenged.

Conclusion

As other chapters in this book show, creating journalism to serve a truly participatory democratic, pluralistic movement is extraordinarily difficult in capitalist economies. Traditionally, within radio and television, people producing alternative media often lacked personal contact with their audiences, yet small-scale and indirect contact has also been rewarding. Interactive media also remove the barriers between sender and receiver, so audiences can participate in the communication process. Producers and readers of the feminist press have enjoyed a sense of community, a literal and spiritual identity, on one hand, knowing their definite, if frustratingly small, mailing list, and on the other, receiving and sharing readers' submissions, including, of course, letters to editors (as well as exchanges from other editors).

Alternative journalists are clearly exploiting the advantages of the Internet to publish magazines, on-line 'zines and journals. This has at least two downsides, however. First, its access is limited to those with computers or Internet access – clearly a problem when wanting to reach poorer women, especially in the developing world. Second, and this is particularly a problem for periodicals available exclusively on-line, how these materials can be preserved, archived and studied is unclear. When on-line periodicals die, their ephemeral presence on the web may disappear without a trace. This leaves future generations unable to study the periodicals or determine their contributions to journalism and history.

Mainstream television, as it currently exists in Britain and in the United States, is oppositional to women's alternative journalism. While scholars may provide readings against the grain that give a feminist spin to a variety of television shows, including in genres 'historically' associated with women, this hardly makes the argument that such programmes serve alternative groups.

Technical, structural and economic demands within cable television's public access channels seem still to present material barriers to access. Cable is not free, of course, but PEG channels are free in the sense that they come bundled into the basic cable package. There are some immediate gratifications, even beyond the personal satisfaction of demystifying technology and the collective satisfaction of demonstrating that women can master complex skills. In a relatively non-bureaucratic way, alternative news media do produce programming and promote debate outside the mainstream. Importantly, alternative women journalists have exposed the limitations of the mainstream news media by offering new ways of thinking, communicating and working outside the mainstream. However, the thin sense of community and the difficulty of sustaining excitement when no one is really working together may be true of many Internet sites. Given utopian rhetoric about the emancipatory potential of the Internet, warnings should also be issued regarding the potential for computer communications to bring people together. None the less, the Internet does seem to demonstrate and facilitate linking of organizations both regionally and internationally and thus to encourage the emergence of transnational and global communities.

10

Women war correspondents

In the wake of the September 11th attacks on the United States in 2001, women figured prominently among the international war correspondents sent to the Middle East to report on the ensuing war in Afghanistan. This sparked a lively debate in the news media about whether women should be allowed to report on wars and thereby put themselves in danger, highlighted by the Taliban's capture of British correspondent Yvonne Ridley. Some journalists and many members of the public argued vociferously that women should not risk their lives by entering war zones, particularly if they are mothers of young children, as is the case with Ridley.

Meanwhile, during the crucial first few days after September 11th, it was the stories of male journalists that dominated the front pages of British national daily newspapers. Madeleine Bunting (2001: 19), correspondent for the *Guardian*, pointed out that women were 'wiped off many newspaper pages', marginalized in a way which would have seemed 'barely possible only two weeks ago'.

The first five pages of five national dailies in the UK (the *Sun*, the *Daily Mail*, the *Guardian*, the *Daily Telegraph* and *The Times*) on 14 and 15 September were dramatically lacking in reports by women. The tabloids were much the same. No women reported for the *Sun* about the crisis on either day, although they had written about a third of the front pages the previous Friday. The *Daily Mail's* front page carried no women's contributions on that Thursday, although it recovered the next day with a major human-interest emphasis. Likewise, during the previous week women writers had taken up two-thirds of the front page and monopolized the comment pages. A similar shortage of women diplomatic correspondents emerged in the broadsheets. *The Times* published no women reporters in its first five pages or on the comment page on the Friday. The *Guardian* contained only one report by a woman, showing a 75 per cent drop from the previous week. As the *Daily Telegraph* is consistently low in figuring women journalists, there was little change.

Although newspapers, especially the broadsheets, have been slow to

advance women in areas of 'serious news' such as war reporting, the broadcast media are beginning to do so. However, we must be cautious in our
optimism, since it is difficult to ascertain whether the proportion of female
war correspondents is rising or whether they merely stand out in a male-
dominated beat. As Matt Wells of the British *Guardian* noted, the British
press sent about eighty extra British-based reporters and photographers
abroad after the September 11th attacks (Wells 2001: 2). And television channels also beefed up their international staffs. Today, women are being sent on
foreign and war assignments in such large numbers that some observers spec-
ulate that women journalists, particularly in television, are being used to
spice up the drama of war reporting in a market-driven profession. By the
1950s, less than 4 per cent of the US foreign correspondents in Europe were
women (Kruglak 1955), although women were 50 per cent of newspapers
staffs in small cities across the United States (Marzolf 1977: 69).[1] By the
mid-1980s, they accounted for 20 per cent of foreign correspondents
(Edwards 1988: 4). Presumably the number is higher now. At the very least,
reporters have suggested that women's visibility in the war zones coincides
with an important trend more generally: the use of women news presenters by
broadcasters trying to boost dwindling news audiences.

This issue was raised most recently with the case of Lara Logan, the lone
independent staffer[2] for CBS News covering the war on Iraq. Logan, formerly
a swimsuit model, had been a favourite British tabloid target – British tabloids
having long been famous for indulging in particularly sexist attacks on women,
with female reporters being no exception – when she was reporting from
Afghanistan for the morning news programme *GMTV*. Logan was no novice.
She had already worked as a staffer or freelancer for several British and US
television and cable news programmes, and had covered crises in the Middle
East, Mozambique, Zimbabwe, India and Kosovo. ITN reporter Julian
Manyon (2001: 16) acknowledged that his competitors had attributed his success in gaining access to Northern Alliance leaders to the 'considerable
physical charms of my travelling companion, the delectable Lara Logan, who
exploits her God-given advantages with a skill that Mata Hari [an exotic
dancer who spied for the German government during the First World War]
might envy'. But in 2003, *New York Times* reporter Alessandra Stanley noted
her 'sex-kitten image' would not help Logan in Iraq (Stanley 2003: B11),
meaning that her professional skills would be paramount. But Betsy West, a
senior vice president for CBS News, took Stanley to task for focusing on sexist
comments rather than framing Logan 'in the tradition of so many intrepid foreign correspondents who just happen to be female' (West 2003: A18).

Women are playing an increasingly conspicuous role in war coverage.
Besides Logan, who was working without protection in Afghanistan, every
television network in the US, for example, included women among its embedded journalism teams to report on Iraq. Many women are praised for their
prize-winning war correspondence. But their prominence has not protected

them from adverse reactions or hostile treatment. Over the decades, they have met public disapproval, military refusal of access to war zones and snide comments from male colleagues, as the response to Logan indicates.

Women war correspondents no longer suffer the same degree of prejudice or barriers confronted by women trying to cover the First and Second World Wars. None the less, they continue to evoke highly gendered attention and curiosity, in part because they are engaging in dangerous forays but also because they disrupt still-lingering stereotypes of women's conventional roles in journalism and the wider society. While their numbers are growing, women remain a minority among war reporters. The attention to war reporters is extreme: not only is this hazardous and challenging work, but it is highly competitive. Careers and reputations are often made on the basis of wartime reporting (see Knightley 1982a, McLaughlin 2002).

The controversy about women war correspondents reached furious heights after Yvonne Ridley's capture in Afghanistan in 2001. The tension between being a parent and taking the kinds of risks involved in war reporting is one that applies to both men and women. But within an ideology that continues to locate mothers' proper place in the home, women war correspondents with dependent children are much more likely to be publicly condemned for taking risks in their careers. Another example is Lucy Sichone, a columnist for Zambia's leading newspaper, who was essentially forced underground with her three-month-old daughter to avoid imprisonment for writing articles critical of the government during a state of civil war there (Stasio 1998). It is worth noting, of course, that this criticism can originate from women. Heidi Evans wondered aloud in the *Nation* whether to praise Sichone as courageous or phone the child-abuse hotline.

The dangers associated with being a war correspondent – whether male or female – are clear. According to the Committee to Protect Journalists, thirty-seven journalists were killed worldwide in 2001 (twenty-four were killed in 2000 and in the first three weeks of the War on Iraq in 2003, twelve journalists were killed[3]). Most of these journalists were not killed while covering war but were murdered in direct reprisal for reporting on sensitive topics, including official crime and corruption. Kathleen Kenna, a journalist covering the Afghan war for the *Toronto Star*, was badly wounded in March 2001 by a hand grenade thrown at her car. Kenna, forty-seven, was the *Star's* South Asia bureau chief and was travelling with three men: a photographer, the driver and her husband. In April 2001, award-winning Marie Colvin, an US-born foreign correspondent for the British broadsheet newspaper the *Sunday Times,* lost her left eye while covering fighting between government troops and suspected Tamil Tiger guerrillas in Sri Lanka. Just a month before, a hand grenade fired by government forces exploded near her. Colvin had been named 'Best Foreign Correspondent of the Year' at the British Press Awards and received a 'Courage in Journalism' award from the International Women's Media Foundation in 2000.

The personal safety risks faced by war correspondents were brought into sharp focus in November 2001 by the news that Taliban leaders promised Afghans 'blood money' for the murder of Western journalists (Traynor 2001). The Taliban leader, Mullah Mohammed Omar, announced a bounty of $50,000 (£30,000) to any Afghan who shot a Western journalist. Eight journalists were killed in seventeen days, including Maria Grazia Cutuli, a reporter for an Italian daily who was killed in a Taliban ambush along with three other journalists; and Johanne Sutton, a thirty-four-year-old journalist for Radio France International, who, along with two male journalists, was killed by Taliban forces while travelling with Northern Alliance troops. Meanwhile the military allied forces' casualty count during the first two months of war was one dead. A United Nations spokesman in Kabul, Khaled Mansour, stated that Afghanistan was too dangerous for the media and aid workers to do their jobs. Being a journalist covering the Afghan war appeared to be more dangerous than being an American or British soldier.

Gender roles are profoundly marked in the context of war, as Joshua Goldstein (2001) explains in his book *War and Gender*. The ways that men and women conform to the needs of the war system are shaped by gender norms which affect women's experiences as war correspondents. As Goldstein shows, the disturbing link between sex and violence is exemplified by the interconnection of a constructed militarized masculinity with wartime conquest, sex, rape and exploitation. Indeed, this relationship is exploited by government campaigns – carried on through the news media – aimed at demonizing the enemy, as exemplified by accounts of the Gulf War.[4] Historically, the masculine discourses of war conspired to exclude women from roles that took them to the front line of conflict, whether as soldiers or reporters. Today, not only are women entering the military, but also certain cultural constraints imposed on women are being turned to advantage by female war correspondents, who can often go undercover undetected.

This chapter details the 'special case' of female war reporters, exposing in the most extreme ways the kinds of debates and tensions continuing about the legitimacy and status of women journalists struggling to succeed in one of the toughest, roughest and most stubbornly male-dominated areas of reporting.

War reporting in the nineteenth century

Margaret Fuller (1810–1850), who began writing for the *New York Tribune* as its literary critic in 1844, is credited as the first woman foreign and war correspondent in the United States. In 1846 Horace Greeley sent her to Europe to dispatch news about the Italian revolution (ultimately it was unsuccessful) led by Giuseppe Garibaldi and to report on social conditions in Italy, France and Britain. She interviewed prominent members of Italy's political and literary community and provided first-hand reports on the French siege of Rome, which was aimed at restoring the rule of the Pope. By the time she became the *Tribune's* foreign correspondent, Fuller was already a distinguished New England intellectual. She had co-edited the Transcendentalist literary journal, the *Dial*, and published two books, including a pioneering treatise on women's rights, *Woman in the Nineteenth Century* (Fuller 1855), which called on women to be self-reliant and to demand equality with men. Through her relationship with a younger man, a twenty-nine-year-old aristocrat named Giovanni Angelo Marchese D'Ossoli, she became a fervent supporter of the struggle for Italian independence. Fuller and Ossoli had a son. In any case, it seems that Fuller and her husband decided to return to the US after their son became ill. On their way back to New York in 1850, the just-formed Italian Republic having been overthrown, all three died in a shipwreck within sight of New York harbour.

Although Margaret Fuller is now acclaimed as an outstanding intellectual, critic and scholar, the scandal associated with Fuller's personal life long coloured her reputation. A few years after her death, her friends and family destroyed a substantial amount of her personal correspondence and papers in order to protect her honour, thereby impeding research about her life. Like many educated and talented women who disrupted social customs about feminine confinement and ignored public disapproval, she exemplifies the way that women journalists' achievements can be overshadowed by a focus on their moral transgressions. During the 1960s, however, her status was publicly recovered when interest in women's history inspired re-examination (Von Mehren 1994).

At the same time that Fuller was writing for the *Tribune*, Jane McManus Storms (1807–1878) was occasionally writing for several newspapers, including the *New York Tribune*, but especially for Moses Yale Beach's *New York Sun*, the country's first successful penny press paper (Reilly 1981). The *Sun* claimed to be politically neutral, but it endorsed the Polk administration's war policies and called for the annexation of Mexico. Storms herself vigorously supported US expansion. So in 1846 when Beach was sent to Mexico on a secret peace mission, the Spanish-speaking Storms, who was then divorced, accompanied Beach to assist with the cover-up and in part to translate for Beach. Meanwhile, she wrote thirty-one letters to the *Sun* with her observations both en route (they were questioned for several days in Cuba) and then from Mexico (Reilly 1981). She reported on what turned out to be two separate battles between Mexican and American troops, as well as a civil war. Indeed, even after Beach fled back to the US, she stayed – to the annoyance of the military. Her wartime correspondence was also published (and reprinted) in several other newspapers. According to journalism historian Tom Reilly, Storms's writing was detached and analytical, and even some of her contemporaries in journalism and politics admired her writing, although Thomas Hart Benton, a powerful senator from Missouri, complained of her 'masculine stomach for war and politics' (Reilly 1981: 21). In 1847 she returned to New York and in 1848 she became the editor of *La Verdad*, a Spanish-language paper distributed clandestinely in Cuba that supported freeing Cuba from Spain (and annexing it to the US). Both her several books and her other writing were published under the pseudonym Cora Montgomery.

A few newspapers, including the *New York World* and the *New York Journal*, published reports by women about the Spanish–American war of 1898. These reports generally adopted a human-interest approach and were labelled as having a 'woman's angle'. Women's accounts tended to focus on the effects of the war, such as the conditions of the wounded and of refugees, while male war correspondents wrote about military technology, tactics and battle strategies.

Reporting on world wars

A small yet significant number of US women journalists served as war correspondents during the First World War, an accomplishment that should be seen in the context of the rise of women's professional associations as well as the larger context of the woman's rights movement, which provided a crucial basis for women's participation in the world of work.

One of the women covering the First World War was Mary Robert Rinehart. The mother of three sons, Rinehart had turned to writing fiction for magazines after a financial panic in 1903. She managed to persuade the *Saturday Evening Post* to send her to Europe well before the US even entered the war, and before many US male journalists reached the battlefields (Rinehart 1948). A trained nurse, Rinehart took special interest in the care of wounded soldiers. She tried to return to France as a nurse after America entered the war. As it turned out, the government was vehemently opposed to her returning, but in 1918 she did make it back as a reporter. Edwards (1988: 31) attributes her forgotten status both to her gender and to journalists' distrust of fiction writers.

Three American women reported on the Russian Revolution: Louise Bryant, Bessie Beatty and, most famously, Rheta Childe Dorr (1866–1948). At age fifty, Dorr went to Russia to report for the *New York Mail*. An active and avid feminist since she was twelve, Dorr had, at the age of thirty-three, separated from her husband and moved with her young son from Seattle to New York to take up a career in journalism. She acquired a job on the woman's page of the *Evening Post* but soon managed to move beyond women's clubs and charities to report on the working conditions of women factory workers. Her 1924 autobiography describes how, after a few years, she switched to freelance reporting, gaining first-hand experience about labour problems by working in several sweatshops. During this period Dorr was the first editor of a radical American suffrage organization, the *Suffragist*; and a series of articles for a reform magazine appeared in her 1910 book *What*

Eight Million Women Want (1971). Dorr joined the *New York Mail* in 1915 and wrote several articles about the Russian Revolution. However, during several subsequent trips to Europe as war reporter, Dorr was denied access to the front as a woman (Dorr 1924).

The stories of several women who reported during the two world wars, and especially during the Second World War, underscore similar degrees of courage and determination, but also point to the heightened sexualization of women reporters, arguably to a far greater degree than women reporting in other arenas. Some women seem not to have been particularly bothered by the attention to their bodies. Perhaps this is because they had no choice or perhaps it is related to their willingness to acquire reporting assignments by claiming that they would provide a different angle from that of male reporters. For example, in a memoir recalling her 'Adventure' reporting in Europe and Asia, Irene Corbally Kuhn (1938: 73) suggested casually that, because of male reporters' First World War experiences, it was always 'sex o-clock' in the newsroom: having lived with death, men now 'seized on life with a rapist's lust, and life meant women and women meant sex'. So Kuhn refused to criticize her editor at the *New York Daily News* for his preoccupation with the human 'mid-section'. When Kuhn's editor concocted a scheme for her to lure a convicted draft-dodger back to France, Kuhn (1938: 140) merely said her editor 'had more confidence in my sex appeal than in the enterprise of any of his male journalists'. The stunt failed, but not because Kuhn did not try. Relying on a Bohemian insouciant attitude, Kuhn, whose journalist-husband died in 1926, remained nonchalant about other people's curiosity about women reporters' bodies. Indeed, she was equally casual, as were most of her memoir-writing colleagues, in attending to other women journalists' bodies, describing her friend Peggy Hull as 'four times as cute' as Shirley Temple (Kuhn 1938: 159). Peggy Hull, the first woman war correspondent officially accredited by the United States War Department, was denied access by her editors at the *Cleveland Plain Dealer* after she decided to travel to France during the First World War. Undeterred, she convinced a news-feature syndicate, the Newspaper Enterprise Association, to take her on and later followed the American expeditionary force to Siberia.

US officials were averse to offering women credentials and mounted many barriers against them. In addition to the harassment they faced – in the form of sexist innuendoes and jokes – the lack of toilet facilities for women was used as an ongoing excuse by successive governments and the military to systematically bar women correspondents from the key events that needed to be reported on. In addition, women faced distinctive obstacles of prejudice in radio broadcasting where men refused to acknowledge their skills, as documented by Hosley and Yamada (1987). For example, Betty Wason, CBS correspondent in Europe in 1940, was asked to 'find a man' to broadcast her reports because she sounded too young and feminine and lacked command and authority to deliver news about war. Helen Siousett, CBS's director of

non-commercial public affairs broadcasting, was paid less than male counterparts but told she should feel privileged to be a department head.

In her account of women war correspondents during the Second World
War, Julia Edwards (1988: 5) claims that women obtained overseas jobs by
arguing that they could deliver more sensitive reports than male journalists
and offer 'a woman's point of view'. Once they arrived, however, women had
to be as competitive, adventurous and hard-headed as the men. On the other
hand, some autobiographical and biographical accounts suggest that a
number of women war correspondents 'took pleasure in maintaining their
feminine identity at the same time they displayed their professional competence' (Beasley 1995: 328). An example is Margaret Bourke-White, a
photojournalist for *Life* magazine who was already famous for her work with
Fortune magazine covering industrial contexts and the poor working conditions of Southern sharecroppers during the 1930s. Accredited to the U.S.
Army Air Force during the Second World War, she captured scenes of the
1941 Nazi attack on Moscow and reported on the battles in North Africa and
Italy. Despite her national reputation, Bourke-White was refused access to air
transport to Europe. She was forced to travel by sea to North Africa to report
on the Allied invasion because the authorities claimed that it was too dangerous for a woman to fly. Her persistent appeals eventually gained her
permission to fly on bombing raids (Beasley and Gibbons 1993: 141).

Bourke-White's biographers describe her as being highly particular about
combining her professionalism with her femininity and meticulous in the
attention she paid to her appearance (Beasley 1995). Bourke-White was portrayed as glamorous, adventurous and courageous. In her autobiography,
Portrait of Myself, Bourke-White (1963) details the whole of her wardrobe for
wartime use, including make-up and the kind of outfits worn during evening
functions. She was proud when *Life* magazine accompanied her photographic
depiction of a bombing raid in Tunis with a pin-up style photograph of
Bourke-White in a flying-suit (1963: 232). Wagner's (1989: 5) study of women
covering the Second World War mentions some women who believed that
being female was a distinct advantage as they could use their feminine attributes to gain favours within a male-dominated field. But, needless to say, this
only applied if they were young, very attractive and confident about their sexuality.

Like Bourke-White, the case of Marguerite Higgins (1920–66) dramatizes
a number of tensions in the lives of women who wanted to report on wars,
and the gendered nature of the attention to ambitious women, a recurring
theme in this book. Through dint of perseverance, Higgins had worked her
way into a foreign reporting job for the *New York Herald Tribune*. She won a
prize for reporting on the liberation of a concentration camp and of Munich
in 1945, and at twenty-six became chief of the *Tribune*'s Berlin bureau.
Attempting to cover the Korean War, Higgins was ordered out of Korea by
the US military with the excuse that there were 'no facilities for ladies at the

front'.[5] General Douglas MacArthur set a major precedent in reversing the order (Higgins 1955: 40), telling Higgins that she should ignore what jealous men said about her. With five male colleagues, Higgins went on to win a Pulitzer Prize for her Korean war reporting.

Several male colleagues, or rivals, as well as male and female biographers (most notably, Edwards 1988), have suggested that Higgins furthered her career by offering sexual favours to men to gain access to news sources. It's the kind of accusation that does not burden men. For her part, Higgins (1955: 56) herself opened the chapter of her autobiography on 'How to be a foreign correspondent (even though a woman)' by saying that her biggest disadvantage was that men associated 'the combination of femininity and blond hair with either dumbness or slyness, or both'. On the other hand, Higgins proudly repeated what she took to be the supreme compliment: a man saying, 'The front line is no place for a woman, but it's all right for Maggie Higgins' (Higgins 1955: 40).

Wartime opportunities were offered to women in newer areas of photo-journalism, radio and television broadcasting. In a speech made in 1944 at the Women's National Press Club in America (where she had taken on several leadership roles), political reporter and war correspondent May Craig (1889–1975) emphasized extraordinary wartime opportunities for women to document the events on the battlefield, in concentration camps and in hospitals. Craig overturned more than one military ruling that barred women from aeroplanes and ships, by convincing the military that women were capable of going about their business without 'facilities'. The Southern-born former suffragist provided eyewitness accounts of V-bomb raids in London, the Normandy campaign and the liberation of Paris. Craig was the first woman on a battleship at sea in 1949 and the first woman to fly over the North Pole in 1952 (Mills 1988).

Born in Glasgow, and educated at Oxford University, Evelyn Irons (1901–2000) had chosen journalism to 'become a great writer'. She joined the *Daily Mail* in 1927 as a fashion correspondent and served as the *Evening Standard* women's editor during the mid-1930s. Irons was determined to report from the war zone after the outbreak of the Second World War. But Field Marshal Montgomery banned women war correspondents from travelling with and covering the British forces. Undeterred, Irons sought and obtained accreditation to the Free French Army. Since the French allowed war correspondents to carry weapons, Irons was armed when she helped the French army capture a Bavarian village and round up prisoners. She was the first woman to be awarded the Croix de Guerre, and the first woman correspondent to reach Hitler's mountain retreat at Berchtesgarten. Later, she reported on a revolution in Guatemala, having entered rebel territory on a donkey purchased for £9 (Wilkes 2001).

The first accredited black woman overseas war correspondent was Elizabeth Murphy. She was one of three sisters who worked for their family-owned *Afro-American* newspapers. Another sister, Vashti Murphy, went to France as a member of the Women's Army Corps and reported on the prejudice and bigotry against black soldiers in the US Army.[6]

Reporting the Vietnam War

Women made significant inroads in war journalism during the Vietnam War. Yet they were still regarded as novel and many news organizations continued to baulk at sending women to cover wars. As late as 1970, for example, no women worked as foreign correspondents for Associated Press.[7] None the less, stretching from 1961 to 1975, the Vietnam War took place during a period of distinctive technological development and involved distinctive forms of combat. Both factors changed the nature of reporting and help explain women journalists' contributions to war reporting. First, the conflict between the United States and Vietnam was the first to be transmitted nearly in 'real time'; reports often reached viewers and readers in Western nations within forty-eight hours. The resulting news product was now less contrived and more improvised, allowing women to contribute to a period of journalistic innovation. This speed of delivery, a crucial factor in the coverage of the Vietnam War (which came to be known as the first 'television war'), was surpassed only when satellite technology allowed images to reach audiences instantaneously during the Gulf War in 1991, which came to be known as the first 'Nintendo-style' conflict.

Second, the Vietnam conflict turned out to present a new war situation. Vietnam war-era journalists enjoyed relatively wide access given that its guerrilla form of combat entailed no front lines and few rigid military restrictions. Some reporters, such as Marguerite Higgins, found that their Second World War experience in war reporting and their familiarity with military protocol and red tape came in handy; their ability to improvise became crucial in dealing quickly with unforeseen events.

Special permission to travel to Vietnam was not required because reporters could book their own commercial airline flights. It was this feature of easy access, rather than significant changes in attitudes about women, that allowed so many women to report from Vietnam (Elwood-Akers 1988). Jurate Kazickas, for example, a reporter who was wounded while covering combat, used the $500 she won on a television game show to travel to Vietnam when her boss at *Look* magazine refused to send her. Indeed, of the nine contributors to a recent collection *War Torn: Stories of War from the Women Reporters Who Covered Vietnam* (Bartimus, Emerson and Wood 2002), five paid their own way over. Vietnam was an 'undeclared war', so a freelance reporter could obtain a press pass merely by showing that three news organizations were interested in using their work. War correspondents found themselves leading double lives, having to face extreme danger and discomfort in recording these extraordinary jungle warfare tactics and then rushing

back to hotels in Saigon to attend embassy cocktail parties in order to network with politicians and gather additional information (Beasley and
Gibbons 1993: 226). The US military supplied credentials to 467 women,
and approximately seventy American women reporters made key contributions to the overall Vietnam reportage (Elwood-Akers 1988).

Nevertheless, the conflict bore certain similarities to the First and Second
World Wars. First, many of those women who reached Vietnam as reporters
had to battle the prejudices, or at least concerns, of the bureau chiefs, fellow
reporters and US and Vietnamese military officials. For example, UPI bureau
chief Kate Webb was captured in Phnom Penh, Cambodia and was thought
to have been killed until her release three weeks later. As a result, access to
combat assignments was denied to Tracy Wood of UPI. When she attempted
to enter front-line units, *Christian Science Monitor* reporter Beverley Deepe
was frequently ordered back to base camp by the military (Elwood-Ackers
1988: 224). Liz Trotta, the first woman to report on Vietnam for US television, attributed her male colleagues' hostility to men feeling threatened by
competition from women (Trotta 1991: 98). Second, since no women were
engaged in combat (women were nurses and in other non-combat roles),
women reporters were profoundly conspicuous. Women stood out even when
they wore combat uniform and carried their own packs (Elwood-Akers 1988:
3). GIs were astonished to see women in the war zone at all. 'Why, for Christ's
sake, didn't they send a man out here? This is no place for a woman', a military officer told Gloria Emerson, a *New York Times* correspondent whose
1976 book *Winners and Losers*, about the Vietnam War's legacy, went on to
win the National Book Award.

Some women reporters said their visibility meant they were noticed at
press conferences and had their questions answered first; and some said that
male soldiers liked talking to women, and would give them rides in their military vehicles (Rouvalis and Schackner 2000). Others complained that
helicopter pilots were reluctant to take women on board. As Elwood-Akers
(1988) emphasizes, the attention paid to them because of their sex was mostly
very unwelcome. 'Military latrine fixation', as Elwood-Akers calls it, persisted. Continuous attempts to use the lack of toilets as an excuse to deny
women access to the front line or attend a unit's mission were, however,
unsuccessful. For women war reporters, the lack of toilets was the least of
their problems. Either way, as Elwood-Akers (1988: 6) points out, 'they
shared the experience of being a woman in a "man's world"'.

The forms and extent of gender differences in Vietnam War reporting continues to be a matter of debate. Some women and men reporters
congratulated women for being more attuned to the 'human side' of the war
and the Vietnamese position, while men zeroed in on military positions and
strategy (Rouvalis and Schackner 2000). Anne Morrissy Merick, an ABC-TV
producer, and Associated Press reporter Tad Bartimus, said they wanted to
cover stories about Vietnam children and nurses – because war is not about

'bang-bang' but about destruction (Rouvalis and Schackner 2000). But other women hated doing these sorts of stories or refused to do 'women's stories', either because it was demeaning to be assigned according to stereotype or because these stories were more likely to be cut. Virginia Elwood Akers (1988: 2) argues that men and women wrote substantially similar kinds of stories:

> Women wrote the so-called 'human interest' stories which have tradition-ally been expected of the woman reporter, but male reporters in Vietnam wrote 'human interest' stories as well. Both male and female reporters wrote of the complexities of the political events that shaped the history of the war. Both male and female reporters analysed the effects of the war on South Vietnamese society.

Women correspondents contributed to the whole gamut of styles of writing, with examples of sentimental or dramatic accounts of the suffering of civil-ians, unemotional reports of battle and even Boys' Own adventure story styles.

Elwood-Akers found no detectable difference in attitudes between male and female reporters towards the war itself. They represented a range of political positions, from Marxist to anti-communist. This is not to say that reporters had no positions. Maggie Higgins, for example, expressed harsh criticism of US foreign policy in Vietnam from the right, while the left-lean-ing Gloria Emerson and Francis FitzGerald opposed US involvement in Vietnam. None the less, 'hawks' and 'doves' were not divided along gender lines.

Although feminists have played a central role in peace movements and protests (such as public protest against nuclear weapons at Greenham Common airbase in the 1980s in Britain), Elwood-Akers emphasizes the pro-fessionalism of women journalists over political motives. Indeed, Elwood-Akers (1988: 7) notes that many women reporters either ignored or marginalized the women's movement. She suspects that given women's diffi-culties in being accepted by the military and male journalists, siding with the women's movement would have constituted professional suicide. Moreover, while these women believed in equal rights for men and women, they chose to fight gender battles individually rather than as part of a movement. They were anxious to be accepted as 'individuals' and experts, that is, not only as 'one of the boys' but also to be respected as professionals first, and as women second. Similarly, Eve Ann Prentice, a journalist for *The Times*, argues in *One Woman's War* (2000: 16) that women journalists rarely write about either women's activism in the peace movement or their wartime victimization because these stories rarely get published: 'Newspapers are still run by men, mostly, and they do like their wars and they do like their blood and guts and thunder.'

Women war correspondents between the 1970s and 1990s

In the last three decades the opportunities to report on foreign conflicts have been numerous, with the Eastern European revolutions, the demise of the Soviet Union, the collapse of Yugoslavia, Bosnia, Chechnya, as well as two Gulf wars and the war in Afghanistan. During this period women correspondents continued to confront sexism while doing their jobs. The Falklands War of 1982 between Britain and Argentina, is a classic example of a conflict whose news media coverage was managed by the British Ministry of Defence (Knightley 1982b: 51). The remoteness of the Falkland islands in the South Atlantic (named the Malvinas by Argentina), being 400 miles from the nearest land mass and 8,000 miles from mainland Britain, required a seaborne task force. Correspondents could not reach the battle zone without Ministry of Defence transport. It was the military authorities who selected the reporters who were to accompany the troop ships to the islands, with only British correspondents being allowed to accompany the task force. When this all-male group of war reporters reached the Falklands, the military also controlled the means of communication from the battle zone and exercised the power of veto over what was reported. No women correspondents were selected and therefore none entered the war zone, except for the official war artist, Linda Kitson (Sebba 1994: 276). However, a few women, such as Edith M. Lederer of the Associated Press, covered the Falklands War from a distance. Women figured in this war only as passive victims in reports on the 'human-interest' angle, as the mothers, wives and girlfriends of the servicemen who died or survived the fighting (Glasgow University Media Group 1985).

BBC reporter Kate Adie may have helped write a new chapter in the history of women war correspondents, however. Dubbed the 'macho male reporter'[8] for having spent so much time with the military, Adie achieved prominence for her coverage of the Iranian Embassy siege in London of 1980 (see Schlesinger 1991) and became a household name in Britain after reporting on the conflict in Libya in 1986 and the Tiananmen Square massacre in China in 1989. Both a Member of Parliament and the *Daily Express* accused Adie of being sympathetic to Colonel Gaddafi's regime in Libya because her reportage on the US bombing of Tripoli in 1986 referred, briefly, to the death of Gaddafi's adopted daughter.[9] Granted, accusations that Adie obtained favours from the regime that were unavailable to other journalists are not necessarily gender based; they have been registered against men, most notably the US broadcast journalist Peter Arnett. In any case, Adie not only resolutely defended herself against the government, but also sued the *Express* and won undisclosed damages from the latter. She won the International News Story of 1986 Award by the Royal Television Society for her reports from Tripoli (Sebba 1994: 267).

Adie found that female television news journalists, even in war contexts, are still much more likely than their men colleagues to be judged by their appearance, regardless of their competence. She has been plagued by remarks about her hair, causing her to take curling tongs along with electric adaptor on her foreign forays (Sebba 1994: 267). At the student uprising in Tiananmen Square, Adie and her crew were caught in the cross-fire while providing eye-witness accounts of the killings of students. Although she was grazed by a bullet, she was more concerned with the injuries and deaths around her. Adie told Sebba (1994), that she did not feel the excitement that some male journalists feel. Staying alive and getting the story out were her priorities. However, an interesting interpretation of Adie's reports by John Simpson, BBC diplomatic correspondent who worked alongside Adie in Beijing, demonstrates the gender inflections of some reports. He stated that he masked his own feelings of the horror by reporting, in 'a good old BBC stiff upper lip piece', only what he had observed and agreed with friends that Adie's piece was 'horribly emotional'. A few months later he compared his and Adie's pieces again and altered his opinion:

> I still thought my piece was fine ... nothing wrong with it, it told you what had happened. But Kate went to the hospital and she gave you a real feeling of the awfulness of it. You felt how frightened she was, as indeed most of us were and I thought she gave a damn sight better account by seeing the aftermath than the real thing.
>
> (quoted in Sebba 1994: 269)

The controversy over Adie again raises the continuing debate regarding whether or how gender might make a difference to styles of war reporting. Lyse Doucet, a BBC foreign correspondent, says gender has made no difference to her career. She admits that women are more likely to talk to women journalists about personal issues such as rape. Otherwise, however, she says 'my view is that I do not believe that coverage of war is affected by gender. I know as many women who are interested in the bombs and bullets as I know men whose main concern is the human cost' (Wells 2002: 3).

On the other hand, British journalist Emma Daly, a Balkans correspondent for the *Independent* who spent 1994 to 1996 reporting from Bosnia-Herzegovinia and then Croatia, emphasizes that 'war is the greatest human-interest story there is'. She observed that after the Bosnian war ended in 1995, some people thought that war reporting had been feminized, that a 'cold, dispassionate ideal had mutated into the more emotive "journalism of attachment" (Daly 1999: 278). Daly highlights the difficult position journalists are placed in when attempting to fulfil the quest for objectivity while under threat, and reporting on events routinely denied by government ministers. She argues that journalists *should* bring 'emotion, passion and commitment to a story' and that this does not necessarily make them 'partisan, unstable, unreliable' (Daly 1999: 280).

During the 1991 Gulf War the United States government wanted positive news media images both to sway public opinion to its side and to attract military recruits, especially since the military draft had been abolished. Yet by 1991 governments were forced to battle not only with the enemy, but also with the news media, which now had satellite links that allowed for 'real-time' broadcasting news of overseas conflicts. During this war, audiences worldwide could witness the 'smart bombs' as they landed in the centre of Baghdad. The US and British governments no longer enjoyed the advantage of extreme geographical remoteness offered by the Falklands conflict. So government manipulation of the news during the Gulf War was bound to be harder.

That said, new technologies are not perfect, as Molly Moore, a *Washington Post* reporter during the first Gulf War, describes in *A Woman at War* (1993). After Iraqi troops had invaded neighbouring Kuwait in August 1990, she was dispatched to Saudi Arabia's oil centre, Dhahran, just 190 miles from occupied Kuwait. She was the only woman reporter working in a pool system with thirty-eight men. She described the 100-hour battle to liberate Kuwait in February 1991 as 'the largest armoured assault since World War II, yet it went unseen by most of the world, missed by the television cameras and the newspapers' (1993: xiii). Poor communications prevented many of Moore's stories from reaching the *Washington Post* in time for use during the ground war itself.

Moore explains that women in Saudi Arabia were prevented from travelling or checking into hotels unaccompanied by a man, but exceptions were sometimes made for Western women who possessed a letter from their nations' consulate authenticating their business. The desk clerk of the 'posh Gulf Meridien Hotel' demanded a letter. 'It was, in essence, US certification that I was not a prostitute. My female colleagues and I called it the "I Am Not a Whore" letter. Indignant, I slapped it on the counter and he gave me a room' (Moore 1993: 31). When Moore phoned the *Washington Post* on the same day, she was told that the style section wanted 'the women's story'. The foreign editor said: 'People here are fascinated by the idea of American women adapting to Islamic culture.' Conscious of the crucial distinction between 'hard' and 'soft' news, and the subordination of the latter, Moore writes in response,

> I winced at the thought that my first war story would be an article on women's problems for the Style section. I wanted to do stories on the US plans for defending Saudi Arabia and how the harsh desert environment was going to affect the capability of American troops and equipment.
>
> (Moore 1993: 31)

But she recognized that the 'women's issue' was in danger of becoming a key political issue since many US military units hesitated in sending women soldiers to the Gulf lest this offend the Saudis.

Women reporting on the war in Afghanistan

During the war in Afghanistan, Gill Swain of the British *Independent* declared that 'a whole new breed' of female war correspondents emerged (Swain 2001). However, the fact that newspapers assigned far fewer women correspondents to the region than did broadcasting media raises questions about whether broadcasting is supporting gender equality or whether, instead, is betraying a market-oriented feminization, that is, female dominance in the medium. Liesbet van Zoonen (1998: 44) agrees that 'femininity' has become an unmistakable ingredient of market-driven war journalism'. She quotes from the British *Times*:

> The world's war zones are chock-a-block with would-be Kate Adies risking their lives for minor stations in the hope of landing the big story because they know that what the major networks want is a front-line account from a (preferably pretty) woman in a flak jacket.

These issues are revisited in relation to confessional journalism in Chapter 11. Meanwhile newspapers seem to be dragging their feet and continue to privilege male correspondents for war reporting.

The apparent rapid upsurge in female war correspondents needs to be understood against the backdrop of an extraordinary boost to foreign news brought about by the terrorist attacks of September 11th. For the last few years, in both the UK and US, newspapers – particularly the tabloids but also the high-quality papers – have been cutting back on their foreign sections in order to give more space and resources to domestic news. Explanations for this shift have been couched in terms of both economic recession and the apparent lack of interest of readers in international news. The foreign departments of all news media, however, were propelled into action after September 11th.

The BBC expanded its broadcasts to cover Afghanistan and the Middle East and launched an extended forty-five-hour news service immediately after the attacks. Challenged by the need to adhere to principles of accuracy, objectivity and range of opinion and analysis, short-wave transmissions to Afghanistan were increased after September 11th and a new medium-wave frequency was added, with expanded output in the regions' major languages of Arabic, Pashto, Persian and Urdu (Wells 2001: 2). As Wells stated, 'The BBC believes the Taliban leader, Mullah Omar, listens to the World Service everyday' (Wells 2001: 2). Meanwhile, both US and British audiences needed more reports about the Middle East. With these kinds of news media expansions, war correspondents found themselves in great demand. This led to expanded opportunities for both male and female journalists. While the *number* of women journalists did not rise significantly, except in broadcasting, their visibility increased.

When Yvonne Ridley was arrested in Afghanistan by the Taliban in October 2001, a backlash against Ridley erupted in the news media. Ridley had disguised herself in the all-enveloping burqa, a typical Afghan dress, and she tea-stained her hands and blackened her fair hair, saying her aim was to 'put a human face on to the people of Afghanistan who had been, week in, week out, demonized by the government and the Americans'.[10] She was caught by the Taliban on her return to Pakistan, only twenty minutes from the border. The US bombing of Kabul began while Ridley was in jail. Her daughter's ninth birthday also took place while she was there. The Taliban deliberated over espionage charges, which carry the death penalty, but they eventually released her. Ridley's (2001) hastily written book about her experiences reveals a poignant tension between the image of a tough, adventurous and driven journalist and the self-doubting anxious single parent.

Fellow journalists in the British news media accused Ridley of several misdemeanours: of being reckless in taking on such a hazardous job and of being insufficiently experienced, as well as failing her parental responsibilities towards her young daughter and pandering to the demands of tabloid journalism. They also complained that she placed her Pakistani male interpreter/guide and Afghan male driver in great danger of long prison sentences and even the death penalty. Members of the journalistic community were concerned that these two men faced the death penalty just to glorify Ridley's career, as Michael Buerk pointed out in a BBC Radio 4 interview with Ridley after her release.[11] Most of the other complaints in the press centred on Ridley's status as a single mother, implying or declaring that she therefore had no right to be a war correspondent.

Echoing fears about women war correspondents in the past, the problems of women placing themselves at risk turned into an obsession in the public debates about women journalists who went to Afghanistan and the surrounding region. While men's parental status is perceived as secondary to their professional status, parental status continues to be emphasized as paramount where women are concerned and is regularly used as an excuse for not treating women as 'proper' professionals. The irony is not lost on women across the world who have been outraged by the oppression of women in Afghanistan by the Taliban regime. Ridley was demonized in the news media after her release, in a way that a man would not have had to put up with. Details about her three marriages were exposed, implying that her 'unstable' family and sex life were evidence of immorality and dysfunctional femininity, thereby discrediting her professional role.

Conclusion: women war correspondents' conspicuous presence

A number of issues emerge from this history of the changing status of women war correspondents. Certainly testosterone is not necessary for war reporting – although bravado may be. However, it is likely that female correspondents who do put their lives on the line to bring us the news will continue to be vilified as irresponsible towards their families for as long as women's professional role is subsumed under their domestic role.

Anne Garrels, a 'roving' foreign correspondent for National Public Radio, covered a number of wars and hot spots, including Chechnya, Bosnia, Kosovo and Afghanistan. She developed a reputation for her courage and intelligence in reporting on sensitive issues under very difficult circumstances, calling for all kinds of improvisional skills (such as carrying around a heavy car battery, to which she could connect her lap top, and experimenting with different ways to hide her satellite phone from Iraqi security forces). Interestingly, Garrels returned to the US at the end of the 'active' phase of the war on Iraq, citing the toll her work was taking on her husband; but by mid-summer of 2003, she was back in Iraq, never far from hot spots.

Even Christiane Amanpour (2000) noted in a public speech the challenge of juggling assignments at work and at home, especially in the context of living in a constant fear: '[F]ear of being shot . . . of being kidnapped, of being raped by some lunatic who hates your stories or blames you for bringing NATO bombs down around them. We manage the fear, but the strain takes its toll.' Amanpour admitted that she had once declared that she would never get married and definitely would never have children: 'If you have a child, I said, you have a responsibility to at least stay alive' (Amanpour 2000). She did marry and have a child, and while covering the war in Afghanistan, she was quoted saying:

> It got a little more difficult when I got married, because you have emotional attachments at home you didn't have before . . . It's even more difficult now that I have an 18-month old baby, who's so difficult to leave. But I'm committed to my work, and I hope I can do it in a way that doesn't take away too much from my family.[12]

Nor is Amanpour the only one to complain that war reporters put their lives on the line only to find their stories killed, never to 'see the light of air' (Amanpour 2000).

Orla Guerin, a BBC foreign correspondent who covered the Israeli and Palestinian conflict in 2001, stated that women and men work differently as journalists. She stressed that it is not just a case of 'women writing about refugees and men about tanks', but that women have a different set of emphases in their interpretation of events. Marie Colvin agrees about these gender differences, using herself as an example: she talked for hours to a civilian whose baby was killed, but she believes a male journalist would not have done this.[13] Similarly, Guerin argued that women journalists personalize stories, but that they put them in an appropriate political and historical context.[14]

In certain circumstances, many women foreign correspondents acknowledge that being a woman can be advantageous, for example getting through a checkpoint without being treated with suspicion. On one hand, then, women's subordination and inferior status in cultures across the world means that, under certain circumstances, precisely because they are dismissed as irrelevant, they can get away with certain subterfuges. On the other hand, there is also plenty of evidence – in the form of personal and institutional aggression towards women from contemptuous staring and innuendoes to systematic sexual discrimination – to suggest that women are perceived as a threat if they breach their subordinate role. So women journalists have to work harder in the kinds of contexts they enter as war correspondents precisely because their gender is marked as 'other'. In any case, given the fine differences between sexist, patronizing and paternalistic management of women's roles, women journalists try to draw attention to the quality of their professionalism, which most of them believe they share with male colleagues, as the critical criterion by which they should be judged and respected.

By the end of the Second World War, over 127 American women had managed to obtain official military accreditation as war correspondents, some with front-line assignments (Wagner 1989). Although in most cases men covered the front-line battles, women were often limited to covering stories about hospitals and nurses or other stories then deemed peripheral to the principal events of war. Today, the human-interest accounts of war victims and the plight of refugees are now considered by the news media to be as critical as the related action on the battlefields.

The influx of women correspondents during the Vietnam era illustrates a crucial and continuing point of relevance that follows from the developments in new media technologies which augment the immediacy of reportage and the shift towards guerrilla and terrorist-led forms of combat from regimental military front lines. Both require flexibility and improvisational skills that women journalists offer. In addition, women correspondents are not only proving that they cope well under conditions of extreme danger, but are being appreciated as journalists who can offer sensitivity to detail and to human-interest angles in stories of conflict. Women are said to report wars differently from men by focusing on what is euphemistically called 'collateral damage'.

Significantly, the trend of using women journalists for their novelty value and attractiveness applies primarily to television; women's appearance continues to play a crucial role in decisions to employ them in television journalism. The ability to broadcast instant images from the field of action means that women journalists can stand in the centre of the action while reporting it. Ironically, MSNCB reporter Ashleigh Banfield, told *Cosmopolitan* magazine that she dyed her hair darker as a security measure before going to Pakistan to cover the war on terrorism. Being blond, Banfield said, could be a nuisance, or even a detriment.(*Cosmopolitan* 2002: 156). Although it went on to highlight Banfield's bravery and heroism,

Cosmopolitan predictably first described her 'sexy black specs'. Anna Sebba (1994), noting the conspicuous rise in the number of women journalists covering the Gulf War argues, somewhat cynically, that women war and foreign correspondents are contributing drama and appeal. She argues that male action is being counterposed with female reporting and even that women are offering a pleasing distraction to television reports on hostilities and violent conflicts around the world.

Meanwhile, Kate Adie herself has criticized TV management for preferring women with 'cute faces and cute bottoms' to those with journalistic experience. In television journalism, they must remain young and attractive. Those who survive broadcasting into middle age are often compelled to move to radio. Of course, women war correspondents' novelty value does not mean that women have to struggle any less with the high risks associated with war and foreign correspondence. But the price women pay for their prominence is that they are still treated as an oddity: conspicuous because they are marked as 'other'.

11

'Postmodern journalism' and its implications for women

Rosie Boycott, one of the founders of the British feminist magazine *Spare Rib* and one of the first women to edit a British national daily, resigned her position as the editor of the *Daily Express* in January 2001 when she found that the paper had been bought by a pornography publisher, Richard Desmond, for £125 million. The *Guardian* commented: 'It was a marriage made in hell – the founder of *Spare Rib* in bed with the owner of *Asian Babes*, *40-Plus* and *50 and Over*, and 40 other pornographic magazines' (Hattenstone 2002: 2). Boycott told the *Guardian* that having sacked a pregnant woman and evicting staff without notice, Desmond was intent on reporting only 'positive news' in the *Daily Express*. This story demonstrates the moral and professional dilemmas that women journalists, and indeed their male colleagues, now face more or less routinely in the news media industry.

In a study of changing trends in British television news between 1975 and 1999, Barnett, Seymour and Gaber (2000) detected a significant shift towards a more tabloid style, with an emphasis on local and parochial (as opposed to global) events in the majority of broadcasts. They found a decline in the amount of coverage of political affairs across all television news programmes in the last ten years, especially among the two commercial bulletins. They also found more sport and consumer stories characterized by 'catchy' stories about crime, Hollywood and sports stars, the Royal Family, and 'quirky trivialities'. They suggest that if 'it continues as a trend rather than a fluctuation, this could lead to the gradual marginalization of serious and foreign news' (Barnett, Seymour and Gaber 2000: 13). The authors raise several questions still to be answered:

Is this proof that there is indeed a degenerative process of 'dumbing down' in television news, or is it a much needed injection of accessibility into what 25 years ago was a deeply serious and dull approach to news? Has the increase in channels and competition given us greater diversity which enriches democracy or lower standards which denigrate public intelligence?

(Barnett, Seymour and Gaber 2000: 12–13)

Women have been involved in the most recent changes in news topics and themes in the last decade in the United States and Britain, both as reporters and consumers of news, although, to the extent that fewer women have reached the top executive positions at newspapers and television stations, they are less central in ordering these changes. A broadening of news agendas and the shift to a more informal, personal and human-interest style of reporting were included in Chapter 5's discussion of gendered newsroom cultures. A close examination of the pronounced move to 'softer' journalism and consumer stories that began in the mid-1990s, however, reveals a cluster of characteristics now common in news content which falls within what one might call a new 'postmodern style' of journalism, if by postmodern one means ideas and styles involving discontinuities, openness, randomness, ironies, reflexivity and incoherencies (see Featherstone 1991).

More specifically, post-feminist journalism is materialistic and consumerist. It is perhaps indicated by the rise of two 'girl' types in the 1990s: the 'ladette', the female version of the young lad, searching for kicks and independence, and who is either applauded or condemned in the news media; and her older sister, the self-absorbed, thirty-something singleton in search of a man, exemplified by the TV series, *Sex in the City*. The latter version literally emerged in 'girl columns': Candace Bushnell's *New York Observer* columns were the basis of *Sex in the City*, whose central heroine is a journalist with the same initials as Bushnell and apparently equally fixated on sex and high-priced shoes. Notably, hundreds of novels and films have been set in newsrooms (whether because newsrooms have some measure of glamour or because journalists have often turned their creative energies to writing novels and scripts). But Bushnell's case is perhaps rare given the extent to which not only is the script autobiographical but also Bushnell may be confused with the actress who plays her character. This may help sell Bushnell's writing, but it does not bolster the professional credibility of the female columnist. This 'new girl writing' has inspired and sanctioned the rise of a whole new feminine, but covertly anti-feminist, journalistic form in the twenty-first century in which it is now permissible for women to expose their own and other women's personal insecurities and vulgar habits, sexual conquests and defeats, and abuses of substances and people. While humour is usually used to make this kind of 'news' broadly entertaining, the discourse of moral panic is also used to develop a sense of moral indignation among audiences and readers regarding topics ranging from youth crime to teenage pregnancies.

Some interesting parallels exist between this new trend in journalism and the 'New Journalism' of the late nineteenth century, described in Chapter 1 on early women journalists. Certainly commercial pressures lie behind both trends. Yet some disturbing current trends within postmodern journalism, such as an emphasis on feminine individualism and consumerism, confirm the distinctiveness of postmodern journalism. This chapter considers the growing popularity of a feminized confessional style of popular journalism modelled on magazine journalism and examines its implications for women journalists, readers and audiences. To assess the impact of these changes on women in the profession, we question the dearth of political, pedagogic and professional feminism and feminist debates in the news media today. After outlining the reasons for the rise in postmodern journalism and specifically the popularity of the magazine-style of post-feminist journalism aimed at women, we offer a critique of confessional and therapy news, characterized as involving an intense but depoliticized exploration of emotion, so that people's 'feelings' about events become more important than the events themselves. .

Confessional journalism and 'therapy news'

Zoe Heller, who has written features both in Britain and in New York and also wrote a 'girl' column for the British *Sunday Times*, highlights the ghettoizing typecasting of women journalists:

> Historically, the role of the female newspaper writer has been to leaven the serious (male) stuff of reportage and analysis with light dispatches – news from the realm of the domestic, the emotional, the personal. Even today, male newspaper editors are inclined, if only subconsciously, to regard their female staff as the people who soften the edges of the paper's main agenda. When a woman journalist is invited to use the first person or inject some more 'attitude' into a piece, it is often a coded entreaty to beef up a specifically female perspective. The request may seem innocuous enough, but in taking such an invitation a woman takes her first step away from the neutrality and freedom of being simply a writer, towards the ghetto of writing 'as a woman'.
>
> (Heller 1999: 10)

Heller's point about history is particularly apt with respect to columnists. In the US, with a few exceptions (most importantly, Dorothy Thompson and Anne O'Hare McCormick, who wrote about international affairs; and then Sylvia Porter on finance and Doris Fleeson on national politics), women steered away from 'serious' topics in their columns. They dished out Hollywood gossip (Hedda Hopper and Louella Parsons) and etiquette (Emily Post), or they offered advice, either strictly domestic (Heloise) or, more especially, advice to the love-lorn (Elizabeth Meriwether Gilmer, Marie Manning, and then the twins Esther Pauline Lederer and Abigail Van Buren, all writing under pseudonyms). Only in more recent decades were women columnists allowed to write more broadly about politics, science, finance; notably, even then, their columns often have an intimate, personal quality associated with the feminine (Braden 2003). This is evident in the work of Ellen Goodman and Anna Quindlen, and explicit in the syndicated 'personal' health columns of Jane Brody and the 'personal' finance columns of Jane Bryant Quinn.

During the 1990s female columnists at tabloid and broadsheet newspapers began borrowing styles and themes from mainstream women's magazine and feature genres, and producing confessional stories. Victims' feelings and exposing the intimate thoughts of the rich and famous are the heart of confessional journalism and 'therapy news'. The trend provoked BBC's foreign correspondent Kate Adie to remark in 2001: 'I am out of step with the kind of journalism which says that to understand anyone's motives or deeds an intimate scrutiny of their private, family and sexual life is necessary'. She astutely added, '[O]ne of the great modern weasel words is "Will you share with us?" meaning "Come on, open up, tell us all". Confession can be useful in certain circumstances but to confess to the masses rather than the individual is a cheapening process' (quoted in Leonard 2001).

Christmas (1997: 3) condemns this trend in journalism as regressive, stating that 'the drive for ever more intimate stories encourages the publication of the bizarre and the prurient'. Likewise, TV journalist and writer Tessa Mayes (2000: 30) argues: '[E]motional indulgence and sentimentalism are replacing informative, facts-based news reporting.' She says that the standard 'Who-What-Where-When-Why' reporting method now includes 'Feel'. It incorporates the feelings of those present at or involved in the incident, their feelings about the feelings of others and, significantly, the feelings of the reporter. Many reporters complain that by focusing on and even inventing trauma at the expense of other issues, 'therapy news' distorts reality. Meanwhile, many reporters are providing 'therapy news'.

The way that tragedies are reported in the British and American news media, according to Mayes, shows that facts are even being ignored or redefined to accommodate 'feelings'. While the eyewitness accounts of rescuers generally constitute a basic element of reports of tragedies and disasters, newspapers such as the *Daily Mail* frame the facts in emotive language and foregrounded emergency workers' feelings over their tasks. Mayes cites the 1999 Paddington rail crash in London, when, similar to the aftermath of September 11th, psychologists' opinions of the feelings of rescuers, the injured, their relatives and witnesses were reported:

The day after the Paddington crash, for example, Sally Cox, a fire-fighter, was shown on the front page of six out of nine national newspapers lifting a hand to her eye. Some reports claimed she was wiping away tears . . . However, even she felt moved to report a day later that 'I was not crying . . . I had a bit of dirt in my eye'.

(Mayes 2000: 31)

The prioritizing of emotions over other issues in news reports gives victims expert status, implying that their suffering embues them with authoritative knowledge about the causes and implications of the event. Another example Mayes mentions was the weight given to the views of the parents of an eight-year-old murder victim. The *News of the World* quoted the parents saying that since 'paedophiles cannot stop themselves' parents should have the right to protect their children. Although the pathologist's report showed no evidence of a sex attack, the *News of the World* produced a campaign against paedophiles, 'naming and shaming', which led to anti-paedophile demonstrations and a series of attacks on suspected paedophiles across the country in the style of a witch hunt. The *Daily Mirror* privileged the parents' views with the headline: 'PARENTS HAVE SPOKEN . . . NOW WE MUST ACT'. That is, it ignored that the parents were not authorities on the legal or medical treatment of paedophiles and later admitted they had not thought things through. In fact, the parents' emotional involvement ensured their inability to offer a measured set of views, according to Geoffrey Wheatcroft in the *Observer* (cited in Mayes 2000).

Mayes (2000) also indicts a blurring of the distinction between journalists' independent evaluation of an event and personal empathy with the victim's feelings. This distinction is further devalued, she says, when correspondents report on their own experiences as victims. This was typified by Sarah Lockett, who, describing her own encounter with a stalker in a report for BBC1 and afterwards, supported new police guidelines regarding stalking. As Mayes points out, the moral authority of the victim-reporter takes on more weight than the principle of impartiality in reporting. The same problem arises in the context of war reporting, illustrated in the previous chapter, when the journalist's personal experience eclipses a balanced assessment of the war from a professional eye witness. 'Failing to distinguish between the professional and the personal means that reporting is in danger of becoming an act of emoting, and objectivity could diminish as a result', says Mayes (2000: 33).

Mayes's explanation for the dominance of therapy news is that it is a journalistic response to the emotionalization of everyday life, symbolized most dramatically in the UK by the public mourning of the 1997 death of Diana, Princess of Wales. But even in Britain, this supplanting of a 'stiff-upper-lip' culture by emotionalization began long before Diana's death. Therapy news is more likely to arise when television news editors, reacting to shrinking viewing figures, assume they can attract larger audiences with excessive emotional coverage emphasizing compassion with the victims of tragedies (Mayes 2000).

This trend of transforming emotion into a spectacle within news reporting causes a serious dilemma for women journalists who have been praised precisely for playing a central role or, as some argue, even leading the way, in changing news agendas and styles and modes of documenting events by 'humanizing' the news. There is, however, an important distinction between, say, exposing aspects of war affecting women and children – such as systematic rape – hitherto treated as peripheral to war coverage and a focus on personal issues at the expense of the political and the systemic. This confessional and therapy style of news is characterized by a profoundly selective tolerance of some people's failings and misfortunes. It usually taps into sympathy for victims drawn largely from white, middle-class, heterosexual social groups of the same nationality as the national or regional newspapers and broadcast programmes. It ignores the misery and distress of migrants and refugees, drug addicts or prostitutes and of millions of people in developing nations suffering from starvation and war.

The kind of therapy news identified by Mayes fails to contextualize the underlying political or socio-cultural causes of and solutions to such disasters. It hinders careful journalistic analysis of victimhood in terms of who and how victims are labelled as such in society and it leads to an individualization and pathologization of offenders and victims within a failure to explore the wider structural causes of, for example, racist and sexist crimes. While radical movements such as feminism have exposed the personal as political by publicizing the power relations operating along gendered lines in the private sphere, therapy and confessional news have quite the opposite effect: a trivialization of public and private issues by avoiding discussions of power, whether about gender, generation, class, race, ethnicity, environmental issues or the developed and developing worlds. Thus, the rise in this particular and potentially exaggerated approach to humanizing the news contributes to the depoliticization of everyday life.

On the one hand, then, women journalists may draw on 'emotionalism' as a creative stylistic device to oppose the stuffy detachment and pose of masculine rationality routinely used in such 'serious' news categories as politics and business. On the other hand, women are being deployed in larger numbers than male journalists to exploit a trend in a hyper-compassionate journalism that systematically devalues issues concerning economic, social and cultural power and techniques of critical engagement and investigation. So we need to be cautious when celebrating those elements of change in journalism that have provided women with an opportunity to stake a claim in news production since there is a continuing tendency for women to be typecast in those areas that commodify news as entertainment.

The sexualization of news

Another feature of market-driven news is the sexualization of news and of female news presenters. This trend is not only about a rise in the reporting of sexual scandal stories about the infidelities of celebrities and male politicians in the tabloid press (see, for example, Lull and Hinerman 1997). As Patricia Holland (1998) claims, the popular tabloid newspapers in Britain changed when Rupert Murdoch transformed the *Sun* during the 1970s by introducing explicit sexual images of women such as the 'Page Three' girl, who symbolizes the division of newspaper readerships by sex and gender. Holland argues that news stories in the 'downmarket' tabloids became structured by sexualization as well as entertainment, thereby marginalizing radical and democratic content. She asserts that women's public participation is disputed by the sexualization of gender difference, because it acts as a tenacious potential constraint on their actions: 'by reinforcing sexual difference, the nature of the democratic discursive space is brought into question' (Holland 1998: 28). This process of sexualization of women's bodies in the context of news persists in new forms.

The emergence of the so-called 'Ken and Barbie' duo in television journalism, where a male and female newscaster are placed together as a couple and encouraged to engage in chatty dialogue, has become typical of television news in the US. The pairing of an attractive female newscaster with an authoritative male anchor has been the general rule for television news for a quarter-century. But increasingly, compatibility between the two presenters through relaxed and even personal banter becomes a crucial mechanism for sustaining a more intimate and personal mode of address. It is an emphasis that not only makes the professional abilities of the anchorpersons irrelevant but also (hetero)sexualizes the news by introducing a frisson between a male and female presenter. Ratings have risen in the US since the introduction of this format, which now characterizes both national and local television news in America, but only local news television in Britain. Interestingly, the British BBC and ITV channels have not yet adopted this style for their national news bulletins, principally because even the commercial channels follow the public service ethos of BBC1 and BBC2. As such the BBC is seen to act as a crucial shield against the public perception of an 'Americanization' of British television, that is, the increasing reliance on market-driven forces.

In the UK, television news programmes are being watched less and less by audiences under the age of forty-five. But with an ageing population, older audiences are increasingly being wooed as an important majority. Nevertheless, within an attempt to attract young audiences, a number of attractive and talented female news presenters, more youthful than their male predecessors, are now being selected (during the last decade) over what some critics regard as more experienced male colleagues in a bid to attract larger audiences (Brown 2002). These women have become household names and are being celebrated as stars. For example, thirty-three-year-old Kirsty Young's face appeared on the front cover of the *Radio Times* magazine (12–18 January 2001).[1] Young anchored the news for ITV1 before returning to *Channel 5 Evening News* in 2002.

An extreme instance of the sexualization of news and newscasters is offered up in Naked News.com, which sells daily newscasts in which the newscasters progressively take off their clothes, until they are entirely nude as they deliver news (national, international, sports, weather). Paying subscribers, who, of course, must be at least eighteen years old, can get both the female version (eleven women, all smiling and cheerful, and certainly all attractive) and the male version, with five male newscasters. Recently the company also began producing Naked News TV!, which its website (at <http://www.nakednews.com>) describes as 'a news and infotainment television program' delivering both serious and lighter sides of the news. The television version has fifty-minute segments, again, with separate all-nude female and all-nude male casts. Certainly one would be very hard-pressed to call this journalism, and news junkies will not be logging on to nakednews.com for the news of the day. But the fact that a company would design a pornographic site in this way at least suggests the vulnerability of journalism as an institution.

Judging women TV news presenters by their looks

While the 'new' TV journalism requires a youthful attractive appearance for male and female newsreaders, a particular kind of appearance is more important for women. This 'particular' appearance is very precisely calibrated, with market research firms undertaking extensive research with audience focus groups to find just what jewellery, lipstick colours, necklines and hairstyles will appeal to audiences. Intense debate continues about whether women are being selected over male colleagues because the public is attracted to images of sexy (but not too overly sexy) young female reporters on TV or because the more feminine, 'human-interest' angle is being favoured over 'proper' (i.e. masculine) factual reporting. On one hand, Kate Adie has accused her BBC bosses of 'filling news bulletins with bimbos because they are more concerned about the "shape of your leg" than professional ability' (quoted in Leonard 2001). She blames this not on sexism per se, however, but 'huge pressures of commercialism' faced even by the BBC. On the other hand, others claim the shift to female news presenters is not simply about recruiting someone with a 'pretty face'. For Channel 5, which presents itself as a 'modern' network catering to the young, the fact that Kirsty Young is a working mother functions to signify her as a 'modern' woman with whom audiences under fifty can identify. When Channel 5's director of programmes, Kevin Lygo, announced Kirsty Young's appointment, he stated:

The main news programmes have all been presented by men in their fifties an upwards, trained in a certain way. The personal has to be brought back. If news is in trouble, the answer is to make it more accessible. News is terribly important to us. To have an intelligent, attractive, talented professional woman at the centre of our news and our channel is equally

important. It is positioning the channel in keeping with what we are. She is
a modern woman, a working mother: she personifies the values we want to
be associated with.

(quoted in Brown 2002: 39)

As yet, the link between the size of news audiences and the gender of the
news presenter has not been proven. Other TV channels are searching for
ways of attracting audiences, with the BBC examining the idea of 'niche
news' to match style of presentation to type of audience. Nevertheless, the
deputy head of BBC television news, Rachel Attwell, anticipates that in ten
years, women will be the main presenters on the main channels (Brown 2002:
40). After all, in contrast to the job of, say, a war correspondent, news presenting is less disruptive for women with children. As Attwell comments, 'it is
a more stable life', potentially a key factor in attracting women to newsreading. Ironically, Attwell claims that young men are increasingly reluctant to
become presenters, despite the much higher salaries of presenters, relative to
correspondents. Attwell suggests that having to conform to a particular
regime of appearance in order to look 'inoffensive and telegenic', with hair in
a particular style, may be offensive to male TV news anchors, who also object
to news presenting as a more passive task than going on forays 'in the field'.
And the director of GMTV, Peter McHugh, claims that women have more
drive and are 'more in touch with the audience' than their male counterparts
(quoted in Brown 2002: 39).

In the United States the formula of using male news 'giants' – currently
men like Dan Rather, Tom Brokaw and Peter Jennings at the three major networks – has been regarded as so crucial to the success of CBS, NBC and
ABC, that their success is what complicates women's efforts to be promoted
to these positions. One large-scale study of US women TV reporters suggests
that they continue to face gender-differentiated obstacles, especially a rigid
approach to the hairstyles, make-up and clothing choices, resulting from
executives' anxieties, as well as gender-based decision-making. Updating their
1986 study, which found that hiring practices are based on the sex and
appearance of applicants, Engstrom and Ferri's 1998 study found that women
TV news anchors continue to agree that traditional gender role expectations
act as a hindrance to their work (Engstrom and Ferri 1998: 794). They also
point out that remarks and faultfinding about women's appearance came
from viewers, management and co-workers. In fact, Engstrom and Ferri
(1998: 798) conclude that 'overemphasis on physical appearance remains the
top-ranked career barrier' against women TV news anchors during the late
1990s; women anchors, in a sense, are part of media content and thus subject
to the appearance standards required of other women who appear on television. This confirms that women continue to be valued for their appearance
rather than their skills. As Lyse Doucet, presenter and foreign correspondent
for the BBC, states: 'One day you're a star, but then you can be a shooting star

and fall to the ground. They'll suddenly say "I don't like her haircut" or something' (quoted in Wells 2002: 4).

Black women journalists on television have had to put up with further difficulties of a racist as well as sexist nature concerning the tyranny of self-presentation. Pamela Newkirk (2000: 81) describes the requirement for African Americans in the United States to mimic white people not only in their behaviour and attitudes but also in appearance:

> As such, the African Americans [reporters] on television spoke in the same clipped diction as their white counterparts and bore no traces of African American culture in their mannerism or appearance. These became, for some black viewers, a source of contention and alienation, although most accepted the affections of black television journalists as prerequisites for middle-class achievement.

Post-feminist journalism

An important question arising from the increase in numbers of women journalists able to draw women readers and audiences is whether it has prompted a revival of feminist debates and approaches in news stories to counterbalance the trend towards the sexualization and trivialization of the news. Examples of this trend include reports entitled 'Why my boyfriend ditched me', 'How I dealt with my weight problem'; 'How I felt when I found husband cheating on me'. Therapy chat shows such as *Oprah*, *Rickie Lake* and the *Jerry Springer Show* in the US and screened in the UK are not journalistic forms, yet their discourse spills over into 'news', signalling the emergence of a style which is written by and for women. As such it is deserves analysis in the context of the trend towards the personalization of news. Such shows promote the trend toward the public exposure of intimate relationship problems framed by a celebrity through the use of a famous presenter.

Heller (1999: 10–11) categorizes the 'new girl writing' – that is, writing by 'jaunty female correspondents in the women's ghetto – in terms of three subgenres: first, the amusing 'home front' column, in which women cheerfully write about lazy husbands and accident-prone children ('Mum – Johnny's stuck a marble up his nose!'); second, the 'stern comment' piece taking a feminist perspective on public affairs ('When was the last time the Foreign Secretary changed a nappy?'); and third, the 'daffy girl' piece, 'in which a youngish single female confides the vagaries of her rackety personal life' ('Never try shaving your legs in a moving taxi'). She points out that the 'daffy girl' piece category gained popularity in the 1990s as part of the fashion for 'personal narratives' exemplified by Helen Fielding's 'Bridget Jones's Diary' published in the *Independent* and later the *Daily Telegraph*. These 'girl' columns are characterized by their frothiness, absence of politics, their emphasis on personal machinations. '[T]hey all tended to an extreme and perhaps ill-advised candour – regularly divulging details of marital breakdowns, sexual peccadilloes, depressive episodes, family rows and disgusting habits' (Heller 1999: 11). Heller points out the emergence of a male equivalent, 'new lad' style of writing, exemplified by Nick Hornby's 'sensitive blokishness', but she argues that it has not enjoyed such appeal despite its confessional element, since it was 'rarely as wincingly indiscreet as the girl's prose'.

Although the 'scurrilous female confessions' sub-genre is not new, the unflattering and self-deprecating quality of the writing is. Heller (1999: 13) sympathizes with this 'new girl writing' and wants to recuperate the genre, arguing that although the girl columns were 'not models of journalistic excellence', they were refreshing because they were simultaneously neurotic and confident, insecure and bold. She acknowledges, however, that one could also argue that the theme of personal humiliation in 'girl columns' demonstrates how unthreatening women journalists are to editors, and how unthreatening women professionals are to men: 'In other words, their alleged "post-feminism" suited the complacent misogynists who were running the show' (Heller 1999: 14).

A key problem is the typecasting of women journalists by insisting that their femaleness should dictate their writing but without addressing the politics of that female experience. As Heller (1999: 16) says, 'To establish a columnar identity, one does have to ham oneself up a little. But for writers in the women's ghetto, what this means, ultimately, is acting out a pantomime version of femaleness. Writing in drag.'

Central to the 'feminization of news' (Holland 1998: 18, van Zoonen 1998: 35) is the rise of a 'market-led feminism'. Market-led feminism indicates a new emphasis in the popular media on a particular materialistic version of femininity, equated with post-feminism, involving career women and focused on consumption and superficial 'style'. Lacking in the news media today are debates about feminism in the context of politics, the academy and various professions. A dominant claim articulated by liberal media is that second-wave feminism no longer speaks to ordinary young women because it is out of touch with their lives, at least in its public form.

Granted, feminism has been dominated by white middle-class women and has tended to marginalize the views and experiences of women from other backgrounds. This remains true of new, individualized models of feminism, characterized by Naomi Wolf's (1993) power feminism, which addresses a white, privileged group with its emphases on the importance of financial power. Moreover, many young women are alienated by the language and rhetoric of feminism. So, the repackaging of feminist ideas and goals as 'new' feminism, post-feminism, power feminism or woman-centred feminism is not surprising, as Imelda Whelehan (2000) points out. Some young independent-thinking women see feminism as a ready-made orthodoxy that *must* be criticized. While old feminists are perceived as incapable of 'taking a joke', many young feminists are demonstrating that they are quite capable of dealing with male sexist jokes and sexual innuendoes by speaking or acting outrageously themselves.

In an attempt to uncouple themselves from the puritanism and political correctness of 'old' feminism of the 1960s and 1970s, post-feminists such as Sophia Phoca and Rebecca Wright (1999) argue that this 'post' signals a 'going beyond' rather than a rejection of feminism. But we argue that male and female journalists use post-feminism to depoliticize feminism; they regard it as proof of the fragmentation and political passivity of feminism (Brooks 1997). Angela McRobbie (1997) argues that the conflict between 'old' and 'new' feminism is commensurate with the clash between older and younger generations, allowing the younger generation to develop a new range of identities. These identities are centred on consumption, hedonism and a celebration of raucous behaviour (McRobbie 1997). As such it merely continues a process begun over a century ago of approaching and appealing to women as domestic *consumers*, rather than as fully fledged citizens within the public sphere. Women's enfranchisement is conveyed through their status as consumers. This post-feminism panders to the advertising needs of news organizations within a market-led journalism. The dilemma facing women journalists is that they are being deployed to pander to women audiences' status as consumers. As such, they are confined to the straitjacket of the type of consumer journalism that leads to the trivializing and depoliticizing process identified in relation to confessional and therapy journalism. Women journalists are peripheral to the male enclaves of political and business news while they are encouraged to visibly bolster the shift towards consumer journalism.

Women professionals' views of new trends in journalism

For many women journalists, especially those in decision-making positions, the rise of confessional and therapy news presents a thorny conundrum with specifically gendered policy implications. Some women see the trend as progressive, arguing that humanizing the news makes it more accessible to women readers. When she was editor of the British *Independent on Sunday* from 1996 to 1998, Rosie Boycott expanded features, because of their emphasis on emotional and personal concerns: 'I want the whole paper to have the sense that it is there for you, talking to you. It's on your side, it is a friend. Magazines sell millions living off that formula' (quoted in Christmas 1997: 27).

On the other hand, other women protest that 'therapeutic news' is pandering to audiences, is 'dumbing down' news and blurring the distinction between features and news. Eve Pollard, former editor of the British tabloid, the *Sunday Mirror*, would therefore restrict features to the magazine sections of newspapers:

Features on skin care are much better done in magazines with colour and space to test one product against another. And how much more space is going to be given to health matters! It's everywhere and it's too much. It can be dangerous as it is frightening people: they are running around diagnosing themselves.

(quoted in Christmas 1997: 27)

Formerly executive editor at the British tabloid, the *Sunday Express*, Amanda Platell identifies the worrying trend that newspapers are becoming like magazines because readers now look to newspapers for entertainment and escape. 'Triumph over tragedy' stories which characterize magazines are popular because they focus on the human drama, not only of television and film stars, but also personal struggles such as 'how I coped with cancer/losing my job/losing my husband' (quoted in Christmas 1997: 27). The reputation of celebrities depends on identifying a triumph over tragedy as part of their psychological make up.

Of course, several women have consistently resisted 'infotainment' and the dumbing down of news (McNair 1998: 121). One woman who tried to practise journalism in a notably different way in the United States is Carol Marin. Starting in 1972, Marin anchored a morning TV talk show and engaged in general assignment reporting in Tennessee before moving to WMAQ, a major NBC affiliate in Chicago, where she was quickly promoted. As anchor of the evening newscast, Marin won awards and acclaim. She also took on what she considered affronts to journalism ethics. In 1990 she criticized her station for hiring a Chicago Bears football lineman as a commentator, in part because, she said, the athlete was known for verbally bashing women and gays and so did not deserve access to the audience. Five years later she criticized the newly hired station manager, Lyle Banks, who, again in the interests of boosting ratings, hired as vice president of news someone without journalism credentials (Finucane 2001: 122). Marin took on Banks a second time after he created a campaign in which advertisers agreed to partner with the station in supporting community outreach programmes in exchange for on-air recognition by journalists. Marin regarded the 'recognition' as a commercial venture and was suspended for three days when she refused to read the copy. She also criticized the 'happy talk' among anchors, news stories that essentially advertised entertainment programmes, and the dramatic increase in the number of stories per newscast – an increase that reduced the length and therefore the depth of each story.

The crowning blow came in 1997 when the station hired Jerry Springer as a commentator, despite protests from Marin and her co-anchor Ron Magers that he was not a serious journalist. Saying that the hiring of Springer – the host of arguably the seediest and more prurient talk show on daytime television – signalled a loss of credibility and integrity in news, Marin gave up her estimated $1 million a year job and resigned, as did others at the station (Finucane 2001: 124). When Springer attacked Marin in his first commentary, alleging that she tried to deny him his First Amendment rights, 1,400 callers responded to the commentary; 1,300 of them supported Marin. Five days later, when ratings for WMAQ continued to plummet, Springer resigned.

Marin won considerable support from various professional journalism organizations, including the SPJ ethics committee which said, 'The steady infusion of pure entertainment into the terrain of journalism troubles all conscientious journalists and threatens the credibility of dedicated professionals' (quoted in Finucane 2001: 124). Marin herself moved to the CBS affiliate in Chicago. And in 2000, promised that she would have control to create a serious in-depth newscast, she became sole anchor of a news programme. Her show initially had high ratings but they were short lived. To the regret of Marin and other television critics and serious journalists, the show was disbanded eight months later – just two days after she won a local Emmy award. She continues to do some reporting for CBS's *60 Minutes*.

Conclusion

The blending of entertainment and information and the blurring of the lines between fiction and news is nothing new. What *is* new is the assumption that today's journalism constitutes a 'feminisation' of news (Holland 1998: 18, van Zoonen 1998: 35), prompted by the influx of women journalists. Yet this kind of influx isn't new either. In the nineteenth century a significant minority of journalists wrote fictitious tales, often with the aim of creating a bit of fun or to stir up political action and highlight what they regarded as a genuine problem. Some of them even labelled their hoaxes as such, although they were not necessarily understood as such and readers often reacted to the hoax as if it were real (Fedler 1989).

This trend in confessional and therapy news also parallels the rise of 'sob sister' journalism and the 'New Journalism' in the US and Britain in the late nineteenth century. As described in Chapter 1, the New Journalism of the 1880s was an emotional and sensational style used to appeal to a reading market just then emerging. Both contemporary postmodern journalism and the New Journalism of the late nineteenth century gave women opportunities to enter the profession as they took on the task of interviewing and writing stories about women. New Journalism's editors, as we saw in Chapter 1, hired women reporters either as 'sob sisters' or to perform investigative stunts that would be regarded as particularly bold for women. This practice is echoed in newsrooms today. Thus, New Journalism shares with contemporary postmodern journalism two key features: heavy criticism for abandoning objectivity and impartiality, and a trend of employing large numbers of women. However, since New Journalism aimed to make newspapers function as agents of social reform, newspapers also vigorously promoted political affairs and public welfare. In contrast, the goal of contemporary news organizations is merely increased market share.

Once again, women journalists are being exploited by the news industry, within the shift to 'soft' journalism, for their potential to provide human-interest stories laced with emotionalism and sympathy. Although the rise of a market-driven popular news media with its emphasis on a 'humanized news' and consumer lifestyle features, is now driving women's inclusion in public communication, women remain typecast as marginal to the 'serious' world of politics and public policies. Nor are women journalists able to use their public forum to promote serious feminist debate or serious debate about feminism. The continuing distinctions between 'hard' and 'soft' news are hardening and institutionalizing a gendered hierarchical division between important, 'masculine' news and inferior, trivialized, 'feminine' news.

To conclude, news is not inherently feminine or masculine. It is therefore not helpful to refer to the postmodern shift to infotainment as a 'feminisation' of news. None the less, this shift has gendered implications, both positive and negative, for women both as journalists and as readers and audiences of the news. It could be argued that, as market-driven journalism intensifies, larger numbers of women journalists are being employed to produce more emotional, sensational and therapy-style news while men get on with the 'real' work of 'hard' news. Crucially, mainstream women journalists are being typecast by being associated with a less prestigious realm of 'news', and as Heller (1999) emphasizes, many end up in what is rendered the 'women's ghetto'. Christmas (1997: 55) asserts that women decision-makers should be questioning the excess of confessional journalism, stating 'pages of intimate details of relationships are becoming banal and often bizarre'. As yet, women are not given more equal access to investigate and report on the privileged 'hard', political and economic news. Notwithstanding these problems, van Zoonen (1998) suggests that women are being given the opportunity to initiate a collapse in the division between 'hard' and 'soft' and to explore ways of allowing women to participate more democratically in the construction of a non-gendered public sphere. In the short run, however, femininity and so-called 'feminine news values' with an emphasis on human-interest stories are more marketable and are being exploited at the very moment when news is shifting as a genre from news to infotainment. While journalism may be in a state of flux – becoming more and more commercialized – this trend does not ensure that women will gain equal status. But, these changes may place pressures on the industry to treat women more equitably in the future.

12

Conclusion

WOMEN, JOURNALISM AND NEW MEDIA

In both the United States and Britain, the institution and profession of journalism has been structured by gender. This chapter begins by summarizing some of the ways in which gender has been deployed both to block or limit women's entry into the profession and yet also to afford certain kinds of opportunities for women. Much debate in media studies now centres on the rise of new interactive media and the Internet's potential for bringing into being an interactive audience. We ask how the Internet and on-line journalism may affect women both in newsrooms and in terms of their relationship to public discourse. Drawing on Habermas's (1989) normative theory about the public sphere, we will explore women journalists' potential contributions to debates and deliberations in the public sphere. We ask whether women can use the Internet as a tool for promoting women's news and for participating in democracy.

Features of the gendered structuring of journalism

The history of women in journalism in both countries reveals that women have been primarily valued either as individual *consumers* of or, better yet, as a collective market for news. As subjects in the news, women primarily interest women; over the last two centuries, they have been widely assumed to be of interest to men only in the context of sexually titillating stories. Even so, women's capacity to generate advertising revenue has been crucial to the success of both print and broadcast news organizations. Therefore, at least in the mainstream news media, women journalists have been valued less for their competence than for their intrinsic femininity and ability to provide a 'woman's angle'. Accordingly, women have been brought into the profession largely to establish a genre of reporting known as 'human-interest' news which, notwithstanding overlaps, has been contrasted with so-called 'serious' news. As such, women journalists have been typecast as either 'feminine' or at least expert in the 'feminine', defined as areas or subjects in which men have no interest and about which male reporters refuse to write. Even when women have managed to escape the confines of the women's pages or to destroy the women's pages, women reporters have been consistently pressured to situate themselves in what has often been called – including by women themselves – a 'female ghetto'. Their association with 'soft' news eclipses the fact that women have worked hard to extend the scope of their accomplishments in a far broader range of journalism. They have been assigned to stories with an emphasis on personalities and personal views. Moreover, they are associated with the shift to confessional journalism. Men have also helped to produce a rise in confessional journalism, and it is typically male managers who have authorized or demanded the therapeutic approach to news. Male journalists are also self-reproachful, even self-critical, in admitting their own complicity with this trend. Yet, the pandering to market interests has often been con-flated with 'feminizing'.

Women have acted as a reserve army of labour in journalism's history in both the United States and the UK. Women's employment in journalism has surged during moments of crisis or innovation across the news media indus-try. Thus, news organizations were essentially forced to recruit women during the First and Second World Wars to fill gaps in newsrooms left by men who entered the military. Many women were forced to leave their wartime posi-tions when the men returned. At other times, editors have hired women to add glamour, novelty or frivolity, and thereby attract desirable audiences. They were recruited as gimmicks when new styles or new trends in journalism were introduced, such as the New Journalism of the 1880s, and have been drawn on as novelties in more recent contexts such as war reporting and in the 'magazine style' of postmodern news journalism common today. Over his-tory, then, women have struggled to be taken seriously as professional journalists.

Individual women have succeeded in establishing themselves as credible journalists reporting on serious issues. They are producing intelligent, useful, important stories about international diplomacy, economic and financial trends, and technological and scientific innovations. They are investigating military abuses, corporate fraud and the downsides of bioengineering. 'Femaleness' is no longer an automatic disadvantage in the reporting world, although many women journalists find that childcare responsibilities continue to be a considerable burden that few men share. Yet women remain a minor-ity within the decision-making positions across the news media.

Previous chapters show several ways in which women journalists have helped transform news agendas and, in so doing, have broadened definitions of news. Women are more likely to report on a wider range of social issues with an emphasis on the human-interest angle, on personalities and personal views. More importantly, women have taken the lead in covering issues affect-ing women's lives, especially with reference to sexual harassment in the workplace, a range of health and medical concerns of specific interest to women, balancing work and family life, and on a range of changes in the nature of work, parenting and family life, including divorce, sexuality and gay rights. However, in doing so they tend to be typecast. They are more likely to be assigned human-interest stories or to cover lower-status beats such as leisure, fashion, lifestyle and cookery.

Many scholars (see van Zoonen 1998) argue that, at least now, critical mass is not the issue, since additional numbers of women entering the profession no longer makes a significant difference. Rather, journalism is changing. The 'new' journalism is marked by the emergence of 'masculine' and 'feminine' styles that can be produced by *either* male or female journalists: 'masculine' styles being traditional, serious journalism and feminine styles referring to consumer-oriented, market-driven news such as 'human-interest, emotional investment and sensationalism' (van Zoonen 1998: 45). As van Zoonen says, the rise in gendered news categories does not necessarily indicate the advancement of women's status in the profession.

We have argued that women have been centrally involved in the shift to a new style of postmodern journalism characterized by a depoliticization of people's lives, especially women's, with a continuing emphasis on addressing women as consumers. Debates about women's issues, women's rights and women's equality are being framed within this commodity culture, leading to a trivialization of feminism. Male journalists are also being pushed into this market-led journalism. Nevertheless, part of this postmodern style has been a renewed emphasis on the sexualization of news such that women as both subjects and producers of news are judged by their appearance rather than their competence.

Meanwhile, the marginalization of women and the trivialization of women's issues in the news, which continued well into the twentieth century, prompted women to develop alternative means of expressing their views, by reporting on and advancing women's rights in a political context through campaigning and activism. The emergence of independent news outlets, from the suffrage press to women's Internet newsgroups, has provided women with the opportunity to promote women's rights generally, to promote the particular interests of specific kinds of women, and to serve women as politically involved audiences for the news of the day. Since these journalistic activities often involve training programmes, women have been able to develop and share their journalism skills with women who otherwise might not enjoy a journalistic voice. In fact, women's alternative news media have, at various historical junctures, disrupted conventional news values and mainstream ways of representing women.

Women's alternative news media throws into sharp relief the way that mainstream news trivializes women and women's issues by unmasking the kinds of themes and issues that the dominant sector reports on. Feminist media expose the sexism of postmodern journalism. It highlights questions about women's use of the Internet as an interactive medium to advance democracy which we examine below. This raises queries about the direction of journalism as an industry and as a profession, and the impact of the Internet in relation to existing gendered structures in journalism, especially given its opportunities for global participation and interactivity.

Gender and on-line journalism

Computer-assisted research is rapidly growing and evolving. Predicting whether on-line reporting will impact journalism's work structures and professional standards in gender-specific ways is difficult, if only because on-line communication is changing so quickly and new processes soon become outdated. Concepts and data from four or five years ago may be wholly irrelevant. Moreover, to date little research has been conducted about on-line journalism and much of what exists is proprietary and therefore not publicly disseminated. Predictions about the impact of on-line journalism on gender patterns in newsrooms are equally difficult, although the initial concerns that women were largely absent in the design and especially in the use of the computer and the Internet now may appear overblown. In both the US and Britain women (and ethnic minorities) are quickly catching up with white men in the extent to which they use the Internet and are becoming the majority of on-line users (Shade 2002: 75).

In terms of competition between on-line news media and traditional news media, research findings remain equivocal. Newspaper readerships have been steadily dropping in Western nations for decades, yet the Newspaper Association of America has concluded that the market for the top fifty US newspapers remains healthy and competitive.[1] Still other surveys indicate decreases in traditional media use but a rise in overall media usage.[2] Whether on-line news will overtake traditional news media remains unclear. Many owners of old media outlets are, however, providing complementary on-line services to offer consumer choice and 'convergence', the newest media buzzword, refering to a blending and combination of print, broadcast and computer dissemination.

During its first few years, on-line journalism simply copied the forms and content of traditional news media. Devising and editing the material for the Internet was largely a technical concern, and was undertaken either by technical workers with elementary journalistic skills or journalists with basic skills in on-line technology. Now an increasing number of newspapers have journalists (reporters, photographers, videographers, editors) who work exclusively for the Internet edition, although this has not yet led to the emergence of a new and distinctive field of journalism. The *Chicago Tribune*, for example, inaugurated its own Internet team in 1996, offering not only digital versions of content from the print version, but additional in-depth stories, special reports, and audio and video material from the *Tribune's* television and radio services. The same is true of the *Wall Street Journal*. Moreover, many journalists and journalism scholars insist that on-line journalism, requiring as it does the same proficiency in reporting and writing skills as other media forms, is not significantly different from print journalism, and that the standards and definitions of good journalism are not medium-specific. Nevertheless, others argue that the unique multimedia, hypertextual and interactive qualities of the Internet will lead to on-line journalism eventually gaining the status of a separate medium (Deuze 1999). In the meantime, in the United States integration or convergence of print and new media is taking on normative status, with shared newsrooms in over 80 per cent of newspapers (Ross and Middleberg 1998, Lasica 1998); European newspapers are likewise continuing to split off on-line activities from traditional newspaper activities (Bierhoff, van Dusseldorp and Scullion 1999). In any case, the question remains whether on-line journalism will merely entail (re)processing the work of 'real' journalists or whether it will require specific journalistic skills for the production of specific on-line content. Evidence is not yet available to confirm whether professional journalism standards are being maintained or undermined by the use of the Internet.

Will on-line journalism evolve into a job for 'the boys', given its 'techy' label or, conversely, is it likely to become a job attractive to women with childcare responsibilities given the 9–5 office-based nature of the occupation? The answer will depend on whether the work is divided off from traditional forms of journalism and what kind of newsroom culture arises within it. What we do know so far is that on-line editors are a relatively young group (Neuberger et al. 1997), and that the rapid pace of change in computer-assisted research and reporting (CARR) and the digitalization of journalism are causing a number of problems for journalists including stress, burn-out and RSI (repetitive strain injury) (Singer 1997a, 1997b; Cottle 1999; Deuze 2001).

Importantly, a recent study by Mark Deuze and Steve Paulussen (2002) in the Netherlands found a significant gender imbalance among on-line journalists: 74 per cent of 137 on-line journalists who participated in their web-based survey were male and, not surprising, the majority were under thirty-five years of age. Less than half of on-line journalists said they leave the newsroom at any period to do reporting. Some 65 per cent of respondents spend over an hour a day engaged in the technical preparation of texts for website editing and coding, so they agreed that technological skills are vital. Three-quarters of these respondents also said that on-line journalism (at least in the Low Countries) is evolving into a new form of professional journalism, to be distinguished from print, radio and television journalism. The researchers did not study the extent to which gender mattered in on-line journalists' professional characteristics. Nevertheless, since these initial survey results suggest that the job has begun to emerge as a masculine domain, on-line journalism needs to be monitored for potential gender segregation.

Mainstream journalism and interactivity

Journalists have marvelled at the Internet's capacity to allow people across the globe not only to seek out information and learn about issues that interest them but also to interact instantly, for example, in on-line polls and chat rooms. What are the implications of new technology developments for women? While interactive media may be seen as part of the democratization of the public sphere, this is more apparent in alternative spaces on the Internet, such as women's news groups, than in mainstream news media. Women's Enews, launched in 2000, is an important Internet news service that, among other resources, provides journalists and other researchers with a database of experts on topics of special concern to women. The news service is a mainstream one in the sense that it is widely used by other media in the US and globally, including the *Washington Post*, the *Los Angeles Times*, the *Chicago Tribune*, the *New York Daily News*, the *Buffalo News*, and MSNBC to newspapers in Kuala Lumpur and the Philippines. Having emerged from a 1996 roundtable discussion hosted by the NOW Legal Defense and Education Fund, Women's Enews is funded by donations, commercial publications using their reports and foundations, including the John S. and James L. Knight Foundation. This news service has received much praise for being ahead in reporting major national and international stories, and for producing stories of depth and breadth.[3] This women's news service is aiming to affiliate with a number of journalism schools and act as a mentor to trainee journalists.

Within mainstream news, interaction by e-mail on live webcasts has been praised for allowing producers to find out more about their audiences and has been referred to as 'user-control journalism', despite the fact that journalists have to decide which e-mails to read out and are inevitably selective. As Kopper, Kalthoff and Czepek (2000: 509) state:

> It seems that we may still need the journalists as mediators, in order to maintain professional standards and in order to help us sort through the jungle of information. What exactly the role of journalists could be in a more participatory system still needs to be explored.

So while the Internet opens up important possibilities for women to participate in the public sphere, questions are raised about the unequal access to new media technology and differing levels of communicative competence structured by class, gender and region, including the divide between the Western and developing world.

Curiously, although interactivity is an important attribute of on-line news media it remains underused (Kopper, Kalthoff and Czepek 2000). Newspaper websites usually provide newsroom e-mail addresses but they are less consistent about offering users the possibility of interacting with specific reporters or participating in on-line polls or discussion forums. This suggests that the journalists remain ambivalent about on-line journalism. Traditional news media have not yet figured out how to 'use' interactivity to break down the traditional distinction between producers and consumers and to transcend conventional modes of 'mass' communication; they do not yet know how to make a profit from it or how to approach the changes to journalism as a profession that are being driven by new media technology.

Women, the Internet and the public sphere

The contrasting histories of women's roles within mainstream and alternative news media say less about gender differences in journalism than they say about a widening gap between market-led journalism and moves towards democratic participation. Nevertheless, the rich and ever-growing opportunities for women to come together on-line to produce and globally disseminate alternative news suggest that traditional forums of public debate are being reformulated by the rise of interest-group websites and that the Internet offers a potential for the reinvention of the 'public'.

For Jürgen Habermas (1989), 'public sphere' is a conceptual resource indicating a space for political deliberation and participation in debate and critique of other spheres, including that of the government, the corporation and the family. Citizens' deliberation in the public sphere has the potential to expose inequalities of modes of communication, among other inequalities. Habermas was deeply concerned that public opinion was being propelled by commercial interests rather than the objectives of information and justice, with publicity reduced merely to public relations. In Chapter 11, we showed how news organizations' market-led attempts – attempts that were largely successful – to redefine citizens as consumers undermined public discourse and ultimately undermined democracy. Traditional journalism is increasingly being eclipsed by entertainment, advertising, sports and fashion within the growing competition between journalism and non-journalism content in news media (Dahlgren 1997, Berger 2000, McManus 1994). Examples of the pressures on news workers to comply with corporate interests and to compete for advertising and audiences include the emphasis on sensationalism in news, a narrowing of the gap in quality between broadsheets and popular tabloid newspapers, a fall in the amount of foreign news in broadcast news and broadsheet newspapers, a decline in the prominence of political coverage and the rise of confessional or therapeutic journalism. The normative ideal of democratic journalism is said to be ending, according to scholars such as Dahlgren (1997). In a society where information is treated as a commodity, market logic overwhelms journalistic logic and undermines the responsibility of journalists to guide citizens through the information jungle.

Many feminist scholars find Habermas's concept of the public sphere to be a useful heuristic device for conceiving democratic communication, although they have criticized his ideas, at least as originally formulated, for ignoring gender and gender difference (see, for example, Benhabib 1992, Holland 1998). The philosopher Nancy Fraser (1992: 116) asserts that the very concept of a 'public sphere' of free and equal dialogue is masculine and depends on the exclusion of women.

The public sphere excludes women precisely because women have functioned historically to prop up men's potential to act as free and equal citizens. Women traditionally catered to men's needs within a subordinate, femininized 'private sphere' of domesticity and intimacy, including sexual subordination. The dichotomy between a public and private sphere is an ideological process that genders space, and in doing so it structures women's subordination. Habermas has responded to feminist critiques by conceding that he had wrongly ignored the relevance of the domestic sphere to politics, power and commerce. Thus, while women *have* been part of the public sphere throughout history, their contribution has been obstructed, unacknowledged and marginalized within a patriarchal assertion of a feminized domestic sphere (van Zoonen 1991). The history of women's alternative media demonstrates both their participation and their marginalization. Activities such as that of the suffrage press in Britain and women's public access in nineteenth-century America described in Chapter 7 show that women have played a central role in public discourse. The question now is whether women's use of the Internet will accelerate this trend.

Despite its limitations, Habermas's conceptualization highlights women's bid for citizenship and democratic inclusion. The feminist project of reworking a Habermasian public sphere aims to further women's emancipation and explain women's participation in public spaces and how their interests and needs can be accommodated. The concept of public sphere initiates a critical analysis of the overprivatization of women's issues in the news media such as rape, sexual harassment, domestic violence, the feminization of poverty and sexual discrimination in employment practices. Identifying the political nature of the private sphere exposes the way that such issues are being depoliticized and treated as 'personal' or domestic rather than as symptomatic of patriarchal structures in society.

In her exploration of an oppositional discursive space for gender politics that may be relevant to contemporary society, Rita Felski (1989: 155–82) develops an alternative model of a feminist public sphere, a 'counter-public'. In contrast to Habermas's model, this counter-public is not and cannot be universally representative. Instead, the counter-public presents a critical analysis of the dominant values and ideals of society from the standpoint of women as a subordinated group. This sphere is 'public' in the sense that its ideas are directed to wider society. Similarly, Fraser (1992) refers to subaltern counter-publics who, because they are marginalized, produce 'counter-discourses' and thereby expand the topics of public discourse by forcing issues that were once ignored to be debated in public. Felski's (1989) model of a counter-public challenges the view that alternative news media is peripheral. The production and circulation of women's alternative news media generates and confirms a feminist identity and notion of community between women.

Although the notion of a counter-public was based on the print medium, one might ask whether the Internet can be used by women as a democratic journalistic tool to produce a counter-public independent of owners, advertisers, and market and corporate interests. Certainly cyberfeminists believe that a feminist counter-public can flourish in cyberspace, and that new communication technologies are liberatory. Indeed, although we are not making this argument, cyberfeminists such as Sadie Plant (1997: 42–3) have even argued that women are better prepared, culturally and psychologically, for the twenty-first century and will do better than men in the digital age. The World Wide Web fosters public discourse and strengthens the public sphere, according to a communitarian logic. The Internet has produced virtual communities linked by social or community issues and is contributing broader and more in-depth political participation by citizens. It also provides the technical means to act as a watchdog against traditional market-led journalism. Independent Internet news groups can operate as oppositional news media both in the West and in the developing world by acting as custodians and challenging both state and commercial media. Interactive electronic technology offers the potential to empower citizens to take part in new democratic debates among one another and with governments.

For women, then, the possibilities of the Internet within the frame of alternative media are enormous, as shown in Chapter 9. Given that women share the experiences of social disadvantage and social exclusion, they continue to constitute a 'minority' group around the world despite their numerical majority. New initiatives in the form of feminist Internet newsgroups and feminist information networks may well expand and seep into the mainstream news media, influencing its form and content precisely because women make up such a vast 'minority' group. Thus, Habermas's normative ideal remains relevant, with women and other marginalized groups successfully exploiting the manifold opportunities to form Internet-based women's groups and have their voices heard within projects aimed at advancing women's rights and civic participation in democracy. However, while women can and do form groups on the Internet, further research is needed to confirm whether this activity supports formation of a genuinely public sphere or instead is merely something closer to Todd Gitlin's (1998) critical notion of tiny, multiple sphericules, emphasizing the narrow and fragmented nature of such in-group communication.

While women in alternative news media have asserted their commitment to women's rights and the democratization of the public sphere, mainstream professional women have, with varying degrees of consciousness and success, battled to advance women's equal employment and professionalization.

Women journalists in mainstream news media have the practical skills to contribute to the enfranchisement of women and the weakening or dismantling of the division between the public and private by ensuring that women's voices are heard in the mainstream through the politicization rather than the commodification of women's experiences. The growth of new media forms and initiatives may release women from traditional stereotypes and constraints; growth of new media forms and the creation of infrastructures may strengthen women's professional and political roles. Unfortunately, this seems unlikely given the concentration of ownership and control of the news media which may worsen existing constraints on employment practices and occupational status, thereby reinforcing a commercialization and sexualization of journalism content. Women journalists must not regard new media technologies as a panacea. For all their opportunities at both the local and global level, and for all the invitations to share information in creative and innovative ways, the Internet is not a universal solution. First, the technology itself is being commercialized and much of the 'news' is an excuse for selling goods and services. Second, the Internet offers more e-commerce than e-commons. Third, the Internet is so fragmented, chaotic and difficult to negotiate that it continues to be difficult to use as a tool for policy-making. Accordingly, the demand continues for newspapers, news magazines and broadcast news, and women need to continue to play a central role in all modes of communication.

Notes

Introduction

1 Extract from Adie's autobiography (Adie 2002) serialized as 'My Gulf War' in the *Guardian, Night and Day,* 15 September 2002: 33.

1 Early women journalists: 1850–1945

1 Equivalent to Britain's state schools.
2 Rayne's book *What Can a Woman Do: or Her Position in the Business and Literary World* was republished in 1974 by Arno Press.
3 Working-class women were effectively debarred from journalism as a profession in the same way that they were excluded from most professions at the time. Women from ethnic minorities were unheard of as journalists, mainly because at the time the ethnic minority population in Britain was very small.
4 William T. Stead (1886) 'Government by Journalism', *Contemporary Review* 49: 656, quoted in Malone (1999).
5 Annie Besant wrote 'White Slavery in London' in the *Link* on 23 June 1888. Other articles she wrote in the *Link* on the same subject in the same year include 'White and Black Lists' (30 June), 'How Messrs. Bryant and May Fight' and 'The Revolt of the Matchmakers' (both 7 July) (quoted in Malone 1999: 52).
6 The major settlement of the immigrant black community in Britain did not begin until the 1950s so a black press was established much later there (see Chapter 4).
7 See Chapter 2 for more details.
8 Those interested in following up women's war writing should consult Sharon Ouditt (1999) *Women Writers of the First World War: An Annotated Bibliography,* London and New York: Routledge.
9 It should also be noted that men suffered because of Reith's moral values as well.

2 Women journalists in the post-war period

1 From anonymous obituary in *The Times,* 12 November 1996.
2 Although the *Guardian* had a woman's page, during the 1950s there was some debate about whether it was considered to be a national paper as it was printed in Manchester. It did not become a Fleet Street paper until it established a London base in 1960.
3 The 'Dear Marje' column in the *Daily Mirror* ran from 1971 to 1996, the last one appearing a week before her death. In 1992 she also wrote a weekly advice column for the *Sunday Mirror.*
4 This situation still existed in the UK in 2000. Research by Caroline Mitchell and Kim Michaels indicates that in 2000 only 14.6 per cent of presenters on main-stream UK radio were female, and 32 per cent of stations have no female presenters at all. See Michaels and Mitchell 2000: 238–49 for details.
5 Quoted in MacGregor (2002: 184).
6 BBC2 was launched in April 1964 and transmitted on 625 lines rather than the existing standard of 405 lines. It was envisaged that there would be a gradual change as old sets broke down, and the new frequency would allow for colour transmissions, introduced in 1968 (see Briggs 1995 for details on the launch of BBC2 and colour transmissions).

3 The education and training of women journalists

1 GCEs were replaced by Ordinary Level certificates (O levels), then General Certificates of Secondary Education (GCSEs). These are national examinations in specific subjects taken at age sixteen
2 Shorthand is still a valued skill among journalists. Delano and Henningham's 1995 survey of UK journalists showed that 56 per cent of journalists believe that without a 100-words-per-minute shorthand qualification, a journalist cannot be considered 'fully trained' (1995: 15).
3 An Advanced Level certificate (A level) is a qualification taken in England and Wales in a specific subject at the end of secondary education, usually around the age of eighteen. The standard requirement for university entry is three A levels.
4 Delano and Henningham state: 'in 1992 more than two thirds (69%) of British journalists have attended university or college, even though fewer than that grad-uated' (1995: 13). Thus the number of graduate journalists is a little less than 69 per cent but still around the two-thirds mark.
5 In the late 1960s, women were about 41 per cent of the student body.
6 Sixteen institutions were contacted by telephone in June 2002. These institutions employed seventy-four men and fifty-nine women to teach journalism.

4 'One of the boys'? Women's experiences of the glass ceiling

1 The International Federation of Journalists' plan can be accessed at <http://www.ifj.org/publications>.
2 'The Great Divide: Female Leadership in U.S. Newsrooms' jointly commissioned and released in 2002 by the American Press Institute and the Pew Center for Civic

Journalism is available on-line at <http: //www.americanpressinstitute.org> or <http: //www.pewcenter.org>.

3 Key findings from Weaver et al.'s (2003) report to the Knight Foundation are available at <http: //www.poynter.org>.

4 Vernon Stone's (1997) survey, 'Women Break Glass Ceiling in TV News', is a report submitted to the Federal Glass Ceiling Commission, and available at <http: //www.missouri.edu/jourvs/tvfunds.html>.

5 Vernon Stone (2001) update and projections in 2001 are available at <http: //www.missouri.edu/-jourvs/gtvminw.html>.

6 Details of the USC/Annenberg study can be found at <http: //www.aaja.org.html/ news-html>.

7 See for example, 'The Connie Chung Phenomenon' by Somini Sengupta (1997).

8 The Freedom Forum is a non-partisan foundation, originally established by the Gannett newspaper chain, to support a variety of services having to do with diversity and First Amendment issues.

9 Henningham and Delano (1998) interviewed 726 journalists employed full time by daily or weekly news media including national and regional daily and weekly newspapers, television and radio news services, and wire services (such as Reuters or Press Association). Freelance journalists were therefore excluded from this study, and those employed by popular or special-interest magazines or those working in non-news information programmes for broadcasting organizations – areas where women predominate.

10 Sixty-seven per cent of women journalists in Britain are under thirty-five years of age, while only 35 per cent of men are under thirty-five. The average age of female journalists is thirty-three and for male journalists it is thirty-eight. British women also represent a minority of journalists in the older age categories, with only 12 per cent of women in the forty to forty-nine age group compared to 27.5 per cent men, and 6.6 per cent of women journalists in the fifty-plus age group, compared to 19.2 per cent of men (Henningham and Delano 1998: 147).

11 Quoted in 'Breaking through the Glass Ceiling', *Ethnic News Watch, The Weekly Journal*, 29 September 1994, p. 5.

12 Quoted in ibid.

13 Quoted in 'Bias in Black and White' by Gavin Bell, *The Scotsman*, 23 June, 2000, p. 10.

14 In 1995 the NUJ's numbers began to rise again, and during the mid-1990s when Henningham and Delano (1998) conducted their study of British journalists, 65 per cent of their sample were members. Aspirations towards professional status were attached to another organization called the British Association of Journalists, but only 1 per cent of the sample belonged to this organization.

15 Only 51 per cent describe the job as a 'profession', according to Henningham and Delano's study (1998: 155). Sixty-seven per cent of the journalists they interviewed do not believe the occupation can be structured as a profession and as few as 5 per cent feel that journalism can be structured into a closed profession along the lines of law or medicine. Yet the majority believe that journalism should have a status similar to that of occupations such as teaching, the law and accountancy.

16 For details of the results of this survey, see Philippa Kennedy, 'WIJ Survey: The Talent that is Squandered by Childcare Failings', *Press Gazette*, 31 May 2001,

available at <http: //www.pressgazette.co.uk/> (accessed 9 July 2003). Also see Women in Journalism (1998).

17 In Britain, there are 260 local commercial radio stations, fifteen local commercial television stations, thirty-nine BBC local radio stations and twelve BBC regional TV stations. Local news therefore provides far more employment opportunities for journalists than national news. See van Zoonen (1994) and Skidmore (1998) for information on women in public relations and advertising.

18 Nancy Cook Lauer, 'Studies Show Women's Role in Media Shrinking', on-line. Available at <http: //www.wenews.org/article.cfm?aid=915> (accessed on 21 May 2002).

19 The *News of the World*'s sales dropped from 8 million in 1955 to 5 million in 1985 and stood at 4.5 million in 1997 (Christmas 1997). Sales of the *Sunday Mirror* dropped from 5 million in 1955 to 3 million in 1985 and to 2.3 million in 1997 (Christmas 1997).

20 Source: Annual Report and Accounts 2001/2002 BBC Facts and Figures <http: //www.bbc.co.uk/info/report8/financial/factsf8.shtm>.

21 Philippa Kennedy, 'WIJ Survey: The Talent that is Squandered by Childcare Failings', *Press Gazette,* 31 May 2001, <http: //www.pressgazette.co.uk/>.

22 Ibid.

23 Anne Perkins, 'WIJ Survey: Working Mothers', *Press Gazette*, 31 May 2001, <http: //www.pressgazette.co.uk/>.

5 Gendered newsroom cultures and values

1 International Women's Media Foundation survey report available at <http: //www.iwmf.org>.

2 See Soothill and Walby (1991) and Meyers (1997) 'for media research on sexual violence', and Kitzinger (1998) on the reporting of 'false memory syndrome'.

3 See note 1.

4 See note 1.

5 *Los Angeles Times*, 9–18 September 1984.

6 However, an award was jointly given for newspaper history in 1918 – the only year this award was made – to Minna Lewison and another Columbia University student for a history they co-authored of the public service rendered by the press. Lewison went on to report for the *Daily Investment News* and *Women's Wear* before being hired as a copy reader for the *Wall Street Journal.*

7 The Pulitzer for commentary has been won by Mary McGrory (*Washington Star*, 1975), Ellen Goodman (*Boston Globe*, 1980), Anna Quindlen (*New York Times*, 1992), Liz Balmaseda (*Miami Herald*, 1993), Eileen McNamara (*Boston Globe*, 1997) and Maureen Dowd (*New York Times*, 1999). The Pulitzer for criticism has been won by three *New York Times* critics (Ada Louise Huxtable, Margo Jefferson and in 1998 by book critic Michiko Kakutani) as well as by two other women. *Miami Herald* writer Madeleine Blais won the Pulitzer for feature writing in 1980, and since then seven other women have won that award.

8 Regional Press Awards are available at <http: //www.regionalpressawards.co.uk>.

9 British Press Awards are available at <http: //www.britishpressawards.com>.

10 BSkyB Annual Report 1998: 29, quoted in Boyle and Haynes 2000: 130.

6 Challenges to sexism and discrimination

1 The decision is available at <http: //www.law.umkc.edu/faculty/projects/ftrials/communications/ludtke.html>.
2 Personal communication with Linda Steiner, 4 September 1998.
3 Also see <http: //www.womeninjournalism.co.uk/about.html> (accessed 14 May 2002).
4 'The Sting of Anti-Discrimination Litigation: Plenty of Pain as Legal Precedents are Set', 2000 *New York Press Club,* no author cited. Posted at New York Press Club's website at <http: //www.bigredhen.com/peckingpaugh.html>.
5 'Anchorwoman Wins $8.3 Million Sex Bias Judgment', no byline, available at <http: //www.cnn.com/US/9901/29/anchorwoman.suit/>, posted 29 January 1999.
6 Ibid.
7 Ibid.

7 The 'first wave' of women's alternative journalism

1 March 1852 issue, p. 24.
2 *Women's Suffrage Journal,* 1 October 1870, p. 79.
3 The Anti-Corn Law League organization was formed in 1839 with the objective of repealing the English Corn Laws. Its leading figures were Richard Cobden and John Bright.

8 Women's alternative print journalism of the 'second' and 'third' waves

1 ABC Total Circulation figures, 1980.
2 In British literature and debates, the term 'women of colour' was later replaced by the term 'black women', or 'black and Asian women'.
3 September 1980, no. 98.
4 April/May 1971, p. 4.
5 Review summary 'Diva's Great But You Don't Get Much for Your Money', Mariandalice, epinions.com, on-line. Available at <http: //www.epinions.com/mags-review-5E2F>.
6 <http: //www.qxmag.co.uk>
7 Texts published and distributed secretly, despite banning by the Soviet regime.
8 <http: //www.hipmama.com>

9 Women's alternative media in broadcasting and the Internet

1 The First Amendment to the US Constitution famously provides for freedom of speech and forbids government censorship or limitations on the press.
2 The WINGS website is <http: //www.wings.org/>.
3 This continues to be a prominent theme. For example, the 'affinity' guerrilla group behind DIVA TV (Damned Interfering Video Activist Television) says it produces MTV-type 'propaganda' on behalf of ACT UP (AIDS Coalition to Unleash Power) (Saalfield and Ravarro 1991).
4 More mainstream Internet news services that focus on women's issues are mentioned in Chapter 12 in relation to the public sphere.

10 Women war correspondents

1 For a list of all accredited American women correspondents during the Second
   World War see 'Women Come to the Front: Journalists, Photographers, and
   Broadcasters During World War II', available at <http: //www.lcweb.loc.gov/
   exhibits/wcf/ecf0005.html>.
2 Independents are sometimes also called 'unilateral', to distinguish them from
   those 'embedded' reporters working under the protection and aegis of the US
   military.
3 Committee to Protect Journalists (2001) '24 Journalists Killed for Their Work in
   2000' available at <http: //www.cpj.org/news/2001/killed_release_01.html>
   (accessed on 9 July 2003). Also see Committee to Protect Journalists (2002) '37
   Journalists Killed for Their Work in 2001' available at <http: //www.cpj.org/
   news/2002/Killed_release_02.html> (accessed on 9 July 2003).
4 Sexual and racial fears were invoked by the George Bush (senior) administration
   to create a demonized image of Saddam Hussein during the 1991 Gulf War.
   Metaphors of Iraqi 'rape', penetration and 'violation' were used throughout the
   war by the US government, evoking the idea that Iraq had 'raped' its neighbour,
   Kuwait (for debates about the media representation of the Gulf War, see Philo
   and McLaughlin 1995).
5 The title of Charlotte Ebener's 1955 memoir *No Facilities for Women* refers to the
   same excuse. Although Ebener had already reported on several wars 'from the
   women's angle', the US military refused to let her visit a Korean island where the
   women were apparently politically and economically independent.
6 F.L. Ingersoll (1993). Women in Journalism project of the Washington Press
   Club Foundation. Available on-line at <http://ncp.press.org/wpfora/murph/htm>.
7 Christine Martin (1988) 'Women War Correspondents in Vietnam: Historical
   Analysis and Oral Histories', Master's thesis, University of Maryland College of
   Journalism, cited in Beasley and Gibbons (1993: 224).
8 Phillip Knightley, *The Times*, 21 January 1991, quoted in Sebba (1994).
9 Colonel Gaddafi's wife and eight other children were all hospitalized, some with
   serious injuries, as the result of the US bombing of Tripoli.
10 Interview on *The Choice*, BBC Radio 4, 30 October 2001.
11 Ibid.
12 Etonline.com, on-line. Available at <http://etonline.com/television/a7795.htm>
    (no byline) (29 November 2001).
13 Interviewed on *Woman's Hour*, BBC Radio 4, 4 October 2001.
14 Ibid.

11 'Postmodern journalism' and its implications for women

1 The *Radio Times* is Britain's famous long-running TV programme listings magazine, produced by the BBC.

12 Conclusion: women, journalism and new media

1 The Newspaper Association of America, on-line. Available at <http://www.naa.org/about/news/10_cmifall99.html>.
2 German public television channel survey, ARD/ ZDF-Arbeitsgruppe Multimedia, 1999, quoted in Kopper, Kolthoff and Czepek (2000: 410).
3 For example, see Narda Zacchino, senior editor, *San Francisco Chronicle* (<http://www.womensenews.org/pressroom.cfm>).

Bibliography

Abrams, R. (1994) 'The Bylining and the Sidelining', *Guardian*, 11 May: 11.

Accrediting Council on Education in Journalism and Mass Communication (2001) *Journalism and Mass Communications Accreditation 2001–2002*, self-published.

Adie, K. (2002) *The Kindness of Strangers*, London: Headline Books.

Ager, S. (2002) 'So Just Why is Paula Zahn So Outraged?' *Detroit Free Press*, 10 January.

Ainley, B. (1994) 'Blacks and Asians in the British Media', Ph.D. thesis, London University

—— (1998) *Black Journalists, White Media*, Stoke on Trent: Trentham Books.

Allan, S. (1999) *News Culture*, Buckingham: Open University Press.

Allen, C. (1999) 'The Failed Case of Hero-Anchor Christine Craft: Contradiction, New Evidence, and What Television News Can Learn', presented to the International Communication Association, annual convention, San Francisco, Calif.

Alwood, E. (1996) *Straight News: Gays, Lesbians, and the News Media*, New York: Columbia University Press.

Amanpour, C. (2000) 'Speech to the Radio and Television News Directors Association', on-line. Available <http://www.unf.edu/jaxmedia/amanpour.htm> (accessed 9 August 2003).

American Society of Newspaper Editors (2000) *A Call to Leadership*, Reston, Va. American Society of Newspaper Editors, on-line. Available <http://www.asne.org/index.cfm> (accessed 20 May 2003).

Associated Press (1994) *Associated Press Stylebook and Libel Manual*, New York: The Associated Press.

Astbury, A. K. (1963) *Freelance Journalism*, London: G. Bell and Sons.

Baehr, H. (1996) *Women in Television*, London: University of Westminster Press.

Baehr, H. and Ryan, M. (1984) *Shut Up and Listen! Women and Local Radio*, London: Comedia.

Baehr, H. and Spindler-Brown, A. (1987) 'Firing a Broadside: A Feminist Intervention into Mainstream TV', in H. Baehr and G. Dyer (eds) *Boxed In: Women and Television*, New York and London: Pandora, pp. 117–30.

Baker, R. T. (1954) *A History of the Graduate School of Journalism*, New York: Columbia University Press.

Barnett, S. (1990) *Games and Sets: The Changing Face of Sport on Television*, London: British Film Institute.

Barnett, S., Seymour, E. and Gaber, I. (2000) *From Callaghan to Kosovo: Changing Trends in British Television News 1975–1999*, London: University of Westminster.

Bartimus, T., Emerson, G. and Wood, T. (2002) *War Torn: Stories of War from the Women Reporters Who Covered Vietnam*, New York: Random House.

Bartley, P. (1998) *Votes for Women 1860–1928*, London: Hodder & Stoughton.

Beadle, M. E., Murray, M. D. and Godfrey, D. G. (2001) 'Pioneering Women in Television, an Introduction', in M. E. Beadle and M. D. Murray (eds) *Indelible Images: Women of Local Television*, Ames, Ia. Iowa State University Press.

Beasley, M. (1986) 'Women in Journalism Education: The Formative Period, 1908–1930', *Journalism History* 13(1): 10–18.

—— (1988) 'The Women's National Press Club: Case Study of Professional Aspirations', *Journalism History* 15(4): 112–21.

—— (1995) 'Women and Journalism in World War II: Discrimination and Progress', *American Journalism* 12(3): 321–33.

—— (1997) 'How Can Media Coverage of Women be Improved?', in P. Norris (ed.) *Women, Media and Politics*, New York and Oxford: Oxford University Press, pp. 235–44.

Beasley, M. H. and Gibbons, S. J. (1993) *Taking Their Place: A Documentary History of Women and Journalism*, Washington, DC: The American University Press.

Beasley, M. H. and Gibbons, S. J. (2003) *Taking Their Place: A Documentary History of Women and Journalism*, 2nd edn, Washington, DC: The American University Press.

Beasley, M. and Theus, K. T. (1988) *The New Majority: A Look at What the Preponderance of Women in Journalism Education Means to the Schools and to the Professions*, Lanham, Md.: University Press of America.

Becker, L. and Kosicki, J. (1997) 'Women Break the Glass Ceiling in TV News', on-line. Available <http://www.missouri.edu/-jourvs/tvfnds.html> (accessed 2 July 2003).

Becker, L., Fruit, J. and Caudill, S. (1987) *The Training and Hiring of Journalists*, Norwood, NJ: Ablex Publishing.

Belford, B. (1986) *Brilliant Bylines: A Biographical Anthology Of Notable Newspaperwomen in America*, New York: Columbia University Press.

Benhabib, S. (1992) 'Models of Public Space: Hannah Arendt, the Liberal Tradition, and Jürgen Habermas', in C. Calhoun (ed.) *Habermas and the Public Sphere*, London: MIT Press, pp. 73–98.

Bennett, A. (1898) *Journalism for Women: A Practical Guide*, London: J. Lane.

Bennion, S. C. (1996) 'Queen Bee', in K. L. Endres and T. L. Lueck (eds) *Women's Periodicals in the United States: Social and Political Issues*, Westport, Conn.: Greenwood Press, pp. 316–21.

Bentham, M. (1996) *A Magazine of Her Own*, London: Routledge.

Berger, G. (2000) 'Grave New World? Democratic Journalism Enters the Global Twenty-first Century', *Journalism Studies* 1(1): 81–99.

Bierhoff, J, van Dusseldorp, M. and Scullion, R. (1999) *The Future of the Printed Press: Challenges in a Digital World*, Maastricht, The Netherlands: European Journalism Centre.

Blair, G. (1988) *Almost Golden: Jessica Savitch and the Selling of Television News*, New York: Simon & Schuster.

Booth, J. (2002) 'The British Don't Like Too Many Changes. They Like to Be Left Alone', *Sunday Telegraph,* 31 March: 5.

Boughner, G. (1926) *Women in Journalism: A Guide to the Opportunities and a Manual of the Technique of Women's Work for Newspapers and Magazines,* New York: D. Appleton and Company.

Bourke-White, M. (1944) *Purple Heart Valley: A Combat Chronicle of the War in Italy,* New York: Simon & Schuster.

—— (1963) *Portrait of Myself,* New York: Simon & Schuster.

Boyle, R. and Haynes, R. (2000) *Power Play: Sport, the Media and Popular Culture,* London: Longman.

Braden, M. (2003) *She Said What? Interviews with Women Newspaper Columnists,* Lexington, Ky.: University of Kentucky Press.

Brennan, E. and Clarage, E. C. (1999) *Who's Who of Pulitzer Prize Winners,* Phoenix, Ariz.: Oryx Press.

Briggs, A. (1975) *The History of Broadcasting in the United Kingdom: Sound and Vision 1945–1955,* Oxford: Oxford University Press.

—— (1979) *The BBC: The First Fifty Years,* Oxford: Oxford University Press.

—— (1995) *The History of Broadcasting in the United Kingdom: Competition 1955–1974,* Oxford: Oxford University Press.

Brooks, A. (1997) *Postfeminisms: Feminism, Cultural Theory and Cultural Forms,* London: Routledge.

Brown, M. (2002) 'Where Have All the Young Men Gone?' *Radio Times,* 12–18 January: 38–40.

Bunting, M. (2001) 'Analysis: Women and War: While the Media's Response to the Destruction in America Has Been Deafening, the Voices of Women have Grown Strangely Quiet', *Guardian,* Comment & Analysis section, 20 September: 19.

Burt, E. (ed). (2000a) *Women's Press Organizations, 1881–1999,* Westport, Conn.: Greenwood Press, pp. xvii–xxxi.

—— (2000b) 'New England Woman's Press Association', in E. Burt (ed.) *Women's Press Organizations, 1881–1999,* Westport, Conn.: Greenwood Press, pp. 153–63.

Butcher, J. (2001) 'Boosting Skills the Real Priority', in *Journalism Training Special Edition,* May, London: UK Press Gazette.

Byerly, C. M. and Warren, C. A. (1996) 'At the Margins of the Center: Organised Protest in the Newsroom', *Critical Studies in Mass Communication* 13(1): 1–23.

Cadman, E., Chester, G. and Pivot, A. (1981) *Rolling Our Own: Women as Printers, Publishers and Distributors,* London: Minority Press Group.

Campbell-Copeland, T. (1889) *The Ladder of Journalism. How to Climb It. A Primer for Beginners in Newspaper Work,* New York: Allan Forman.

Carter, A. (1988) *The Politics of Women's Rights,* London: Longman.

Carter, H. (2001) 'Just Doing Her Job', *Guardian,* G2, 4 October: 9.

Christmas, L. (1997) *Chaps of Both Sexes? Women Decision-makers in Newspapers: Do They Make a Difference?* London: BT Forum/Women in Journalism.

Chun, L. (1992) 'Public Lives: Lest We Forget', *Guardian,* 11 March: 20.

Conciatore, J. (1995) 'Longtime Reporter Katie Davis Accuses NPR of Gender Bias', *Current,* 1 May, on-line. Available <http://www.current.org/rad/rad601d.html>.

—— (1996) 'NPR Settles Discrimination Suit with Ex-reporter Katie Davis', *Current,* 15 January.

Connery, T. B. (ed.) (1992) *A Sourcebook of American Literary Journalism*, New York: Greenwood Press.

Cook Lauer, N. (2002) 'Studies Show Women's Role Shrinking', *Women's Enews*, 21 May, on-line. Available <http://www.feminist.com/news/news45.html> (accessed 16 October 2002).

Cottle, S. (1999) 'From BBC Newsroom to BBC Newscentre: On Changing Technology and Journalistic Practices', *Convergence* 5(3): 22–43.

Covert, C. L. (1981) 'Journalism History and Women's Experience: A Problem in Conceptual Change', *Journalism History* 4: 2–6.

Coward, R. (1987) 'Women's Programmes: Why Not?', in H. Baehr and G. Dyer (eds) *Boxed In: Women and Television*, New York and London: Pandora, pp. 96–106.

Craft, C. (1986) *An Anchorwoman's Story*, Santa Barbara, Calif.: Rhodora.

—— (1988) *Too Old, Too Ugly, and Not Deferential to Men*, Rocklin, Calif: Prima Publishing.

Creedon, P. (1993) 'The Challenge of Re-visioning Gender Values', in P. Creedon (ed.) *Women in Mass Communication*, 2nd ed, Newbury Park, Calif: Sage, pp. 3–23.

—— (1994) 'Women in Toyland: A Look at Women in American Newspaper Sports Journalism', in P. Creedon (ed.) *Women, Media and Sport: Challenging Gender Values*, Thousand Oaks, Calif: Sage, pp. 67–108.

Crisell, A. (1997) *An Introductory History of British Broadcasting*, London: Routledge.

Cronin, M. (1996) 'The Lowell Offering', in K. L. Endres and T. L. Lueck (eds) *Women's Periodicals in the United States: Social and Political Issues*, Westport, Conn.: Greenwood Press, pp. 186–94.

Croteau, D. and Hoynes, W. (1992) 'Men and the News Media: The Male Presence and its Effect', in S. Craig (ed.) *Men, Masculinity and the Media*, London: Sage, pp. 154–84.

Daddario, G. (1994) 'Chilly Scenes of the 1992 Winter Games: The Mass Media and the Marginalization of Female Athletes', *Sociology of Sport Journal* 11(3): 275–88.

Dahlgren, P. (1997) 'Media Logic in Cyberspace: Repositioning Journalism and its Publics', *Javnost – The Public* 3: 59–72.

Daly, E. (1999) 'Reporting from the Front Line', in S. Glover (ed.) *Secrets of the Press: Journalists on Journalism*, London: Allen Lane, Penguin, pp. 272–80.

Dancyger, I. (1978) *A World of Women: An Illustrated History of Women's Magazines 1700–1970*, Dublin: Gill & Macmillan.

Davies, D. R. (1996) 'Far and Near', in K. L. Endres and T. L. Lueck (eds) *Women's Periodicals in the United States: Social and Political Issues*, Westport, Conn.: Greenwood Press, pp. 78–82.

Davis, E. (1996) *Lifting As They Climb*, New York: Simon & Schuster (originally published 1933, Washington, DC: National Association of Coloured Women.)

Davis, P. W. (1854a) 'The Introduction', *The Una*, February: 4.

—— (1854b) 'The Moral Character of Woman', *The Una*, June: 72–3.

Dear, J. (2001) 'Employers Must Do More', in *Journalism Training Special Edition*, May, London: UK Press Gazette.

Delano, A. (2000) 'No Sign of a Better Job: 100 years of British Journalism', *Journalism Studies* 1(2): 261–72.

—— (2003) 'Women Journalists: What's the Difference?', *Journalism Studies* 4 (2): 273–86.

Delano, A. and Henningham, J. (1995) *The News Breed: British Journalists in the 1990s*, London: London Institute.

De Moraes, L. (2002) 'CNN Caught in "Zipper" Ad for Paula Zahn', *Washington Post,* 7 January: C1.

Denker, D. (1971) 'Eleanor Medill Patterson', in E. T. James (ed.) *Notable American Women 1607–1950*, Vol. III, Cambridge, Mass.: The Belknap Press, pp. 26-8.

Deuze, M. (1999) 'Journalism and the Web: An Analysis of Skills and Standards in an Online Environment', *Gazette* 61(5): 373–90.

—— (2001) 'Online Journalism: Modelling the First Generation of News Media on the World Wide Web', *First Monday* 6(10), on-line. Available <http://www.first-monday.org/issues/issue6_10/deuze/index.html> (accessed 22 May 2003).

Deuze, M. and Paulussen, S. (2002) 'Research Note: Online Journalism in the Low Countries: Basic, Occupational and Professional Characteristics of Online Journalists in Flanders and the Netherlands', *European Journal of Communication* 17(2): 237–45.

DiCenzo, M. (2000) 'Militant Distribution: Votes for Women and the Public Sphere', *Media History* 6(2): 115–28.

Dick, S. J. (2001) 'Marcia Yockey: A Force of Nature in Evansville, Indiana', in M. E. Beadle and M. D. Murray (eds) *Indelible Images: Women of Local Television*, Ames, Ia.: Iowa State University Press.

Dillard, I. and Schusky M. S. D. (1971) 'Ellen Browning Scripps', in E. T. James (ed.) *Notable American Women 1607–1950*, Vol. III, Cambridge, Mass. The Belknap Press, pp. 250-2.

Dorr, R. C. (1917) *Inside the Russian Revolution*, New York: Macmillan. .

—— (1924) *A Woman of Fifty*, New York: Funk & Wagnalls.

Dougary, G. (1994) *The Executive Tart and Other Myths*, London: Virago.

Drew, B. (1874) *Pens and Types: Or, Hints and Helps for Those Who Write, Print, or Read*, Boston, Mass.: Lee & Shepard.

Drew, J. (1995) 'Media Activism and Radical Democracy', in J. Brook and I. A. Boal (eds) *Resisting the Virtual Life: The Culture and Politics of Information*, San Francisco, Calif.: City Lights, pp. 71–83.

Duncan, M. C. and Messner, M. A. (1998) 'The Media Image of Sport and Gender', in L. A. Wenner (ed.) *MediaSport*, New York: Routledge, pp. 170–85.

Dykewomon, E. (1987) 'Notes for a Magazine: A Dyke Geography', *Sinister Wisdom* 33 (Fall): 3–7.

Edwards, J. (1988) *Women of the World: The Great Foreign Correspondents*, Boston, Mass. : Houghton Mifflin.

Ellerbee, L. (1986) *And So It Goes*, New York: G. P. Putnam's Sons.

Elliott, P. (1978) 'Professional Ideology and Organisational Change: The Journalist since 1800', in G. Boyce, J. Curran and P. Wingate (eds) *Newspaper History*, London: Constable.

Elwood-Akers, V. (1988) *Women War Correspondents in the Vietnam War 1961–1975*, Metuchen, NJ: Scarecrow Press.

Emerson, G. (1976) *Winners and Losers: Battles, Retreats, Gains, Losses, and Ruins from a Long War*, New York: Random House.

Emery, E. and Emery, M. (1984) *The Press and America: An Interpretive History of the Mass Media*, 5th edn, Englewood Cliffs, NJ: Prentice-Hall.

Endres, K. L. (1996) 'Introduction', in K. L. Endres and T. L. Lueck (eds) *Women's Periodicals in the United States: Social and Political Issues*, Westport, Conn.: Greenwood Press, pp. xi–xxv.

Endres, K. L. and Lueck, T. L. (eds) (1996) *Women's Periodicals in the United States: Social and Political Issues*, Westport, Conn.: Greenwood Press.

Engelman, R. (1990). 'The Origins of Public Access Cable Television, 1966–1972', *Journalism and Mass Communication Monographs* 123 (October).

Engstrom, E. and Ferri, A. J. (1998) 'From Barriers to Challenges: Career Perceptions of Women TV News Anchors', *Journalism and Mass Communication Quarterly*, 75 (4) winter: 789–802.

Farrell, A. E. (1998) *Yours in Sisterhood: Ms. Magazine and the Promise of Popular Feminism*, Chapel Hill, NC: University of North Carolina Press.

Featherstone, M. (1991) *Consumer Culture and Postmodernism*, London: Sage.

Fedler, F. (1989) *Media Hoaxes*, Ames, Ia.: Iowa State University Press.

Feldman, S. (2000) 'Twin Peaks: The Staying Power of BBC Radio's *Woman's Hour*', in C. Mitchell (ed.) *Women and Radio: Airing Differences*, London: Routledge, pp.64–72.

Felski, R. (1989) *Beyond Feminist Aesthetics: Feminist Literature and Social Change*, Cambridge, Mass.: Harvard University Press.

Finucane, M. O. (2001) 'Carol Marin: Chicago's Courageous Newscaster', in M. E. Beadle and M. D. Murray (eds) *Indelible Images: Women of Local Television*, Ames, Iowa: Iowa State University Press, pp. 121–9.

Flatlow, G. (1994) 'Sexual Harassment in Indiana Daily Newspapers', *Newspaper Research Journal* 15 (summer): 37–8.

Fleming, C. (2000) 'The Home Front: An Examination of the Position of Women in Broadcast Journalism', MA dissertation, Leicester University.

Fornoff, S. (1993) *Lady in the Locker Room*, Champaign, Ill.: Sagamore Publishing.

Franklin, B. (1997) *Newszak and News Media*, London: Edward Arnold.

Fraser, N. (1992) 'Rethinking the Public Sphere: A Contribution to the Critique of Actually Existing Democracy', in C. Calhoun (ed.) *Habermas and the Public Sphere*, Cambridge, Mass.: MIT Press, pp. 109–42.

Fuller, M. (1855) *Woman in the Nineteenth Century*, Boston, Mass.: Jewitt.

Furman, B. (1949) *Washington By-line: The Personal History of a Newspaperwoman*, New York: Alfred A. Knopf.

Gallagher, M. (1995) *An Unfinished Story: Gender Patterns in Media Employment*, Reports on Mass Communication, 110, Paris: UNESCO.

Gates, H. L., Jr. (1996) 'White Like Me', *The New Yorker*, 17 June: 66–81.

Gellhorn, M. (1988) *The View From the Ground*, New York: Atlantic Monthly Press.

George, P. (2003) *Never Say Never: Ten Lessons to Turn You Can't into Yes I Can*, New York: McGraw-Hill.

Gershick, Z. Z. (1998) *Gay Old Girls*, Los Angeles, Calif.: Alyson Publications.

Gibbons, S. (2003) 'Women's Media Transformed by Internet', *Women's Enews*, 29 January, on-line. Available <http: www.womensenews.org/article.cfm?aid=1201> (accessed 24 May 2003).

Giddings, P. (1984) *When and Where I Enter: The Impact of Black Women on Race and Sex in America*, New York: W. Morrow.

Gitlin, T. (1998) 'Public Sphere or Public Sphericules?' in T. Liebes and J. Curran (eds) *Media, Ritual, Identity*, New York: Routledge, pp. 168-74.

Glasgow University Media Group (1985) *War and Peace News*, Milton Keynes: Open University Press.

Goldberg, K. (1990) *The Barefoot Channel*, Vancouver: New Star Books.

Goldie, G. W. (1977) *Facing the Nation*, London: Bodley Head.

Goldstein J. (2001) *War and Gender: How Gender Shapes the War System and Vice Versa*, Cambridge: Cambridge University Press.

Gottlieb, A. H. (2000) 'National League of American Pen Women, 1897–Present', in E. Burt (ed.) *Women's Press Organizations, 1881–1999*, Westport, Conn.: Greenwood Press.

Graham, K. (1997) *Personal History*, New York: Alfred A. Knopf.

Griffin, P. (1992) 'Changing the Game: Homophobia, Sexism and Lesbians in Sport', *Quest* 44: 251–65.

Grunig, L. A. (1993) '"The Glass Ceiling" Effect on Mass Communication Students', in P. Creedon (ed.) *Women in Mass Communication*, Newbury Park, Calif.: Sage, pp. 276–300.

Habermas, J. (1989) *The Structural Transformation of the Public Sphere: An Inquiry Into a Category of Bourgeois Society*, trans. T. Burger with the assistance of F. Lawrence, Cambridge: Polity Press (first published in German in 1962 as *Strukturwandel der Affentlichkeit*).

Hall, T. V. (2000) 'Association for Women in Sports Media, 1987–Present', in E. Burt (ed.) *Women's Press Organizations, 1881–1999*, Westport, Conn.: Greenwood Press, pp. 21–6.

Halper, D. L. (2001) *Invisible Stars: A Social History of Women in American Broadcasting*, Armonk, NY: M. E. Sharpe.

Hamamoto, D. Y. (1994) *Monitored Peril: Asian Americans and the Politics of TV Representation*, Minneapolis, Minn.: University of Minnesota Press.

Hann, M. (2001) 'Media Studies? Do Yourself a Favour – Forget it', *Guardian*, 3 September: 4.

Hargreaves, J. (1994) *Sporting Females: Critical Issues in the History and Sociology of Women's Sports*, London: Routledge.

Harrison, B. (1978) *Separate Spheres: The Opposition to Women's Suffrage in Britain*, London: Croom Helm.

—— (1982) 'Press and Pressure Group in Modern Britain', in J. Shattock and M. Wolff (eds) *The Victorian Periodical Press: Samplings and Soundings*, Leicester: Leicester University Press.

Harwood, D. (1927) *Getting and Writing News*, New York: George H. Doran.

Harwood, R. (1991) 'Dirty Talk', *Washington Post*, 27 October: C6.

Hattenstone, S. (2002) 'Rosie Outlook', *Guardian*, G2, 30 July: 2.

Healy, P. (1966) *Cissy: A Biography of Eleanor M. "Cissy" Patterson*, Garden City, NY: Doubleday.

Heller, Z. (1999) 'Girl Columns', in S. Glover (ed.) *Secrets of the Press: Journalists on Journalism*, Harmondsworth: Penguin, pp. 10–17.

Hemlinger, M. A. and Linton, C. C. (2002) *Women in Newspapers. Still Fighting an Uphill Battle*, on-line. Available <http://www.mediamanagementcenter.org/center/web/publications/data/WIN2002.pdf> (accessed 20 August 2003).

Henningham, J .P and Delano, A. (1998) 'British Journalists', in D. H.Weaver (ed.) *The Global Journalist: News People Around the World*, Cresskill, NJ: Hampton Press.

Henry, S. (2004) 'But Where Are All the Women?: Our History', in R. R. Rush, C. E. Oukrop and P. Creedon (eds) *The Search for Equity: Women in Journalism and Mass Communications Education*, Mahwah, NJ: Erlbaum.

Higgins, M. (1955) *News is a Singular Thing*, Garden City, NY: Doubleday.

Hilmes, M. (1997) *Radio Voices: American Broadcasting, 1922–1952*, Minneapolis, Minn.: University of Minnesota Press.

Hitchcock, N. (1900) *What a Reporter Must Be: Helps to Success in Newspaper Work*, Cleveland, Ohio: Ralph Hitchcock.

Hoge, A. (1966) *Cissy Patterson: The Life of Eleanor Medill Patterson, Publisher and Editor of the Washington Times–Herald*, New York: Random.

Holland, P. (1987) 'When a Woman Reads the News', in H. Baehr and G. Dyer (eds) *Boxed in: Women and Television*, London: Pandora, pp. 133–50.

—— (1998) 'The Politics of the Smile: Soft News and the Sexualisation of the Popular Press', in C. Carter, G. Branston and S. Allan (eds) *News, Gender and Power*, London: Routledge, pp. 17–32.

Horn, P. (1995) *Women in the 1920s*, Stroud: Alan Sutton Publishing Ltd.

Hosley, D. H. and Yamada, G. K. (1987) *Hard News: Women in Broadcast Journalism*, Westport, Conn.: Greenwood Press.

Howarth, J. (2000) 'Women in Radio: Making a Difference?', in C. Mitchell (ed.) *Women and Radio: Airing Differences*, London: Routledge, pp. 25–61.

Hunter, F. (2000) 'Hilda Matheson and the BBC, 1926–1940', in C. Mitchell (ed.) *Women and Radio: Airing Differences*, London: Routledge, pp. 41–7.

Hutson, J. B. (1971) 'Victoria Earle Matthews', in E. T. James (ed.) *Notable American Woman 1607–1950*, Vol. II, Cambridge, Mass.: The Belknap Press, pp. 510–11.

Inglis, F. (2002) *People's Witness*, New Haven, Conn.: Yale University Press.

International Women's Media Foundation, on-line. Available <http://www.iwmf.org> (accessed 22 May 2003).

Jordan, E. (1938) *Three Rousing Cheers*, New York: Appleton-Century.

Karpf, A. (1980) 'Women and Radio', in H. Baehr (ed.) *Women and Media*, Oxford: Pergamon Press.

Kasper, A. (n.d.) 'Interview of Helen Kirkpatrick', Washington Press Club Oral History Project *Women in Journalism*, on-line. Available <http://www.pres.org/wpforal/int1.htm>.

Kassell, P. and Beasley, M. (1996) 'New Directions for Women', in K. L. Endres and T. L. Lueck (eds) *Women's Periodicals in the United States: Social and Political Issues*, Westport, Conn.:Greenwood Press.

Kaul, A. (ed.) (1997) *American Literary Journalists, 1945–1995*, Dictionary of Literary Biography, first series, Detroit, Mich.: Bruccoli Clark Layman, 185.

Keeble, R. (2001) *The Newspapers Handbook*, 3rd edn, London: Routledge.

Kellner, D. (1990) *Television and the Crisis of Democracy*, Boulder, Col.: Westview Press.

Kitzinger, J. (1998) 'The Gender-politics of News Production: Silenced Voices and False Memories', in C. Carter, G. Branston and S. Allan (eds) *News, Gender and Power*, London: Routledge, pp. 186–206.

Knight, M. (1990) 'Inteview of Ruth Cowan Nash', Washington Press Club Oral History Project *Women in Journalism*, on-line. Available <http://www.pres.org/wpforal/int1.htm>.

Knightley, P. (1982a) *The First Casualty: The War Correspondent as Hero, Propagandist and Myth Maker*, 2nd edn, London: Quartet.

—— (1982b) 'The Falklands: How Britannia Ruled the News', *Columbia Journalism Review* September–October: 51–3.

Kopper, G. G., Kalthoff, A. and Czepek, A. (2000) 'Research Review: On-line Journalism – a Report on Current and Continuing Research and Major Questions in the International Discussion', *Journalism Studies* 1(1): 499–512.

Kroeger, B. (1994) *Nellie Bly: Daredevil, Reporter, Feminist*, New York: Random House.

—— (1996) 'Nellie Bly: She Did It All', *Journalism History*, 28(1): 7–15.

Kruglak, T. E. (1955) *The Foreign Correspondents: A Study of the Men and Women Reporting for the American Information Media in Western Europe*, Geneva: Librairie E. Droz.

Kuhn, I. (1938) *Assigned to Adventure*, Philadelphia, Pa.: J. B. Lippincott.

Kurth, P. (1990) *American Cassandra: The Life of Dorothy Thompson*, Boston, Mass.: Little, Brown.

Lasica, J. D. (1998) 'Keeping Online Staffers in Exile', *American Journalism Review* May, on-line. Available < http://www.ajr.org/Article.asp?id=429> (accessed 22 May 2003).

Lawson, T. (2002) 'Artificial Intelligence Spare Rib Memories', *Scotsman,* 19 June: 5.

Leab, D. J. (1970) *A Union of Individuals: The Formation of the American Newspaper Guild, 1933–1936*, New York: Columbia University Press.

Lee, A. J. (1976a) 'The Profession of Journalism in England, 1855–1914', in J. Tunstall (ed.) *Media Occupations and Professions: A Reader*, Oxford: Oxford University Press.

—— (1976b) *The Origins of the Popular Press, 1855–1914*, London: Croom Helm.

Leman, J. (1987) '"Programmes for women" in 1950s British Television', in H. Baehr and G. Dyer (eds) *Boxed In: Women and Television*, London: Pandora, pp. 73–95.

Leonard, T. (2001) 'Kate Adie Starts Uncivil War over BBC "Bimbos"', on-line. Available <http://news.telegraph.co.uk>.

Leonard, T. C. (1995) *News for All: America's Coming-of-Age with the Press*, New York and Oxford: Oxford University Press.

Leslie, A. (1999) 'Female "Firemen"', in S. Glover (ed.) *Secrets of the Press: Journalists on Journalism*, London: Penguin, pp. 221–36.

Loach, L. (1987) 'Campaigning for Change', in H. Baehr and G. Dyer (eds) *Boxed In: Women and Television*, New York and London: Pandora, pp. 55–69.

Logie, I. M. R. (1938) *Careers for Women in Journalism*, Scranton, Pa.: International Textbook Company.

Low, F. H. (1904) *Press Work for Women: A Text Book for The Young Woman Journalist*, London: L. Upcott Gill; New York: Charles Scribner's Sons.

Lucas, M. and Wallner, M. (1993) 'Resistance by Satellite: The Gulf Crisis Project and the Deep Dish Satellite TV Network', in T. Dowmunt (ed.) *Channels of Resistance: Global Television and Local Empowerment*, London: British Film Institute, pp. 176–94.

Luce, R. (1889) *Writing for the Press*, Boston, Mass.: The Winter Publisher Company.

Lull, J. and Hinerman, S. (1997) *Media Scandals*, London: Polity Press.

McAdams, K. and Beasley, M. (1994) 'Sexual Harassment of Washington Women Journalists', *Newspaper Research Journal* 15 (Winter): 130–1.

McCann, P. (2000) 'I Sent Out for Tampons not Underwear', *The Times*, 24 March: 19–20.

MacCarthy, F. (2002) 'Obituary: Mary Stott: A Great Campaigning Journalist, She Founded the Guardian Women's Page and Gave a Liberating Voice to a Generation', *Guardian,* 18 September: 20.

MacGregor, S. (2002) *Woman of Today*, London: Headline.

McLaughlin, G. (2002) *The War Correspondent*, London: Pluto.

McManus, J. (1994) *Market Driven Journalism: Let the Citizen Beware?* London: Sage.

McNair, B. (1998) *The Sociology of Journalism*, London: Arnold.

McRobbie, A. (1994) *Postmodernism and Popular Culture*, London: Routledge.

——. (1997) 'Pecs and Penises: The Meaning of Girlie Culture', *Soundings* 5: 157–66.

Malone, C. (1999) 'Sensational Stories, Endangered Bodies:Women's Work and the New Journalism in England in the 1890s', *Albion* 31 (1): 49–71.

Manyon, J. (2001) 'Bribe and Seek', *Spectator*, 3 November:16–17.

Marzolf, M. (1977) *Up From the Footnotes*, New York: Hastings House.

—— (1983) 'American "New Journalism" Takes Root in Europe at the End of the Nineteenth Century', *Journalism Quarterly* 61(3): 529–36.

—— (1993) 'Women Making a Difference in the Newsroom', paper prepared for the annual conference of the Commission on the Status of Women in Journalism, Association for Education in Journalism and Mass Communication (AEJMC), Kansas City, 11–14 August.

May, A. (1983) *Witness to War: A Biography of Marguerite Higgins*, New York: Beaufort Books.

Mayes, T. (2000) 'Submerging in "Therapy News"', *British Journalism Review* 1(4): 30–5.

Melin-Higgins, M. and Djerf Pierre, M. (1998) 'Networking in Newsrooms: Journalist and Gender Cultures', paper presented to the 21st General Assembly and Scientific Conference of the International Association for Media and Communication Research, Glasgow University, July.

Meyers, M. (1997) *News Coverage of Violence Against Women: Engendering Blame*, London: Sage.

Michaels, K. and Mitchell, C. (2000) 'The Last Bastion: How Women Become Music Presenters in UK Radio', in C. Mitchell (ed.) *Women and Radio: Airing Differences*, London: Routledge, pp. 238–49.

Miller, A. V. (compiler) (1990) *Our Own Voices: A Directory of Lesbian and Gay Periodicals, 1890–1900*, Toronto: Canadian Gay Archives.

Miller, P. and Miller, R. (1995) 'The Invisible Woman: Female Sports Journalists in the Workplace', *Journalism and Mass Communication Quarterly* 72(4): 883–9.

Mills, K. (1988) *A Place in the News: From the Women's Pages to the Front Pages*, New York: Columbia University Press.

—— (1997) 'What Difference Do Women Journalists Make?' in P. Norris (ed.) *Women, Media and Politics*, New York and Oxford: Oxford University Press, pp. 41–55.

Mitchell, C. (ed.) (2000) *Women and Radio: Airing Differences*, London: Routledge.

Moore, M. (1993) *A Woman at War: Storming Kuwait with the U.S. Marines*, New York: Charles Scribner's Sons.

Morley, A. with Stanley, L. (1988) *The Life and Death of Emily Wilding Davison, with Gertrude Colmore's The Life of Emily Davison*, London: Women's Press.

Moss, M. L. and Warren, R. (1984) 'Public Policy and Community-Oriented Uses of Cable Television', *Urban Affairs Quarterly* 20: 233–54.

Mott, F. L. (1962) *American Journalism*, New York: Macmillan.

National Women and Media Collection, The, on-line. Available <http://www.system.missouri.edu/whme/womedia.htm>.

Nelson, J. (1993) *Volunteer Slavery: My Authentic Negro Experience*, Harmondsworth: Penguin.

Neuberger, C., Tonnemacher, J., Biebl, M. and Duck, A. (1997) 'Die Deutschen Tageszeitungen in World Wide Web', *Media Perspektiven* 12: 652–63.

Newkirk, P. (2000) *Within the Veil: Black Journalists, White Media*, New York: New York University Press.

Newman, J .(1995) 'Gender and Cultural Change', in C. Itzin and J. Newman (eds) *Gender, Culture and Organizational Change: Putting Theory into Practice*, London and New York: Routledge, pp. 11–29.

O'Dell, C. (1997) *Women Pioneers in Television*, Jefferson, NC: McFarland.

Olin, C. (1906) *Journalism*, Philadelphia, Pa.: Penn Publishing.

Oukrop, C. and Rush, R. (2003) 'Women Say Salary is Key Discrimination Source', *Women's Words*, Spring, on-line. Available <http://www,mdwebsolutions.com/womens%20word/>.

Papper, B. and Gerhard, M. (2001) 'Up From the Ranks: Grooming Women and Minorities for Management', on-line. Available <www.rtnda.org/research/2001womin.shtml> (accessed 22 May 2003).

Paton, M. (1991) 'Obituary: Jean Rook', *Independent,* 6 September: 26.

Paxson, M. (1991) Oral interview, with Diane Gentry, sponsored by the Washington Press Club Foundation, on-line. Available <http://www.press.org/wpforal/pax3.htm (accessed 24 July 2003).

Pember, D. R. (1987) *Mass Media Law*, Dubuque, Iowa: William D. Brown.

Penn, I. G. (1969) *The Afro-American Press and Its Editors*, New York: Arno Press and the New York Times. Originally published 1891, Springfield, Mass.: Willey & Co.

Philo, G. and McLaughlin, G. (1995) 'The British Media and the Gulf War', in G. Philo (ed.) *The Glasgow Media Group Reader*, Vol. 2, London: Routledge, pp. 146–56.

Phoca, S. and Wright, R. (1999) *Introducing Postfeminism*, Cambridge: Icon.

Pichanick, V. K. (1980) *Harriet Martineau: The Woman and Her Work, 1802–1876*, Ann Arbor, Mich.: University of Michigan Press.

Plant, S. (1997) *Zeroes + Ones: Digital Women + the New Technoculture*, London: Fourth Estate.

Porterfield, E. (1999) 'Sportswriter Settles Lawsuit against P-I', *Seattle Post-Intelligencer*, 6 May, on-line. Available <http://seattlepi.nwsource.com/local/with06.shtml> (accessed 7 August 2003).

Powell, C. (2003) *My American Journey*, New York: Ballantyne Books.

Preece, C. (1990) *Edward Willis and Ellen Browning Scripps: An Unmatched Pair*, Chelsea, Mich.: self-published.

Prentice, E. A. (2000) *One Woman's War*, London: Duckworth.

Radio-Television News Directors Association and Foundation (USA) (2001) *Survey of Women and Minorities in Radio and Television News*, Ball State University, on-line. Available <http://www.rtnda.org/research/womin2000.shtml> (accessed 22 May 2003).

Rakow, L. F. and Kranich, K. (1991) 'Woman as Sign in Television News', *Journal of Communication* 41(1): 8–23.

Rayne, M. (1974) *What Can a Woman Do: Or Her Position in the Business and Literary World*, Salem, NJ: Arno Press (originally published 1893 by the Eagle Publishing Company).

Reilly, T. (1981) 'Jane McManus Storms: Letters from the Mexican War, 1846–1848', *Southwestern Historical Quarterly*, lxxxv: 22–44.

Richardson, A. (1996) '"Come On, Join the Conversation!": 'Zines as a Medium for Feminist Dialogue and Community Building', *Feminist Collections* 17(3–4): 10–13.

Ridley, Y. (2001) *In the Hands of the Taliban: Her Extraordinary Story*, London: Robson Books.

Rinehart, M. R. (1948) *My Story*, New York: Rinehart & Co.

Robarts, S. with Coote, A. and Ball, E. (1981) *Positive Action for Women*, London: National Council for Civil Liberties.

Roosevelt, E. (1949) *This I Remember*, New York: Harper & Brothers.

Ross, I. (1936) *Ladies of the Press*, New York: Harper.

Ross, K. (2000) *Women at the Top 2000: Cracking the Public Sector Glass Ceiling*, King-Hall Paper No. 9, London: Hansard.

—— (2001) 'Women at Work: Journalism as En-gendered Practice', *Journalism Studies*, 2(4): 531–44.

Ross, S. S. and Middleberg, D. (1998) 'The Middleberg/Ross Media in Cyberspace Study, Fifth Annual National Survey', on-line. Available <http://www.middleberg.com/toolsforsuccess/cyberstudy98.pdf> (accessed 22 May 2003).

Rouvalis, C. and Schackner, B. (2000) 'Female Correspondents Recall their Historic Role Reporting from Vietnam', on-line. Available <http://www.Post-Gazette.com/magazine/20000330namwomen2.asp> (accessed 30 March 2003).

Rowe, D. (1999) *Sport, Culture and the Media*, Buckingham: Open University Press.

Rush, R., Oukrup, C. and Creedon, P. (eds) (2004) *Seeking Equity for Women in Journalism and Mass Communication Education*, Mahwah, NJ: Erlbaum.

Rush, R., Oukrup, C., Bergen, L. and Andsager, J. L. (2004) '"Where Are the Old Broads?" Been There, Done That . . . 30 Years Ago: An Update of the Original Study of Women in Journalism and Mass Communications Education, 1972 & 2002', in R. R. Rush, C. E. Oukrop and P. Creedon (eds) *Seeking Equity for Women in Journalism and Mass Communication Education*, Mahwah, NJ: Erlbaum.

Rutenberg, J. (2002) 'News Anchors and the Cathode-Ray Ceiling', *New York Times*, 3 June: C1–C8.

Ryan, M. P. (1992) 'Gender and Public Access: Women's Politics in Nineteenth Century America', in C. Calhourn (ed.) *Habermas and the Public Sphere*, Cambridge, Mass.: MIT Press, pp. 259–88.

Saalfield, C. and Ravarro, R. (1991) 'Shocking Pink Praxis: Race and Gender on the ACT UP Frontlines', in D. Fuss (ed.) *Inside/Out: Lesbian Theories, Gay Theories*, New York: Routledge, pp. 341–69.

Sanders, M. and Rock, M. (1988) *Waiting for Prime Time: The Women of Television News*, Urbana, Ill.: University of Illinois Press.

Saunders, L. (1993) 'Writing Wrongs', *Guardian,* 30 March: 13.

Savitch, J. (1982) *Anchorwoman*, New York: G. P. Putnam's Sons.

Scannell, P. and Cardiff. D. (1991) *A Social History of British Broadcasting*, Vol. 1, London: Blackwell.

Schilpp, M. G. and Murphy, S. M. (1983) *Great Women of the Press*, Carbondale, Ill.: Southern Illinois University Press.

Schlesinger, P. (1991) *Media, State and Nation*, London: Sage.

Sebba, A. (1994) *Battling for News: The Rise of the Woman Reporter*, London: Hodder & Stoughton.

Sengupta, S. (1997) 'The Connie Chung Phenomenon', *Media Studies Journal* Spring: 149–54.

Shade, L. R. (2002) *Gender & Community in the Social Construction of the Internet*, New York: Peter Lang.

Shamberg, M. (1972) *Guerilla Television*, New York: Holt, Rinehart & Winston.

Shapiro, L. (1990) 'Minorities: Still Talking But Are We Hiring?', *APSE Newsletter*, 13 April: 15.

Shapley, O. (2000) 'Broadcasting A Life', in C. Mitchell (ed.) *Women and Radio: Airing Differences*, London: Routledge, pp. 29–40.

Shingler, M. and Wieringa, C. (1998) *On Air: Methods and Meanings of Radio*, London: Arnold.

Shoemaker, P. J. and Reese, S. D. (1991) *Mediating the Message: Theories of Influence on Mass Media Content*, White Plains, NY.: Longman.

Shuman, E.L. (1899) *The Art and Practice of Journalism: How to Become a Successful Writer*, Chicago, Ill.: Stevans & Handy.

—— (1903) *Practical Journalism: A Complete Manual of the Best Newspaper Methods*, New York: D. Appleton and Company.

Sieghart, M. A. and Henry, G. (1998) *The Cheaper Sex: How Women Lose Out in Journalism*, London: Women in Journalism.

Sims, M. (1985) *Women in BBC Management*, London: BBC.

Singer, J. (1997a) 'Changes and Consistencies: Newspaper Journalists Contemplate Online Future', *Newspaper Research Journal* 18(1/2): 2–18.

—— (1997b) 'Still Guarding the Gate? The Newspaper Journalist's Role in an Online World', *Convergence* 3(1): 72–89.

Skidmore, P. (1998) 'Gender and the Agenda: News Reporting of Child Sex Abuse', in C. Carter, G. Branston and S. Allan (eds) *News, Gender and Power*, London: Routledge, pp. 204–18.

Sloan, W. D. (1990) 'Preface', in D. Sloan (ed.) *Makers of the Media Mind:. Journalism Educators and Their Ideas*, Hillsdale, NJ: Lawrence Erlbaum Associates, pp. xi–xiii.

Sloan, W. D., Stovall, J. G. and Startt, J. D. (eds) (1989) *The Media in America: A History*, Worthington, Ohio: Publishing Horizons.

Smith, A. (1979) *The Newspaper: An International History*, London: Thames & Hudson.

Smith, C., Fredin, E. S., Ferguson, N. and Carroll, A. (1993) 'Television: The Nature of Sex Discrimination in Local Television News Shops', in P. Creedon (ed.) *Women in Mass Communication*, 2nd edn, Newbury Park, Calif: Sage, pp. 171–82.

Smith, H. L. (1998) *The British Women's Suffrage Campaign, 1866–1928*, London: Longman.

Smith, J. (1994) 'What's My Line?', *Guardian*, 15 September: 13.

—— (2002) 'Beverly Williams Sues Channel 3', *Philadelphia Daily News*, 25 May, on-line. Available at: <http://www.current.org/rad/rad60Id.html>.

Smith, R. N. (1997) *The Colonel: The Life and Legend of Robert R. McCormick 1880–1955*, New York: Houghton Mifflin.

Sontheimer, M. (1941) *Newspaperman. A Book About the Business,* New York: McGraw-Hill.

Soothill, K and Walby, S. (1991) *Sex Crime in the News*, London: Routledge.

Stanley, A. (2003) 'In the 24/7 TV War, Reporters Young and Old are Making Their Mark', *New York Times*, 8 April: B11 .

Stasio, M. (1998) 'When Death is a Constant Companion', *On The Issues*, Spring 7: 2. Also available on-line (*OTI* online):<http://www.echonyc.com/~onissues/sp98death.html>.

Stead, W. T. (1886) 'Government by Journalism', *Contemporary Review* 49: 656–73.

Stearns, B-M. (1932) 'Reform Periodicals and Female Reformers 1830–1860', *American Historical Review* 37: 678–99.

Steinem, G. (1994) *Moving Beyond Words*, New York: Simon & Schuster.

Steiner, L. (1983) 'Finding Community in Nineteenth Century Suffrage Periodicals', *American Journalism* 1(1): 1–16.

—— (1991) 'Evolving Rhetorical Strategies/Evolving Identities', in M. M. Solomon (ed.) *A Voice of Their Own: The Woman Suffrage Press, 1840–1910*, Tuscaloosa, Ala.: University of Alabama Press, pp. 183–97.

—— (1992) 'Construction of Gender in Newsreporting Textbooks, 1890–1990', *Journalism Monographs* 135: 1–47.

—— (1993) 'Gender in Journalism Textbooks', in P. Creedon (ed.) *Women in Mass Communication*, Newbury Park, Calif.: Sage, pp. 301–16.

—— (1997a) 'An Annotated Bibliography of Autobiographies of Women Journalists', *Journalism History* 23: 13–15.

—— (1997b) 'Gender At Work: Early Accounts by Women Journalists', *Journalism History* 23(1): 2–15.

—— (1999) 'New York Times Coverage of Anita Hill as a Female Cipher', in M. Meyers (ed.) *Mediated Women: Representations in Popular Culture*, Cresskill, NJ: Hampton Press, pp. 225–50.

Stephens, N. (1963) *Journalism*, London: Robert Hale Ltd.

Stone, V. (1997) 'Women Break Glass Ceiling in TV News', on-line. Available <http://www.missouri.edu/-jourvs/gtvminw.html> (accessed 23 October 2002).

—— (2001) *Minorities and Women in Television News*, on-line. Available <http://www.missouri.edu/-jourvs/gtvminw.html> (accessed 23 October 2002).

Streitmatter, R. (1994) *Raising Her Voice: African-American Women Journalists Who Changed History*, Lexington, Ky.: The University Press of Kentucky.

—— (1995) *Unspeakable: The Rise of the Gay and Lesbian Press in America*, Boston, Mass.: Faber and Faber.

Strupp , J. (2002) 'A Feminine Touch', *Editor and Publisher* 135(33) (16 September): 10.

Sutton, A. A. (1948) *Education for Journalism in the United States from Its Beginnings to 1940*, Evanston, Ill.: Northwestern University Press, reprinted New York: AMS Press, 1968.

Swain, G. (2001) 'The Women in the War Zone', *Independent,* 2 October: 8.

Talese, G. (1970) *The Kingdom and the Power*, New York: Bantam.

Television and Cable Factbook (1997) Washington, DC: Warren Publishing.

Thompson, D. (1932) *I Saw Hitler!*, New York: Farrar & Rinehart.

Thompson, M. W. (1998) 'Breaking Through the Glass Ceiling', *American Journalism Review* 20 (December): 10.

Thumim, J. (1998) '"Mrs. Knight *Must* Be Balanced": Methodological Problems in Researching Early British Television', in C. Carter, G. Branston and S. Allan (eds) *News, Gender and Power*, London: Routledge, pp. 91–104.

Toynbee, P. (1993) 'Tribute to Jill Tweedie', *Guardian,* 13 November: 25.

Traynor, I. (2001) 'Taliban Offer £30,000 a Head to Kill Reporters', *Guardian,* 30 November: .

Trotta, L. (1991) *Fighting for Air: In the Trenches with Television News*, New York: Simon & Schuster.

Tunstall, J. (1971) *Journalists at Work*, London: Constable.
—— (1993) *Television Producers*, London: Routledge.
—— (1996) 'From Gentlemen to "Journos"', *British Journalism Review* 6(3): 54–9.
Turner, R. D. (1991) 'Black Women Sportswriters and the Locker Room Wars', *Ebony* 46(4): 170–8.
U.S. Bureau of the Census (2001) *Statistical Abstract of the United States*, Lanham, Md.: Bernan Press.
Van Wingerden, S. A. (1999) *The Woman Suffrage Movement in Britain, 1866–1928*, London: Macmillan.
Van Zoonen, L. (1991) 'A Tyranny of Intimacy? Women, Femininity and Television News', in P. Dahlgren and C. Sparks (eds) *Communication and Citizenship*, London: Routledge.
—— (1994) *Feminist Media Studies*, London: Sage.
—— (1998) '"One of the Girls": The Changing Gender of Journalism', in C. Carter, G. Branston and S. Allan (eds) *News, Gender and Power*, London and New York: Routledge, pp. 33–46.
Vincenzi, P. (1996) 'Obituary: Marjorie Proops', *Independent,* 12 November: 16.
Viswanath, K., Kosicki, G. M. and Creedon, P. J. (1993) 'Women in Mass Communication Education: Progress, Problems, and Prospects', in P. Creedon (ed.) *Women in Mass Communication*, Newbury Park, Calif.: Sage, pp. 237–63.
Viva! (1994) *An Application to the Radio Authority for a Greater London Licence*, London: Radio Authority.
Von Mehren, J. (1994) *Minerva and the Muse: A Life of Margaret Fuller*, Amherst, Mass.: University of Massachusetts Press.
Voss, M. (1991) 'Pulitzer Prize Women', *Journalism and Women Symposium Newsletter*, August: 1.
Wagner, L. (1989) *Women War Correspondents of World War II*, New York: Greenwood.
Walker, S. (1934) *City Editor*, New York: Frederick A. Stokes.
Walsh Childers, K., Chance, J. and Herzog, K. (1996) 'Sexual Harassment of Women Journalists', *Journalism and Mass Communication Quarterly* 73(3): 559–81.
Weaver, D. H. (1992) 'A Secret No More', *Washington Journalism Review*, September: 23–7.
—— (1997) 'Women as Journalists', in P. Norris (ed.) *Women, Media and Politics*, New York and Oxford: Oxford University Press, pp. 21–40.
Weaver, D. H., Beam, R., Brownlee, B., Voakes, P. and Wilhoit, G. C. (2003) 'The American Journalist in the 21st Century: Key Findings', presented to the Association of Education in Journalism and Mass Communication, July, on-line. Available at <http://www.poynter.org>.
Weaver, D. H. and Wilhoit, G. C. (1986) *The American Journalist: A Portrait of U.S. News People and Their Work*, 2nd edn, Bloomington, Ind.: Indiana University Press.
———— (1996) *The American Journalist in the 1990s: U.S. News People at the End of an Era.*, Mahwah, NJ: Erlbaum.
Webb, M. (1980) 'Marilyn Webb, Co-founder of oob', *on our backs*, February: 5.
Weill, S. (2000) 'Hazel and the "Hacksaw": Freedom Summer Coverage by the Women of the Mississippi Press', *Journalism Studies* 2(4): 545–61.
Wells, M. (2001) 'Caught Short', *Media Guardian*, 1 October: 2.
—— (2002) Interview with Lyse Doucet in 'Shooting Star', *Guardian, G2*, 8 January: 3–4.

Werden, F. (1996) 'The Founding of WINGS (Women's International News Gathering Service): A Story of Feminist Radio Survival', in D. Allen, R. R. Rush and S. J. Kaufman (eds) *Women Transforming Communications: Global Intersections*, Thousand Oaks, Calif: Sage,.pp. 218–25.

West, B. (2003) 'A War Reporter First' (letter to the editor), *New York Times*, 9 April: A18.

Whelehan, I. (2000) *Overloaded: Popular Culture and the Future of Feminism*, London: The Women's Press.

Whitehorn, K. (1997) '"We Never Had Orgasms on the Front Page . . . Of Course, it's All Changed Now"', *Observer Review*, 7 December: 1.

Whitt, J. (2000) 'Adele Arakawa: A Commitment to Professionalism', in M. E. Beadle and M. D. Murray (eds) *Indelible Images: Women of Local Television*, Ames, Ia.: Iowa State University Press.

Wilkes, R. (2001) 'Inside Story: A Woman of No Little Importance', Telegraph.co.uk, on-line. Available at <http://www.telegraph.co.uk/property/main.jhtml?xml= property/2001/06/27/pimpor23.xMl&secureRefresh=true&_requestid=111218> (accessed 11 November 2003).

Williams, K. (1998) *Get Me a Murder a Day: A History of Mass Communication in Britain*, London: Arnold.

Wilner, J. (1993) 'Judge Clears Wente of Racial Discrimination Charges', *Current*, 16 January.

Winship, J. (1987) *Inside Women's Magazines*, London: Pandora Press.

Winslow, B. (1996) *Sylvia Pankhurst: Sexual Politics and Political Activism*, London: UCL Press.

Witt, L., Paget, K. M. and Matthews, G. (1994) *Running as a Woman: Gender and Power in American Politics*, New York: Maxwell Macmillan International.

Wolf, N. (1993) *Fire with Fire*, London: Chatto & Windus.

Woman's Hour (2001) Interview with Michael Carney on the publication of his biography of Hilda Matheson, November, BBC Radio 4.

Woman's Hour (2002) 'Domesticating the Airwaves', interview with Maggie Andrews, 11 September, BBC Radio 4.

'Women Come to the Front: Journalists, Photographers, and Broadcasters During World War II', on-line. Available <http://lcweb.loc.gov/exhibits/wcf/ecf0005.html>

Women in Journalism (1998) *The Cheaper Sex: How Women Lose Out in Journalism*, London: Women in Journalism Monograph.

Women in Military Service for America Memorial website, on-line. Available <http://www.womensmemorial.org/history.html>.

Woodruff, J. (1997) 'Covering Politics–Is There a Female Difference', *Media Studies Journal*, Spring 11(2): 155–8.

Yamane, N. T. (2000) 'Pacific Coast Woman's Press Association, 1890–19(41)', in E. Burt (ed.) *Women's Press Organizations, 1881–1999*, Westport, Conn.: Greenwood Press, pp. 189–98.

Ziamou, T. (2001) 'Women Make the News: A Crack in the Glass Ceiling', Paris: UNESCO, on-line. Available <http://www.unesco.org/webworld/march8/2001/ wmn2000eng.pdf>.

Index